THE GREEK GENOCIDE IN AMERICAN NAVAL WAR DIARIES

Book and cover design by Alex Dimeff

Cover image: "Trekking to the Sea," originally published in *Certain Samaritans* by Esther Lovejoy. New York: The Macmillian Company: 1927.

ISBN: 978-1-60801-180-3

First Edition
Printed on acid-free paper in the United States of America.

THE UNIVERSITY OF NEW ORLEANS PRESS
unopress.org

THE GREEK GENOCIDE IN AMERICAN NAVAL WAR DIARIES

Naval Commanders Report and Protest Death Marches and Massacres in Turkey's Pontus Region, 1921–1922

Edited by
Robert Shenk and Sam Koktzoglou

With a Foreword by
James Stavridis, Admiral, USN, Retired

CONTENTS

To my maternal grandfather, Stavros Xygalas, who was executed in Amasia on September 21, 1921. Also, to my late parents Lefkothea and Ioannis, who as children in the course of this genocide lost many family members and were forced to leave their homeland of Pontus in Asia Minor to find refuge in Greece.

—Sam Koktzoglou

To the victims of all the genocidal actions that took place in Turkey's Pontus both during and after World War I.

—Robert Shenk

ACKNOWLEDGMENTS

The editors both want to thank our anonymous reviewers and Dr. Herb Gilliland for their insightful comments on the manuscript. Thanks also to the experts of the Center for Asia Minor Studies for their review of the book typescript and the comments provided. All these experts taught us much—though any errors remaining are those of the authors. We are both also obligated to Costas Apostolidis, Chairman of Raycap S.A., for supporting the project financially.

The editors also express the following personal acknowledgments:

I am indebted to my late father Ioannis Koktzoglou, a survivor of the massacre at the village of Ada near Samsun. It was after he showed me a book, that mentioned the presence of an American destroyer in the port of Samsun at the time of the massacre, that I decided years later to look for documentation. This book wouldn't have been possible without the help and support of others. I am grateful to the late Professor Harry Psomiades, of the City University of New York, who directed me to the U.S. National Archives where I located the war diaries presented here. Many thanks to historian Dr. Theodosis Kyriakidis, of the University of Thessaloniki, Greece, for his valuable input. Last but not least I would like to thank my wife, Venise, for coming with me to Washington D.C. twice and assisting me with photographing and later transcribing the diaries.

—Sam Koktzoglou

UNO English graduate student Toria Danielle Smith helped me greatly in getting this manuscript closer to publication. And thanks to

Chris Robinson for putting the maps together for another book project of mine.

Going back further, though, I should particularly express my appreciation for the help that the late Marjorie Housepian Dobkin gave me personally by her encouragement of my naval research, and by her example. Her study of innumerable naval documents having to do with the American flotilla that was sent to Turkish waters shortly after World War I constituted building blocks for her ground-breaking study of the great fire at Smyrna, *The Smyrna Affair.*

—Robert Shenk

FOREWORD

by James Stavridis, Admiral, USN, Retired

What do you do when you are captain of a small but powerful naval vessel, a destroyer stationed for several weeks at a port in a foreign country, and you see and hear that terrible things—torture, massacres, rapes, forced deportations—are happening widely to a minority group in that country? Beyond that, such atrocities are now threatening thousands of terrified people who live on the very streets of the port you visit every day. From your anchorage, you see events unraveling before your eyes.

Although you have expressed your concern to local officials and even have protested strongly at what is threatening to occur, these protests have been almost wholly ignored. Meanwhile, your boss, the navy admiral back in the capital, either seems to have other things on his mind or at any rate seems less concerned than you about the events your messages have described to him in detail.

To be sure, from the very beginning of your ship's assignment to duty at this port, you have had directions to "remain neutral" between differing internal groups.

But shouldn't you do *something*? You're a representative of *America*, after all! And these are essentially *slow killings* of men and then the heartless deportations of women and children, which will end with the death of many of the latter as well.

What might you do, though: Shoot your big guns in warning? Argue further with the local officials? Argue even more strongly with the admiral? Send sailors ashore to save the weeping women and children even now being rounded up in front of your ship's boat?

Or, instead, just shake your head, report what you see and learn as best you can, and continue to watch (and listen) helplessly?

Such were the kinds of challenges repeatedly confronting the commanding officers of American naval destroyers, one or more of which vessels were continuously moored just off the harbor of the Black Sea port of Samsun, Turkey beginning in the spring of 1921 and extending well beyond the calamitous burning of Smyrna in September of 1922.

The two authors who have ferreted out in America's National Archives the "naval war diaries" found in this collection were first of all intent upon showing just what was happening to the Ottoman Greeks in the Pontus Region of Turkey after World War I.

And so this book is, for one thing, a unique and until now unpublished record from an impartial source of all the multiple atrocities that were then being inflicted upon the men and women of Greek heritage in Turkey. These included the burnings of hundreds of Greek villages; the murders of many of the villagers, some of them being *burned alive*; the sending of Greek males to hard labor camps with impossibly insufficient food and no shelter so that their deaths were virtually inevitable; and the terrible death marches of tens of thousands of women, children, and elderly, along with the incidental rapes, murders, and abductions of young Greek women, as well as the repeated robberies of all these people along the way. All the above, and some Greek armed retaliations as well. It was a terrible time in the Levant, and of course the Armenians suffered horribly as well. There were brutalities everywhere.

But this book is more than that. It is also a record of the inquiries, reports, recommendations, and other actions of what were apparently the first American naval officers ever to be confronted almost directly with (in the events mentioned above) the terrible twentieth century phenomenon that we have come to know as ethnic cleansing. Such a totally unprecedented situation is what these officers generally found themselves facing, and the war diaries record what actions they took in response.

Naval servicemembers at all levels might profitably study the extraordinary circumstances that these officers faced, as well as their varied responses to the narrow options open to them. Such consideration would be valuable even if it seems, and hopefully is, very unlikely that any of today's naval men and women will ever face anything quite like this again.

Other readers might also greatly profit from such reflection, for all manner of circumstances are involved here: written directives, standard naval protocol, the discovery and consideration of all relevant circumstances, the weighing of various points of view, the reviewing of all the options, and—most weighty—individual conscience. The latter would include the larger responsibility of an officer both to his fellow human beings and to his country, *whatever* the effect upon his own career.

These diaries are brief panoramas into events of a particular time and place that ended with the death of tens of thousands, and the birth of a new nation in Turkey at a terrible cost which has never fully been counted or acknowledged. This, along with snapshots of a few American naval ship captains who saw, reported, made recommendations, and in other ways responded to it all, and perhaps through a deterring role helped save several thousand lives in the process, as will be seen within.

Could they have done more? Should they have taken bold and independent steps beyond what they did? History will judge them, and this volume of primary source material will help. It is a fascinating and disturbing tale that helps illuminate not only the past, but the hard choices we face going forward in this turbulent twenty-first century.

PREFACE

In mid-1921, in the northeast coastal region of Turkey that has been called "Pontus" for centuries, the Nationalist Turks, who were by now in charge in most of Anatolia, began moving a whole body of people inland. Many tens of thousands of ethnic Greeks and other Christians were being marched south, ostensibly because of the Turkish Nationalist fear that this population—Ottoman citizens of Greek descent whose ancestors had lived in this area for nearly three millennia and who at this period included many partisans in the mountains—would support a Greek Army's landing on this coast. It was said that such a landing might form the basis of a martial "second front" to aid Greece in its campaign against an opposing Nationalist Turkish Army in the fierce war that was taking place a couple of hundred miles away in the western part of Anatolia (also known as Asia Minor).

But this forced migration was being imposed with conditions horrible to behold. Greek women, children, and elderly were being marched hundreds of miles to the south, even as far as Syrian deserts, by Turkish Nationalist forces, deprived of food except what they could carry or buy and sometimes deprived of water even when crossing streams. Moreover, the deportees were frequently robbed and sometimes killed, and many young women were either raped or abducted and taken into Turkish homes as concubines or slaves. Beyond all that, just because of the terrible conditions, these deportations became death marches for a great many.

Accompanying events were equally awful. Most local Greek men were being marched off to "labor battalions" in which conditions were so harsh that few of them ever returned. Many leaders among the Greek community throughout Pontus were arrested and publicly hung after trials in which they were allowed no defense. And near the Pontic port of Samsun, massacres took place whereby as many as half of the 3,000 Ottoman Greeks who had been rounded up there for the labor camps were immediately killed by the Turks.

The deportations or death marches inland, the labor battalions, the execution of Greek leaders of Pontus, and the multiple killings seemed an intentional repetition of specific actions taken by Turkish authorities against the Armenians during World War I.

In late 1921 and early 1922, American Near East Relief workers far inland would witness and testify to many thousands of deaths and the terrible conditions of the surviving Greek deportees of Pontus after weeks or months on the road. However, the *beginnings* of these Pontic deportations and associated events near the Black Sea coast were also noticed.

For as it happens, United States Navy warships were continuously present at the port of Samsun for over two years, beginning in May 1921. As a result, American naval officers there often saw towers of smoke from Greek villages in the area, which were being burned daily by the Turks, while they also heard reports of village burnings near other Pontic port cities. At Samsun, American businessmen, relief workers, or naval officers sometimes saw firsthand the deportation parties of hundreds or even a thousand at a time being sent south.

The American ship captains recorded these events and other observations in daily records of a few paragraphs or several typed pages. They recorded conversations with Turkish civilian and military leaders, as well as their own protests about what they were seeing. They reported conversations with American relief workers who could tell of conditions deep inland where they were stationed. And they also described, in writing, conversations with local American businessmen, fluent in Turkish, who had lived in Turkey for years and who could offer much additional perspective. Of course, the naval ship captains also sent frequent messages about what was occurring to their admiral, Mark Bristol, back in Constantinople (modern Istanbul).

Admiral Mark Bristol, shown at Constantinople in 1922. Although Bristol protested the deportation of noncombatants at Samsun to Mustafa Kemal in late 1921 at the plea of one of his ship captains, after that he obstructed the publication of American relief reports on the widespread deaths of Greek deportees.

We have found over a year's worth of these "war diaries" in America's National Archives, and we have photographed them and reproduced the bulk of six months of them here and summarized others. Sam Koktzoglou and I have teamed up to select, edit, and introduce these records. I'm a professor of English at the University of New Orleans, and Sam is a retired engineer and a descendant of Pontic Greeks. We produce these records in the hopes of providing for the first time a unique window from an impartial source on events in Samsun and the Pontus region in general—the Pontic Coast being the starting point of the long deportation trails that tens of thousands of women, children, and elderly were forced to travel usually by foot with little or nothing to hope for at the end of the road.

At the same time, the American naval officers' urgent responses to what they were seeing constitute a critical part of this account.

My interest in this project is partly professional, for it is a follow-up to my 2012 study, *America's Black Sea Fleet*, which told a story never heard in detail before of the American Navy's deployment of a flotilla of destroyers and other vessels to Turkish waters for better than four years (1919–1923). This book is an expansion upon Chapter Five of that earlier work, a chapter entitled "Death in the Pontus." I'm a retired captain in the naval reserve, and for some fifteen years, I have studied the American Navy's deployment to Turkish waters and events that took place in post-World War I Turkey.

Sam Koktzoglou's interest in this project is partly personal as his father and mother were survivors of events described in this book; his father was the only survivor of his entire family. His mother's father was among the notable Pontic Greeks executed in Amassia (by the so-called "Independence Tribunals") on September 21, 1921 (see the report of those hangings within). Sam has been studying the history of Asia Minor and Pontus for many years. Sam and I met at a conference in Chicago in 2013.

We hope that the account rendered here will make more clear what happened to the Ottoman Greeks under the Turkish Nationalist revolutionary regime and its leader, Mustafa Kemal, and how on-the-site American naval officers responded to these startling, terrible events.

Within, the war diaries speak to these subjects:

* *The terrible suffering widespread in Pontus in 1921–1922 and the desperate situation of Ottoman Greeks in all of mainland Turkey*

* *The rationale provided by the Turkish Nationalists for imposing such suffering*

* *The responses of the American naval officers as they learned of the impending brutal inhumanity to be inflicted upon women, children, and the elderly*

* *Protests by some of those naval officers and how such protests were responded to by Nationalist authorities*

* *Examples of how responsible leadership combined with an eloquent report to a superior can have a greatly beneficial effect*

* *The actions of "extremist" Turkish leaders Osman Agha and Nureddin Pasha, which resulted in atrocities affecting many tens of thousands, men and women both*

* *Pontic Greek guerilla activity against Turks and Turkish villages near Samsun*

* *Anti-Nationalist activities of the Hellenic Navy in the Black Sea*

* *Protests about the deportations made to Nationalist leaders (at much personal risk) on the part of Turkish civilians and leaders in Samsun*

* *The noteworthy integrity of American businessmen in Samsun whose Turkish former employees entrusted them with witness accounts of atrocities*

The story of the later burning of Smyrna has been related in four major histories since 1971, and the American Navy's war diary records of those terrible events have been widely studied. The U.S. Navy's war diary record of the 1921–1922 sufferings of the Pontic Greeks has been, until now, mostly unnoticed. We intend this book to amend that record.

Robert Shenk and Sam Koktzoglou

View of Samsun and harbor

GENERAL INTRODUCTION

The Armenians are not the only subject people in Turkey which have suffered from this policy of making Turkey exclusively the country of the Turks. . . . Indeed the Greeks were the first victims of this nationalizing idea.

—Henry Morgenthau Sr.
American Ambassador to the Ottoman Empire, 1913-1916

Why the American Navy was in Turkey

One of the most astonishing though little-known stories of recent history is the role of American naval officers as witnesses to and protesters of one of the first acts of genocide of the early twentieth century, these acts being committed by Nationalist Turks against the Black Sea Greeks.[1] The daily experiences of these officers have seldom been studied, and their written reports have never been published before.

Following World War I (1914–1918), the American Navy sent a flotilla of warships to Turkish waters with a homeport based in Constantinople (modern Istanbul). This small naval detachment's mission was to speed teams of investigators and relief personnel in reponse to reports of great atrocities being committed throughout Turkey, particularly against the Armenian people. These reports had spread around the world during World War I and, in particular, had raised great concern throughout America.

In early 1919, a motley group of U.S. Navy steam yachts and submarine chasers was assigned to Admiral Mark Bristol, who had recently arrived at his new headquarters at Constantinople to initiate that promised flotilla. For months, American naval ships would help transport American investigatory commissions and relief workers to ports, providing them access throughout Turkey including those parts of Asiatic Turkey or Asia Minor known as Armenia. The investigating commissions were seeking to understand exactly what had happened to the Armenians and what should be done in response, and the relief workers of America's "Near East Relief" (NER) organization were seeking to help the survivors. (The immensely important work of the Near East Relief in reducing suffering and saving lives at great personal sacrifice, a contemporaneous story intertwined with ours, was simply remarkable.) Besides transporting these groups, the naval officers were also charged to protect the life and property of Americans who lived in the region. Some of those Americans were missionaries who had remained with their flocks deep in the interior of Turkey throughout the Great War.

After transiting the Mediterranean and Aegean Seas, the naval vessels navigated up the Hellespont into the Sea of Marmara and then sped on to Constantinople. There they visited the American naval headquarters at the United States Embassy for briefings as to their mission and about current circumstances in the region. After orientation, they steamed on through the Bosphorus Strait into the Black Sea to ports throughout Turkey (ports that had seldom or never been visited before by American warships)—the Pontic ports (from west to east) of Inebolu, Sinop, Samsun, Ordu, and Trebizond (modern Trabzon), and the then-Georgian port of Batoum, among them. At the same time, British Army units briefly occupied strategic sites in Turkey to restore order in the postwar period, and Allied tribunals in Constantinople began to investigate the reported massacres, death marches, and other outrages that had occurred in Turkey during the World War.

As has been recounted in detail elsewhere (Shenk, *America's Black Sea Fleet*, 41–42), in May 1919, Admiral Bristol was given a small number of destroyers (usually he had four, six, or eight at a time) to replace the steam yachts. For four years, the admiral sent these versatile warships on a variety of missions throughout the waters touching much of what was then known as the "Near East"—in particular, the waters of the Black Sea, Aegean, and Eastern Mediterranean. Before long, however, the British occupation units went home, and the Allied tribunals investigating atrocities against the Armenians ended mostly in futility (Göçek, 44–45, 262, 354–73). Then another war began, this involving a Hellenic Army against newly formed Nationalist Turkish forces (under their leader Mustafa Kemal) in western Asia Minor.

The Greco-Turkish War in Western Anatolia

The background of this war is complex. To pare it down to its essentials, in 1919, elements of the Hellenic Army had been requested to land in Smyrna by leaders among the World War I Allies so as to forestall Italian forces taking over some of Western Anatolia, including the great port of Smyrna. Elements of this Hellenic Army consequently landed and occupied Smyrna and the nearby region. Before long, the same national Greek Army was encouraged by the Allies to occupy much of western Anatolia. The Allied leaders stipulated that these Hellenic forces were to hold and govern the area for five years, after which there would be a plebiscite in which the local population would decide whether they would continue to be ruled by the Greeks.

This task delighted the government of Greece, whose Prime Minister Eleutherios Venizelos was a strong proponent of what was called the Megali Idea, an irredentist concept of expanding the Greek nation into a greater Greece. This expansion would include parts of Turkey, Smyrna, and western Anatolia (traditionally called Ionia, which, like Pontus, also had a strong Ottoman Greek population), in particular.

However, the whole idea of any Greeks ruling Turks was anathema to the Turks, ethnic Greeks in Anatolia having for centuries been subservient to the Ottoman rulers. So a great popular uproar in Constantinople and Anatolia was created by the Allies having the Hellenic Army—rather than British troops, say—given charge at Smyrna. Such Turkish outrage, aided by much propaganda, helped to ignite a fervent nationalism among the Turks throughout Anatolia. This movement in turn happened incidentally to feed into the plans of the World War I Turkish war hero Mustafa Kemal, who had landed at Samsun almost simultaneously with the Hellenic landing in Smyrna with the purposes of building a Turkish Nationalist Army and government to replace the Sultan and his government and of defeating and ousting the occupying Hellenic Army. (The Sultan's government with concurrence from the Allies had appointed Kemal inspector of the 9th Army and sent him to Anatolia to reestablish order, but Kemal had different plans.) Meanwhile, the Sultan's government, which had replaced the government of the "Young Turks," was being propped up by three of the European Allies of World War I: Britain, France, and Italy. In 1920, these three countries would send in troops to occupy Constantinople.

By mid-1920, the Hellenic Army was battling against a Turkish Nationalist Army a couple of hundred miles east of Smyrna. Even though some of the Allies soon began to withdraw support from the Greeks (Italy and France actually began to support the Nationalists), when the Greek Prime Minister Venizelos fell from power on November 1, 1920 in part because of the unpopularity of this war back in Greece, the new Greek King Constantine unaccountably did not withdraw the Greek Army from Anatolia but fought on.[2]

Some argue that it was partly because of the severity and threat of this war that the Turkish Nationalists chose to enhance their persecution of the Greeks of Anatolia, especially those of them living on or near the eastern Black Sea coast of Turkey, the area traditionally called "Pontus."

The Renewed Deportations

In early 1921, reports began being sent to Constantinople revealing that some of the same kind of atrocities that had been perpetrated in 1915–1916, especially upon the Armenians, were occurring once again in Turkey, particularly against the Greeks in the Pontic region.

Deportations had been one of the preferred methods of decimating the Armenians in 1915–1916 but had then been used to a significant extent against the Ottoman Greeks as well. By claiming that they were simply moving the Christian residents elsewhere, perhaps because a particular area was subject to enemy invasion, Turkish officials could deny malicious intent as they marched long lines of Armenians and Greeks away from a populated area. (Sometimes, as Göçek notes, 63, this intentional destruction via deportation was even justified by saying the Christians were being moved out of their traditional homelands for their own safety.) As for the results of the deportations and associated massacres, these methods had both been so widely used back in 1915–1916 against the Armenians in particular that a great proportion of Turkey's Armenians had already died. But now, long after the war, deportations of Greeks were beginning again in Pontus, and elsewhere in Anatolia, and other atrocities were occurring as well.

Even without outright killing, the effects of deportation upon the Pontic Greeks were devastating—particularly if the men were first separated from their families and sent away, as was often the case. Their sources of income being lost with the deported breadwinners, families would soon become impoverished even if their villages were not immediately destroyed. But food and shelter would become very hard to come by if the Pontic Greek families suddenly found their villages destroyed and themselves forcibly conducted hundreds of miles away, which had typically been the case with the Armenians (and with tens of thousands of Ottoman Greeks too) back in 1915–1916. Often, in the past, such deportations also involved kidnapping, robbery, rape, and outright killings, especially once the deportees were far away from population centers and prying foreign eyes.

By the late summer of 1921, numerous killings, some massacres, the burning of innumerable Greek villages, and many forced deportations into the interior, which soon became death marches, had become commonplace throughout Pontus. Although all Christian minorities in Turkey had suffered great depredations in 1914–1918, this time the suffering affected the Ottoman Greek minority even more profoundly than it did the ethnic Armenians who had been most severely ravaged before.

The political forces responsible for these acts had also changed. No longer in charge were the "Young Turks," whose political party (the "Committee on Union and Progress") had taken control from the Sultan in 1908. The three leaders of the Committee on Union and Progress who had been primarily responsible for the Armenian Genocide had fled Constantinople in the final days of World War I, and within three years, they were all dead—two by assassination. The newly formed revolutionary government and armed forces of the Nationalist Turks had come to power in Asia Minor. Under the leadership of Mustafa Kemal, this new Nationalist government, its police, and its armed forces (which included many lawless irregular or "chettah" forces[3] and also a great many former Ottoman officials who had earlier carried out the Young Turk policies) began arresting, killing, and "deporting" the remaining Christian minorities of Turkey just as the Young Turks had done in 1915–1916.

As mentioned above, Mustafa Kemal had landed in the Pontic port of Samsun in May 1919 and immediately began forming an organization to help him build a new Turkish Nationalist Army and government in Anatolia, replacing almost everywhere the European-supported government of the Ottoman Sultan in Constantinople, often with the aid of former Young Turk or Committee on Union and Progress officials (Göçek, 297–99). On June 16, 1921, following the June 9, 1921 bombardment of the small Pontic town of Inebolu by a Hellenic warship operating in the Black Sea, Mustafa Kemal was persuaded to deport the Pontic Greek population away from the northern coast of Turkey entirely (Fotiadis, 391; Mango, 330).

This was defended as a move to prevent the Pontic Greeks from supporting any possible "second front" for the Greeks in the Greco-Turkish War, in face of fears that Greek naval units that had just begun operating in the Black Sea might attempt to land large contingents of Greek troops. There was some possible validity to such a concern, especially since in June of 1921, the wartime Allies occupying Constantinople and controlling the sea lanes—the British, French, and Italians—had allowed Greek warships to move into the Black Sea,[4] where they began bombarding Pontic port cities. (Among other things, the Hellenic Navy was attempting to keep the Nationalists from bringing in arms and ammunition through those Pontic ports and was trying to destroy what warmaking material was already there.)

Were the Greek Navy to go further and attempt to land large numbers of troops at one or more of those Pontic ports, Turkish leaders were said to fear that such a new Hellenic force might find itself welcomed by a supportive population, including armed guerilla bands. This rationale was sometimes cited when Turkish Army officers made the "Turkish case for the deportations" as they sometimes are said to do in the war diaries. (That case is sometimes roughly outlined in the conversations reported by the American officers.)

It is also possible, of course, that this stated rationale—to move the Pontic Greek population so as to prevent those people from assisting Hellenic armed forces intending to form a second front—was more of a convenient pretext so that the Turks could cause the eventual (if deniable) death of most of those being deported. This view is supported in the diaries by a message that Captain Joyce of the *Fox* sent to Admiral Bristol as early as May 24, 1921. In that message, he concludes that "there is a definite policy here for the extermination of the Greek inhabitants. Everything indicates that hundreds of Greek villages have been completely devastated." On May 27, he goes on to say that the local Turkish military authorities in Samsun itself had voted for the extermination of the Black Sea Greeks. And all of this occurred *before* the initial Greek naval bombardment on June 9, 1921 at Inebolu.

American Near East Relief workers in the interior, who often witnessed the terrible effects of the deportations right in front of them, would sometimes conclude that what they were seeing was simply a Turkish endeavor to get rid of the Pontic Greek population. In these war diaries, we see some American naval ship captains in Samsun coming to a similar conclusion but much earlier than even the relief people did.

The Admiral's Reasons to Station His Warships at Samsun

The Americans, who had been involved with the Allies in the First World War, were not invited to take part in the postwar occupation of Constantinople or to help Britain, France, and Italy make decisions on policy with respect to what remained of the Ottoman Empire—this because America had never declared war on the Ottoman Empire. Hence an antagonism grew between American and other European forces in Constantinople. This antagonism was particularly strong between American and British officials and especially in terms of their countries' competition for business (Housepian Dobkin, 79–83).

Admiral Bristol, the leader of America's naval forces in the region and the country's "High Commissioner" in Constantinople, became America's leading representative in the Near East upon his arrival in 1919. He had his offices at the American Embassy at the old Ottoman capital. The admiral came to see as perhaps his major mission the promotion of American commercial interests throughout the Near East, and he viewed the European powers as America's chief competitors, although Greeks and Armenian businessmen could be strong competitors too. Before long, the admiral came to believe that a Turkish Nationalist government, which the Allies initially opposed, would provide the best support for American business interests (Shenk, *ABSF*, 48). For this and other reasons, such as the protection of American relief and missionary personnel deep in the interior of Turkey, Bristol was concerned to retain close contact with the Nationalist headquarters in Angora (modern Ankara), as well as to gain as much information as possible about conditions all over Anatolia.

For such reasons, in the late spring of 1921, Admiral Bristol began stationing a regular rotation of destroyers at Samsun, the largest port on Turkey's Black Sea Coast and the one that provided best access both to Angora and to other Turkish cities inland where American missionary and Near East Relief stations were located. Beyond that, two substantial American tobacco companies were doing business at Samsun itself—another reason to keep a naval presence there. So the admiral made sure that at least one of his destroyers anchored off this port continuously from May 1921 through the fall 1922 (except for a few days at Christmas) and beyond. The reports of these vessels helped him monitor things from his offices back in Constantinople. (For four years, Admiral Bristol headed both a naval and a diplomatic staff there.)

The American Naval War Diaries and Their Contents

The admiral's destroyer captains at Samsun kept detailed records of occurrences in the city and the region, these being found in the naval documents of the era officially entitled "war diaries" (the American Navy continued to use this standard document title for years, whether America was involved in a war at the time or not). Periodically the captains sent or delivered war diary sets back to their boss at Constantinople, but copies of all the war diaries for Samsun were also kept *on station.* As a result, each captain new to Samsun could read a chronological record tracing several months' to a over a year's worth of recent events when he arrived at the port (Shenk, *ABSF*, 206).

What was in those diaries? Many records of little importance to the focus of this book—issues of internal American naval affairs; of American relief work and commercial operations in the city and the area; of American missionary operations deep in Turkey's interior; of visits to Samsun by commercial ships from several nations; and so on.

But they also contained reports covering very different subjects: word of the burning of hundreds of Pontic Greek villages accompanied by many killings; reports of widespread deportations of ethnic Greeks into the interior of Turkey; reports to American businessmen by former employees of terrible massacres in which the former employees themselves had barely escaped death; pleas for help from starving Greeks in the hills brought to the destroyers by intrepid young swimmers; and, as time went on, oral or written reports from American Near East Relief workers about the terrible death marches they had encountered at their inland stations or while traveling from Samsun to stations throughout Turkey's interior.

Near East Relief poster

The war diaries also recorded information less favorable to the Greeks. They outlined discussions between the American naval officers and Turkish Nationalist civilian officials and army officers, some of the latter making the "Turkish case" for the deportations. The diaries described raids by Greek partisans from the hills upon Turkish villages and upon Turkish soldiers or police. They reported the presence of Hellenic naval vessels spying upon or even bombarding Black Sea ports. And they pointed out that many draft-aged Ottoman Greek men (subject to induction into the labor battalions) were being hidden away in Samsun or spirited away to the mountains by friends or families.

In short, these sets of war diaries provide a continuous and even-handed account of what was going on in one of the most prominent ports of Anatolia from mid-1921 on. The war diaries record the observations of responsible and mid-level American naval officers at the beginning of a long deportation trail stretching south through Turkey as far as Syria.

These documents also show how frequently American officials discussed the atrocities with and made protests to Turkish civil and military authorities. While the naval officers often had to rely on secondhand reports, they were also locally connected. They were in contact with decision-making Turkish civilian officials, whom they knew well enough to assess their integrity. They also had contact with some Kemalist military officers charged with committing these atrocities by the Nationalist government or taking upon themselves the commission of depredations. They consulted American businessmen who, from their long experience in Turkey, could offer much perspective. The naval officers sometimes were able to feel viscerally the enormous angst and sorrow of Pontic Greek women citizens of Samsun and refugees who begged their help. They also heard of protests to Nationalist leaders from Turkish civilians who opposed the Nationalist atrocities. This proximity and these connections allowed American naval officers to know what was occurring and gave them opportunities to take actions in response.

Assembling the Samsun War Diaries and Their Potential Value

It has been possible, by searching into America's National Archives, to assemble the better part of a year's worth of these war diaries, stretching from the spring of 1921, with the initial village burnings, followed by massacres that began the major phase of Turkish atrocities in the Pontic region, all the way until the early fall of 1922. By that time many tens of thousands of Pontic Greeks had perished while most of the remaining population had become utterly impoverished and homeless (usually also starving and diseased) and permanently displaced far to the south.

The record presented in these pages is of value for several reasons. For one thing, it supports reports of the Turkish genocide of Armenians, Greeks, and Syriacs (the latter people sometimes called Assyrians or Arameans), the truth of which remains denied by the Turkish government, which has also denied the part played in these actions by Turkish Nationalists following the World War.

This collection is valuable, too, in another way. Most of the reports or testimonies available about the treatment of the Greeks in the period the war diaries cover are either from Ottoman Greeks themselves, from various foreign diplomats, or from American relief workers or missionaries returning from months or years stationed far inland. What we provide in this book is a new portrait and a perspective from a relatively new angle.

Moreover, the recorded observations of American naval officers offer a generally impartial source. Yes, the ship captains had heard of all the massacres and death marches that the Armenians had suffered during World War I (Who in America had not?), but as far as we know, none had witnessed it directly in 1915–1916. Indeed, these war diaries show how American naval officers attempted to deal with terrible, genocidal circumstances apparently never before confronted in American naval history.[5]

America was a neutral power in the Greco-Turkish conflict in western Anatolia, and the orders the ship captains received from Admiral Bristol upon being sent into the Black Sea and its Turkish ports insisted that they "remain neutral." Nevertheless, several of these officers soon recognized such horrors were occurring or were about to occur in the area under their cognizance that they felt that they had to speak out or urge their admiral to do so.

Admiral Bristol, again due to his hopes to aid American business interests in Turkey (especially with the Nationalists), became increasingly more sympathetic to the Turks than to Turkey's various Christian peoples despite the terrible sufferings of the latter groups during the "Great War" (World War I) and now under the Nationalists. Eventually he was to develop such a deep bias for the Nationalists that the American-educated Turkish academic and journalist of the day, Ahmed Emin Yalman (who was imprisoned for a term by the British for his Nationalist leanings), would say in a memoir that Admiral Bristol's "activities from the beginning to the end of our struggle for independent existence amounted, in effect, to almost an informal alliance between [Nationalist] Turkey and the United States."[6]

As a result of these command circumstances, sometimes the officers reporting back to American naval headquarters about Turkish transgressions were risking their careers to speak out on behalf of those minority people who were suffering atrocities of terrible proportions to a superior who seemingly didn't want to hear anything of what they had to say.

The American Officers Get Their Admiral to Protest

Despite his Turkish sympathies, however, as we will see here, the admiral at one point was persuaded by particularly strong arguments by one or two of his ship captains at Samsun to protest via telegraph directly to the Nationalist leader, Mustafa Kemal, arguing specifically that the Nationalists should refrain from deporting Greek women, children, and elderly (all of them noncombatants) from Samsun—such a deportation having just been ordered. And so he did. His protest, along with other, more local protests from the ship captains themselves, saved several thousand women and children natives of Samsun from being forced out on the death marches. Moreover, it appears from a careful review of these diaries and other war diaries extending beyond September 1922 that these people in particular—Pontic Greek women, children, and elderly native to Samsun proper—never lost their protected status, even long after the admiral's official protest.[7]

However, as the diaries and other records indicate, with one or two other exceptions, the deportations never slowed down in the Pontus region as a whole. Not only were most Pontic Greek men sent to virtual death sentences in the labor battalions or massacred outright, but beyond that, the deportations of women and children continued at and near Samsun itself. Thousands of Pontic Greeks who had lived not in Samsun proper but in the hundreds of Greek villages near the city that the Nationalists or Turkish irregulars had burned down—women and children who the Turkish scorched-earth policy had made utterly destitute and who were ever seeking food and shelter in the city (but who were usually denied entry there)—were frequently gathered up and deported as time wore on.

It should be noted that many warnings of impending deportations from Samsun proper made by the American destroyer capains were not immediately proven true. The very presence of the American naval vessels and American officers itself had some deterrent effect upon the implementation of Turkish plans as a couple of ship captains take care to note. For one thing, the American ship captains' persistent inquiries and complaints about pending deportations sometimes may have caused deportations to be postponed. Also, the simple, constant presence of one or more American warships and their officers no doubt inhibited Turkish authorities somewhat from allowing many outright atrocities to be committed right in Samsun.

It is also true that American warship commanders were seldom allowed out of Samsun to search into the myriad reports of Greek villages and occasional Turkish ones having been burned or to investigate the many fires and columns of smoke they saw nearby, often daily. Nor did the naval officers ever get to take trips inland to the cities of Malatia (Malatya), Sivas, Marsovan (Merzifon), or Harput (Elazığ).

But as we will see in the diaries, the American officers frequently spoke with or heard from those American relief workers and missionaries who did take such journeys and who before long, upon their return to Samsun, began to tell of the unburied, fly-covered refugee bodies lying along the roads, as well as the enormous sufferings of thousands of emaciated Greek women, children, and elderly they had met who were forced by Turkish guards to trudge along hopelessly southward—or die in the process.

The ship captains also heard from the American tobacco managers whose former Turkish and Greek employees often came to them with reports of massacres or other atrocities. And once, even the local Turkish mayor or governor (the "Mutasariff") of Samsun and the region admitted to Captain Arthur LeRoy Bristol of the *Overton* that terrible massacres had indeed been committed at nearby Kavak of many of those male Greeks of Samsun who had just been marched out of their homes and places of work despite official Turkish assurances that they were being moved simply so they could practice their trades and businesses in another location.

As for the burning of Greek villages near or far, that was reported so often and so credibly by these officers that even the skeptical admiral back in Constantinople eventually admitted in a letter to an official back home something that he would almost never admit in public, writing, "I don't think there is any doubt that the Greeks have been pretty well cleared out of the whole region and deported to the interior and the villages wiped out" (Shenk, *ABSF*, 111).

Actually, within a few weeks of his own 1919 arrival in Turkey, after a visit to Samsun, Admiral Bristol himself had written back home to his wife about the "White Death" that Greek women and children in the region had suffered during the Great War: deaths inflicted by forced exposure to the winter cold, sometimes after Turkish baths, and starvation rather than by direct killing or orders to kill. In an official report of this visit, besides reporting wartime deportations of both Armenians and Greeks from the Pontic region, he also witnessed the wartime devastation of Greek and Armenian villages in the countryside not far from Samsun: "'the houses were burned and leveled to the ground'" (Shenk, *ABSF*, 54).

Now in mid-1921, however, American relief workers were reporting that, once again, many thousands of poorly clothed, ill-fed, and feeble Pontic Greek women, children, and elderly were being forced along the deportation trails inland. These journeys to uncertain destinations were treks that usually took *months* to complete—for those who survived them, that is. Often, deportees were purposely sent into the teeth of a winter blizzard after a brief rest stop in a town. The term "White Death," or a related term like "White Massacre," was beginning to be used again, this time in reference to the 1921–22 deportations from Pontus (for example, see the Italian Catholic priest's use of the latter in *Brooks* WD, July 13,1921).

Because relatively few atrocities occurred in Samsun itself (the Kavak and Marsovan massacres and extensive burning of Greek villages are frequently reported and spoken of, but they took place outside the city), we support the war diary accounts by frequently reproducing what we call "testimonies," reports by reliable eyewitnesses from other sources. These testimonies make clear much of what was happening in parts of Anatolia that the naval officers could not personally see. Following are brief descriptions of the kind of testimonies we present. These details, we think, make clear the importance of these testimonies for war diary readers:

* Two of the testimonies as to the massacres at Kavak and other atrocities eventually were added to the war diaries but find their place much later than the war diaries we present. Quoting them where we do allows us to provide convenient firsthand witness of those events for diary readers from a few who escaped the massacres.

* Village burnings in Pontus are mentioned everywhere in the war diaries, and two reliable accounts from Pontic Greeks we have obtained, one of them from our search of the archives, allow us to present firsthand descriptions of some of the worst of such episodes. Both of these specific atrocities were said to have been committed by the chettahs of Osman Agha, who

is a major figure in the war diary reports—another obvious reason for their inclusion.

* At one point, a group of three NER witnesses of what happened inland on the death marches were interviewed by a ship captain when they returned to Samsun. The captain discounts in the diaries much of what the men report—but presentation of their subsequent written reports allows diary readers to judge the reliefers' veracity for themselves.

* American officials' reports of great suffering of deportees deep inland at Harput were typically scoffed at by Admiral Bristol in Constantinople, who assured the Turks that nothing of the kind was going on, as one war diary records. However, the relief workers soon wrote about what they had seen, and hence we can present parts of these reports, which soon found their way into British newspapers.

The cutthroat Osman Agha ("Lame Osman") and his irregulars killed many thousands of Greek and Armenian civilians throughout the Pontus region. Shortly after his widespread destruction at Marsovan, he was promoted to colonel in the regular army by Mustafa Kemal.

These testimonies are often quite vivid. For example, one testimony eventually sent to the American Secretary of State, which we produce within, came from Ethel Thompson, an NER worker who had spent some time in Samsun before being allowed to proceed by truck south to her NER station at Harput in August of 1921. Her journey inland introduced her graphically to the woeful situation of the deportees.

> We crossed Anatolia under a blazing sun, passing groups and groups of the old men of Samsun and the inhabitants of other Black Sea ports walking on, God knows where, driven by Turkish gendarmes. The dead bodies of those who had dropped during the hard tramp were lying by the roadside. Vultures had eaten parts of the flesh so that in most cases merely skeletons remained.

Once she reached Harput, Ethel would soon discover that, despite their great compassion, the Americans were seldom allowed to help the desperate deportees:

> Our Director had begged for permission to take into the orphanages the Greek children whose mothers had died on the way. It was always refused. Finally, after many weeks of continual appeals, they promised that we could take an old building formerly belonging to German missionaries and keep the Greek children there. We did this and issued a week's rations of food and gave them some clothes, but in a very few days the building was empty. The Turks had driven the children over the mountain.

Rather than these testimonies, of course, the diary accounts themselves are always the chief things. Among the key portraits in this collection are the self-portraits drawn in their diaries of the American Navy captains themselves. The diaries record how they try to enforce their admiral's policies, whether reasonable or misguided. The officers do their best to understand local conditions, consulting with American and foreign businessmen in the port, as well as Near East Relief personnel coming from the interior or working in Samsun, and they report on what they hear and see. They argue with Turkish authorities, register protests both to those authorities and to their boss (the admiral back in Constantinople), and, in general, attempt diligently to decide how to respond to the great inhumanity occurring within their purview. After all, genocide is not an event that naval duty brings one to confront every day.

Greek women trekking toward the seacoast. "Trekking to the Sea" *from Esther Lovejoy's* Certain Samaritans, *published by the Macmillan Company.*

The City of Samsun Itself

Writing home, the *Overton* officer Alfred Murray once described the port of Samsun in this way:

> The town is right down on the shore with a great bank of hills back of it. The hills are wonderfully rich with no trees—covered with grass and with the grasses one can see great herds of cattle sheep and camels feeding on them. The hills are covered with square farms mostly planted with tobacco.[8]

Tobacco was one of the region's major exports. For years, the two major American tobacco firms in the city had each employed several hundred Ottoman Greek men and some Turks as tobacco sorters. This work slowed substantially when almost all the Greek men were deported inland, about half being massacred almost immediately while the others were sent onward to uncertain fates.

Often, the tobacco was transported by camel train. The brand name of the famous "Camel" cigarettes perhaps was inspired by such tobacco caravans in Turkey or by postcards featuring them.

Arriving by ship at the port of Samsun, a traveler could journey on to Angora from there. However, Samsun also was the entry port for American relief workers and missionaries who traveled by carriage ("araba") or in NER trucks to distant American mission stations located near or in Marsovan, Sivas, Malatia, Arabkir (Arapgir), Harput, Diyarbekir, and Cesarea (Kayseri).

Camel caravans like this one transported tobacco to and from Samsun and Bafra in days of peace, but in 1921–22, they transported guns and ammunition to the Turkish Army far inland. *Turkish postcard, probably published prior to 1920.*

Before the 1915–1916 deportations, Samsun had been a thriving port city, boasting a population of forty to sixty thousand inhabitants (contemporary estimates differ as to the number). However, the city had suffered greatly from the 1915–1916 deportations targeting its ethnic Armenians and Greeks, and after the Great War, the population was down substantially. Even during the postwar period covered by the war diaries, we will hear how Turkish civilians in Samsun protested the renewed deportations of Greek men and the additional commercial disaster it now was wreaking upon the city (the latter being part of a country-wide commercial disaster that has been catalogued recently in the Turkish memoirs surveyed by Göçek, 268–70).

The Region Called Pontus

As for the larger region in which Samsun was located, Pontus is a coastal region of northeast Turkey that stretches along the Black Sea. As generally described during this period, it runs some 400 miles from just beyond the small port of Sinope in the west to very near the Russian port of Batoum in the east and extends from 50 to 100 miles inland. It is generally composed of low, sloping, and often forested hills near the coast reaching up to or backed by mountain ranges several miles inland (the mountains to the east, especially, are known as the "Pontic Alps," with the highest peak reaching almost 13,000 feet). In the period covered by these diaries, besides the ports and a few small inland cities, many hundreds of small villages dotted the region. Greeks and Turks plus a very small number of Armenians comprised most of the population of Pontus in 1920.

Ionian Greek settlers and merchants had colonized Pontus way back in the eighth century BCE. Some of their trading posts grew into towns with stone walls and eventually became maritime cities. As recorded in Xenophon's *Anabasis*, when the famous 10,000 Greek mercenaries fought their way north from Persia to the Black Sea (near what is now Trebizond or Trabzon) around 370 BCE, they found the inhabitants of this area spoke their language. They also discovered that these local Greeks had been living there for some 300 years.

Pontic Greeks continued to speak Greek and retain Greek customs under the long subsequent reigns of the Roman and the Byzantine Empires. In the centuries after St. Paul preached Christianity in Asia Minor and Greece in the first century CE, the Pontic Greeks became Christian, as did Greece itself. Indeed, according to the New Testament text, inhabitants of Pontus were among the very first converts to Christianity (Acts 18:2; 1 Peter 1:1). The Pontic Greeks kept their Greek language, their customs, and their Orthodox Christianity even while the Venetians and Genoese enlarged the Black Sea trade and built their own trading posts in the Pontic region. By the Byzantine period, the city of Trebizond had become the capital of the "Empire of Trebizond," and was known as a center of culture and learning.

When the Turks conquered Constantinople and took over Anatolia in the fifteenth century CE, the Pontic Greeks survived that too, "negotiating and conceding a little, converting to Islam a little" as Neal

Ascherson in his book *Black Sea* puts it (176–77). Even those Pontic Greeks who converted to Islam often continued to speak Greek and retained many Greek customs.

Under the Ottoman Empire, the Greek Orthodox Church, to which most Pontic Greeks belonged, was a semi-autonomous *millet*, or religious community, which meant that the Ottoman Greeks throughout Anatolia, though much oppressed, were partly tolerated. Especially in the coastal cities, churches and monasteries remained prominent institutions, and during the nineteenth century, hundreds of schools were built throughout Pontus. Both from their expertise in trade and business as by their comparatively advanced education, the Pontic Greeks prospered to a degree, particularly as compared to the backward Turkish peasants living alongside them. Ottoman Armenians, subjects of another Ottoman *millet*, also excelled in business and trade. The relative prosperity of both these religious and ethnic groups—dampened considerably as it always was by their lack of political and legal freedom—increased during this period, even as the Ottoman government continued to rule, sometimes very oppressively.

This prosperity of the indigenous Christian peoples eventually brought about much envy from the Turks, as did the growth and vocal publicity of some Armenian Nationalist groups. Originally, the Armenian community was the greatest object of the Turks' attack. Indeed, under Sultan Abdul Hamid, the Turks had massacred somewhere between 80,000 and over 200,000 Armenians in Asia Minor from 1894 to 1896, this before the Committee on Union and Progress, or "Young Turks," took over from the Sultan in 1908. Even after that, a massacre of between 15,000 and 20,000 Armenians occurred in Adana in 1909.[9]

Besides Armenians, Ottoman Greeks were also sometimes targeted by the Young Turks even prior to the World War, specifically as early as the Ottoman Empire's Balkan Wars of 1912–1913. In 1913-1914 in Eastern Thrace and Ionia (western Anatolia) and in the Sea of Marmara region, Ottoman Greeks were summarily deported away from Turkey into Greece or deep into the interior of Turkey. However, once World War I began, the Turkish antagonism turned again toward the Armenians. Leading figures of the Armenian population in Constantinople were suddenly executed in the spring of 1915, and Armenians suffered many massacres and death marches throughout Turkey after that, especially in the rest of 1915 and in 1916. In comparison, fewer Ottoman Greeks than Armenians were murdered outright during the Great War. Yet large deportations of Pontic and other Ottoman Greeks were also conducted then.

A widely cited estimate is that at least 500,000 Ottoman Greeks were deported into the interior of Turkey between 1914 and 1917 with much loss of life.[10]

Not all the Ottoman Greeks had been forced out of Samsun or the surrounding Pontus region during the World War, to be sure, and many Pontic Greeks, though very few Armenians, would eventually return from deportation. As a result, many Greek men in Pontus were still in business, or had returned to Pontus to take up their trades or professions, in the postwar period.

Map of the Pontus region

The Hope for a "Pontus Republic"

Because of the Great War depredations, some Armenians had dreamed of a new homeland for themselves via an "American Mandate" for Armenia (building upon the arguments of their American supporters who often voiced this hope; Shenk, *ABSF*, 31–33). Similarly, in the postwar period, some of Turkey's Ottoman Greeks—especially those from the Pontic Diaspora, that is, former residents of Pontus now living in Constantinople or Europe—began campaigning for a "Pontus Republic" that might revive a self-governing small Christian empire that had once existed in the late Middle Ages.

One can download the memorandum signed by Greek Orthodox Archbishop Chrysanthos Filippides of Trebizond of the "Pontus Delegation," which was presented at the Peace Conference in Paris on March 10, 1920.[11] This document proposed an independent nation governing the Pontus region or if not that, at least a successful "autonomous region" like Lebanon was once said to have been. This memorandum was formally addressed to Lloyd George of Britain, but reportedly Chrysanthos also discussed the subject with American President Woodrow Wilson.

The idea did not gain much traction. To be sure, we read in the war diaries of an American ship captain saying that the Pontic Greeks often rejoiced outright upon hearing of successes of the Hellenic Army in the war against the Turkish Nationalists far inland. However, there is no mention in the diaries of 1921–1922 of a public endorsement by ethnic Greeks of a Greek Republic. We only hear about the general subject in occasional Turkish Nationalist accusations.

Mobilization in the Pontus Region: The Labor Battalions

Some of the male population of Pontus had already been mobilized by the Nationalists by the late spring of 1921. Turks were pressed into the new Nationalist Army, while Ottoman Greeks were inducted into the notorious "labor battalions," which had been re-established by the National Assembly in Angora on March 2, 1921 (Hofmann, "Cumulative Genocide," 73). The latter assignments had comprised one of the major tools of minority destruction during World War I.

Labor battalions were regarded as death sentences for those sent to them; in 1922, British diplomat George W. Rendel estimated that life expectancy in these groups was two months, an estimate widely cited.[12] The conditions as dictated by the Turks included very difficult work, such as breaking rocks for road construction and repair—this combined with meager food and inadequate clothing, little or no shelter from the elements, rampant diseases and lack of medical care, and occasional outright killings. All of this ultimately brought about a horrific and apparently intentional result. For instance, the Greek writer Elias Venezis (born Melios), a survivor of a post-Smyrna labor battalion of Greek men from Ayvali (Ayvalik; just north of Smyrna), tells us that of the roughly 3,000 men that were sent to those groups, only 23 survived.[13]

As we learn from the diaries, some Greeks were able to pay a tax that allowed them to evade such labor force mobilization. This is another reason that, in early 1921 before the renewed deportations and massacres, many Greek men still lived and worked in local businesses or for American tobacco companies in Samsun.

Greek Irregulars in the Pontic Mountains

Another important characteristic of the Pontic Region in 1919–22 was the existence of several partisan or bandit groups in nearby mountains. Such groups had originated during the World War or even before, but they grew in number as the war between the Hellenic and Turkish Nationalist armies went on and as labor battalion mobilization threatened the Pontic Greek males. Both Turkish bands (comprised mostly of deserters from the Nationalist Army) and, more significantly, Pontic Greek partisan or guerilla groups could be found throughout the Pontic mountains. The latter groups were composed of draft-age men of Pontic Greek heritage who had deserted from the labor battalions or escaped other deportation parties, or who had left Samsun and coastal villages before being taken by the Turks, just to attempt to survive.

How many Greeks joined these bandit or guerilla groups can be hard to nail down. For the Samsun region, the figure of 15,000 Greek bandits once listed in the diaries (*Sturtevant* WD, Dec. 30, 1921) seems exaggerated. Another figure mentioned is 5,000 (*Overton* WD, Oct. 21, 1921), and this number correlates more closely to the 3,500 armed fighters estimated by a Greek military report in mid-1922.[14] Whatever the number, the potential local Greek support of possible seaborne assault by Hellenic troops—a possibility that, in theory, might provide a second Greek front in the war against the Turkish Nationalists—was another oft-cited reason for the Nationalists to pacify the northern region of Anatolia as they had decided to do in early June 1921 via deportations (Mango, 330).

These armed Greek groups could be fierce fighters. As one bandit remembered, "We lived in the mountains. We were being killed, and we killed. We were being burned down and we burned" (Michael Papadopoulos in an interview with Clark, 65). Moreover, they were certainly feared by the Turks. Excerpts from the diaries of the Soviet general Mikhail Frunze (traveling with a Ukrainian mission to Angora that passed through Samsun) reveal that Turkish soldiers throughout Pontus greatly feared Greek partisan attacks (see Nicolopoulos).

However, although they certainly carried out raids on nearby Turkish villages or Turkish military groups, sometimes to get food simply in order to survive and sometimes in reprisal for killings or massacres on the part of the Turks, the Greek partisans hardly seemed to have been a significant military force. They were armed mainly with rifles, typically German Mausers (Fotiadis, 482), and appear to have lacked artillery, radios, or formal military training.

Beyond that, they were usually hampered by the presence of their families. As Fotiadis comments:

> Pontian partisans took their women, children and old people into the mountains with them to save them from the attacks of the Chetes and the regular army. A. Makridou-Kalliga writes that, apart from the battles they fought . . . they also had to feed the women and children and shelter them in caves, forests, and high mountains that were inaccessible to the enemy. Every rebel move was of necessity accompanied by a parallel move from one shelter to another of the women and children, and this in hostile territory where there was no possibility of obtaining supplies of arms and food from Greek villages, as these had been razed to the ground by irregular Chetes. (480–81)

These partisan groups were almost always in hiding and apparently had little, if any, radio communication with other Greek guerilla bands or with the Hellenic Navy, nor did they possess a regular command and control structure that we are aware of. They lacked support from the Hellenic military or perhaps enjoyed it "only spasmodically" (Clark, 69).[15]

True, some Greek partisans may have contacted the Hellenic warships once they appeared in the Black Sea, perhaps by swimming out to them. This is much more likely than the notion that they were in communication with the Hellenic Army, engaged as it was with the Turkish Nationalist Army a couple of hundred miles to the west. Partisan contact with the warships in the Black Sea cannot be verified, though some brigands bragged of it (*McFarland* WD, Sept. 3, 1921). Diary reports of conversation with Hellenic naval commanders indicate that their ships were focused on stopping guns being landed in the Pontic region, guns that were meant for the Turkish Army far inland.

In their war diaries, the American naval officers often report seeing trans-shipments of arms and ammunition inland toward the war zone, so it appears that the Hellenic Navy was not very successful in stopping those arms shipments. Moreover, an indication of the questionable martial competence of Pontic Greek guerilla bands might be that there are no war diary reports of them capturing Turkish arms shipments. However, American naval officers lacked good local sources for information either about the Nationalist military's battles with the guerillas or about the activities of the Greek partisans themselves.

An American captain from one of the destroyers in Samsun (possibly Captain Haas of the *Sturtevant*) among three ethnic Greek guerillas from the mountains. Photo provided by Stergios Theodoridis.

As revealed in the diaries, Ottoman Greeks evading Turkish forces often entered Samsun seeking food, as did escapees from labor battalions, deportations, and massacres. Local support of male escapees and guerillas by friends and families in Samsun became another Nationalist rationale or pretext for the 1921–1922 deportations. Bruce Clark explains: "Irregular fighters, with a modicum of popular support, can never be defeated without removing the civilian population that succors them. That is what any Turkish or pro-Turkish historian, faced with Greek allegations [of atrocities], would invariably point out." We see this logic outlined in the diaries, and at least one American Navy captain seems to agree with it. However, the specific historical parallels that Clark cites in support of "removing the civilian population" so that guerillas would lose local support—modern Russians against Chechens, for instance, and Turks against Kurds—hardly assure one either of the humanity or reasonableness of such a tactic. Clark himself (69) recognizes that such "iron logic" may have "terrible consequences," which it certainly did in Pontus in 1921-22.

Greek Refugees from Burned Pontic Villages

The initial war diaries indicate that the burnings of the villages, often accompanied by much killing, had started even before the policy of deportation was formally initiated by the Nationalists, which was right after the bombardment of Inebolu in early June 1921. These burnings were typically carried out by Turkish chettahs. The deportations throughout Pontus began a bit later, and usually the males were deported first. As Greek villages near Samsun went up in smoke, an increasing number of women and children sought refuge in Samsun—those who were not killed, that is. At one point, some ninety Greek village children, newly orphaned by Turkish raids on their villages, found their way on their own to the American Near East Relief station at Samsun. Eventually, and certainly by the summer of 1922, a scorched-earth policy of Nationalist military and irregular forces rendered most of the hundreds of Greek villages in the Pontus region completely unlivable.

When word got out that Greek village refugees were getting into Samsun, they were searched out by Turkish soldiers or police; those found were detained. (We see in the war diaries that censuses were frequently conducted by Turkish police or soldiers, apparently to see which Greeks actually were residents of Samsun and which were refugees.) Before long they were deported inland.

Nationalist officials were unconcerned that Greek women and child survivors had become destitute. Although civilian Turkish officials sometimes insisted that they would be protected and provided with food, deportees forced south seem never to have been fed by the Turks. Moreover, even sympathetic American relief teams stationed deep inland were often prohibited from feeding them.

The Navy Destroyer Captains

The American destroyer captains were commanders or lieutenant commanders (mid-level officers) in rank. The term "captain" used here normally refers to their status as ship captains rather than as captains in military rank. Most in their thirties, all were graduates of the United States Naval Academy, as were most (although not all) of the eight or so other naval officers aboard each ship. The ship captains were typically competent at running and navigating their vessels, but few of these officers had any diplomatic experience or much knowledge of history. Some had hurriedly read the 1918 book *Ambassador Morgenthau's Story* about the 1915-1916 Turkish massacres and deportations while en route their Near Eastern duty. However, as we will see, two or three of the ship captains seem to have been relatively well informed about what had happened to the Armenians.

Of course, these officers would have been briefed by the admiral or his chief of staff in Constantinople before taking their ships on their wide-ranging tours of the Black Sea. From these briefings, they would have learned the admiral's policies, and some would imbibe his prejudices as well. In addition to their assignments in Turkey, the destroyers also visited several ports in southern Russia, where American grain was being sent to help end a terrible Russian famine (Shenk, *ABSF*, 137-53). Beyond that, these warships often spent a day or two a month at the legendary Turkish port of Trebizond (for centuries, a terminus of camel caravans from the East) before steaming a couple of hundred miles farther west to Samsun, where they typically spent from two to four weeks apiece.

Some of these ship captains were men of considerable ability as their later careers would indicate; two are worth mentioning in particular. Commander Arthur LeRoy Bristol (no relation to Admiral Mark Bristol) had been a flag secretary for two major shore commands, had won the Navy Cross and Distinguished Service Medal during the First World War, and had commanded other destroyers before assuming command of the destroyer *Overton*, the position he holds for several months in these war diaries. Not long after graduating from the Naval Academy at Annapolis, he had been chosen to serve on the presidential yacht, *Mayflower*. Thus, by the midway point in his naval career when we meet him in the diaries, he was already manifesting considerable talent.

After his command assignment on the *Overton*, Commander Bristol would become a naval aviator, be given command of the first ship built from the keel up as an aircraft carrier (USS *Ranger*), and eventually be promoted to rear admiral and given a series of major combat leadership positions. In 1941, he would be assigned to head up America's effort to help Britain by providing convoys partway across the Atlantic, this in the tense period before America entered World War II. He apparently excelled at this vitally important task because he was promoted to vice admiral in February 1942. Had he not died of a heart attack in Newfoundland in April of that year, we might well have heard Arthur LeRoy Bristol being named in the same breath as famous American admirals of the Second World War.[16]

It was Commander Bristol's strong handwritten missive of July 18, 1921 (presented in full within) that probably moved the reluctant Admiral Mark Bristol to directly contact Mustafa Kemal and to protest the already-ordered deportations of Samsun's Greek women and children. Such a major protest from America's senior representative throughout the Near East, for that was Admiral Bristol's position, seems to have had a permanent impact on some Pontic Greeks, halting the deportation of as many as 10,000 Greek residents of Samsun itself—that is, the Greek women, children, and elderly there, as virtually all of the Greek men of Samsun had already been deported or sent to labor battalions, had died or been killed, or had joined Greek guerilla groups.

Another noteworthy commanding officer who visited Samsun was Captain William Leahy of the cruiser *St. Louis*, which was sent briefly to Samsun in September 1921. Already holding the naval rank of captain, William Leahy would eventually be promoted to admiral and rise to become Chief of Naval Operations in 1937-1939. Upon retirement, he was appointed governor of Puerto Rico and then served briefly as America's ambassador to France. After Pearl Harbor, though, Leahy was recalled to active duty in the navy as President Roosevelt's personal chief of staff, making him, in effect, the first head of America's Joint Chiefs of Staff, a group of senior military leaders that made many major decisions under Leahy's leadership throughout World War II. Leahy served ably in a similar capacity under President Truman, overall from 1942-49. In 1944, he was the first American general officer ever promoted to five-star rank (in his case, "fleet admiral").

Reproduced in this volume are several pages of Leahy's personal diary, which record the *St. Louis's* visit to Samsun. Admiral Bristol had reportedly sent Captain Leahy to the port to make a personal evaluation of the situation there, but the admiral probably also intended the cruiser's voyage to be a show of force, as a cruiser was a much larger warship than a destroyer and had larger guns. No doubt the admiral intended to continue to encourage the Nationalists not to deport Greek noncombatants from Samsun into Turkey's interior, where their futures—indeed, their very lives—would be in jeopardy.

Captain Leahy, interestingly, is the only figure among the American ship captains in Turkish waters who is heard to contemplate the use of armed force to protect the minorities of Turkey, although he wrote this in his personal diary and as far as we know not in an official document. Specifically, he speculates that he could command the whole of the city of Samsun with his cruiser's guns. Had a man of his competence and initiative been present at Smyrna a year later or even been in naval command at Constantinople, it is possible that things might have ended differently for the many tens of thousands of Greeks and Armenians who were slaughtered or died at Smyrna in September 1922 and before.

Other American captains were less alert to the reality of what was going on in Anatolia than these two men. I think in particular of the ship captain who, later in this collection, writes with approval of Faik Bey, a Samsun mutasariff who served several months in this job. This ship captain reports that Faik Bey had not allowed any atrocities to occur during his tenure.

While it is true that this mutasariff is on record as committing himself to allow women and children who were original residents of Samsun to remain in the city after their husbands and fathers had been deported, he carried out other policies that were not so benign. For instance, he directed the deportation of many other groups of Pontic Greeks into the interior, such as women and children whose original villages right near Samsun had been destroyed by Turkish forces and other Greek villagers who had once been protected by the Greek partisans in the mountains but had now come down to Samsun, fleeing starvation. Rather than support these groups, Mutasariff Faik Bey deported several thousand of these women and children south, which would almost certainly result in the death of a significant percentage of them. The navy captain who so praised this Turkish official seems utterly oblivious to the nature of the horrors put into effect by the Greek death marches that were taking place all over Pontus region and elsewhere in Anatolia.

Admiral Mark Bristol's own pro-Turkish bias, often pronounced strongly to his officers, caused increasingly pro-Turkish views to obtain place among his ship captains—particularly in 1922, when, out of support for the Turkish Nationalists, the admiral sought to quash reports from American journalists, missionaries, and Near East Relief officials about the terrible things they were seeing deep inland (Shenk, *ABSF*, 112-19; Housepian Dobkin, 95-97).

The Navy Destroyers Themselves and Their Crews

The destroyers that the ship captains commanded were newly built, sleek, *Clemson*-class destroyers, colloquially named "flushdeckers" or "fourstackers," 314 feet long with a breadth of 31 feet and a draft of almost 10 feet. They each had a complement of 8 officers, 8 chief petty officers, and 106 enlisted men. These vessels each featured four 4-inch or 5-inch guns, as well as several torpedo tubes—although apparently none of this considerable armament was ever used on the Turkish station. These destroyers had a top speed of about 35 knots.

Hence, though an economical speed of 11 knots would require almost two days for them to travel the nearly 500 miles from Samsun to Constantinople, they could usually reach the old Ottoman capital overnight from Samsun if need be, and more than once the senior American naval officer present at Samsun sent a destroyer at high speed to Constantinople to deliver an urgent message to the admiral.

One of America's "four-stack" or "flush deck" destroyers. These versatile warships were slender but fast and powerful, with a crew of just over a hundred. The one pictured is a *Wickes*-class destroyer; the *Clemson*-class destroyers that saw duty at Samsun were very similar.

Usually the destroyers could send and receive radio messages from Samsun, but sometimes atmospheric interference inhibited electronic communications. In the occasional ships' messages reproduced in the diaries, "Stanav" (for "Naval Station") was the name of the naval command in Constantinople while "the Detachment Commander" (or, less often, the American "High Commissioner") was Admiral Bristol.

Sometimes sailors and officers were allowed into the small city of Samsun, where they typically played baseball after they constructed a diamond and field. More rarely, sailors or officers went hunting locally with Turkish guides. Except during crises, the sailors and officers ashore watched races between Arabian thoroughbreds at the city's track or competed with other navy ships' crews at rowing, sailing, or diving. However, few sailors stayed overnight in the city of Samsun, and often they were not allowed ashore in the first place. As for the commanding officers, on the rare occasions when weather and surf made it difficult to return to their ships, captains would board overnight with the family of the manager of an American tobacco business.

Seldom—indeed, almost never—do the destroyer captains mention interaction of members of their crews with the Greeks or Turks ashore.

Lack of shore leave was not a severe problem for the navy ships' crews, however. Constantinople was the sailors' main liberty port, and a fantastic one it was, and the destroyers returned "home" to USN *Buoy #1* just off the European sector of "Constan" to take a rest (and go on liberty) every four to six weeks (Shenk, *ABSF*, 121-36, 155-74).

Ship captains and officers sometimes attended parties or picnics of the small American community in Samsun or brought those Americans out to the ship to entertain, or offer them hot showers, while their ships visited. For a few months during mid-1921 (when the diaries begin), while tensions were at their height, the admiral stationed two destroyers at Samsun.

Other Nations' Ships at Samsun

Commercial ships from several nations regularly stopped at the port. Once in a great while, French, Italian, or British warships also visited the city.

However, from 1921-1922, Greek warships came by regularly, stirring local fears of bombardment. This had occurred at other Black Sea Turkish ports, including Trebizond in July 1921, and would eventually take place at Samsun. It had been a Greek warship's bombardment of the small port of Inebolu (east of Samsun) on June 9, 1921 that is said to have moved the Nationalists to decide that all local Greek males—some of whom might support a Greek Army's landing—had to be deported inland (Mango, 330; but see also Fotiadis, 393).

The American ship captains had orders to stay out of the Greco-Turkish War, but they regularly visited Hellenic warships upon their arrival at Samsun to warn them of the presence of American civilians in the city, asking for time in which the Americans ashore might move these civilians to safety. Such actions may have protected the city from bombardment on occasion and may have aided the Turks in a minor way. On the other hand, as any bombardment of a port usually resulted in retaliation upon the city's Greeks, perhaps this American "interference" also helped protect those beleaguered people who remained at Samsun. Sometimes, indeed, on steaming out to meet the Greek warships, the Americans informed the Hellenic naval officers they met that any bombardment would make things much worse for the Ottoman Greeks ashore (see, for instance, the *Overton* WD, July 21, 1921).

Other Americans and American Organizations at Samsun

The Near East Relief was a private charity initially, but one that had become an official American governmental organization shortly after the end of the Great War. Its relief workers had begun arriving in Turkey in 1919. The Near East Relief organization in Samsun itself operated a hospital and also ran separate orphanages for Armenian, Greek, and Turkish orphans. One Mr. Van Toor ran the hospital until very late in the diaries, when a man named Green took his job. Usually several other American NER workers were present in the city, typically working at one of the aforementioned sites while they awaited Turkish permission to travel inland. This included the NER worker Gertrude Anthony, a niece of Susan B. Anthony, who is mentioned early in the diaries. She was awaiting permission to travel to the American mission and relief station of Marsovan, where she had been assigned. A few young American women worked long-term at the NER orphanages at Samsun, where they were helped by young, English-speaking Greek or Armenian women who had been educated at American schools in Turkey such as "Anatolia College," the American mission college at Marsovan.

American relief was distributed at several sites throughout Turkey, most commonly at the several substantial missionary stations in the interior, for American missionary work had been conducted in Turkey since the mid-nineteenth century. Churchgoers' contributions had gone into substantial buildings for churches, schools, and hospitals, as well as homes for staff, salaries, and so on. The missionaries proved vital to the postwar relief work. Because they had often spent years or even decades in the country, they typically knew one or more of the local languages, understood the various peoples and knew some of their leaders, and were acquainted with the geography. Worthy of note, more than half of the NER volunteers who worked in Turkey were women, as were many American missionaries. Often the missionary women had been educated at then-prominent Eastern women's colleges in America like Wellesley, Smith, and Mount Holyoke.

Samsun was also the home of two substantial American tobacco businesses: the Alston Tobacco Company, managed by William J. King along with the "younger King" (apparently William J.'s son Preston King) and a third manager named Johnson; and the Gary Tobacco Company, headed by a man named Currin. There were originally some 600 workers in the Alston company, mostly Ottoman Greek men (though there were also Turkish employees), some of whom had been working for King and Johnson for years. The Gary tobacco business also employed hundreds. After the deportation of all the Greek men, many of them to be massacred shortly afterwards near the small town of Kavak, the firms hired hundreds of Greek women in their place, partly to keep their businesses in operation but also partly to keep the families of the deported or killed Greek males from destitution.

There were other, smaller American companies, including the Melachrino Tobacco Company and a Standard Oil outlet that sold some gas and oil in Samsun. The American Trade Corporation, whose supervisor, an American named English, seems to have also managed the Melachrino firm, sold shoes, cotton, woolen goods, and toilet articles (*Sturtevant* WD, Sept. 21, 1921). Altogether, there were between fifteen and twenty American civilians in Samsun at any one time, plus the families of the businessmen, as well as a few NER workers or missionaries awaiting permission to travel to interior assignments or to leave the country.

A few other foreigners were present in Samsun, having lived there for years, chiefly Italians. Most notable was Stanislas Count Schmecchia, who represented the Italian Lloyd Triestino steamship company and who served as a kind of informal Italian consul (he had once been the official Italian consul here). American Navy ship captains found the Count highly emotional but generally quite trustworthy. He was typically greatly saddened by the terrible atrocities occurring in the region.

The Turkish Leaders in Samsun and Elsewhere in the Pontus Region

The Turkish civilian official that the navy captains interacted with most was the mutasariff, who served both as the mayor of Samsun and the governor of the local district, and who was changed out every few months. One of the Turkish men assigned to this post was very weak or corrupt; another man was more responsible. A less important official, the Turkish censor, was actually working for the Americans to some extent. As Captain Bristol remarked in April 1921, back when the destroyers were coming to Samsun only occasionally:

> It appears that all affairs connecting with Americans are left almost entirely in the hands of Haidar Bey, the interpreter. Haidar Bey is employed by the Near East in the fore[n]oon, is Official Censor for the Americans, and acts as interpreter and general utility man for the Senior Naval Officer [the senior American captain in port]. It is practically certain that he has a fourth job, as spy for the Angora Government. But all in all, the arrangement appears to be very satisfactory. (*Overton* WD, April 28, 1921)

While early captains, like Bristol, regarded Haidar Bey as an asset—and he is relied on by the Americans throughout these diaries—eventually his reliability was questioned.

Concerning censorship, the civilian Americans in the port, like Gertrude Anthony, went out of their way preliminarily to self-censor the letters of local Americans because of occasionally "scandalous" letters or magazines being included in the Turkish mail to and from the mission stations. (These letters were apparently regarded as scandalous either because they told the truth of what was going on in Turkey or because they took a marked anti-Turkish slant—or both.) Had the Turks seen such letters, they might have stopped the mail from the inland mission stations, which would have included all letters and reports from NER officials there. As it was, some mission workers hundreds of miles inland were quite isolated. At Arabkir, Armenia, a bit off the beaten track to the east, at one point the two or three Americans there said they had not seen any other Americans for a year and a half.

Besides the Mutasariff, there was also a military governor in the Samsun area who the Americans talked to occasionally. He was in charge of the Nationalist military forces in the city, which sometimes numbered several hundred, and perhaps more troops in the region.

Two Turkish leaders spoken of frequently in the diaries, whose actions adversely affected the Greeks in Samsun and in Pontus generally, were among the most brutal ethnic Turkish leaders in all of Turkey, which is saying something.

One was Osman Agha (Feridunzade or Feridunoğlu Osman Ağa), also known as Topal or "Lame" Osman, who the recent biographer of Mustafa Kemal, Andrew Mango, rightly labels "a sadistic ethnic cleanser of Armenians and Greeks" (Mango, 383). Indeed, the Russian General Frunze on his visit to Turkey heard Turkish civilians refer to this man with revulsion as "Osman Ağa the Strangler" (Nicolopoulos, 50). Originally the leader of a private army of hundreds of cutthroats of the "Laz" ethnicity, Osman was responsible for extortion, mass killing, brutality, robbery, and/or rape of many thousands of Pontic Greeks under the general approval of the Nationalists (Mango, 213). Lame Osman had also organized massacres and greatly enriched himself and others back in 1915-1917 (Akçam, 326, 342).

Andrew Mango points out that Kemal relied on outlaws in the early period of his Nationalist leadership (Mango, 227, 254), and that is certainly true. According to Fotiadis, Mustafa Kemal made contact with Osman at Havza ten days after he entered Turkey at Samsun in May 1919, called him a patriot, and entrusted this leader of cutthroats with the initial "cleansing" of the Pontus region (Fotiadis, 285-87). Later, after he had fomented much disorder in the Samsun area likely including the massacres at Ada and Kavak, Osman was ordered to leave Samsun and report to Angora. This order was given to him at the time of Admiral Bristol's protest and perhaps partly because of it—and in the *Overton* diary entry of July 19, 1921, Captain A.L. Bristol happens to witness personally Osman's great distress on the likely occasion of his first hearing of that order.

However, instead of immediately reporting to Angora, Osman and his chettahs moved on to Marsovan. As reports in this book depict, at that small city, the Laz forces of Osman Agha killed perhaps a thousand Greeks and Armenians, raped many minority women, and burned some 400 houses. Yet once Osman arrived in Angora, Kemal promoted him to colonel in the army (Fotiadis, 389). As an indication of Mustafa Kemal's continued and apparently substantial alliance with this utterly abominable man, Osman provided Kemal a rotation of his Laz irregulars to be Kemal's personal bodyguard for some two and a half years beginning in late 1920 (Mango, 284, 381-82).

To finish the story of Osman Agha, in March 1923, Osman invited an outspoken opponent of Mustafa Kemal named Ali Şükrü to his house and on his arrival had him strangled and buried. Since Şükrü was a member of the General Assembly, Kemal ordered the regular military to arrest Osman. Osman and his men resisted, and Osman was killed in the ensuing gunfire (Mango, 381-82). He was decapitated and his body hung publicly. Mango claims that Kemal had not ordered the killing of Şükrü but that it was convenient for Kemal not only to have this political opponent done away with but also, with the death of Osman, to finally have gotten rid of "the last detachment of irregulars" who Kemal had depended on in his first years as the Nationalist leader (Mango, 383). Göçek, however, says that in his death cries, Osman claimed that Kemal had ordered the murder (336).

The other Turkish leader active in the Pontus region who was known for his brutality was Nureddin Pasha (Nureddin or Nurettin İbrahim Konyar), rightly described by Kemal's biographer as "a forceful, ambitious, xenophobic, and cruel soldier" (Mango, 330). Mustafa Kemal had formally put this Turkish Army general in charge of pacifying the whole of the Pontus region in December 1920 by appointing him head of the new Nationalist "Central" Army, which was being built up to 10,000 men. Much of the widespread devastation of Pontus that we read about in the diaries was due to Nureddin. It was Nureddin's recommendation to the general staff at Angora that, "in view of the danger of a Greek landing in Samsun, all male Greeks aged between 15 and 50 years should be deported to the interior" (Mango, 330). The approval of this recommendation gave him deportation authority, which authority Nureddin seems to have relentlessly pushed to expand so as to deport Greek women and children as well. The diaries indicate that Nureddin was something of a potential rival of Kemal, who was said to be comparatively moderate in his policies as compared to the "extremist" Nureddin.

The local Nationalist military commander in Samsun mentioned above would have reported to Nureddin.

As we will see, Kemal would relieve Nureddin of his Pontic military command in November 1921, apparently due to the great severity of his repression of a Kurdish revolt near Sivas in March 1921 in which Nureddin employed Osman Agha's cutthroats (Mango, 330). The action of Nureddin had reportedly upset members of the Nationalist Assembly. However, the measures Nureddin employed to eliminate the ethnic Greeks of Pontus in nearly a year's command there were probably even more brutal.

Nationalist leader Mustafa Kemal. *From the collection of Admiral Thomas Kinkaid at the Naval History and Heritage Command.*

That Mustafa Kemal seems to have cared little about taming Nureddin's methods is made clear by the fact that he would choose Nureddin as one of the leading generals of the Nationalist Army in 1922, apparently because of his "savagery in battle." This assgnment would ultimately allow Nureddin to settle a score with the Greek Orthodox Metropolitan (or bishop) Chrysostomos of Smyrna, a religious and civic leader and Greek Nationalist, who, according to Ureneck, "mixed Greek territorial ambitions with his spiritual duties."[17] Chrysostomos not only had welcomed the Greek Army with blessings when it landed in Smyrna in 1919 but before then had also successfully pressed the British to depose Nureddin as postwar governor of Smyrna. When Nureddin came into control at Smyrna in late 1922, he would take the opportunity to retaliate, delivering the bishop to a Turkish mob by which he was beaten and stabbed, his eyes gouged out, and his nose and ears severed before someone shot him, ending his misery (Ureneck, 171-73).

And it was into the hands of this man that Kemal had given military control of the Pontus in late 1920.

Political Leadership in Angora

In 1921, most Nationalist *political* leaders were at Angora when they were not at the front. Mustafa Kemal, who was from the very beginning the leader of the Nationalists, was of course the key figure there, although he took personal charge of the embattled Nationalist Army to the west for a period. There seems to be no question that to Kemal was due both the initial directive to pacify northern Anatolia *and* the backing off of the deportation order hanging over the Greek women and children in Samsun proper when Admiral Bristol protested the deportations directly to him. Yes, Nureddin Pasha was thought by those in Samsun to be mercilessly pressing the burning of the Greek villages and deportations. However, in the diaries, local Turkish officials at Samsun are frequently quoted saying the orders for deportations come from Angora—that is, directly from Mustafa Kemal and his administration.

Americans occasionally met Mustafa Kemal, including not only General Harbord of the United States Army, who in 1919 made an intensive investigatory journey across Anatolia, but also American journalists, naval officers, and relief workers too. Conferring with him during the period the diaries cover were the American naval intelligence officer Lieutenant Robbie Dunn from Constantinople (see the *Brooks* WD, July 13-14, 1921) and the widely and rightly respected missionary-turned-NER worker Annie T. Allen, who had been sent by Admiral Bristol to lead American relief efforts at Angora and who is mentioned occasionally in this book. In effect, Allen became Admiral Bristol's (and America's) informal representative at the Nationalist headquarters.

Early on, Allen found herself not only invited to dinner amongst the Nationalist leaders but was allowed to observe the Nationalist parliament in action. After the Nationalist suppression of the peasants' revolt at Konia, which she had observed firsthand under the very guns of the rebels while shepherding a group of orphans to a place of safety, Allen protested some Nationalist actions there in person to Kemal upon traveling to Angora. She received a thoughtful written response from him.

Allen was well treated in Angora and generally spoke with respect of Kemal and the Nationalists, but, in the midwinter of 1921–1922, she took a carriage journey to Harput to assist American reliefers deal with obstructive Turkish officials there. On the journey, she witnessed death marches similar to those she had seen take place during the Great War despite assurances she had recently received from authorities in Angora that nothing of the kind was taking place! In fact, these deportations were in full force and had been occurring for months. Sadly, this remarkable woman failed to change the attitude or policies of the Turkish officials at Harput toward the deported minorities or toward America's Near East Relief there. On her return journey, she was accidentally thrown from her carriage, and shortly later she died of typhus. Her sickbed comments about her experience at Harput were somewhat cryptic, but it was clear that she had been much demoralized about Kemal and the Turkish Nationalists before she died (Shenk, "Ethnic Cleansing," 200).

Events chronicled in these diaries suggest that Allen's demoralization was warranted.

Our Presentation of the War Diary Accounts

The main corpus of the Samsun war diary records—that is, the group of records stretching from May to early November 1921—has been shortened by omitting much irrelevant reference to internal naval, commercial, and relief business; insignificant visits to various quarters of the town; discussion of miscellaneous visitors to the city (Russian, German, American); and so on. These deletions are marked by ellipses. Reference to every Turkish or Greek military-related event of any size at all has been included in this six-month record. All references to either Greek or Turkish offenses or atrocities have been included, and all relevant comments by American ship captains are also to be found here. Reports of Turkish and Greek arguments about these events and conversations between the Americans and Turkish officials have also been retained.

We have summarized the last eight months or so of the Samsun war diaries that we examined (from November 1921 to June 1922) rather than reproducing them in detail, both to save space and because most critical actions had already taken place by November 1921. However, village burnings and substantial deportations continued well into 1922, as our summary notes. Other important information can also be found in our summary, including a brief account of the Hellenic Navy's June 1922 ineffective bombardment of Samsun.

Besides the Samsun war diaries, in a separate section we reproduce many of the Trebizond war diaries that the naval captains recorded from July 1921 to June 1922, which were far shorter than the Samsun diaries as the destroyers typically only visited Trebizond for a couple of days every three or four weeks. These diaries from the destroyers' visits to the second-largest Pontic port provide yet another window on the overall Pontic experience. The male Greeks at this city were not deported as early as the Samsun Greeks had been, but a December 1921 war diary notes that, by then, these minority males had also been sent inland, probably to labor camps. As the Trebizond diaries show, the Greek women and children at this city somehow were never threatened with deportation, perhaps because Osman Agha and his Laz cutthroats never came there. Nevertheless, terrible events in the local region outside of the city of Trebizond itself were certainly occurring. In the spring of 1922, thanks to the persistence of a reporter from the *Christian Science Monitor* who got ashore at Trebizond and searched out news as to what was happening there and nearby, post-war news of such events as death marches, forced starvation, and massacres being inflicted upon Greeks of Pontus got into an American newspaper—this despite Nationalist attempts (which were seconded by Admiral Bristol) to keep things quiet.[18]

Finally, in all the diaries and some supporting documents, obvious grammatical errors and errors in punctuation, as well as some spelling deviations, have been silently corrected. Harput, for instance, in the original diary entries is also spelled Kharput, Harput, and Harpout; usually we correct diary reference to Harput. We regularly use modern spelling for the city of "Samsun" rather than "Samsoun"—the Americans typically used the latter spelling in the war diaries. The Americans also usually spelled the Nationalist leader "Mustapha" Kemal, which we have changed everywhere to "Mustafa" Kemal. References to "Nurettin" or "Noureddin" we change to "Nureddin." For most other names, we typically use the spellings found in the diary text.

All parentheses in the text are original, but brackets in the text indicate either (a) a probable reading of a word obscured or partially obscured in the original typescript, (b) a word indicating the likely intended meaning, or (c) additional information added for explanation, such as "all the arabagees [drivers of carriages]." A bracketed mark of ellipses [...] indicates that we simply cannot read the original. Asterisk marks in the text refer the reader to further information or commentary at the bottom of the page. These serve as explanatory footnotes for the diary text itself. Commas have occasionally been added to the diary texts for clarity, and on a few occasions, addition of paragraphing has cut the density of some long, shapeless diary passages. Full-length references that appear in the footnotes are sometimes made use of for publications referred to only once; a few of these documents do not appear in the selected bibliography.

Finally, we need to comment on our rather technical use of additional ellipses.

Standard ellipses such as those mentioned above occur within a diary entry (see, for example, the end of the first paragraph of the *Fox* WD, May 24, 1921).

However, occasionally at the very end of an entry, at the beginning of an additional line, we have placed an ellipsis of four periods (see the very end of the *Fox* WD, May 17, 1921). These marks indicate that a whole day's entry or perhaps several days of entries have been omitted in the succeeding material. (In the case mentioned, we have omitted entries for May 18, 19, and 20, which would ordinarily follow.) We have usually omitted one or a few days' entries in these cases because we have judged the material within them to be irrelevant for our purposes—often they are very short, or the captain did not come ashore that day (or nothing happened), or they only deal with material such as naming the ships in the harbor or commenting upon the comings and goings of those ships, etc.

Also because of irrelevancy, we sometimes omit material within a day's entry but before any verbiage begins, either using an ellipsis of four periods on the first line of the day's entry to indicate that one or more sentences have been omitted within the opening paragraph (see *Fox* WD, May 22, 1921) or that the material preceding the first printed paragraph of verbiage has been omitted (see *Fox* WD, May 27–28).

Footnotes to "General Introduction"

1. We need to comment about our use of ethnic or nationalistic titles in the foregoing Preface, in this General Introduction, and in later sectional introductions, footnotes, and other editorial remarks.

There were obvious differences between Pontic and other Asia Minor Greeks compared to the Greeks of the nation of Greece referred to as "Greeks" in documents of this period. Greeks in Asia Minor or Anatolia were ethnic Greeks who were born as citizens of the Ottoman Empire rather than ever being citizens of Greece. Many spoke a Greek dialect different from that spoken in Greece; indeed, a significant number spoke only Turkish. So, in our comments, we often make use of the title "Ottoman Greeks" to clarify that our reference is to those ethnic Greeks who were born in and lived in Anatolia. However, since the American naval officers writing the diaries who used the term "Greek" were usually referring to Ottoman Greeks, we often leave off the qualifier. Of course we also regularly use the term "Pontic Greeks" for natives of Pontus, since what happened to these particular Ottoman Greeks is central to this work.

We sometimes use the term "Hellenic," especially in referring to the army from Greece that in 1919–1922 was fighting the Nationalist Turks in western Anatolia or to officers and crewmen of warships from Greece that were operating in the Black Sea and sometimes bombarding Turkish Nationalist facilities at Pontic ports.

As for the terms "Turks" and "Turkish Nationalists," we are well aware that the Nationalist forces and the government of Mustafa Kemal included several Muslim ethnicities, including (most particularly in these diaries) the Laz forces of Osman Agha but also, for example, Circassians, Arabs, and Kurds, as well as Muslims of mixed descent. Yet in the American documents we are editing or citing, Mustafa Kemal's forces or the civilian officials working for him are known as "Nationalists," "Turkish Nationalists," or simply "Turks," and when American officers refer to "Turks" or "Turkish officials," except in the case of the Laz, they regularly ignore (or fail to perceive) ethnic differences that might have been distinguished among those oppressing the Pontic Greeks.

Besides American usage of such labels, one notes that the motto "Turkey for the Turks" was prominent not only among the earlier Young Turks but among the Nationalists too. For instance, in 1923,

Kemal himself spoke very favorably of the specific concept "Turkey of the Turks" while explaining his idea of nationalism. He said in an interview, "We are now Turks—only Turks," but since his idea of nationalism meant "a people of *kindred birth, religion and temperament*" (our italics), he was obviously including all Muslim ethnicities in Turkey, not just ethnic Turks, under a Nationalist label (Marcosson, 144).

Overall, then, the lumping together of several Muslim ethnicities under the label "Turk" being not just an American practice in the diaries but also a Nationalist habit of the day, in our introductions and editorial work we also normally use the term "Turk" as a nationalistic label, although the person being spoken of is often ethnically Turkish as well.

2. Housepian Dobkin points out that Premier Venizelos had been away at the Paris Peace Conference for two years when he returned to Greece, that some Greek troops had been absent ever since the Balkan Wars had ended in 1913, and that there had been little noticeable improvement in the Greek Army's position in Ionia. Apparently because of such factors, not only did Venizelos lose the election in November 1920, but after the death of King Alexander, King Constantine's return was soon accomplished by a plebiscite. Housepian Dobkin goes on briefly to discuss the paradoxical continuation of the war (*Smyrna, 1922*, 92–93).

3. The Turkish word for bandits, irregulars, or partisans was "çeteler." However, throughout the diaries and in other American documents of the day, the term "chettah" is customary, so we also use this Americanization rather than the Turkish term in our introductions and editorial material.

4. Lieutenant Arthur Murray of the *Overton* reported the beginning of this new activity in a letter to his mother June 5, 1921 in *Black Sea: A Naval Officer's Near East Experience*, Kindle book, Location 591.

5. We use the term "genocidal" here advisedly. Although the word "genocide" itself did not exist until Raphael Lemkin coined it during World War II, from what the naval officers were hearing and seeing, most of them concluded pretty early on that the Turkish policies were intended to "exterminate" the Ottoman Greeks in Anatolia (e.g., Captain C.S. Joyce, *Fox* WD, May 24 and 28, 1921, and Captain A.L. Bristol, *Overton* WD, July 17 and 22, 1921; similar comments appear in

several later war diaries). As far as we can see, such a "policy of extermination" amounts to virtually the same thing that modern scholars now denote by the term "genocide." Indeed, the terms we find in the diaries parallel close to those of the originator of the term in his own definition. For instance, this same word "extermination" appears in the English version of Lemkin's 1945 proposal to the United Nations for "*an international treaty on genocide,*" as was published in the April 1946 *American Scholar* (15:2, 227–30):

> The crime of genocide should be recognized therein as a conspiracy to exterminate national, religious or racial groups. The overt acts of such a conspiracy may consist of attacks against life, liberty or property of members of such groups merely because of their affiliation with such groups.

Should someone ask us what our definition of genocide is, we would refer to this definition of Lemkin's. Notice, too, in connection with this original formulation, that attacks against "life, liberty, and property," such as Lemkin denotes above as qualifying actions to be genocidal are all three described in the war diaries as frequently taking place in the Pontus in 1921–1922.

6. *Turkey in My Time* (Norman: Univ. of Oklahoma Press, 1956, 94, 79). For additional outlooks on the admiral, see Shenk, *ABSF*, 41–48; Housepian Dobkin, 65–83; Ureneck, 48–64, as well as Bryson, Buzanski, and Dunn.

7. For example, the executive officer of the *Overton* in either his October 1st or November 1st, 1922 war diary from Samsun (date partially obscured) estimates that "there are about seven or eight thousand people in Samsun who will have to be evacuated" or moved by ship out of Turkey altogether. Almost all of these would have been Greek women, children, and elderly from Samsun proper who seem to have been kept from deportation by the admiral's protest to Mustafa Kemal.

8. Arthur Murray, *Black Sea,* Letter of June 5, 1921, to his mother.

9. Taner Akçam mentions several estimates as to how many Armenians were killed from 1894–96 in *A Shameful Act,* p. 42. On p. 69 of the same

work, he mentions the casualty estimate cited in our text of the massacres at Adana. See also Göçek, 204–06, concerning details of the massacres at Adana.

10. This estimate, cited by several scholars, comes originally from a memorandum written by British diplomat Rendel of March 20, 1922. Hofmann, "Cumulative Genocide," 102–03, cites this source and then, while noting other estimates, describes various methological difficulties involved in such accounting. Psomiades, *Fridtjof Nansen*, 13, Shirinian, "The Background," 53, and others use this same estimate, though sometimes indirectly.

11. See this URL: https://archive.org/details/pontusquestionme00pontiala.

12. For instance, see Psomiades, "Near East Relief," 27. He documents the Rendel memorandum as follows: Great Britain, FO 371/7960, E11885/10524/44, *Memorandum by Mr. Rendel on Turkish Atrocities between March to October, 1922,* October 30, 1922.

13. Speros Vryonis, Jr., summarizes Venezis's experiences and frequently translates from Venezis's Greek account in "Greek Labor Battalions in Asia Minor," *The Armenian Genocide: Cultural and Ethical Legacies*, ed. Richard G. Hovannisian (New Brunswick, NJ: Transaction, 2007), 275–309; the numbers cited are from p. 288.

14. Psomiades in "Bombardment," 146, cites a June 7, 1922 Greek naval report written at Constantinople estimating that 3,500 armed fighters were scattered in guerilla bands in the Bafra-Samsun region. This was after the Nationalist Minister of the Interior had come to Samsun with a strong force that attacked the Greek partisans in the mountains and perhaps reduced their numbers substantially. He had arrived in the city on February 11, 1922 according to the *Williamson* diary of that date.

15. Clark references (262) the work of Nikos Marantzidis on the "irregular warfare which raged around the Samsun area in the early 20th Century," found in that author's book, *Yasasin Millet, Zito To Ethnos* (Iraklion, Papepistemiakes Ekdoseis Kritis, 2001).

16. Vice Admiral Arthur L. Bristol's naval biography can be found in the Naval History and Heritage Command profile, to be found at https://www.history.navy.mil/research/histories/ship-histories/danfs/a/arthur-l-bristol.html, accessed on May 3, 2018. Similar information on Bristol can be found in the *Dictionary of American Naval Fighting Ships.* Incidentally, through a mistaken reading of Bristol's handwriting, Shenk, *ABSF*, 99, mistakenly named this officer "G.L. Bristol."

17. Note that for many Ottoman Greeks, Chrysostomos's welcoming of the Hellenic forces at Smyrna would not have been regarded as excessively nationalistic. Instead, those people would have received the Hellenic forces as liberators, hoping that centuries of "slavedom" would end under the Hellenic occupation of Ionia. Chrysostomos is a patriot to Greek Orthodox Christians, and he has been declared a martyr and saint by his church.

18. See the Herbert Gibbons newspaper article that we reproduce at the end of the section of Trebizond war diaries. During much of the period the diaries cover, the Nationalists normally did not allow foreigners traveling on transiting commercial vessels to go ashore in Pontus. This would have helped to keep anyone from reporting atrocities that were occurring there (see the *McFarland* WD, August 27, 1921). It was probably by pretending to be an NER worker that Gibbons managed to evade this Turkish order and learn much about the Greeks' situation in the Trebizond region (see *Sands* Trebizond WD, June 3, 1922).

TIMELINE OF EVENTS REPORTED IN THE AMERICAN WAR DIARIES FOR 1921–1922

Prior to the period covered by the American war diaries of this collection, major Turkish aggression against the Ottoman Greeks involving deportations, massacres, or forced labor took place in 1913-1914 in Eastern Thrace, Ionia (western Anatolia) and the sea of Marmara region; and during World War I throughout Anatolia, including Pontus.

In 1919–1922, the Hellenic Army and Greek civilian governor protected the Greeks and other nationalities at Smyrna and in much of Western Anatolia, including the Greek part of the war zone. However, elements of the Hellenic army allowed, encouraged, or committed some atrocities against Turks in the Sea of Marmara region, the latter actions often being reprisals for earlier atrocities of Turks against the Greek population of Nicomedia (see Shenk, *ABSF*, 96–98, 305–06, and Faltaits).

Otherwise, in most of the rest of Anatolia for this period, Ottoman Greeks increasingly came under Turkish Nationalist governance and became increasingly subject to the same kinds of Turkish attacks as the Young Turks had inflicted upon the Armenians (and, to a lesser extent, upon the Greeks) during World War I.

On their side, Greek partisans in Pontus increasingly attacked Turkish forces and Turkish villagers during this time, either seeking food or in reprisal for the Turkish attacks upon them.

The timeline produced below principally covers events that are mentioned in the war diaries of the American destroyers reproduced in this collection, though some details come from secondary works or the testimonies presented here.

Noteworthy Events in the Pontus Region Shortly Before the War Diaries Begin

December 1920: Nureddin Pasha is appointed head of the Central Army.

January 18–19, 1921: The first Greek leaders from Samsun, Bafra, and other Pontic cities are arrested and imprisoned at Amassia. Many others are arrested later.

Map of the main Pontic ports,
along with various other sites mentioned in the war diaries

Significant Events Reported By War Diaries of this Collection

May 1921: American destroyers begin maintaining a rotating station at Samsun; destroyers also visit Trebizond periodically. War diaries in this collection begin.

May 15, 1921: The large village of Ada (near Samsun) is destroyed, and the residents are massacred by Turkish irregulars.

May 23, 1921: Reports begin being heard of great numbers of Greek villages devastated in the Samsun region and near Bafra, and inhabitants are being driven out or killed.

June 9, 1921: Hellenic warships bombard Inebolu (to the east of the area mapped above), the first of several such Hellenic naval actions in Pontic ports of the Black Sea.

June 16, 1921: Mustafa Kemal and his government agree with Nureddin Pasha's recommendation (in view of the possibility of a Greek landing at Samsun) that all male Greeks, fifteen to fifty, should be deported to the interior (Mango, 330).

June 17, 1921: Some 3,000 draft-age Greek males are arrested in Samsun, including tobacco workers from American companies in the city, and are deported inland. Roughly half of these deportees are soon massacred at or near Kavak.

July 17–19, 1921: An order is issued to deport all the Greek women and children of Samsun. Commander Arthur LeRoy Bristol convinces Admiral Mark Bristol to protest this order via telegraph to Mustafa Kemal.

July 19, 1921: Osman Agha is suddenly recalled to Angora and ordered to report from Pontus.

July 20, 1921: Hellenic warships bombard Trebizond. Subsequently, the first group of some 300 male Greek residents are deported from this city.

July 23, 1921: Youssuf Kemal, Kemal's foreign minister, cancels the deportation of women and children from Samsun proper, probably in response to Admiral Bristol's protest.

July 24, 1921: Osman Agha and his Laz forces begin four days of murder, rape, looting, and burning at Marsovan. Afterwards, he reports to Angora.

August 11, 1921: Nationalists announce a wide commandeering of 40% of all supplies useful for military purposes. The NER and both local and foreign businesses must comply.

September 2, 1921: About 900 women and children from near Samsun are deported. Deportation of women and children not native to Samsun proper continues regularly afterwards, as do deportations elsewhere in Pontus and Anatolia generally.

September 5, 1921: Some 6,000 women and children are reported to have been deported from Bafra. Americans hear that many local Turks had unsuccessfully tried to stop these deportations, which reportedly were very cruel.

September 21–23, 1921: The American cruiser *St. Louis*, commanded by Captain William Leahy, visits Samsun.

September 1921: Hangings of Greek leaders of Pontus are conducted in Amassia; partial lists of those hung are published in Samsun. In August and October, Nureddin Pasha comes to Samsun reportedly for more such "tribunal" work.

September 27, 1921: The NER Director at Sivas reports via message that 50,000 deportees are en route to Sivas from Amassia; from 1,000 to 3,000 arrive there daily.

October 30, 1921: Kemal relieves Nureddin Pasha of his command of the Central Army.

November-December 1921: Almost all Greek and Armenian men are deported from Trebizond.

1922

February 12, 1922: The Nationalist Minister of the Interior visits Samsun while a large Nationalist military force attempts to eliminate the Greek partisans in nearby mountains.

May 3, 1922: Dr. Mark Ward and Forrest Yowell, exiled from NER at Harput, reach Constantinople, are quoted in British papers about death marches and untold suffering in the interior. Admiral Bristol blocks these reports in American papers.

May 31, 1922: A major article on Turkish atrocities in the Trebizond region is published in America's *Christian Science Monitor* by Herbert Adams Gibbons.

June 7, 1922: Hellenic warships bombard Samsun without substantial effect.

July 18, 1922: The NER Director at Samsun reports frightful Turkish atrocities in the Trebizond region but asks that they be kept quiet lest they interfere with relief work.

Significant Events Taking Place After the War Diaries of This Collection

August–September 1922: The Kemalist Army decisively defeats the Hellenic army. The Hellenic Army retreats, burning Turkish villages as it goes. Myriads of Greek refugees flee to Smyrna.

The great conflagration at Smyrna takes place, as do terrible events during and after the fire.

In late September, the American Navy, with the help of British sailors, begins the evacuation of nearly 200,000 remaining women, children, and elderly from Smyrna, cooperating with American missionary Asa Jennings, who has located and brought twenty Greek transports to the port.

October 1922: Except for thousands of Christian males retained in Turkey for forced labor, the majority of the remaining Christians in the interior begin their trek to the sea; transports eventually will take most of those who survive on to Greece.

July 1923: The Peace Treaty of Lausanne and population exchange are agreed on between Greece and Turkey. In 1924, remaining Greeks in Asia Minor are exchanged for Turks from Greece. Greeks in Constantinople can stay, though tens of thousands leave.

September 1923: American Navy ships leave Turkish waters permanently. Most American civilians and civilian agencies leave Constantinople. Allies also leave. Nationalists enter, take over Constantinople, and now rule all of Turkey.

SAMSUN WAR DIARIES
FROM MAY 1921
TO NOVEMBER 1921

FINDING OUT WHAT'S HAPPENING ASHORE

In early May 1921, some 3,000 male ethnic Greek residents remained in Samsun, operating businesses or otherwise working there. Even though a large number of Greek men had been pressed into labor battalions before this, many others had paid the required exemption tax, thus legally avoiding the labor requirement.

As a result, commerce in Samsun in early 1921 continued as it had for decades, mostly in the hands of the commercially adept Greeks. At the same time, the two large American tobacco firms in the city, taken together, employed perhaps 1,000 men, mainly Pontic Greeks but some Turks as well.

Such strong bonds existed between the employees or former employees of the latter firms and their American managers that both Greeks and Turks would confide to their former managers some of the terrible things they had witnessed or learned of. Besides the perspective offered by the managers' years of experience in the country, their political knowledge, and their fluency in Turkish, what the managers learned from their former or current employees also made the American tobacco bosses great assets to the navy ship captains seeking knowledge of the city and region.

Another reason the naval captains depended so heavily on the local Americans is that their ships had to anchor out in the harbor, no dock space being made available for them, though commercial vessels were allowed to offload on the docks. The captains typically arrived in the city in the morning and often returned to their ships for dinner. Occasionally, rough surf confined the American captains to their ships during the day as well.

Because of this, not only were the American businessmen more well informed on some matters than the destroyer captains, but Near East Relief workers like Gertrude Anthony sometimes had a better grasp of lo-

cal affairs than the navy men. As we'll read here, Anthony first witnessed a Turk murder a Greek near the NER Personnel house, where she probably had rooms, and later, seeing the perpetrator walking free, realized that Turkish civilian authorities were not going to hold him responsible for his actions. This tells us something about conditions in Samsun, especially upon the arrival of many of Osman Agha's men in the late spring of 1921. Later, Anthony heard and saw the despair of the Greek women as they learned that their husbands, fathers, and brothers were about to be deported and as they feared that soon they might share the same fate.

The local Americans didn't know everything, of course, and the naval officers also frequently sought information from Turkish officials, including the Samsun Mutasariff, as well as the regional military commander. But these men were not always forthcoming. So the destroyer captains sought advice and information from foreign nationals as well, such as the Italian referred to as Count Schmecchia.

Some things they were able to witness directly, such as the arms and ammunition frequently being landed at the port and sent inland by truck, wagon, or camel caravan, or the importation of Russian bullion. However, often the Americans could only guess why the Turks wanted to kill or deport the Greeks of Pontus, and sometimes they were unable to know for sure whether these dread decisions were being made locally or at Nationalist headquarters in Angora.

Finally, the American captains had to evaluate the honesty and competence of the Turkish officials they spoke to daily and to understand and give due credit to the "Turkish case" for the deportations, which we as readers must evaluate too. Overall, they did their best rightly to assess what was occurring in the region each day and to decide whether to tell their admiral about it in their war diaries by message, to protest to Turkish authorities, or simply to wait for future events.

It is important to note that two of the ship captains in particular—Captain Joyce of the Fox *and Captain Bristol of the* Overton*—had considerable background for this work of evaluation. They and the destroyers they commanded had both spent a year and a half in Turkish waters before we meet them in the war diaries, some of that duty involving occasional visits to Samsun. So if these two officers seem to be making rather incisive judgements early on, their own recent Turkish experience was helping to make that possible.*

USS *FOX*, COMMANDER C.S. JOYCE WAR DIARY SET FOR MAY 11-29, 1921

The Fox *arrived at Samsun on May 12, 1921 to relieve the* Overton, *which was just completing a visit there. With this contact relief, the continuous destroyer presence in Samsun began.*

Prior to the arrival of the Fox, *the* Overton *had recently visited Samsun from April 28–30, 1921 and then had visited both Samsun and Trebizond beginning on May 2. Little of substance for our purposes was reported in the war diaries for these earlier* Overton *visits.*

When the Fox *arrived, the Muslim season of "Ramazan" (Ramadan) was in progress, and Commander Joyce records that a few shots were being fired and rockets set off every night, apparently in connection with those ceremonies. Otherwise, the most substantive comments in the first five days of the* Fox *diaries concerned the presence of several hundred Georgians, these being Circassians who the government had once fed but who they were no longer feeding. The Circassians were now leaving the city.*

Captain Joyce also reports that the current Mutasariff's name was Sezaye Bey and that he seems "more keen" than his predecessor.

On May 17, very ominous events begin being reported.

May 17, 1921

. . . . Went ashore in the morning and met Miss Anthony* of the Near East Relief near the dock. I rode up with her to the Near East Relief Offices and she told me that she had received very authentic news that the Turks had burned about one hundred Greek villages to the southward of Bafra, or in that neighborhood. She stated that she had received this information from two different sources, in one of which she placed great confidence. However, none of it was firsthand information.

There appears to be no doubt that the activities against the Greeks are increasing and reports come in every day of villages being devastated and the inhabitants being driven out. They are not allowed to come to the large towns and are made practically homeless. All the

* Gertrude Anthony had taught biology in high school in Berkeley, California before she volunteered for the Near East Relief. In May 1921, she was awaiting Turkish permission to travel inland from Samsun to Marsovan, where she had been assigned by the Near East Relief. Part of her detailed record of events in Marsovan is presented in a "testimony" section later.

Greeks in Samsun are being listed and are compelled to report any visitors they may have in their houses. This is apparently for the purpose of preventing the homeless villagers from becoming refugees in Samsun. The Greek inhabitants appear to be in a frenzy of fear about half of the time. All those of military age have been mobilized. Many of those living in Samsun have gained exception for twelve months by paying six hundred (600) pounds (Turkish paper), and I believe that much of the trouble with the Greek villagers is due to their failure (as usual) to comply with the orders for military service.*

Went ashore again in the afternoon and saw most of the tobacco men and had tea at the Near East where I found four workers who had recently returned from Cesarea or Caesarea [Kayseri] on their way to the United States. They expect to leave on the Italian ship Palacky, tomorrow. The consensus of opinion among the Near East workers seems to be that all through the country the Greeks were in imminent danger and they expressed the belief that the Armenians had their turn on suffering and that it was now the Greeks' turn. They had encountered no particular troubles in coming from Cesarea.

The former Mutasariff who was deposed last fall (while Mr. Tuck† was here) is still in town, and he told me that he had been trying for some time to get permission to go to his old home in Macedonia and that he is expected to be able to leave before long.

. . . .

May 21, 1921

. . . . Went to tea at the Near East, and Miss Anthony reported that the rumors were very persistent that all the Greek villages in this neighbor-

---

* After the Young Turks took power in 1908, all non-Muslims were liable for military service, although the previous Ottoman system of draft evasion by paying a special tax still persisted at times and places. Armenians and Greeks, especially physicians, sometimes played important roles in the Ottoman Army, during the Balkan Wars, for example. However, most who were drafted under the Ottomans ended up doing forced labor under awful conditions. By 1921, the Nationalists had resurrected the earlier practice of sending ethnic Christians to the notorious "labor battalions" rather than to the Turkish Army. The labor battalions were a death sentence within a few months if you didn't escape them. Hence male Greek villager resistance to "mobilization" by flight to the Greek partisans in the nearby mountains is neither surprising nor unreasonable.

† Pinckney Tuck Jr. had been the American consul in Samsun until early 1921. With his departure, the American consul position in the city lapsed.

hood are being destroyed and the inhabitants killed. She reports further that the priests are being crucified. One small girl came to her today for assistance, and reported that she was the only one left out of her family, that the soldiers came to her house and at first behaved in a friendly manner but that they soon turned and killed the men and then commenced a struggle with the women. The little girl did not know what to do, so she crawled into the oven and thereby escaped and finally made her way to Samsun. Miss Anthony reports that there have been four children who came to her with similar stories within the last few days.

May 22, 1921
. . . . The baggage belonging to Mr. Van Toor and Miss Wood was very expeditiously and courteously handled, but a great many contraband things were found. Mr. Van Toor had an automatic pistol and considerable ammunition, which he was not allowed to keep. . . . He had a large bundle of newspapers which were distinctly debarred. These I threw in my boat to save Haidar Bey the necessity of destroying them. In addition, they had two mail bags, one containing letters and the other containing magazines, in spite of the fact that it is well known that magazines are not allowed. . . .

May 23, 1921
Went ashore in the forenoon and was informed by Miss Anthony that the mail had come in a very unsatisfactory condition. The magazine bag contained a number of copies of the "Literary Digest", which is not permitted. There were also a number of copies of "Asia". Concealed in the pages of these were two typewritten articles by Mr. Chater. These articles were scurrilously anti-Turk, which can do neither the Americans nor the Near East any good anywhere, and are especially out of place in Anatolia. These may or may not have been concealed in the magazine purposely but their presence there was sufficient to establish criminal negligence on the part of some one of the Near East, at the very least. . . .

Fortunately, Miss Anthony was able to get the articles by Mr. Chater* for destruction before Haidar Bey had read them. The following is a paraphrase of a dispatch sent today:

> "Recommendation is made that the Senior Naval Officer at Samsun not be required to assist Near East personnel to enter

* Melville Chater was an American journalist who sometimes wrote articles critical of the Turks.

> Samsun in the future. It neither improves the prestige of the Navy nor helps the Americans in Anatolia when the Senior Naval Officer connives at all sorts of violations of rules that are laid down by the local authorities. Mr. Van Toor brought in newspapers and magazines which are known to be debarred. Some of the articles criticize the Moslem faith and the Angora government, besides which there were two typewritten articles by Mr. Chater which were concealed in a copy of "Asia", and which were of a very scurrilous nature. It is only a question of time when the mail for Americans will again be stopped unless drastic action is taken in Constantinople."

Went ashore in the afternoon and saw most of the tobacco people but found nothing new. It appears from all accounts that a definite policy of extermination is being pursued against the Greek villagers, and day after day reports come in of villages having been destroyed. Every day groups of young men are brought in under guard and some women and children (refugees) are beginning to drift in. A large herd of cattle (mostly buffaloes) were driven through the streets this afternoon by soldiers and it was said that these cattle were part of the loot from the adjacent villages. Mr. Johnston* told me that a few days ago a number of Ottoman Greeks waited on him and asked if they could make arrangements to see me. They desired for me to intercede for them with the Mutasariff. Their proposal was that they would abandon their property in Samsun if they were given permission to leave. I told Mr. Johnston that unfortunately this was entirely a matter of internal Turkish affairs and that we could not intrude in it, and I therefore have not seen the people concerned.

May 24, 1921

Went ashore in the forenoon and found nothing of importance had transpired. In the afternoon when I went ashore, I saw Mr. Van Toor in the Near East office and he told me that there had been a shooting affray in front of the Near East Personnel House about one o'clock and that one Greek had been killed and one badly wounded. . . .

I saw Miss Anthony at the Personnel House and she had seen the shooting that took place in the street this afternoon. She said that ap-

* After this entry, we have corrected the occasional "Johnston" entries to "Johnson," who was a senior manager with the Alston Tobacco Company.

parently none of the participants were in uniform and that the shooting appeared to be on one side. The man that was killed and the one that was badly wounded did not return the fire. The assailants apparently got away although there were a number of people on the street at the time. No information could be obtained regarding the matter except that the men who had been shot were Greeks. From the present indication, it would appear that the idea has gotten abroad that immunity is granted anyone who kills or attacks Greeks and incidents of this sort have been on the increase of late.

Miss Anthony told me that in the last two days there had been over ninety applicants for admission to the Greek orphanage and that these were all small children who had found their way into Samsun from the destroyed villages, and in some instances were accompanied by a few women. The women are not allowed to remain in the town and [instead] sleep in the fields outside the city during the night. Miss Anthony said that these children represented a number of villages and that they all stated that their villages had been completely destroyed. On account of the shortage of funds, the Near East was only able to give food and shelter to a few of these refugees and the ones selected were those who apparently had no friends or relatives left. It is not known what the effect will be of the Near East Relief sheltering these refugee children who are not permitted to come into Samsun by the authorities. The following is a paraphrase of a dispatch sent this date:

> "It is apparent that there is a definite policy here for the extermination of the Greek inhabitants. Everything indicates that hundreds of Greek villages have been completely devastated. A few of the young men have been captured and taken for the army and some of the women and children have escaped. The survivors have been prohibited from coming to Samsun or going to other large places. However, some have managed to get into Samsun. During the last two days, about ninety children have asked the Near East at Samsun for relief but only a few of them could be accommodated. It is impossible for us to take any action in the matter. It is believed that the Near East in Constantinople should be notified that there will be a great increase in the number of orphans in this section in the near future. Practically all Greek property is being seized. This includes residences, tobacco magazines and retail stores."

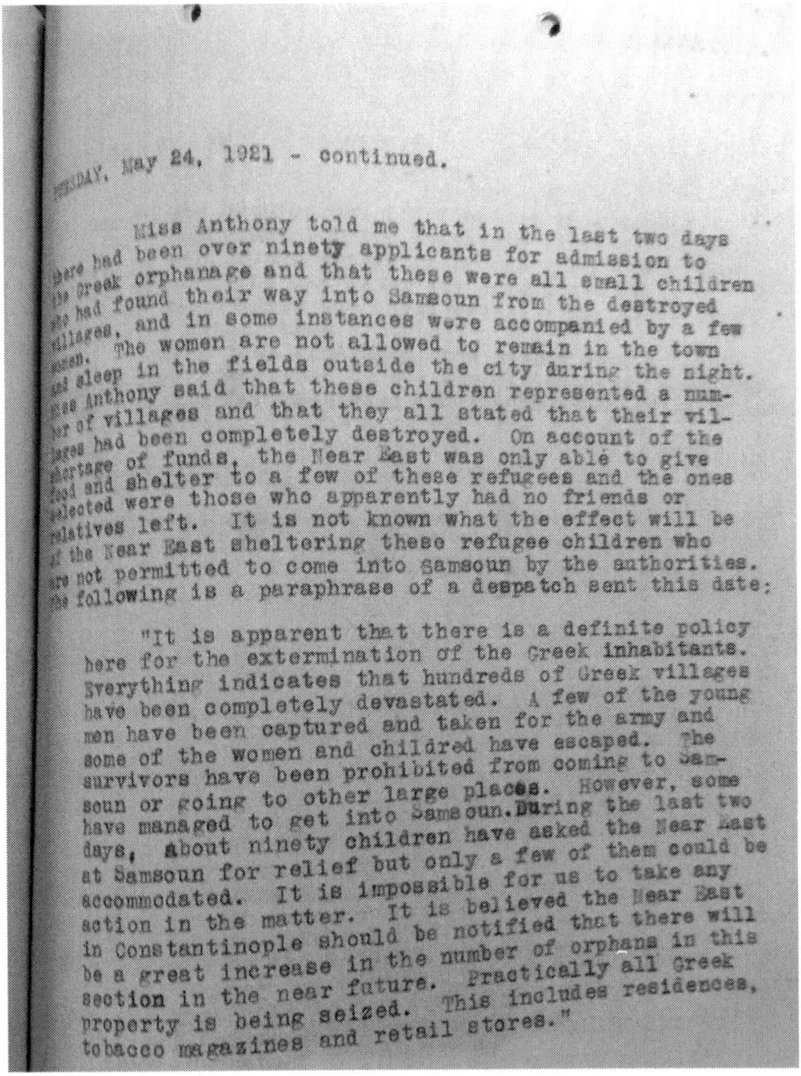

ESDAY, May 24, 1921 - continued.

Miss Anthony told me that in the last two days there had been over ninety applicants for admission to the Greek orphanage and that these were all small children who had found their way into Samsoun from the destroyed villages, and in some instances were accompanied by a few women. The women are not allowed to remain in the town and sleep in the fields outside the city during the night. Miss Anthony said that these children represented a number of villages and that they all stated that their villages had been completely destroyed. On account of the shortage of funds, the Near East was only able to give food and shelter to a few of these refugees and the ones selected were those who apparently had no friends or relatives left. It is not known what the effect will be of the Near East sheltering these refugee children who are not permitted to come into Samsoun by the authorities. The following is a paraphrase of a despatch sent this date:

"It is apparent that there is a definite policy here for the extermination of the Greek inhabitants. Everything indicates that hundreds of Greek villages have been completely devastated. A few of the young men have been captured and taken for the army and some of the women and childred have escaped. The survivors have been prohibited from coming to Samsoun or going to other large places. However, some have managed to get into Samsoun. During the last two days, about ninety children have asked the Near East at Samsoun for relief but only a few of them could be accommodated. It is impossible for us to take any action in the matter. It is believed the Near East in Constantinople should be notified that there will be a great increase in the number of orphans in this section in the near future. Practically all Greek property is being seized. This includes residences, tobacco magazines and retail stores."

Photo of a page from one of the war diaries in original typed form, typical of the original war diary reports found in the National Archives.

After leaving the Near East Personnel House, I saw Mr. Currin and he corroborated some information Miss Anthony had given regarding the seizure of Greek property in Samsun. It appears that practically all Greek stores have been seized (eighteen of them today). Many of the Greek-owned tobacco magazines which were not being used by either the Americans or the Regie* have been seized and sealed, and day after day Greeks are being evicted from their homes and their property sealed or used by the Turkish authorities.

During that afternoon the French merchant ship Circassie came in escorted by the French destroyer Tonkinois. They sailed again for Trebizond and Batoum about seven o'clock.†

. . . .

May 26, 1921

Went ashore in the morning and found nothing new. Told everyone to have mail ready so that we could sail promptly upon the arrival of OVERTON. Made arrangements to take Mr. Hieatt [apparently an NER official] to Constantinople, as there appeared to be no merchant transportation immediately available.

Found that the government had appointed Haidar Bey official censor for English and French incoming mail, but he apparently gets no pay for this duty. There was considerable mail from the Near East workers in the interior which had not been censored, and Miss Anthony has censored most of it. She was much exercised over the things she found in some of the letters, and she had to destroy many of them. Haidar Bey accepted her censorship and we took all Near East Mail to the post office and had stamps put on them and the censor's mark added.

When I went ashore in the afternoon, there was a new policeman at the gate and he would not allow me to pass, and directed me to see the inspector. When I went to the inspector's office, he apparently did not know what I wanted and after considerable conversation during which neither I nor the inspector understood what the other was saying, I was directed to proceed. . . .

---

* The "Regie" or Regis Tobacco Company was originally a French firm, which eventually was taken over by the Turkish government (Nicolopoulos, 288).

† We omit many such shipping reports, which were routinely recorded in these diaries.

May 27, 1921

. . . .

During the afternoon, Mr. Van Toor [Director of the NER hospital in Samsun] came on board, accompanied by one of the customs inspectors or policemen on the dock and said that he had come to see me about the imminence of a Greek massacre in Samsun. He said that Miss Anthony and the Greek woman who is in charge of the Near East Greek orphanage were very much wrought up about the matter. It appears that a large number of Greek women have been warned by their Turkish women friends that they were in great danger, and there is no doubt that the Greeks are terrorized and are fully convinced that they are to be massacred in the near future. Mr. Van Toor wished my advice and wanted to know if there was any way in which I could intercede with the authorities. He said that the consensus of opinion was that the civil authorities did not desire any trouble but that the present activities against the Greeks were being pushed by the military authorities. I told Mr. Van Toor that without definite instructions, I could not interfere with internal affairs of Turkey so long as our Americans were not molested.

He asked what I thought could be done by his approaching the Mutasariff on the subject. I advised him that if he did so, it would be well to say that these stories were told to him by people coming to the Near East orphanages and to the soup kitchen for relief and that these rumors appeared to be well founded, that they were bound to get out and that he had therefore come to headquarters in order that he might deny the intention of any authorized severity towards the Greeks. I advised him against making a protest about what was assumed was going to happen, and to concern himself solely with what facts he had been able to glean from the statements made by the orphans and refugees who had come to him for relief, and to lay stress on the fact that these stories getting about could not do anything but injury to the authorities and their government. Mr. Van Toor then left the ship and returned to the city.

About 7:30, U.S.S. OVERTON stood in and soon afterward Commander Bristol came on board. He reported that Mr. Wiley had returned to Constantinople on the steamer Sparta and that there was no need for me to go to Ineboli.* As I have not yet received the writ-

* The destroyers often carried American businessmen and others to Constantinople or other ports while en route to their next stop.

ten statement from Mr. Van Toor, I arranged to go ashore with Commander Bristol in the morning.

May 28, 1921

. . . .

Went ashore in the afternoon and saw Mr. Van Toor, also Miss Anthony, both at the Near East. They were still convinced that a massacre of the Greeks was imminent. Mr. Tuck's [former] clerk, who now works for the Near East,* stated that sixteen Greek teamsters had been killed today on their way out of the city to their villages. Several others were killed yesterday and the work of killing has been going on as reported previously. He stated that he knew for a fact that the Turkish civil authorities were not in favor of this severity towards the Greeks but that the military authorities were forcing the matter. He was firmly convinced of the idea that the military forces under Osman Agha were entirely out of control.† He further stated that in a council meeting held about a week ago, the military authorities voted for the extermination of the Greeks, whereas the civil authorities were against it. As the military authorities were in the majority, they carried the vote, but nothing was done about it, and another meeting was to have been held yesterday. It was not held, however, and the Greeks believe that the military authorities are determined to abide by the previous vote.

Miss Anthony stated that she had seen the man who killed the two Greeks in front of the Personnel House, with a crowd of what appeared to be bandits, going over the district in which the Personnel House is located (the rich Greek district). He was pointing out the various houses and apparently detailing the men for something and telling them what to do. She stated that it was apparent to her from his gestures and demonstrations, that the recompense they were to receive was to consist of wearing apparel and only that. She further stated that she had seen these people peering into yards, windows and over walls, with the idea apparently of getting the lay of the land for making an attack. She said that from such information as she had, which came through Greek sources, of course, she was convinced that all

---

* Tuck's clerk was no doubt a Pontic Greek. He was later deported with all the other Greek men.

† Osman Agha's men were chettahs or irregulars. They often cooperated with the Nationalist forces, and sometimes gendarmes, in actions against the Greeks, but were known for atrocities of all kinds.

the Greeks were to be massacred within the next three days. She laid a special stress on the fact that a great number of the Greek women had been warned by their Turkish women friends that the end had come.

After talking with Miss Anthony and Mr. Van Toor, I saw Mr. Johnson and asked his opinion of it, as he seemed better qualified to judge than most of the others. He said that there was no doubt that the next three days would see the end of the matter, one way or the other; that the majority of people believed that a massacre was to take place; that Osman Agha's men were concentrating in the town, coming in from all the outlying villages, and with their coming into the city meant only one of two things, either they were being gotten together in order to stop their depredations in the villages, or they were being gotten together in order to complete the work in Samsun. He did not think there was any menace intended towards the Americans but fully realized that with riot and disorder going on, everyone would be in danger.

About 3:30, Commander Bristol, Lieutenant Commander Lanphier and myself returned to the ship, and it was noticed that the city was full of soldiers, most of whom however were unarmed, though many of them carried their cartridge belts and some their bayonets. After talking the situation over with Commander Bristol, I decided it was best to return direct to Constantinople and lay the matter before the High Commissioner.* This especially in view of the fact that the lives of the Americans in Samsun would be menaced by any general riot and slaughter. In view of Commander Bristol's reporting that Admiral Bristol will be out of town Sunday afternoon, I sent a dispatch, of which the following is a paraphrase:

"The situation in Samsun is such that I am returning to Constantinople direct. I would like to explain to Admiral Bristol when I arrive, which will be about Sunday noon."

DEPARTED Samsun 6:35 p.m., 28 May 1921.

ARRIVED Constantinople 1:05 p.m., 29 May 1921.

---

* Admiral Bristol had fought for the title of America's High Commissioner in Constantinople so as to be in parity with the senior English, French, and Italian officials there, who were all titled "High Commissioners." In mid-1919, the State Department agreed he could use the title.

USS *OVERTON*, COMMANDER A.L. BRISTOL WAR DIARY SET FOR MAY 27-JUNE 7, 1921

. . . .

May 29, 1921

From interviews with foreign company representatives and Near East Relief personnel in Samsun, the American ship commander* formed the following definite impressions which I have embodied in a dispatch to the Detachment Commander. They are as follows:

1. That the present time constitutes a crisis for the Greeks in a large area surrounding Samsun.

2. That there is a definite movement against these Greeks and that this movement is directed by [higher] authority—probably Angora—and that the movement is under strict control.

3. That the coming week will show whether or not this movement contemplates the complete extermination of all Greeks in this area.

4. That foreigners in Samsun are not in danger.

I am of the personal opinion, based on no particular facts, but the above general impressions, that disturbances of a serious nature, i.e., wholesale massacre, rioting, etc., which would endanger the lives of Americans, will not occur in the town of Samsun proper.

It is rumored today, that the troops who have been engaged in destroying Greek villages have been called in and are now quartered in the barracks on the hillside behind Samsun. It struck me as important to learn as much as I could regarding the status of these troops. Repeated inquiry brought no positive information, but from all the replies, I am of the opinion that these are troops of the regular army, they were probably at one time Osman Agha's men and may still be attached to his command, but I am fairly positive that they have been incorporated in the army and they are [under strict control] of the

* The "ship commander" referred to is no doubt Commander Bristol himself.

military; numbers of them were seen around town without arms and still wearing the Lars headdress.*

I sent the usual liberty party and baseball party ashore this afternoon and on my return to the ship found that these men had all been searched on the dock by the customs officials before being allowed to pass the gate returning to the boat. This is contrary [to] the understanding which I have with the Mutasariff. I will take the matter up with him.

May 30, 1921

Received Detachment Commander's dispatch, serial 73,† directing us to make representation to the local authorities concerning the movement against the Greeks. Because of electrical storms which are occurring every afternoon and evening, communication with Constan-

---

* Osman Agha's 3,000 or so cutthroats were mostly of the "Laz" nationality (often spelled "Lars" in the diaries) who lived in the coastal region of northeast Turkey, from Kerasund (Giresun) eastward. Ethnically, they were a branch of the Georgian people. The Turkish Laz were Muslim, while most of the Laz back in Georgia remained Christian. The small Turkish Lazistan "sanjak" or county was under the administrative control of the Turkish province of Trebizond.

A few months later, Osman Agha would be made a colonel in the army, incorporating his men more directly into the military. But the famous Turkish patriot and propagandist Halide Edib, herself one of the first Turkish graduates of the American Women's College in Constantinople, once noted in marked understatement that these men were "'not amenable to discipline'" (Shenk, *ABSF*, 107). As Mango points out, Mustafa Kemal had been making use of some of the most notorious outlaws (Osman Agha and others) since he first began building his organization in Anatolia (227, 284).

† It appears that, after steaming the *Fox* overnight to Constantinople in order to speak to the admiral in person, Captain Joyce had persuaded Admiral Bristol to telegraph Captain Bristol of the *Overton* back at Samsun and order him to complain to the Mutasariff in the admiral's name about the inhumanity threatening the local Greeks.

Although Captain Bristol decides not to deliver the admiral's message at this moment, later, when the Americans learn that a formal order has been issued for the deportation of all Greek women and children from the city, Commander Bristol and Commander Spears of the *Humphreys* would deliver it to the Mutasariff. This letter to the local officials (see *Humphreys* WD, June 8, below) may have had the effect of temporarily keeping women and children from being deported with the men as apparently had been originally ordered. See below as the story proceeds.

tinople is difficult and this dispatch was the only one received after repeated attempts. Before going on shore I transposed the meaning of this dispatch into language such as I hoped to be able to get through to the Mutasariff through an interpreter. While Haidar Bey's English is improving and is quite good for ordinary conversation, most of the interviews with the Mutasariff must be conducted in most simple language in order to avoid misunderstanding.

Went on shore at ten thirty a.m. and arranged with Haidar Bey for an interview with the Mutasariff at five p.m. I directed Haidar Bey to meet me promptly at four p.m. as I intended to drill him with what I had to say to the Mutasariff. Before the interview, called on the Near East and gossiped with Van Toor and Miss Anthony for some time.

Lunched with Johnson and later had a long talk with King* in his office. During this talk with King, a Turk who was the former Mutasariff here and who was removed from office last fall came in. He and King talked together in Turkish for about half an hour. After his departure King told me that his information was as follows: that twelve locally prominent Turks had gone to the Mutasariff and informed him that the present conditions must cease; that the economic prosperity of this locality was being completely destroyed; that the people doing the damage and conducting the massacres were all strangers and not from the Samsun province; and that it was very certain that at some future time Samsun and its people would be called upon to pay the price. He further stated that the Mutasariff had been forced to telegraph Angora and that these twelve men had themselves sent telegrams to Angora; that a halt had been called in the whole affair and that there was every hope that the whole movement against the Greeks would be stopped.

Haidar Bey did not arrive until ten minutes to five. It was then too late to have a long talk with Haidar Bey before the interview with the Mutasariff, and in view of this and of the news which I had just heard, I decided not to deliver the Detachment Commander's message today. After five p.m., called on the Mutasariff and after exchanging greetings took up the question of the liberty party.

* The man named simply "King," who appears so often in the war diaries, is William J. King, the manager of the Alston Tobacco Company. The "younger King," apparently King's son, is Preston P. E. King, who also works for Alston and serves occasionally as the interpreter for the American officers. His mentions usually involve his first name or initials to differentiate him from his father.

Informed the Mutasariff that my men had been searched on the dock and that this was not in accordance with my agreement with him and was something which I could not permit. The Mutasariff replied that he regretted very much that it would be necessary, as strict orders had recently been received directing that all persons, without exception, be searched (this statement of the Mutasariff I do not believe to be true in any particular). I replied to the Mutasariff that in such case I quite understood that orders must be carried out, but under the circumstances, it would be impossible for me to permit any of my men to go on shore. I further stated that in the future I would greatly appreciate a word from him [when] any conditions under which we might be operating were changed. Interview ended after a few unimportant observations on both sides.

May 31, 1921

Went on shore at ten a.m., and visited Near East Offices and Tobacco offices. Was everywhere informed that conditions seemed to be constantly improving; that the tension among the Greek population was relaxing and that apparently things were returning to normal. During last week, before my arrival, the newspapers had been daily publishing violent anti-Greek articles. The Tobacco men informed me that these articles no longer appear and that they had been told by their employees that during the past two days, several editions of newspapers containing such articles had been suppressed. . . .

LETTER OF COMMANDER A. L. BRISTOL TO ADMIRAL MARK BRISTOL

At this point, Captain Bristol has become convinced that the Greeks are no longer threatened. Shortly, he expresses very strong conclusions along these lines in a naval letter to Admiral Bristol that he sends by an American businessman traveling by steamer in case his messages can't get through by radio. We provide this informative letter in place of the next six days of war diaries.

U.S.S. OVERTON, #239
Samsun, Anatolia
4 June 1921

My dear Admiral :

I'm writing you a brief note to send to you by Mr. Gary as I have just heard that his steamer is going direct to Constantinople. I am sending you two radios tonight, but as transmission has been difficult, you may possibly receive this before radios arrive.

Situation Samson, is briefly, as follows:

1. I consider that the anti-Greek movement is over. What appear to be regular troops have arrived in town and practically all of the former Osman Agha men have left town headed East. They may do some damage enroute Kerasunda. Tremendous damage has been done in the villages back of Samsun, but this all occurred previous to the arrival of the OVERTON and measures to stop these Greek murders and killings began to take effect here about the time I arrived.

2. The Greeks have a report, received from Angora by telegraph, that a Greek warship has bombarded the towns of Krekly and [...] near Ineboli, hence my request for information. Samsun has been in a state of great excitement ever since this news arrived two days ago and hundreds of people and troops have been engaged in digging trenches, [making] machine gun pits and stringing barbed wire in the hills back of the city ever since. All the streets and waterfront are under strong patrol. After your message, I do not believe that Greeks are in the

Black Sea and consider that nothing will happen at Samsun, but I have taken necessary steps to assemble Americans and take off the women at least, in case anything happens.

3. There has been great shipping activity in the harbor in the last four days: five Turks, two French, one Italian and one [Polish] vessel. Large quantities of ammunition have been landed. One night the whole population of the town was turned out and sent to the docks to get all the ammunition away from the waterfront before daylight.

4. Haider Bey informed [me] today that the Mutasariff had been relieved from office, that his successor has not arrived, and no one knew who it would be, but that the present Mutasariff while still here, had ceased to act. Further that the head of the military would be relieved in a day or two. That the local Government had practically ceased to function, except through subordinate officials who still carry on their jobs. . . .

Captain Bristol went on to tell the admiral that now was not the time to send two Americans to Angora as the admiral had apparently asked the captain to try to do.

So, having assured the admiral that "the anti-Greek movement is over," it must have been with great alarm that Captain Bristol heard the totally opposite news when his ship's boat took him from his destroyer's anchorage into Samsun on the seventh.

CONTINUATION OF USS *OVERTON* WAR DIARY

June 7, 1921
Went on shore at 10 a.m. and met with King. He informed me that the Greek situation had become very serious and that practically all of the Greeks, at least all of the influential Greeks in Samsun, had been directed to get ready to proceed to the interior in five days. He stated that these Greeks would be sent back to the towns from which they originally came. It appears that [most of the Greek families] in Samsun are not native, but have come here from other places, in many cases as far back as forty or fifty years ago. Most of them are from Cesarea and Sivas. I asked King to verify as much of this as possible and then called on the Near East Relief where I found that McDowell [Director of the Near East Relief at Samsun] had just returned from the interior. Had a long talk with McDowell on his experiences and the conditions which he had encountered and asked him to write me a brief summary of what he had found. Returned to King's office to obtain further information from him, also sent for Haidar Bay. From both of them I found that the order against the Greeks is as stated. My "estimate of the situation" which this has created will be found attached.* In the afternoon returned to the ship to await arrival of HUMPHREYS.

ESTIMATE OF SITUATION SAMSUN JUNE 7, 1921

FACTS OR NEAR FACTS

1. Numbers of Greeks (exact number not known but all important people and probably all Greeks) have today been told that they have five days to prepare to go with their families to the interior.

2. Each Greek has been told that he must return to the place from which he originally came.

* An "estimate of the situation" is a formal military appraisal of difficult circumstances facing a military force, a genre of the day that was taught at the Naval War College and elsewhere. Although Commander Bristol had not yet attended the Naval War College, he probably had become familiar with the use of this kind of document when serving (with considerable distinction) as an aide on two major staffs while a lieutenant.

3. Most Greeks (heads of Greek families) in Samsun are strangers, that is, they were not born in Samsun, although some have lived here as long as forty years.

4. The Mutasariff is not acting on any official matters and is said to have been relieved. This on good authority.

5. There are numerous troops in the town and these appear to be regulars—that is, troops with more military discipline and [training] than the Osman Agha men who were recently here or the [former] regiment here who were newly raised troops.

6. The town is under strong patrol. Trenches have been constructed and it is evident there is expectation of a Greek landing in this vicinity.

7. Large quantities of ammunition and arms have been landed here in the past week and today field pieces are being landed from Turkish steamer.

8. No anti-Greek movement of any proportion has occurred in Samsun proper, but numerous attacks upon and murder of Greek individuals have taken place.

9. Such attacks have not been punished and there are indications that a lawless element is strong enough to either defy the local authorities or else are working with the sympathy and connivance of local authorities.

10. Deportations similar to these ordered here have occurred in the interior and Greeks have arrived safely at their destinations (authority- McDowell).

11. Angora is not aware of the wholesale destruction of Greek villages in Samsun area (authority- McDowell). (I doubt this).

12. Messages which have been sent by influential Samsun Turks to Angora protesting anti-Greek policy have not reached Angora (authority- McDowell).

13. One man in present Angora Government (the Minister of Interior*) is most influential and most feared in anti-Greek campaign (authority- McDowell).

14. This Minister of Interior is probably responsible for suppression of telegrams and keeping Angora Government in ignorance (opinion by McDowell).

15. Angora Government believes Greeks on coast [are] disloyal [and fear] for their influence and actions in case of Greek landing (authority- McDowell).

16. Angora determined to take strong measures to deprive these Greeks of any power for harm, but also determined to do this without massacres or confiscations of all property (authority- McDowell).

17. U.S. Destroyer in port has certain deterrent effect on any anti-Greek actions in this town.

18. Senior Naval Officer [Captain Bristol himself] has message from Detachment Commander protesting in name of humanity against Greek massacres.

19. Possibility that Senior Naval Officer can locate Mutasariff during Bairam [a Turkish festival] or that he will receive message is doubtful.

20. That Mutasariff will forward message to Angora is doubtful.

21. That message will have effect to stop present move is doubtful.

22. Bairam excitement at high pitch. No work going on and no one to be found in their offices or homes.

23. There is much news to be had but very little of it reliable.

* Ali Fethi (Okyar) had been appointed Minister of the Interior for the Nationalists shortly before the date of this estimate.

OPINIONS BASED ON ABOVE AND ON GENERAL OBSERVATIONS; AUTHENTIC NEWS AND RUMORS.

1. It is generally accepted that the Mutasariff [has] been relieved but I am inclining to the opinion that his move is a subterfuge. He knows that the Americans are watching the situation and probably does not want to be talked to or to be in any way hindered in what he is doing. If what McDowell says is true, and I think it is about fifty-fifty, there is a determined effort on the part of the anti-Greek party (Extremists) to get through with the [deal] before they can be stopped. They probably believe that if they can successfully accomplish the practical extermination of the Greeks, that their act will not be seriously disapproved by the Government or country as a whole, although their action be officially denounced.

2. The Mutasariff is reported to be the brother of the man who carried out the Armenian massacres and who is now a prisoner of the British in Malta. There is no question in my mind that many of the Turks here in Samsun deplore the present situation and are doing all that they can to prevent it. A number of them have confided in King and Johnson, and Haidar Bey has practically [admitted] to me this morning that the lawless element is in control in this area.

3. It is possible that the deportations may be only such as stated [and] that the Greeks will all arrive at their destinations safely, [but] even so, this means that they will eventually perish in large numbers as they will be without means and in crowded areas. As I understand the Turkish side of the case, it will be as follows—The Greeks along the coast, although Ottoman subjects, are disloyal and some of them are guilty of direct acts of treason. Their presence in the coast, where the Greek landing may occur at any time, is [prejudicial] to the safety of the Government. Therefore, they are [forced] to move them back from the coast where they can do no harm.

4. The Turks have plenty of proof of their assertion of the disloyalty of the Greeks. During the British occupation* particularly and recently during the successful Greek advance, the rejoicing of the Greeks

* The British had sent a small force of 200 troops to Samsun for several months beginning in early March 1919 to help establish order (Mango, 213).

was very open and loud. The Turks will undoubtedly [deny] that the deportation in any way means harm to the Greeks and [will] insist it is merely a military move essential to the [safety] of the Nationalist Government. It is not considered that Americans or their affairs are in any danger from this new situation.

COURSES OF ACTION OPEN

The first course of action open to the Senior Naval Officer is to deliver the Detachment Commander's message. The actual delivery of the message will be difficult, as it will be hard to locate the Mutasariff during Bairam and more difficult to get an interview. It can however be accomplished by sticking to it. After obtaining an interview, I consider it extremely doubtful that the Mutasariff will give the message [any official response]. He will simply state that he is not acting until the new Mutasariff arrives or that he cannot receive messages of a political nature. Assuming however that message is delivered and accepted, I do not believe that, in the present state of affairs, it will have the effect of stopping the movement. Once having spoken, the Senior Naval Officer will have shot his bolt and no further action will be left to him. It is not conceivable that any direct assurance will be given to the message. The delivery of the message may affect the status of the Americans in the interior.

The second course of action is to sit and watch things until some direct act occurs. I am assured, and believe it, that certain Turks are still working to stop the deportation and hope to be able to prevent its taking place. The Senior Naval Officer will still be able at any time he sees fit to protest to the Mutasariff.

The third course of action is for OVERTON to proceed Constantinople at earliest possible time after arrival of relief and lay whole situation before the Detachment Commander. It is not known what means of communication exist between Constantinople and Angora direct, but it is believed that a message of protest direct to the Angora Government would have the greatest effect at this time. In any case, OVERTON could arrive Constantinople, obtain views of Detachment Commander and return to Samsun before any positive movement would take place in Samsun.

CONCLUSION

Not to deliver message at this time. To watch situation and in the meantime to have OVERTON proceed to Constantinople with full information.

USS *HUMPHREYS*, COMMANDER W.O. SPEARS WAR DIARY SET FOR JUNE 7-14, 1921

June 7, 1921

Anchored in Samsun harbor at 7 P.M. with the following named passengers: Lieutenant (junior grade) R.S. Dunn, U.S. Navy*; Mr. J.M. English, Melachrino Tobacco Co; and Mr. W.H. Alston, President of Alston Tobacco Co. Commanding Officer of OVERTON (239) came aboard immediately with previous diaries, records, etc. Also, with information that the situation in Samsun had taken a decided turn for the worse. The OVERTON had been unable to communicate with Constantinople on account of static conditions. And Commander Bristol was of the opinion that unless radio communication could be established tonight, the OVERTON should proceed immediately to Constantinople to lay the situation before Admiral Bristol.

The situation was that in the afternoon it had been learned that the police authorities in Samsun had ordered a number of Greeks to prepare to be deported and it was generally understood ashore that all Greeks including women and children were to be deported five days from 7 June. Upon the advice of Commander Bristol and Lieutenant Dunn it was decided to try to send the below quoted message to Constantinople and if unsuccessful the OVERTON should sail at 3:30 A.M. Fortunately we were able to make communication and upon Commander Bristol's advice the following message was sent:

---

* Lieutenant (junior grade) Robert Steed Dunn was a journalist, adventurer, and Harvard graduate who had worked for journalist Lincoln Steffens. Perhaps with the help of a ship captain friend, he enlisted in 1917 in the U.S. Navy at age forty-two and initially served as an ordinary seaman (and lookout) on one of the first American destroyers to steam from New England to Britain when America entered the war in 1917. Dunn was soon promoted to the officer ranks and in 1919 joined the staff of Admiral Bristol when the latter was sent to Turkey. He served as Bristol's intelligence officer until 1922 when he was directed to leave Turkey by the State Department. Upon returning to the States, he left the navy.

Dunn had come to Samsun at Admiral Bristol's direction in order to travel to Angora to interview Mustafa Kemal on Admiral Bristol's behalf, which he did on or about July 5, 1921. His message about his interview appears below.

GOVT STANAV:

TRANSMITTED FOR COMMANDER BRISTOL PERIOD GREEK SITUATION CHANGED PERIOD TODAY MANY GREEKS INCLUDING ALL INFLUENTIAL FAMILIES TOLD BY POLICE TO BE READY TO START FOR INTERIOR WITHIN FIVE DAYS AND TO TAKE WITH THEM ALL WOMEN AND CHILDREN PERIOD EACH FAMILY TO BE SENT TO TOWN FROM WHICH THEY ORIGINALLY CAME PERIOD TURKS BASE ACTION ON PROBABILITY OF ATTACK BY GREEK MEN OF WAR AND FEAR DISLOYALTY OF LOCAL GREEKS AND I CONCUR PERIOD GREEKS IN STATE OF EXTREME PANIC PERIOD DELEGATION OF MEN APPROACHED [ALSTON TOBACCO MANAGER WILLIAM] KING TO HAVE ME INTERCEDE WITH MUTASARIFF TO PERMIT THEM TO CHARTER VESSEL AND LEAVE COUNTRY ON PROMISE NOT TO RETURN AND LEAVING BEHIND ALL POSSESSIONS PERIOD THIS I DECLINED TO DO PERIOD UNABLE TO SEE MUTASARIFF TODAY PERIOD WILL ARRANGE TO DELIVER YOUR MESSAGE TOMORROW IF CONTINUES SERIOUS BUT DOUBT THAT THIS WILL TURN LOCAL AUTHORITIES FROM ANY INTENTIONS THEY MAY HAVE PERIOD.

HUMPHREYS

Message [received] from Stanav stating that the Greek Battleship KILKIS was in the Black Sea for a demonstration against the Turks. Carefully studied all previous records [previous war diaries] until about 2 a.m. Decided that if conditions ashore have not improved to deliver Admiral Bristol's message to local authorities, which had been held [back] as not being necessary on account of supposedly improved conditions ashore.

June 8, 1921

Went ashore at 10:30 with Commander Bristol. . . .

There seemed to be no change in the Greek deportation orders so Commander Bristol and I decided to present Admiral Bristol's message, changing the wording somewhat to simplify translation. Haidar Bey was requested to arrange an interview for us with the Mutasariff. In the meantime Bristol, Dunn, and I had lunch with the Currins at their house. After lunch while Bristol and I were working on the message we were going to present to the Mutasariff, Mr. McDowell, who [had] recently returned from Angora came into Currin's office where we were working, with the information that he had just interviewed the Mutasariff and that he had been assured by the Mutasariff on his word of honor that the deported Greeks would not be molested while enroute to their new place of abode. The Mutasariff also told him that no definite day was fixed for deportation and that only a limited number of Greeks would have to go; furthermore the Mutasariff was waiting to see us.

As I had previously been warned by Mr. Currin that McDowell was not to be trusted; was not trusted by any Americans in Samsun; and by Dunn, that he lived in the same house with him in Tiflis when he [McDowell] was in the British Secret Service; and by [Commander] Bristol, that he also was suspicious of him under the circumstances; after consulting with Bristol, decided to adhere to our previous intentions and deliver the Admiral's message.* Whereupon, we immediately visited the Mutasariff in his office and were cordially received, Haidar Bey interpreting. After observing the usual polite formalities in which the Mutasariff expressed regret that Bristol was being relieved and hoped that he would feel free to consult with him at any time, I told him that I had a message to deliver to him from Admiral Bristol which I would like to read to him. He made the usual explanation that of course he could not receive any official message as we had not recognized his government. I also made the usual explanation that it was not an official message to his government but simply a message to the local ruling authorities regarding certain excesses committed, information of which had been brought to Admiral Bristol's attention. He agreed to receive the message unofficially whereupon I read him the following, Haidar Bey interpreting:

"His Excellency the Mutasariff:

The High Commissioner of the United States of America has recently been informed of certain excesses committed

* Commander Spears speaks as if this was his decision, and if he were senior to Commander Bristol, it would have been; the ship captains strictly observe naval seniority. However, obviously, Spears has just arrived and has been consulting with Bristol in depth. Note that some punctuation has been changed to clarify Spears's expression here.

> by both the Greek and the Nationalist Military against the noncombatant civil population under their respective control. The High Commissioner of the United States of America was particularly shocked to learn of the outrages committed by the Nationalist Military against the civil population in the Samsun district. The High Commissioner of the United States of America has therefore instructed me to deliver to Your Excellency the following message:
>
> 'The High Commissioner of the United States of America deprecates any enmities and excesses against the civil population no matter by whom committed. The American people will always without prejudice or partiality strongly condemn any acts committed which are against the recognized methods of humanity and civilization. Likewise the American people will always praise and sympathize with those who refrain from excesses and show patience as well as humane action. The High Commissioner of the United States of America hopes for immediate action by the authorities of Samsun which will protect all life and property and for the maintenance of law and order in accordance with recognized procedure.'"

As we purposely left the Mutasariff with the impression that this message was more recent than it actually was, and that it was actually caused by the recent crisis, and due to the very frank and lengthy interview which followed, it is thought that it was presented at the most effective time.

The Mutasariff then proceeded to give a long discourse on the whole situation which can be summed up as follows:

(1) Present difficulties with the Greeks started in the late world war when they were armed by the Allies to harass the Turkish Army – have been in continuous state of revolt ever since.

(2) Committed excesses and crimes on Turkish subjects in Samsun vicinity making it necessary to send Nationalist troops to protect the loyal subjects.

(3) Attacks by Greeks on Turkish troops causing retaliations.

(4) Upon the arrival of Nationalist troops at numerous villages, the Greeks instead of surrendering their arms when demanded, became bandits and united in attacks on Nationalist troops.

(5) Upon being disbanded by the numerous fights with Nationalist troops, numerous Greek bandits have taken refuge in Samsun.

(6) The local government has a record of numbers of such Greeks with arms and have demanded the delivery of their arms which they refuse to deliver.

(7) The deportation orders which will be issued are to get rid of these armed desperados which is considered a military necessity.

(8) No native-born Greeks or Greeks well known to the authorities will be deported, others will have to return to the places from which they came.

(9) It is optional with the deported Greeks whether or not they take their wives and children[, the] government preferring that they go so that they will not be dependents here.

(10) The Mutasariff personally guarantees that they will not be molested enroute, it being optional whether or not they leave singly or in groups, with or without escort.

(11) The deportation order is also necessary on account of the state of feeling of the local Turks who have been informed that 65,000 Turks were massacred last month by the Greeks.* They are extremely bitter toward the local Greeks and the Mutasariff fears a general massacre unless he accedes to the general feeling and deports some of the Greeks.

The interview lasted about an hour and a half and ended with the usual forms of politeness of our promising to assist the Mutasariff in

* Probably a reference to vastly exaggerated Turkish propaganda that had been widely dispersed after Greeks and other minorities had attacked Turkish villages to the east of the Sea of Marmora in 1921. See the note to Youssuf Kemal's answer to Admiral Bristol's protest to Mustafa Kemal of July 23, 1921, below.

enforcing local laws as far as Americans were concerned and his inviting us to visit him often, that he would always be glad to discuss privately and unofficially any matter with us.

We had not been in Currin's office ten minutes when the Governor's secretary arrived and spoke privately with Currin. We later learned that he told Currin that our interview had been effective and that not as many Greeks would be deported as was intended.

Arriving on wharf found heavy surf running requiring the use of shore boat to get out beyond the breakers to embark in the ship's boat. Turkish officials on the dock very polite. Bristol remained on board for dinner and after a conference we decided to send the following message [to the admiral]:

We omit the repetitious parts of the message, which ended this way:

> "Have impression that your message will have beneficial effect but unable to decide now to what extent period Mutasariff reply was in more detail and apparently more frank than expected but must discount same until many of police orders for deportation are revoked period Still consider that the lives of any Greeks deported will be in jeopardy period No news of Greek man of war but consider that a demonstration by Greek vessels off Samsun would precipitate matters most unfortunately for local Greeks period."*

The following is the opinion of Commander Bristol regarding the interview with Mutasariff which is a very good summary showing events leading up to present crisis:

---

* The last statement was certainly true. A month or so later, 300 Greeks were deported from Trebizond after a Greek bombardment there (see *Cunningham* WD, July 27, 1921). This negative effect on the Greeks brings up a larger question. Since the Hellenic Navy's incursion into the Black Sea was an apparent cause of the decision of the Turks to begin deporting the Black Sea Greeks, and since the Greek bombardments overall seem to have done little substantial injury to the Turks (Psomiades in "The Naval Bombardment of Samsun," p. 153, concludes for instance that the Greek bombardment of Samsun in 1922 was merely a "blip")—is it not likely that these Greek naval actions were, altogether, massively counterproductive?

First, a long preamble by the Mutasariff in which he went into the subject of the Greek bandits who have always been more or less in force in the mountains back of Samsun. He made a long story of how all the Greeks had been furnished arms by the Greek government just after the war and that these Greeks still held these arms and refused to give them up; that the Turks had actual documentary proof of the existence of Greek organizations which had been in existence for some time and which were known to be working in the interest of the Greek government in certain Pontus schemes.* He then went on to state that the Angora government had been too busy to deal with the matter until very recently when armed forces had been sent against them. He stated that unfortunately some regrettable things had happened (he insisted on the number four and not more than five cases) during this military move. He vehemently maintained, however, that just such things would occur in any country in a movement of this kind and that reports had been greatly exaggerated. The Mutasariff then went into the present order against the Greeks in the town of Samsun; he stated that no deportation orders had been issued, but that the government had determined to send away from Samsun certain Greeks who were considered a menace to the safety of the town. He said that these would be Greeks not native to Samsun and who had not come here recently, but Greeks who had come after the commencement of the war in '14 and who were known to be working on Greek treasonable schemes. He said that he had thought these men would desire to take their families with them, as they would be returning to towns in which their homes were, but that no orders would be issued for women and children to go and that it would be entirely op-

* "Certain Pontus schemes": As noted in our General Introduction, during and after the end of World War I, just as some Armenians had been seeking a country of their own, ideas had been floated of a "Pontus Republic," which would recreate a republic of the ancient Greek colonies in the northwest coast of Asia Minor, an Empire of Trebizond that had existed from roughly 1204 to 1461 CE.

Also, there were certainly partisan or guerilla forces composed of ethnic Greeks in the hills and mountains near Samsun and elsewhere in Pontus, and this allowed the Samsun Mutasariff to claim that these groups were connected with the "Pontus schemes."

> tional whether they went or not. He then stated that no definite time had been set for anyone's departure; that when they did go, they could make arrangements to go by arrabaugh [araba or carriage] if desired, singly or in groups and that no plans for military escort had been made but that he would consider a military escort if they desired. He then stated that he gave his personal guaranty that no harm would come to any one and that they would all arrive safely at their destination.

June 9, 1921

Went ashore at 10:30 with Bristol and Dunn. Visited Near East and delivered several messages to Haidar Bey to be censored. Arranged by telephone to visit the Mutasariff and introduce Lieutenant Dunn who asked permission to visit Angora. Mutasariff replied that he would telegraph Angora and request permission; reception cordial. Visited King's office and found situation unchanged, that is, still tense. Certain employees of the Tobacco men had received orders for deportation.

Had lunch at King's house with Bristol, Dunn and Mr. Alston as guests. Family very much excited over King's sister-in-law, married to a Turk, having received order from police to depart. According to Mrs. King, all Greeks are to be rounded up, started out to the hills, and there turned over to the Turkish soldiers, who are going to kill all of the men and take all the pretty girls. Also that all the young Greek girls had bought up all the strychnine and corrosive sublimate in town, deciding to kill themselves rather than be at the mercy of the Turks. She further remarked that so great was the demand for poison by the Greek girls that the Turk druggists here had increased the price ten-fold and were profiteering on it.

The gravity of this discourse was somewhat upset when, after listening to a steady flow of it for some time, Lieutenant Dunn very gravely interrupted to say that he thought corrosive sublimate was a bad thing to take as it worked too slowly and the Turks would probably be able to accomplish their purpose on the young ladies before it became effective. It is my opinion that Mrs. King is responsible for most of the excitement among the American Tobacco people as she seems to be very fond of making sensational statements.

Two Italian steamers in harbor discharging and taking cargo. Sent following code message to Stanav:

> "Situation tense and unchanged period Police continue to warn Greeks of all classes to prepare for deportation comma including women and children period Our impression is that only certain Greek males will actually be deported period Your instructions not to interfere with deportation of Greeks have been and will continue to be carried out.
>
> Humphreys"

June 10, 1921

Went ashore at 10:30 with Bristol and Dunn. Made usual rounds. Rumor that two Greek vessels bombarded Ineboli,* first heard from Abdullah [the contractor who the Americans use] and later confirmed in conversation with prominent Turk in King's office. Russian Mission landed this morning, reported to have considerable gold.† Observed many new Turkish officers on street, evidently showing new troops have arrived. Turks continue building trenches back of city. Samsun [navigation] light still not functioning, evidently extinguished to prevent aiding Greek ships in the Black Sea. Reported that fourteen members of the "Bristol Club" have been arrested and will be tried. According to Tobacco men this club composed of ex-officials is responsible for the present movement against the Greeks. Their arrest would indicate that the regular Military have the upper hand now and [that the military is] probably responsible for the reports that the deportation orders of Greeks will be modified. Mr. King states that the Military Commander sent word to him that his sister-in-law would not be deported and for them not to worry about it, although the police have not rescinded their order.‡ First group of Greeks to be deported tomorrow. Sent following to Stanav:

---

* The bombardment of Ineboli (Inebolu) took place on June 9, 1921.

† Since 1920, the Bolsheviks had provided gold to help finance the Nationalists' war with the Greeks, as well as quantities of ammunition. The war diaries regularly note such importation of bullion.

‡ Local police had recently learned that some fifty men in town were members of what was called the "Bristol Club," though why they chose this particular name for their group—that of both the American admiral and the captain of the *Overton*—is unknown. The club had a former Samsun police chief as its head, and many members were former bandits. They used a coffee house near the tobacco magazines as a club house and were responsible for several killings in town (*Overton* WD, June 1, 1921).

> "Situation unchanged period It is believed that first group of Greeks will be deported tomorrow period Reported on reliable authority that two Greek war vessels bombarded Ineboli yesterday afternoon firing about fifty shots period Extent of damages and casualties not known period Russian political mission landed here today reported to have brought considerable gold period.
>
> Humphreys"

June 11–June 14, 1921

On June 11, it was reported ashore that 25 Greeks had been handcuffed together and sent out of town; on June 12, 115 more Greeks had been deported. Tobacco managers King and Currin called on the Mutasariff and told him that unless the deportation of their skilled employees ceased, they would have to close up business. On June 13, there were wild rumors as to to the fate of the recent deportees and that many Greek warships were in the Black Sea. Fox *was to arrive shortly.*

USS *FOX*, COMMANDER C.S. JOYCE WAR DIARY SET FOR JUNE 14–JULY 1, 1921

. . . .

June 16, 1921

Went ashore with Commander Spears at 10:30. Upon our arrival on the dock we were met by Abdullah, the contractor, who reported that all the Greek men in town were being arrested. We proceeded in a Near East automobile to the post office, where we met Haidar Bey and gave him some press news.* I also had him censor a letter containing some money for Mr. Currin. At the post office, we met Mr. McDowell of the Near East, who was there getting some mail censored which he was going to take to Constantinople with him.

He told us there was a wild excitement in town this morning on the strength of a rumor that the Greek fleet had passed Sinope and were going to attack the town [Samsun] today. As a result of this, all the Turkish women and children started to make for the hills, as they expected the Greek ships to shoot into the Turkish quarter of the town. The Greeks were also greatly excited as they did not know what would happen to them. In the meantime, the Turkish authorities apparently had made up their mind to take some action and were arresting all the Greek men in town.

After leaving the post office, we went to Mr. King's office where we saw Mr. Alston, Mr. King, Mr. Johnson, Mr. Currin, Mr. Harris, Mr. Van Toor and the younger Mr. King. Later on, Mr. Fitzgerald of the Gary Tobacco Company also came in. The Alston Tobacco Company's magazines had been visited by the police an hour or so earlier, and all the men employees placed under arrest. This resulted in the magazines being closed, as they could not continue their work. The Gary Tobacco Company's magazines had not been interfered with up to this time, but while we were there, Mr. Currin was sent for and it is believed that all their men are also to be taken, which will result in all the tobacco manipulation being stopped.

The Turk who was in Mr. King's office stated that the reason for the arrest of all the Greeks was for the purpose of identification and that

* "Press news" is a summary of world news available to the destroyer via its communication circuits, which the captains usually distribute to the Americans ashore. They sometimes also give a copy to the Mutasariff.

all those who could not prove that they were natives of Samsun would be deported immediately. On the other hand, another rumor had it that all the male Greeks, over a certain age, were to be deported, regardless of whether they belonged in Samsun or elsewhere. Of course it is difficult to ascertain what is really taking place. The streets were very quiet and well patrolled, though there were large groups of Greek men under guard at various places and it was reported that there were five or six hundred of them in the courtyard of the Mutasariff's office awaiting investigation or final orders. We did not visit the Mutasariff as we had no special mission under the circumstances and doubted his accessibility. Therefore, on account of tomorrow being Friday, Haidar Bey was instructed to make arrangements to visit the Mutasariff Saturday morning.*

Commander Bristol and Commander Spears had made arrangements with the Americans in town to congregate at Mr. Currin's house on the beach, should any trouble arise and especially in case the Greek warships attempted an attack. However, in view of the fact that trenches are being constructed on the beach, it is now a question of whether it would not be more dangerous to the American personnel to endeavor to embark [on the American destroyer] without permission, or to remain. It is therefore doubtful if the authorities would grant permission for the Americans to embark, as they no doubt feel that a certain amount of protection comes to them from the presence of the Americans in the city, so that if an attempt is made to bring all the Americans [to the ship], it must be done against the wishes of the authorities and it might prove dangerous to embark these people under a machine gun or infantry fire from the beach. In as much as they all live in the Greek section of the town, it is unlikely that they will be subjected to any great amount of firing from the Greek ships. It is also very doubtful if the Greeks will have force enough to attempt a landing.

It appears that the city has been fortified and that therefore the Greeks have a right to bombard the port without warning. It therefore seems probable that we will have very little time to take action should the Greeks arrive. . . .

* Friday would have been the Muslim day of rest, and the Mutasariff would not have been in his office.

June 17, 1921

. . . .

Sent the following dispatch this date:

> "The arrest of all male Greeks between the ages of fifteen and fifty has been completed. It is reported that two thousand have been marched into the interior in the last twenty four hours. About one hundred and fifty were seen by us leaving under guard this afternoon with one priest among them. No deportation of women and children but there will be great suffering from hunger. Tobacco business stopped."

Due to the delay occasioned by the Russian refugees,* we were unable to go ashore in the forenoon. About 11:30, I went on board of HUMPHREYS and stayed for luncheon with the intention of going ashore immediately afterward but before departing, a very heavy rain squall started which lasted for about two hours. Soon after three o'clock, Captain Spears and I started ashore, stopping alongside the steamship Remo to find out if Mr. Alston and Mr. King had gotten aboard. A Turkish policeman came to the foot of the gangway and told us that he had orders from the Commandant that we must not come aboard as Mr. King and Mr. Alston were not on board. We therefore went ashore and found Mr. Alston, Mr. King, Mr. McDowell and Mrs. McDowell on the dock preparing to embark. Haidar

---

* Five Russian men had swum to the *Humphreys* from the Italian merchant ship *Marininia*, upon which Nationalists at Inebolu had placed them, during the night of June 16–June 17. They believed they were in danger of being taken to Bolshevik Russia, from which they had escaped, and they had asked for asylum. Captain Joyce of the *Fox* eventually decided they were not in imminent danger nor entitled to asylum, and as Senior Naval Present, he had them returned to the *Marininia*, which was en route to Batoum. However, Captain Spears of the *Humphreys* disagreed with Joyce's action and wrote fourteen numbered paragraphs (!) in his war diary arguing that as the Russians had asked for asylum and as the Americans had earlier evacuated Russian political refugees from the Crimea, it was the Americans' duty to grant it to them. (On the earlier occasion, nearly 150,000 "White Russian" refugees had been evacuated by several allied navies to Constantinople; see Shenk, *ABSF*, 69–87 for this episode.) Overall, five full pages concerning the Russian refugees open the June 17 war diary entry and precede the message above. These pages we have omitted.

Bey was there [working] them through. They afterward got aboard and the ship left in the evening. We then walked out to Mr. Johnson's house and had tea. On the way out we saw about one hundred and fifty Greek men being marched out of the town under guard and among them a priest.

The Turkish school house was filled with Greek men and had a guard of soldiers around the outside. However, the soldiers did not prevent a large crowd of women and children accumulating nor did they prevent them from passing food etc. to the men inside. The yard near the Mutasariff's office was filled with boys. Upon arrival at Mr. Johnson's house, we found out from him that all the male Greeks between the ages of fifteen and fifty have been arrested and deported. This is regardless of whether they were Samsun natives or not. He further said that about two hundred of them had been marched out of the city during the night and that they would probably all be gone by tomorrow. There is no news as yet of what has happened to those who had already been deported.

June 18, 1921

Went ashore with Commander Spears in the morning and found very little change in the situation. Mr. Van Toor said that he had seen a large party of Greeks being deported this morning (he thought about five hundred) and that he was very much pleased with the arrangements made for them. They all had packs on their backs which contained a certain amount of food and apparently an adequate guard. Following them were four Arabas [carriages], two of which apparently contained provisions and the other two of which were apparently empty and he thought were provided for those who might fall sick or become unable to march. No news as yet has been obtained of how the men have fared on the road, but so far as is definitely known, nothing has happened to them. Mr. Johnson reported today that they were bringing in a number of the men from villages that had not already been depopulated and in a few days the deportation would be completed. . . .

I told Haidar Bey to make an appointment for us tomorrow morning to see the Mutasariff at 10:30. It is the intention to lay before the Mutasariff that it is our duty to evacuate the Americans in case of an attack on the town by Greek warships and that we looked to him to assist us in every way in fulfilling this duty.

Sent the following dispatch:

> "Conditions unchanged. Deportation of male Greeks continues and the parties appear to be well protected and supplied."

June 19, 1921

Went ashore with Commander Spears and saw all the Americans. Found conditions about the same and that both the Tobacco and Near East people are finding it extremely difficult to do business without the Greeks, as most of their clerical force were Greeks.

Had an interview with the Mutasariff and told him that it was our duty in case of any hostile action on the part of Greek men-of-war to evacuate the Americans at Samsun; that any neutrals would only be a source of embarrassment and responsibility to the authorities on shore and that I depended on the local authorities to lend me every assistance in fulfilling my duty toward the American citizens. The Mutasariff stated that if the Greek ships attacked, he would immediately lose control of the situation and that the city would be under military law and the [local] Military Commander would have full authority in that event. He further said, however, that he would find out from the Military Commander what his attitude would be and let me know tomorrow. He wished to know my personal opinion as to as to whether the Greeks would be likely to confine themselves to a bombardment or would attempt to land. I told him that of course I did not know but could only assume from their reported action at Ineboli that they would confine themselves to a bombardment. He then said that there must be some cloud in the sky, as he expressed it, or I would not be concerned about this question.

Captain Joyce and the Mutasariff continue to discuss the possible evacuation of the Americans and also the circumstances of the Russian refugees. After this, the captain's war diary continues.

I then spoke to the Mutasariff about the question of propaganda and called his attention to the fact that every other country published to the world their side of all the political and economic questions that were of importance, whereas the Turks never told the world anything of their side of the situation. This was done with the idea of perhaps drawing him out on what the present activities of the Turks were in regard to propaganda and missions. Particular stress was laid on the fact that in America the people all knew about Armenians and Greeks and almost every one, but they knew nothing about the Turks except what the Greeks or Armenians said. The Mutasariff agreed that this was so, that it was a great mistake but that the people higher up in Turkey did not realize the advantages of propaganda, but he said he thought they would be better in this respect in the future. He did not, however, vouchsafe any information regarding their present plans.

The deportations still continue and it is expected that within the next twenty-four hours they will be completed. So far as is known, they have all arrived safely at Kavak, and the consensus of opinion seems to be that they will be safe beyond this point so far as massacres are concerned.* The buyer for the Near East was arrested and was afterwards released on the ground that he was a Protestant and not an Orthodox Greek, but so far as is known, he is the only one that has been released as yet who was under fifty years old and over fifteen.

Had luncheon at Mr. Currin's house and later went to the Near East where I saw Mr. Van Toor. He said that he had no assurance yet that Admiral Bristol's message to Mardin† had been delivered but would make further efforts tomorrow. He further said that Haidar Bey had some hesitancy about it as he thought it might not get by the telegraph censor. However, I told Mr. Van Toor to make such necessary changes in the wording as to make it satisfactory to the censor and yet get the information that Admiral Bristol desired. The Near East received a telegram a few days ago from Diarbekir which is not far from Mardin and it seems reasonable that the message will get through.

Sent the following dispatches:

> "No changes in the conditions ashore. It is expected that the deportations will be finished inside of two days. As yet there

---

* This statement might seem curious, and admittedly it has different possible interpretations. For example, it may refer to local conditions near Kavak—where Osman Agha's notorious band of cutthroats were then located. However, massacres of minority men had been widely practiced over the last several years by the Turks, and some Americans who knew of the 1915-1916 massacres of Armenians might naturally have been concerned about deportee safety.

† Admiral Bristol was for some reason concerned about the conditions at the American mission at Mardin, which was hundreds of miles inland.

has been no news of massacres enroute. Your message to Mardin has not gone yet but hope to get if off tomorrow. There is no information here about the mission."

"Expect to hold full power trial tomorrow.* When is HUMPHREYS to be relieved? Expect to send her to Trebizond on Tuesday and take her excess oil when she returns."

. . . .

June 20, 1921

Held full power trial. Upon our return, Commander Spears came on board and reported no particular news from ashore except that Mr. Van Toor was anxious to give up the hospital and that he suspected Haidar Bey of being in some way responsible for the loss of the Greek employees in the Near East Office. He also reported that it was rumored that several Greeks in the first party had been killed just after leaving Kavak.

Sent no dispatch as there appeared to be no authentic news.

June 21, 1921

The HUMPHREYS got underway for Trebizond at 7:00 o'clock. About 10:30, I went ashore and visited the Near East. It appears that, after all, the Near East buyer had been deported, he being the one who was released the other day on account of being a Protestant. Mr. Tuck's former clerk is to be deported in a day or so and it is expected that he will go out on one of the Near East trucks that is going into the interior. Mr. Van Toor was rather of the opinion that Haidar Bey was the cause of his losing these people but I very much doubt it. Mr. Van Toor also said that it was practically impossible to operate the hospital now as all their wardmen and druggists had been taken away and he was therefore very anxious to give the hospital up. . . .

The tobacco people have been having a very hard time trying to straighten up their payroll on account of the confusion that everything was left in by their clerks when they were suddenly arrested. Both com-

* Every destroyer conducted an annual "full power trial" to operate the vessel at differing proportions of full power for a standard distance so that engineers could measure such things as steam pressure and quality of steam at various propeller-shaft rpms. These trials took a good part of a day to perform.

panies are trying to get started again, using women and children. Mr. Johnson says that the story is going around that the first party of Greeks, when being marched out of Kavak, were to be marched down into a little valley, and they thought the conditions suspicious, so refused to go. Apparently there was a stampede and several of the Greeks tried to run away when they were shot down by the guards. Another story has it that when these men tried to run away, and the guards fired upon them, the other Greeks in the party attacked the guards and took their guns away whereupon several of the guards were killed. The story has it that there were forty-five Greeks killed and fourteen Turks, while another story has it that they were as many as two hundred Greeks killed. It is impossible to tell anything about the facts in the case as yet. The Turks claim that they were marching them down into the valley to rest them as all the houses and places where they could stay in Kavak were filled. These people have been allowed to send telegrams and letters from every town they had passed through, though as yet no communications have come from beyond Kavak.*

A tobacco factory in Samsun, with both Greek and Turkish employees (see cigarette packs being filled on a small table in the foreground). Well over a thousand men worked in these factories in peacetime.

* Such telegrams were suspect, some of them being from Turkish gendarmes using the identities of massacred Greek men to extort money from the Greeks' relatives.

When Miss Anthony left for Marsovan, she arranged to indicate by the signature on her dispatch regarding her arrival, of the conditions on the road and her dispatch arrived yesterday and her signature indicated that conditions were suspicious, but as she was in a very suspicious state of mind, this may be discounted to a certain extent.

Mr. Johnson said that the only institution in town who has been allowed to keep their Greek employees was the Ottoman Bank. When these employees were arrested, the Director of the bank went to the authorities and told them that he would simply have to close the bank and go out of business. So the authorities released the employees, as the bank handles all the government funds. In the meantime, so they said, they are taking the matter up with Angora. Haidar Bey seemed to think that it would be possible in a few days to get a nucleus of the important employees back for the tobacco firms. He seemed quite confident of it but whether or not he had any real basis for the statement could not be ascertained.

Up to the time I left to return to the ship, the Mutasariff had not received a reply from the Military Commander regarding the proposal I made him on Sunday, so I expect to hear tomorrow. . . .

Three short dispatches to Constantinople follow. As these basically repeat the conclusions mentioned above, they have been omitted.

June 22, 1921

Went ashore at 10:30, and saw Van Toor, Currin, Johnson and Haidar Bey. Haidar Bey said that the Mutasariff was unable to give me a reply on the questions I put to him on Sunday, and Haidar Bey further said that he was sure that the authorities here had telegraphed to Angora in regard to this matter. He said that he thought that even the military commander was afraid to act on his own responsibility and that he would ask authority from Angora. . . .

Then I visited Mr. Currin. He told me a well known Turk had come to him this morning with tears in his eyes and reported that what might have been expected had happened and that most of the first three parties of Greeks that left here had been massacred on the road.

He stated that all the arabagees [drivers of carriages] coming in over the road reported a great number of dead Greeks lying by the roadside. Mr. Johnson's information corresponds with this in all essentials, and he has received a telegram from a town beyond Kavak which was sent by one of his men. This man stated that he and three others had arrived and were proceeding immediately toward Amassia. From the fact that this man mentioned three others who were with him, none of whom Johnson knew, Johnson has arrived at the conclusion that the rest of his men who were in the party had been done away with, because had they survived, they would have been mentioned in the dispatch.

The Turks claim, as usual, that the parties were attacked by bandits, either by Greek bandits who were endeavoring to release the Greeks, or by Turkish bandits who were endeavoring to rob the Greeks, but in either case the authorities absolved themselves from responsibility. Johnson is now convinced that practically all his leading men and office force have been killed.

Mr. Currin states, and apparently on good authority, that about one hundred and fifty women and children have been deported within the last two days. These were people who had come in from the outlying villages comparatively recently. The general opinion in town is, that is only a question of time when the rest of the women and children will be deported.

All the skilled artisans in town are gone and it is difficult to understand how the Turks expect to get along without them, not to mention the tradesmen who own and operate most of the wholesale and retail stores. Practically all the jewelers, tailors, shoe-makers, barbers, bakers, etc., have been deported.

Made arrangements to land any mail which the WILLIAMSON may bring, tomorrow morning at ten o'clock, and have Haidar Bey on the dock to meet it.

At 7:45 p.m., the U.S.S WILLIAMSON arrived and anchored. . . .

While the Williamson was at Ineboli, the Greek destroyer *Jerax* steamed slowly by the city with her guns trained on the town but she did not fire and made no other demonstration. Also, [it was] reported at Ineboli that this destroyer had been cruising up and down the coast for several days, sinking small coasting vessels. We have had no information of any Greek ships being in the Black Sea up to this time, though they cannot get out of the Bosphorus without passing our ships. There was a small motor boat with a load of oil belonging to the Standard Oil Company which was overdue in Samsun and it was feared it had been sunk by the Greeks, but she arrived this evening safely.

The Commanding Officer of the WILLIAMSON reports being well received in Ineboli and reports of having seen several buildings that were damaged by the bombardment of the Greek ships.

The following are paraphrases of dispatches sent this date:

"Have reports from Turkish sources that most of the Greeks in first three parties were killed. Number believed to be five to six hundred. Johnson believes from telegram received that most of his men have been killed. Some women and children have been deported but none belonging to Samsun." . . . .

June 23, 1921

. . . .

Upon going ashore saw Mr. Van Toor of the Near East and all of the tobacco people. They are still having a difficult time due to the loss of their Greeks and Mr. Van Toor has somewhat of a problem on his hands, as he has a number of orphans in his orphanage who are over fifteen years of age and who are subject to deportation. He is in a quandary as to what to do about them. If he asks the local authorities for advice, he will precipitate their arrest and deportation, whereas, if he continues to say nothing about it, the authorities will blame him for having secreted them which in itself is a grave offense in the eyes of the authorities.

Further reports continue to come in of the Greeks having been massacred on the road. Mr. Farqua, who is a member of the firm that represents the Standard Oil in Samsun, and a French citizen, reports that he sent his clerical force out in an araba, that the very next day the araba returned but the Tartar driver was afraid to say anything, as he had been threatened by the Turkish soldiers and told to say nothing. He finally came around yesterday and stated that all the Greeks had been taken out from his araba, and their money taken away from them, all blankets and provisions seized, and the araba told to return to Samsun. It appears from the arabagee's story that they were bringing up the rear of the column, that some sort of melee took place ahead of them and that a great many of the Greeks were killed; that he stopped and waited and after all firing had ceased, started to proceed again but was soon captured by the soldiers and turned back, as stated above. No information could be obtained as to what started the trouble but this occurred six or seven hours from Samsun.

A ring belonging to one of the clerks of the Melachrino Tobacco Company was brought in by a Turk, to identify a man who was badly wounded and lying in a Turkish village up in the mountains. This ring bore the name of a Greek to whom it belonged and it appears that he was shot through his shoulder and otherwise injured but in some way survived and was later picked up by a Turkish villager and taken to his house. The Turk who brought the ring in wanted some medicines for his relief. . . .

. . . .

June 25, 1921

Went ashore with the Commanding Officer of the WILLIAMSON at 10:30, and found Mr. Van Toor on the dock waiting for us. He stated that the Greek section of the town had been surrounded with soldiers that morning and that everyone had been ordered to remain indoors. He was unable to get permission for anyone to leave the orphanages, even to get bread, so he had been out himself scouting up enough bread to keep them going. As we left the dock, we found a number of guards in naval uniform with a field gun on the beach. All business was stopped in town and none of the natives were permitted to pass in or out of the Greek section of the town. It appears that a house to house search was being made and all boys and men were being arrested and taken to the Police station for investigation. . . .

As none of the Greeks were permitted out of their houses, the tobacco magazines were closed and practically all business in the town was stopped. However, the Americans were not interfered with to any extent; the only exception being Mrs. Austin of the NER who was stopped and interfered with by soldiers on her way from the house to the office. The Gendarmes Commander stated that the search was being made for men between the ages of 15 and 50 who were believed to be in hiding and that as soon as the search was completed, all the old men and boys would be released again and the whole affair would be finished. However, no one, not even Haidar Bey appeared to have any confidence in this statement.

Haidar Bey was more open in his statements and condemnations of the proceedings than he has ever been before and said that he had told the governor [the Mutasariff] that the present policy was disastrous and had told him that it was impossible for this news to be kept secret and that when it became known, it could not but result disastrously for the Turks. He said he fully realized that the Turks could not expect the same recognition as the other European powers if they were going to conduct their government in this fashion. Haidar Bey said that the governor told him that he talked too much and interested himself too much in things that did not concern him, and he replied that anything that concerned Turkey concerned him and he must use such influence as he had to prevent further disgrace. Haidar Bey suggested that it might be possible that the Mutasariff would ask me to remain in Samsun for a while on the plea that he would prefer to deal with me than some of the other officers but that his real motive would be to prevent me from laying the situation before Admiral Bristol immediately. . . .

June 26, 1921

. . . .

It was reported that, in the search of the town, about one hundred and fifty Greeks, between the ages of fifteen and fifty, were found in hiding, and these are being deported. It is well known to nearly everyone that there are many others in hiding in Turkish houses, but it is not known if these houses are to be searched or not.

June 27, 1921

In visiting with the Mutasariff, Captain Joyce began a conversation in which he emphasized the neutrality of the Americans, how much money they were bringing into the country via the tobacco business, and the importance of the charity work of the Near East Relief—as well as how much the deportations (and various regulations) were interfering with all this important work.

In reply, the Mutasariff made in effect the following statement: That he realized the neutrality and friendliness of the Americans; that he realized the great benefit to the whole country of having the Americans here to buy the tobacco crop and that he realized it was his duty to do everything he could to further the interests which were so tied up with the interests of the community of which he was governor. He further said, however, that the orders for the deportation of the Greeks were absolutely mandatory and came from Angora and that all the tobacco firms, of whatever kind, were treated in exactly the same way; that the Regie [the Turkish-managed Regis Tobacco Company] had lost all of their employees in exactly the same way as the American tobacco firms. He promised faithfully to endeavor to obtain authority for a limited number of the important employees to return in order that the tobacco firms might carry on their business. He further said that the Near East had made an agreement in Angora that they would conduct their relief work for the benefit of all the needy regardless of creed and that as the hospital and the Turkish orphanages in Samsun were both Moslem institutions, it would not be in accord with this agreement if they removed assistance and he said that of course if the Near East could not afford to continue with the hospital, that he could not compel them to continue but that there was no money in the budget for him to operate it and that he would have some difficulty in finding a way to do it.

It will be noted that the Mutasariff assumed that the question regarding the hospital was purely a religious one and tried to make it appear that the Near East was endeavoring to give up the Turkish orphanages as well. He was immediately corrected in this misinterpretation of my words.

In continuing, the Mutasariff said that the restrictions in Samsun were very much more severe than anywhere else and he insisted that the orders came direct from Angora for both the restrictions on Americans and for foreigners and for the deportations. . . .

TESTIMONY AS TO THE MASSACRES NEAR KAVAK
–FROM THREE WITNESSES

About the Testimonies in This Book

We present these testimonies to demonstrate what actually was happening in the interior of Turkey, which often the ship captains (given their isolation at Samsun) could only guess at.

For instance, no one in Samsun directly witnessed the reported massacres of two of the first three parties of ethnic Greek men deported from Samsun. Local Americans in the city witnessed the men being marched off but heard only second- or third-hand reports of the killings that followed, conflicting accounts that will keep coming in for weeks. So we present below some eyewitness accounts testified to by survivors.

As will be seen, such testimonies often come from interviews or from reports submitted to official panels or governing offices, such as American Embassy officers in Constantinople, officials at the State Department in Washington, D.C., or—as is the case here—other local offices or officials.

A Greek Who Tells of Faking Death

After suddenly being deported from Samsun in late June 1921, the young Greek Cosmas Lilidas was among a group of deportees assaulted by their guards who were using rifles, knives, and bayonets, but by faking death, he managed to save his life in the midst of all the carnage. He then was marched on with other massacre survivors to Sivas. After several months, through the intervention with Nationalist officials by Ms. Annie Allen, America's NER representative at Angora, Lilidas was allowed to return to Samsun. A day before Van Toor of the Samsun hospital interviewed him, he and another young man had just returned to the city after traveling on the road by wagon (accompanied by a gendarme) from near Marash in southern Turkey, a journey that took twenty-seven days.

Mr. Van Toor said he had talked a little to one of the two Greeks who returned yesterday; that he was going to talk more to him soon. This boy is a Greek, 19 years old, a former Near East employee, named Cosmas Lilidas. He said that he was deported on 20 June in a party of 1,000 men and boys. When they had walked four hours to the village of Djinbush they stopped to eat lunch. They sat down surrounded by their guards, who in turn were joined by another party of guards, making a total of about 1,000 guards. The guards suddenly opened fire on the deportees. Then after firing a short time they went about with knives and bayonets making sure that those who had been shot were dead. This boy rolled over in a ditch and made believe he was dead. He was stabbed with a knife in the arm and back, but not fatally. In the afternoon they continued their march, 292 remaining out of the 1,000. At Sivas, Liladas went to the Near East Relief hospital to have his wounds treated and the party of deportees was broken up and sent in different directions. In the meantime the Near East Relief at Samsun had received telegrams from this party saying all was well. It is not yet known if these wires were "faked," or whether the deportees were forced by their guards to send them.

The above passage was found in the Sands *WD of November 30, 1921.*

A Greek's Letter about Evading the Massacre at Kavak

The second testimony is a translation of an abridged letter from an Ottoman Greek resident of Samsun who had evaded death in one of the massacres and who later wrote his brother, a merchant in Constantinople, from somewhere in the Turkish interior about his experience. The letter was thought important enough to be recorded in the minutes of a British committee in Constantinople.

Along with two other deportees, this witness had feigned death (as had Liladas, above) and later escaped the massacre scene. What happened to the author after he wrote this letter is not known.

I do not remember the date of the events which I am going to relate to you. I only remember that one Thursday afternoon [at] 2 o'clock a rumour spread out in the town [of Samsun] that the Greek Fleet was coming. Upon that, Policemen and Gendarmes surrounded the streets and arrested all the Greeks from 13 to 55 years of age. Next morning they started sending them into the interior of Anatolia. I had locked myself up in my shop for two days, but fearing that my wife and children [might] suffer, I came out and surrendered.

Our convoy was composed of 2,000 men. A few days previous to this, two convoys composed of 2,100 and 1,900 men respectively had already left Samsun. We heard that after us another two convoys left the town. In the evening we arrived at Kavak (40 miles distant from Amisos [an older name for Samsun]) and were told that we were to pass the night in the inns one hour from Kavak. But on the way, as we were descending the slope, we heard shots and soon found ourselves between two fires. [Two] men from our convoy and I laid ourselves down among the wounded and the killed pretending to be dead; we had only time to do this when the guards came up and stripped us of all our clothing leaving us our shirts and pants only which were soaked with blood of the killed near us. After a few hours we managed to get away. From our convoy 660 were killed and 530 from the first one. I do not know how many killed had the other convoys.

Those who were saved were in a deplorable condition, they were left without food or water and almost naked they were sent to Sivas on foot and thence to Kangal. For the present we have no news of them. . . . We are now in comparative safety on the heights of the mountains. We have been so much altered by the hardships and sufferings we have gone through that nobody can recognize us any more. If no help is sent to us we are lost; all the villages around us have been burnt and no woman or child has been left; all have been massacred. We heard that the Turks were about to deport also the women and children of Samsun, but through the interference of the Americans, this was postponed. . . .

This account was originally published in the minutes of the September 14, 1921 meeting of the "British Armenian-Greek Section," meetings organized by the British occupation force in Constantinople. It can be found in Vartkes Yeghiayan, compiler, British Reports on Ethnic Cleansing in Anatolia, 1919–1922: The Armenian-Greek Section, *Glendale, CA: Center for Armenian Rememberance, 2007, 223.*

An Italian Deposition About the Kavak Massacres and Other Atrocities

A third testimony about occurrences at Kavak and other atrocities is a deposition given by several male members of an Italian family to a church official in Constantinople. At least one of these men had been deported with the Greek males from Samsun, but upon reaching Kavak, he had been released due to a telegram from officials in Samsun who had learned of his Italian nationality. At Kavak, he heard gunshots and cries from the massacre and later saw some bodies.

Although he was rescued from these deportations, all the members of his family were soon afterwards deported from Samsun to Constantinople because of their Greek Orthodox religion despite their being longterm resident workers at Samsun. The Brooks *war diary, July 14, 1921, records Count Schmecchia's complaint of Italians being deported from Samsun, which likely refers to this family, among others.*

Besides speaking of the Kavak massacre, this particular deposition also mentions many other killings, village burnings, and other crimes said to have taken place in Samsun or the region. Some of these atrocities are confirmed in the war diaries. The source of the Italians' information is not always clear, although the deposition opens with a confirmation that the Italians were "in many cases eyewitnesses" of what they report—perhaps this note refers specifically to early events at or nearby Samsun.

A note: The Italians here characterize the Turks as being possessed by "brutal passion." No doubt this is understandable given what they had seen and sometimes barely escaped themselves. Certainly there were also bitter feelings about being evicted from their homes and workplaces. The war diaries, however, manifest many different local Turkish attitudes about the atrocities. Some Turks were reported weeping at what was happening or confessing to American tobacco managers their shame upon learning of the actions by their fellow Turks.

Deposition sworn to

by Jocob Cantoni, aged 48 years, his brother George Cantoni, 46 years old and their children—Constantine 21 years, George 20, and Philip 18 years old—all Italian subjects, orthodox christians, deported from Amisos (Samsun), here, on the boat "Cleopatra", the 5/18 July 1921.

They have been deported in spite of their Italian citizenship, as belonging to the Greek nation. The steps taken by the Italian Consul at Samsun, Mr. Stanislas Count Schmecchia have been without results.

. . . These men swear that prior to their deportation they always lived at Samsun and were employed in the American Tobacco Society. Philip was employed at the Italian Agency. They have been in many cases eye-witnesses of the horrible events that lastly took place at Samsun and its environments. They declare the following:-

1) For months past the excesses of the Turks in the towns and chiefly in the Christian villages that were spared after the [World War I] armistice—murders, robbing and pillaging—were the order of the day. These were perpetrated by the organizations in authority, by Turkish bands and by armed Turks of the neighbourhood. This evil got worse every day. It was a recreation for any Turk and especially for the bands of Osman Agha to kill in full daylight, in the town, with any kind of weapon, the first christian that they met, so as to satisfy their savage instinct.

So it was in the case of Djineklou Anesti and of many others. It cost nothing for a Turk if excited by his brutal passion, to attack a christian quarter and to seize the first woman met. It was in this way that some young naval cadets carried off from the door of her house Mlle Athinas Asli, sister in law of Mr. King, Director of the "American Tobacco Company". They also forced the house of Mlle Simian. . . . .three days later they were freed. This criminal state of things still continues; no complaints to the authorities are taken into consideration; besides, the terror and anarchy do not allow of any complaints being made.

2) Towards the end of May last it was announced that all the inhabitants of Samsun who were not originally of the country including immigrants, would be deported in seven days time. This deportation was begun by deporting the Greek refugees from Russia* and from Epes and Siva. Then the inhabitants of Samsun who came from different parts of Anatolia but had lived 30 or 40 years [consecutively] at Samsun, submitted, through a commission composed of priests and ladies, a petition that the Government, taking into consideration their living so long in Samsun, would allow them out of

* Many Pontic Greeks had fled to Russia during the Great War, and some had returned afterwards. Apparently they were then sent to the interior.

philantropy to stay in their homes. For all answer the Government had the commission arrested and thrown into prison. The priests were sent into the interior; the women—H. Rossidou, Hel. Sonoglou, Ph. Symionidou, Andavaloglue and Mlle Nicolaidou, teacher—were, after much trouble, released.

[3)] The Government made known to the christian population that they had nothing to fear and that everybody could peacefully continue their occupations. In spite of this, several days after the 3/16th of June 1921, the town was surrounded by soldiers and gendarmes and the police proceeded to the arrest of all the Greeks at market and even forced their way into the stores of the American Tobacco Society where thousands of men were at work.

In this way, without any preparation for departure, without food or money—about 2950 people of the male population, from 14 to 50 years, were arrested most brutally and imprisoned in the Turkish school and in that of Kutsuk-me'arif. The next day they were deported to the interior of Anatolia—barefoot, hungry and under the menace of the sticks of the gendarmes.

The first party of 999 people began their march on foot. 11 carriages were used for the ill people accompanied by the doctor Cheraffedine. Two days later a second party of 1200 people followed the first, and a third of 751 people took the same direction. The first party after a march of 13 hours, without stopping, came to Kavak at 10:45. After brief control they were divided into two parties, the first counting fewer people was sent far from the town, the others were taken to a grange, which was surrounded by gendarmes and bandits. At the order to shoot, they fired simultaneously and ferociously exterminated their prisoners. This work was continued till about 2 hours after midnight. Eye-witness of these tragic fact[s] was George Cantoni, son of Jacob, who by mistake, though Italian subject, was made one of the first party of prisoners. and was liberated only after a telegraphic order from Samsun.

Having passed the night at Kavak, he heard the shots and the cries of the victims. The next day he counted 20 corpses that were being transported on carts to the Local of the Government.

The second party arrived at Kavak after being robbed of even their clothes but they were not killed. The third party was terribly massacred and mutilated by the hordes of Osman Agha, even before their arrival at Kavak, at the foot of Mahmour Dag.

4) After the two monstrous act[s] of these terrible arrests, public cryers at Samsun announced that anybody hidden in their houses would be hung together with the members of their families and that all the men from 14 to 50 years must give themselves up to the authorities. After this order 3000 men gave themselves up to their executioners, including those that had found refuge at Samsun after their [village] homes had been burnt down. From these were separated all men aged from 20 to 36 years, fit for military service, not taking into consideration their having or having not served in the army or paid the exoneration tax. All the arrested men were imprisoned in the school and were afterwards sent away in parties, the fate of most of which is unknown.

5) After this extermination of the male population came the turn of the terrified women and children.

Saturday 3/16 July the mouhtar Stavros Djerkezoglou with some police agents announced that in the length of three days the inhabitants had to prepare themselves for exile and could sell all their belongings. This murderous order caused such horror and agony in all the families that they declared they would rather die with their children in their homes than submit to dishonor and infamous death. Some poor people in fatal agony sold all that remained to them for a piece of bread. Such was the tragic situation of Samsun when we left on Monday.

6) In what concerns the towns in the environments of Samsun—such as Bafra, Alatsan, Tsarchamba, Oumah, Ordou, Kerassundo as far as Trebizond—it is known that a party of arrested inhabitants of Bafra passed through Samsun as well as the arrested of Ouniah, Ordou and Kerassundo that were sent into the interior. The rest of the inhabitants of Bafra and Alatsan passed through Kiopru and Kirze. The inhabitants of Kavab, Kadjas, Merzifoun, Hadjikeny etc., have also been deported into the Interior. The people deported from Tsarchamba were nearly all massacred between Samsun and Tekekeuy.

7) More than 70 villages in the environs of Bafra, which were not destroyed after the armistice, have now been burnt and only ruins remain. The inhabitants have been exterminated. The big village of Ada, half an hour from Samsun, with the surrounding villages has suffered a fearful fate: the pursuing corps, commanded by Demir Ali, aided by the famous band of Osman Agha, after having concentrated all the surrounding inhabitants in Ada, surrounded the village and fired it from four sides burning everybody and shooting those that escaped

from the fire. More than 3500 persons succumbed to this death by fire and steel. The same fate overtook Karaberdjin and its environments: the villages of Dere, Avden, Dzinarchi, Tsandir and others were also burned and their inhabitants massacred. At the American hospital at Samsun more than 40 girls aged from 6 to 12 who were brutally violated by the savage Turks, are being taken care of. Some of the villages near Samsun which had remained half destroyed—Papazmahales-si, Devkerid, Tekne bounar, we saw completely burned the last day before our departure.

All the preceding was deposited under oath by the men in question, who fully understood their responsibility, in all christian conscience.

The Locum Tenens of the Grand Vicariat
Me'tropolite of Ne'ocesare'e and Cotyora
(Signed) Polycarpos.

This testimony was found in the Overton *war diaries under a one-sentence covering note (dated August 17, 1921) from Admiral Bristol's chief of staff, Captain Lyman Cotten. Cotten had sent this deposition to the captain of the* Overton *for his "verification and comment"; Captain Arthur LeRoy Bristol of the* Overton *would have been the captain addressed. Although he had not actually been at Samsun during the Kavak massacres, Commander Bristol was probably the most knowledgeable of all the ship captains who acted as senior naval officer at Samsun and was clearly the one most trusted by the admiral.*

A copy of this deposition had apparently been given to the American embassy by the church officials, who had it deposed on July 21, 1921.

THE SMOKE FROM BURNING VILLAGES

The smoke from burning villages seemed to billow up daily in varying directions from one day to the next. This destruction was part of various Turkish attempts to move all Greeks into the interior or simply to get rid of them. We have heard before that surviving Greek women and children from destroyed villages fled to Samsun for food and shelter, and for the next year or so we will continue to hear both of such burnings and of the subsequent deportation of remaining villagers inland.

A letter delivered by an exhausted swimmer to the Williamson *(included in the next set of war diaries) comes from a spokesman for a group of men who have also lost their village homes. They were probably hiding in the forest when their villages were attacked and now were seeking desperately for help from the American destroyer in Samsun, whose captain, however, had been ordered not to take sides. Without help, the men might well starve.*

In the same letter are reports of the terrible destruction in May of the large village of Ada, about three miles west of Samsun, in which inhabitants were burned alive (the Italian deposition immediately above also describes the Ada atrocity). That letter also mentions similar events occurring more recently at Tekekeuy.

Some groups of Greeks fought against the destruction of their homes with mixed success, often provoking Turkish authorities to further measures. However, little provocation was needed to arouse the worst instincts of Osman Agha's men.

USS *WILLIAMSON*, LIEUT. COMMANDER J.C. CUNNINGHAM WAR DIARY SET FOR JUNE 22-JULY 7, 1921

June 22, 1921

U.S.S. HUMPHREYS (236) stood in from Trebizond at 6:05 and went alongside FOX (234). . . .

Went with Comdr. Joyce and met the following Americans: Messrs. Johnson and W.J. King, of the Alston Tobacco Co.; Messrs. Currin, Fitzgerald and Harris of the Gary Tobacco Co.; Mr. English of the Melachrino Co.; Messrs. Van Toor and Plimpton and Miss Pickering of the N.E.R., and Mr. Farqua, a French subject who is an employee of the Standard Oil Co.

The war diary of this day essentially repeats the information of the Fox *war diary of the same date (both captains having attended the same meetings) and is therefore mostly omitted.*

. . . .

June 24, 1921

Did not go ashore. Underway at 6:15 to hold full power trials. Anchored at Samsun at 2:15 p.m.. Called on the FOX.

June 25, 1921

At 10:00 went ashore with Cmdr. Joyce to meet the Mutasariff. Met Van Toor on the dock.

As Captain Cunningham of the Williamson *had attended the same meeting and encountered the same conditions as Captain Joyce of the* Fox, *the war diaries are similar and are omitted here, except this final comment that doesn't appear in the other war diary:*

Returned to ship about 1:30. About 3:30 observed from the ship 75 to 100 camels on the hillside and saw a caravan of probably 50 wagons, moving over a road to the southward. Some officers ashore reported that these were loaded with ammunition and some machine guns and were being escorted by soldiers.

June 26, 1921

The two captains heard similar information in their conversations of this date, and we omit the first half of this war diary. A bit more information was added afterwards:

Noticed a number of Greek men and boys assembled in a courtyard at the Mutasariff's office. This afternoon, Abdullah, the contractor, informed one of my officers that about 150 Greeks were deported yesterday, and that two old Greek men, who had been advising Greeks to hide, were killed 10 or 12 kilometers outside of town. This contractor also said that arms, ammunition and clothing were received yesterday from Batum and Novorrossisk.

Little happened over the next several days, except for Captain Cunningham noticing considerable ammunition on the waterfront, probably offloaded from a Turkish schooner lying alongside a small dock and meant for the Turkish front lines.

July 1, 1921

. . . .

Went ashore at 10:00 with the Commanding Officer of the STURTEVANT. Observed a quantity of ammunition on the waterfront—some was being loaded into arabas and a number of arabas were seen going toward the waterfront. There was no ammunition on the dock yesterday.

Went to the Near East and discussed the situation at the hospital with Van Toor. He no longer desires to turn the hospital over to the Turkish authorities and is perfectly willing to continue running it as before until instructions are received from NER headquarters in Constantinople. With conditions as at present, I consider NER should continue to operate the hospital. Went to Mr. King's office and saw all the Alston people and Haidar Bey. The American [civilians] have been given permission to visit the ships on July 4, and we are arranging for boat races, swimming races, etc., on that date. The Americans had planned a picnic for the Officers on July 4, but now that they can visit the ships, the picnic is to be held on Sunday, July 3, near the lighthouse. Haidar Bey says that this is perfectly all right.

The Commanding Officer of STURTEVANT and I went through Alston Tobacco Co's magazine with Mr. Johnson. There were about thirty old men there, only four or five of whom are experienced in the tobacco business, and as many women employees as can be used.

Mr. Johnson stated that some wounded Turkish soldiers were brought into Samsun yesterday evening from a small Greek village two hours to the eastward of here and that these soldiers had been wounded in attempting to capture Greek brigands. For several hours this afternoon, the flame and smoke from burning houses to the eastward have been observed from the ship. With practically no wind, it was easy to distinguish the fires and it is estimated that at least 50 houses were burned. As many as 15 distinct fires could be counted at one time. This is probably the village where the Turkish soldiers were wounded yesterday. . . .

July 2, 1921

Went ashore at 10:00 with the Commanding Officer of the STURTEVANT and made the usual rounds. The fact that two Greek villages had been burned the day before and that wounded Turkish soldiers had been brought to Samsun was common knowledge. While in the Alston Tobacco Co.'s office, a Turk came in and called Mr. King outside. When Mr. King returned, he announced that this Turk had just told him that yesterday two Greek villages had been burned by Turkish soldiers and that about 250 Greeks had been killed, most of whom were women and children. These villages were Tekekeuy and Tsinik. Mr. King stated that 17 Turkish soldiers had been killed and that 9 wounded soldiers had been seen being brought into Samsun. The above statements were corroborated by Mr. Currin and Abdullah, the Contractor.

Tekekeuy, which was one of the largest and prosperous villages in this district, was inhabited by a type of Greek peacefully inclined and above the average. This village was one of the few which was not molested throughout the war. According to Mr. King, and from what I have been able to find out from other sources, this seems the most probable, the men fearing deportation had taken to the mountains, but, when the Turkish soldiers began destroying the village, the Greek men attacked them. According to Haidar Bey, the Turkish patrols on the outskirts of the above villages were attacked by Greek brigands after which they, the soldiers, burned the villages as a retaliatory measure.

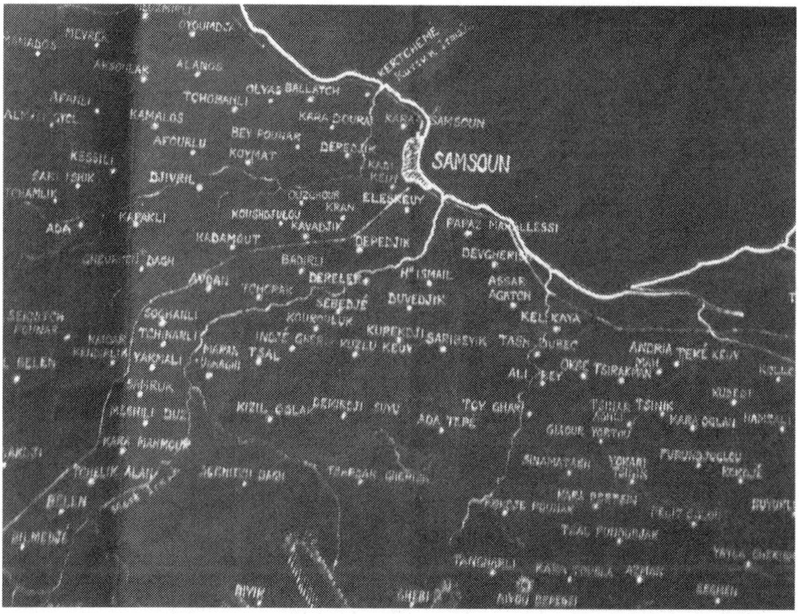

Massacres of Greeks took place at many Greek villiages shown on this contemporaneous map, including Ada, shown to the far left, three miles from Samsun, and Tsinik and Tekekeuy to the right. *National Archives and Records Administration.*

Although I believe Haidar Bey sincerely regrets such occurrences, he is nevertheless always prepared, like the Mutasariff, to attribute everything to brigands.

It is reported that the Turks and Greeks have been fighting near Bafra for several days. The Commanding Officer of the STURTEVANT and I, in going to Mr. Currin's office for lunch, observed about 50 Greek men in the courtyard at the Mutasariff's office. These men came from around Bafra. Haidar Bey stated that while these Greeks were marched to Samsun, a band of Greek brigands attacked their escort in an endeavor to release the Greeks, but the escort was too strong. A few on both sides were killed.

A telegram was received yesterday by Haidar Bey from a Turkish congressman in Angora stating that he expected to obtain permission, through the Minister of the Interior, for some of the experienced employees of the tobacco people to return to work. Mr. King knows where three of his men are, but has heard nothing from the others since their deportation. . . .

The following message paraphrased, sent to STANAV:

> "Turkish soldiers yesterday destroyed the villages of Tekekeuy and Tsinik, killing about 250 Greeks, most of whom were women and children. Seventeen Turkish soldiers reported killed. Private message from Turkish Congressman of Angora states that some employees of tobacco firms will be allowed to return to work. Conditions inside Samsun itself quiet."
>
> ....

Conditions in Samsun itself are quiet and unchanged. Received message stating that BROOKS would sail on July 5 for Samsun to relieve WILLIAMSON.

.....

July 4, 1921

Went ashore at 10:00 to bring all Americans off to the ship. Fifteen of them came and remained on board until late in the afternoon. They all enjoyed the boat and swimming races and other stunts. All Americans were searched on the dock before embarking. As there was nothing new, no message was sent to STANAV. The conditions here are the same—very quiet. There still are a number of soldiers in Samsun and they are going in and out practically all the time. About 300 or 400 were seen marching into Samsun yesterday. No reports of villages being burned have been received in the past two days. Greeks from the destroyed villages are hiding in the mountains.

July 5, 1921

Soon after midnight last night a Greek went on board the STURTEVANT having swam from shore. This Greek who came from Carapece, a village near Tekekeuy, brought a letter from the people in the destroyed villages telling of the conditions there and begging protection from the Americans. The Captain of the STURTEVANT sent him on board here. He was still in a very exhausted condition, having collapsed soon after arriving on the STURTEVANT. Several times while enroute to Samsun, this Greek encountered Turkish soldiers and he only succeeded in reaching Samsun after much difficulty. When asked if he wished to return to his village, he became very much frightened, stating that he would certainly be killed if required to land, and begged to be landed in a port where there were no Turks. As I feel certain that he would be killed if put ashore here, even during the night. I am keeping him on board and will land him in Constantinople. The following is a copy of the translation of the letter from the village—the original letter was in French:

TO: COMMANDING GENERAL OF THE CRUISERS OF THE UNITED STATES IN SAMSUN

EXCELLENCY:

After the particular catastrophe which happened to all the Greek villages subject to the Turks between Bafra and Samsun, which happened the 25[th of] May, 1921, the government of Mustafa Kemal in Samsun, having even burned alive several families assembled in several houses at Ada, a village of Samsun, the same government made general at a still more savage way—the Turks on the 16 June, 1921 which happened to all Orthodox Greek Christians condemned by fate to be subject to a barbarous government to get (?) the Turks. *[Note: The preceding question mark in parens apparently indicates some problem in the translation from the French.]*

After having assembled in Samsun all the Greek Christians between the ages of 12 and 50, having explained and promised to them that nothing further except that a further exile to the back country would happen to them, and each one would be free to follow out his trade at his convenience, they were cut down and killed like cattle, between Samsun and Kavak at a distance of thirty to forty kilometers from Samsun. About 3,000 strong were officially killed by this government. They were thought to have been killed by the savage[s] stationed in Samsun, killed in having to meet stations in the Eliaskey quarter of Samsun.

After having killed the men from Samsun, there were assembled 22 men and taking them to Eliaskey, the savages cut them down. One of these victims, the said Lazaros Techelenz, being able to escape and save himself, explained to us in a savage manner [the way] they have been cut down.

As to the families of the particular village of Tekekeuy, the savages, after having violated their honor, killed them all like cattle, without having spared the little children. A few men escaped to the mountains, some of them slightly wounded, and others dangerously wounded, of which group, I have a detailed list to present to you.

After Tekekeuy, the government commenced work on the villages on 30 June, 1921, in a more systematic way, setting fire to the houses (which you certainly saw burning yesterday evening). Up to this writing they have set fire to four villages of about six hundred houses.

Not knowing any other manner of notifying you, we have thought to send it by Nicholas Tetheophilon, to present my letter to you, which you are prayed to take under your protection.

Taking into consideration, your Excellency, [all] the Orthodox Christian people which live under the government of Mustapha Kemal Pache at Samsun, you are infinitely begged to interest yourself as soon as possible to save them. Let it be, your Excellency in the name of God, in the name of International Law, finally in the name of your own children, and your own conscience, do not leave us unprotected, and open to being cut down and killed like cattle by the Turkish barbarians. Such manner of indifference and delay exposes us still more dangerously.

All the men who were able to escape into the mountains have at this writing been able to find nothing to eat, and are starving.

You are infinitely begged to advise us by electric signal at nine (9) o'clock in the afternoon in the direction towards the mountains of Samsun in the direction of Tekekeuy where we are holding ourselves during the month after your reception of my letter. Signal to explain to us that you have received my letter and will interest yourself as much as possible to save us by every manner of your convenience.

Recommending you in advance in the name of all the despairing Greeks, I beg [you] to accept, Excellency, my consideration:

Signed: Kassandros Phkyriskidy,
General Agent of the Several [?] Companies
in Samsun affiliated with the Gresham Life Union
and Phoenix Company, Paris, etc.

Following this document in the Fox *war diary are a couple of pages of questions and answers, whereby the navy people questioned the young Greek. As a competent and slightly more informative summary was produced in the* Sturtevant *war diary of July 4, 1921, reproduced following this war diary set, we omit the questions and answers found here.*

July 6, 1921

Went ashore at 10:00 with the Commanding Officer of the STURTEVANT. Mr. King stated that he had been informed that Turkish soldiers had been raising havoc in the interior, that they had been killing the Greeks in the towns of Tokat and Niksar, and that all the property of the Greeks was being sold and the proceeds from such sales were being appropriated by the Turkish Government.

A short time before this, I met Mrs. King and she told me that she wanted to see Mr. King and tell him of the terrible conditions in the interior. So I feel certain that Mr. King obtained the above information from his wife and as she is inclined to greatly exaggerate reports, I do not believe that much dependence should be placed upon the above. . . .

About 11:00 the Commanding Officer of the STURTEVANT and I had an interview with the Mutasariff. He was very pleasant and seemed in a better humor than before. I stated that I had come to say good-bye and to introduce Captain Haas of the STURTEVANT. . . .

THE DESTRUCTION OF VILLAGES
–TESTIMONY OF KOKTZOGLOU AND YPHANTIDES

In the message sent to the American destroyer via the swimmer mentioned in the Williamson *diary set, just above, a massacre at the village of Ada near Samsun is mentioned, widely considered one of the worst acts of village destruction in the Samsun region. But in other respects, the burning of Ada is consistent with the actions of Turkish chettahs, who have killed all the Greeks they can find whether by direction or on their own initiative. (The Italian family's deposition that mentions the atrocity at Ada attributes it to Osman Agha's chettahs. The message also mentions the village of Tekekeuy being destroyed by similar violence.)*

As it happens, the father of this book's researcher and author, Sam Koktzoglou, who sought out the Samsun and Trebizond war diaries in the National Archives, survived the massacre of the village of Ada, which lies three miles west of Samsun. Ioannis Koktzoglou and two women may have been the only village members who escaped the massacre that occurred on May 15, 1921. Below is his son's summary of his father's circumstances, drawn from Ioannis's autobiography. It is followed by a brief description of the event in Ioannis Koktzoglou's own words.

The Massacre at the Village of Ada

The village of Ada was near the town of Samsun, approximately three miles away. According to Ioannis, he was born around 1905 and had three brothers and a sister. His mother died when he was six or seven months old. His father was drafted in 1914 and never returned from his service (in the Turkish Army's labor battalions).

Thus it was when he was about ten years old that Ioannis and his siblings became orphans of both parents and were left without the care and security of an immediate family. His brothers were killed by the Turks under various circumstances, and his sister died from malnutrition. Ioannis became a goat shepherd. He even changed his name to Mustafa to avoid harassment and bullying.

He was about fifteen or sixteen years old at the time of the massacre. He happened to be at his aunt's house up until several hours before the event. He was the only one who left the village when he learned that Turkish troops were on the way from Samsun toward Ada. In his account he says that the local Turkish authorities/Army had recently assured the leadership of the village that they would be safe if they stopped assisting/harboring Greek bandits. This was most likely the reason that the villagers stayed and did not leave as he did. For some reason, Koktzoglou had reservations about the Turkish Army's assurances, so he left the village and joined his uncle, who was heading up a Greek guerilla group in the nearby hills.

He returned to the village the next day along with his uncle and his uncle's men and witnessed the results of the massacre and of the destruction of his village. Below is an excerpt from his notes/autobiography. His testimony must be a compilation of what he heard from the other survivors of the massacre (two women) and what he witnessed when he returned to the village after the event.

His account was edited regarding the year of the event, which he cited as 1917. From various sources, it was determined that the event took place in 1921. There are at least four independent sources that document the massacre and destruction of Ada—see notes below. The description of this event varies to some extent from source to source, but the main story is the same.

Ioannis Koktzoglou's account:

> On May 15, 1921, thousands of irregular Turkish troops surrounded the village forming seven rings around it. At 7:30 pm they gathered all the inhabitants of the village. They killed some of them outright. They forced the rest into a number of houses, poured fuel oil on the houses and set them on fire. They shot those attempting to flee and threw them back into the fire. The Turkish troops had another method to kill those who tried to escape from the fire. They soaked a rope in oil and put it around their victim's neck. Two men would pull on the rope, each holding one end. They then stabbed the victim in the forehead or abdomen with a bayonet. Finally they threw the dying victim back into the fire.

Notes on the Ada atrocity can be found in these sources:

1. *Pages from the Black National Tragedy of Pontus*, Antonios I. Gavrilides, 78, 89, and 161. (This book is in Greek.)

2. Italian Family's Deposition on Deportations and Massacres in Samsun area, dated 8/21 July 1921, U.S. National Archives, Washington D.C. (This testimony is reproduced above in these war diaries.)

3. Letter from a village Near Samsun to the Commander of the USS *Sturtevant*, received on July 5, 1921, begging for help/protection from Turkish massacres/atrocities, U.S. National Archives, Washington D.C. (See the diary set immediately above for this letter.)

4. Newspaper article dated August 13, 1921 from *The National Herald*, New York, on the deportation and massacres of Greeks in the Pontus region.

Massacre at a Village in the Mountains Near Ordou

Although the episode recounted below occurred in February 1922, a good deal later than the war diaries presented right here, the burning of villages with associated massacres (including many near Ordou and Bafra, as well as those near Samsun) have already been reported and will continue to be reported throughout the diaries. This account well illustrates the methods of Osman Agha at villages like these.

The following document was sent to State Department Near East expert Allen Dulles from Boston by Ernest W. Riggs, who may have known Dulles when both were working in Constantinople; Dulles was a diplomat under Admiral Bristol's direction for a period before reassignment to the State Department. The document originally came from Riggs's brother, C.T. Riggs, a missionary in Anatolia. The events described here occurred in a mountain village above the small port city of Ordou, which lies on the Pontic coast between Samsun and Trebizond. Savvas Yphantides, one of the fifty or so Greek men who hid in the forest and furtively looked on, describes the events, including his own wife's death at the hands of the Turks.

The Riggs brothers were long-term missionaries of the American Board and knew the Yphantides family. C.T. Riggs may have seen Yphantides while on a visit to Constantinople.

A trustworthy Greek of the village of Bey Alan, ten hours' distant from Ordou in the mountains, arrived in Constantinople last week from Batoum, after a most remarkable escape from his native place. He states that he was in Bey Alan from June 15, 1921, to March 18, 1922.

There were during the summer of 1921 five different orders for the deportation of Greeks from the Ordou region. In the first deportation, or sevkiat, all the men from 18 years to 50, almost 850 to 1000 in number, were exiled. Two or three weeks later came the order to send off those of from 50 to 60. A few were not sent for various reasons. In the fifth or last deportation were about 75 men, including all up to 65 years of age. By the end of August, 1921, all the Greek men of the Ordou region had been exiled; but Bey Alan, which was in the district of Kerasoun, though really dependent on Ordou, bought itself off, as did nine other villages near by. Many, however, of the men were sent off, and the rest, in fear of being likewise deported, hid in the mountains. In August came the order that all women and children from these villages go down to Ordou. By some means this order was countermanded and the women and children remained.

On January 25, 1922, it was rumored that Osman Agha, the famous chief of the chetes, or irregular bands, was coming to the region of Kerasoun and the Greeks realized that this boded no good for them. A few days later the Turkish villagers from nearby villages (Urmalu and Chukdouman) came to Bey Alan and demanded ten liras and a "top" [bolt] of cloth in consideration of which they would save that village from deportation. But it was evident that their real purpose was to spy out and see that these villagers got no word of what was happening at other points. They further demanded that one coppersmith and one blacksmith be given to their villages, and this was done. This was merely a blind.

On Wednesday, February 15, the men hiding in the forest nearby heard 5 or 6 rifle shots, and saw two houses burning in the village. They crept as near as they could and saw that there were at least 200 or 300 soldiers of these bands of Osman Agha in the village, and also a lot of Turkish women who had evidently come to carry off the plunder, which they were doing. All the cattle, as well as the household goods, were being taken off. The women and children of the village were not to be seen, which roused fears that they had been killed. The destruction continued all that day, till finally all the houses in both upper and lower quarters of the village had been burned except two. Out of about 175 women and children, and a few men hiding in cellars, only four persons escaped, and that as if by a miracle. Their story confirmed the worst fears of those hiding in the woods. All the women and children had been gathered up into the two houses, with the exception of about fifteen girls of over sixteen years old, and the houses then burned over their heads, any who attempted to escape being shot down. One woman succeeded in escaping by feigning death in a valley. The wife of the man giving this report ran off as far as a garden in this valley, but was followed up by the Turks and shot there, while lying down to hide herself. The young girls were subjected to the most horrible treatment all night, and all butchered the next day. Some say that 5 or 6 were reserved for the harem of the Pasha.

The other nine villages near Bey Alan had all received already the same treatment, and had been annihilated. Their names were:

Mikro Tepe Keuy	Bozat
Meghalo Tepe Keuy	Kale Gennu
Paxar Souyou	Ghouzere
Yoma	Kara Sar
Demirji Keuy	

About fifty of the men were saved, having hidden in the woods before the slaughter began. They watched for the withdrawal of the Turkish troops who stayed there for several days. At last, after 23 days, the men came back and buried the corpses.

Deponent, at much risk to his life, succeeded in getting to Ordou, and later to Batoum, and after spending some time in prison at the instigation of the Turkish Consul, finally escaped and came to Constantinople.

Source: National Archives, State Department document 867.4016/598

THE TURKISH ORDER TO DEPORT THE SAMSUN WOMEN AND CHILDREN, AND CAPTAIN BRISTOL'S URGENT PLEA THAT THE ADMIRAL INTERVENE

In the opening pages of the following diary sets, we read more reports of burning villages near Samsun (associated with the reported torture and killing of 250 Greek women) after which a visit by Hellenic warships to the port will cause a brief excitement. Also mentioned is the situation of the local American tobacco companies. Their male Greek employees have all been lost either to massacre or some other unknown (but ominous) fate, so the American managers are attempting to provide for the destitute Greek families left behind by hiring some of their wives and daughters to work with the tobacco.

*However, before long a more consequential issue arises: the order for the imminent deportation of all the remaining Greek women, children, and elderly in the city. The current Mutasariff insists that this order has come from Angora (*Overton *WD, July 17, 1921), and Captain Bristol seems to agree. He writes after visiting the Mutasariff that he believes this deportation "is part of an official plan which contemplates extermination of the Greeks insofar as they can get away with it" (*Overton *WD, July 17, 1921). However, the war diaries also regularly speak of a very active military element in the Samsun area ever pushing for the extermination of the Greeks (*Fox *WD, May 28, 1921;* Overton *WD, July 22, 1921). Haidar Bey's mention of a long telegram from Nureddin Pasha, which insists that the Mutasariff carry out the deportations (see* Overton *WD, July 19, 1921, below), would seem to identify Nureddin Pasha as the key deciding figure. But Osman Agha might have been involved* *as well, as a British report would suggest (see the third explanatory note in the* Overton *WD, July 19, below).*

Yet even if the deportation order originated not in Angora but at the insistence of Nureddin, or Osman Agha, or both, not only had these vicious men been appointed or supported by Kemal in the first place, but clearly the Nationalist government in Angora had gone along with the order when they first heard of it.

In any case, this ordered deportation of the women and children of Samsun becomes the central concern of the two American naval officers who have to confront it most directly and who describe the circumstances in the second and third sets of war diaries below: Captain Victor Stuart Houston of the Brooks *and Captain Arthur LeRoy Bristol of the* Overton.

Readers will remember Admiral Bristol's original protest to local Turkish officials against deporting noncombatants, likely written at the behest of Captain Joyce of the Fox. *The captains who were then present in Samsun had delivered this message to the Mutasariff when the original deportation seemed imminent. It is possible that this early protest to local officials at Samsun convinced the Turks to spare the women and children back when they deported the men, for according to the war diaries, originally* all *the Greeks in the city had been ordered to go.*

Now, however, all the remaining Greeks have been threatened again. Captain Bristol protests vehemently to the Samsun Mutasariff but concludes that this local protest will have no effect. The Overton *captain becomes so convinced that the Greek women, children, and elderly are about to be deported that he decides to send Captain Houston on the* Brooks *overnight to Constantinople, carrying a hastily handwritten letter to the admiral. The letter explains that if Admiral Bristol does nothing, the deportations are almost certain to proceed and furthermore that America might find itself being blamed for the atrocities about to take place!*

We believe that it was Captain Bristol's powerful letter that convinced Admiral Bristol to protest via telegraph to Mustafa Kemal in Angora against the ordered Samsun deportation. By this action on the part of the admiral, which caused the Nationalists to back off, many thousands of lives of the women, children, and elderly of Samsun proper were saved—and permanently saved too. To be sure, Admiral Bristol's protest would neither save all the Greeks in the region nor reverse what many Americans looking on believed was the intended goal: the exter-

mination of virtually all the Greeks in the Pontus region and of Christians throughout Anatolian Turkey.

It was certainly Captain Bristol's advice rather than anything Captain Houston told Admiral Bristol personally that convinced the admiral to take action, for when the Brooks *reached Constantinople, the admiral would not even admit Captain Houston to his presence! This provoked Houston to go outside the chain of command and inform the Greek Orthodox Primate in Constantinople (the supreme head of the Greek Orthodox Church, whose headquarters were in the city) of the impending death marches. For a mid-level officer to pass this information along to a major non-American official (incidentally, a person for whom Admiral Bristol had no use) was a major divergence from standard military protocol. This action would earn Houston the admiral's great ire and an unsatisfactory fitness report, which would have ended any possibility for Commander Houston to be promoted to captain.*

In Houston's required reply to this decidedly adverse report, he would explain that on arrival in Constantinople, he found that the Turkish order to deport 15,000 Greek women and children from Samsun was not being taken seriously at the American Embassy. This was the case, Houston argued, despite the death of "thousands upon thousands of Armenian women and children" via similar methods during the infamous Young Turk atrocities that had taken place during the Great War.

But this ultimately futile challenge to Admiral Bristol by the destroyer captain Houston is told in more detail elsewhere (Shenk, ABSF, *101–03). In the three war diary sets that follow, we present in their full context events beginning with the first word of the orders for deportation of the Greek women and children from Samsun and ending in that order's sudden cancellation. Within the concluding* Overton *report, we publish Captain Bristol's handwritten letter to the admiral followed by the admiral's telegraphed protest to Mustafa Kemal at Angora. A couple of days later, Nationalist Foreign Minister Youssuf Kemal's telegraphed response to Admiral Bristol (also presented here) calls off the ordered deportation.*

Finally, also of some interest in this war diary set is Captain Bristol's war diary description of his firsthand witness of Osman Agha's great anguish, which seems to have resulted from the latter's suddenly being ordered to leave Samsun and report to Angora. For the moment, at least, Osman seems to have become something of a "loose cannon" for the Nationalists, who find it convenient to order him out of the Pontus area though they will soon have use for this cutthroat elsewhere. To be sure, before moving on to Angora, where Kemal will appoint him a colonel in the regular army, Osman will have his irregulars terrorize, loot, rape, and kill many of the Greek and Armenian inhabitants of the small city of Marsovan, something that American NER workers at Marsovan describe.

USS *STURTEVANT*, LIEUT. COMMANDER E.G. HAAS WAR DIARY SET FOR JUNE 29-JULY 14, 1921

...

June 30, 1921

Discussed the different phases of the situation with Johnson and Fitzgerald, neither of whom reported any startling changes or new developments. Very favorably impressed with Johnson and Currin, both of whom appear to possess a thorough understanding of the situation which they follow in a calm and dispassionate manner; they are very affable, possess tact and judgment, and are, I believe, very accurate observers. Haidar Bey is superficially clever. He is sagacious, tactful, very reticent and more or less of an opportunist. I regard him as a decided asset, however. . . .

Observed several boxes, who gave every appearance of containing small arms ammunition, on the docks and in small boats alongside the docks.

July 1, 1921

Went ashore with the Commanding Officer of the WILLIAMSON at 10:00 and called at Near East Relief and Tobacco Company offices. Discussed situation with King, Johnson, Currin and Haidar Bey. No changes; conditions quiet and peaceful. Commanding Officer of the WILLIAMSON and myself inspected the magazines of the Alston Tobacco Company, the activities of which have been greatly curtailed and circumscribed as a result of their loss of their trained employees who were deported a short time ago. The employees (about six hundred) now in the magazine are, for the most part, young and inexperienced Greek and Turkish girls. Both tobacco companies are giving employment to as many families of their former Greek employees as possible, in an endeavor to alleviate the misery and suffering of these poverty stricken families. Haidar Bey assured Mr. King this morning that the Mutasariff is doing everything he can to persuade the Angora government to allow at least fifteen former Greek employees of the Alston Tobacco Company—and presumably about the same number of Gary Employees—to return to Samsun to resume their work in the tobacco magazines. Speaking for the tobacco companies, "'Tis a consummation devoutly to be wished."

At 3:00 p.m. observed four columns of dense smoke rising from the valley behind the hills to the south-eastward of Samsun. Received station ship diary from Commanding Officer of WILLIAMSON which I read very carefully. Observed more ammunition on the dock today.

July 2, 1921

Went ashore with the Commanding Officer of the WILLIAMSON and called at the Near East Relief and tobacco company offices. Discussed situation at great length with Van Toor, King and Currin, no changes; everything quiet ashore. Everybody particularly anxious for news concerning the reported evacuation of Greeks from Asia Minor. Learned that Tekekeuy and Tsinik, two Greek villages located about six miles to the south-eastward of Samsun, had been pillaged and burned last evening by the Turks—presumably by the Lars troops who are known to have been in that vicinity recently. Reported that two hundred and fifty Greek women and children were tortured and killed. Haidar Bey is of the opinion that this latest Turkish atrocity was committed by way of retaliation for the predatory tactics employed by certain Greek brigands who, at the time of the Greek deportation, fled to the nearby forests and are now conducting a sort of guerilla warfare against the Turks.

. . . .

July 4, 1921

Everything quiet ashore. It is reported that forty Greek men who evaded the recent deportation were found in hiding and were marched into the interior. It is also reported that several Turkish villages in the interior have been destroyed by the Greeks.

American Colony and Haidar Bey spent the day on board the WILLIAMSON. Crews of WILLIAMSON and STURTEVANT conducted swimming races—honors about evenly divided. About 12:10 A.M. was attracted to the ship's side by a voice calling for help in appealing tones and observed a man swimming along the starboard side of the ship and making for the gangway, which he finally succeeded in reaching. He endeavored to pull himself out of the water, but was unable to do so owing to his weakened physical condition, and consequently it was found necessary to pull him out of the water. Upon reaching the deck it developed that the man was a Greek and it was quite apparent that he had been in the water for quite some time. The man wore no clothing except a pair of swimming trunks, in which he had very ingeniously concealed a sealed bottle about six inches in length and one inch in diameter, containing a letter in French addressed to the Commander of the United States ship in Samsun, and which was delivered to me. [See *Williamson* WD, July 5, 1921 in the section just above for the letter itself.]

The boy, after receiving hot coffee and dry clothes, appeared to be greatly refreshed and showed a willingness to talk; but as he spoke only Greek it was found impossible to extract any information from him. The Commanding Officer after reading the letter dispatched Ensign T.H. Robbins, U.S. Navy, to the WILLIAMSON, Senior Officer present, with the letter and boy. Ensign Robbins read the letter to the Commanding Officer of the WILLIAMSON who thereupon interrogated the boy through the medium of a member of his crew who spoke Greek.* The substance of the boy's statement, as accurately as it could be recalled by Ensign Robbins upon his return to the ship, is as follows.

"I am from Carapece, a small village one and a half hours walk from Tekekeuy. All the men were marched out of the city of Tekekeuy by Lars troops, and I hear they were slaughtered (about 600 of them). Then on Friday a few remaining Greeks got some pistols and killed about 25 Turks; then a Turkish commissioned officer issued arms to all Turks, civilians and troops, and told them to kill the Greeks on sight. The men with the pistols were all killed; and the Lars troops took all the women and defiled them, killing them by slashing them with sabers; then they gathered all the children in the city and killed them, the favorite method being to lift them up by one foot and to cut their

* It was not unusual in those days that some U.S. Navy crewmembers (the children of immigrants from Europe to the United States) remained fluent in their parents' language and could thus become translators here and there. Even in World War II, similar things happened. In 1944, aboard an American escort carrier, a Polish crewmember of a German submarine captured on the high seas noticed a Polish-American seaman's namebadge, spoke to him in Polish, and eventually was separated from the captured German crew. He claimed to have been forced into the German Navy, and he helped the American seamen learn to operate the *U-505,* righting the submarine and towing it back to Bermuda. See C. Herbert Gilliland and Robert Shenk, *Admiral Dan Gallery: The Life and Wit of a Navy Original*, Annapolis: Naval Institute Press, 1999, 127–31.

heads off with one sweep. I escaped by swimming out of sight, where I stayed until the killing and burning was over. I spent the night on the beach and then the next day made my way inland to find a group of men (500) in the hills. There are many more (600) twelve hours march toward Bafra. The former men gave me the letter, and I made several attempts to get through the Turk lines; I succeeded in getting through at 2:00 P.M. today (Monday). I reached the beach and swam to your ship. The men said signal on the mast as soon as I came on board so they would know that I did not drown. Please do not put me ashore, they will kill me. Take me to a place where there are no Turks. The men in the hills are starving; they went into Tekekeuy and found no food so they are eating grass and killing dogs and any other living things to eat. I do not know of any villages been burned to-day."

July 5, 1921

Went ashore with the Commanding Officer of the WILLIAMSON at 10:00 A.M. and called on Van Toor, King and Currin. No new development in situation ashore. It is reported that the Greeks in this section have resorted to retaliatory measures and are now destroying the Turkish villages and violating the Turkish women. It is possible that these reports which are now being assiduously spread by the Turks are part and parcel of their propaganda disseminated to justify or distract our attention from the bestial outrages which they have committed. Commanding Officer of the WILLIAMSON and myself discussed the case of the Greek boy who swam to the STURTEVANT last night and both are agreed that it would be an inhumane act, for which there would be no justification, to deliver the boy to the Turks here who would, I am certain, inflict upon him unspeakable tortures.

July 6- 8, 1921

Captain Haas reports on these dates that three Greeks trying to re-enter Samsun on the night of the sixth had been shot; that several field pieces and ammunition had been observed on the pier awaiting shipment inland; and that reports were heard that large numbers of cattle, presumably cattle stolen from the Greeks, would be sold at auction soon, the proceeds to be turned over to the Turkish Army. Also, the Brooks, *as it approached Samsun, reported in its war diary for the seventh that it observed several very conspicuous fires along the coast near or in back of Bafra.*

July 9, 1921

. . . . Called on the Colonel Ismael Haky Bey, Military Commander, who received us very cordially and appeared genuinely glad to have us call. He was quite talkative, frank, and apparently sincere. He stated, most emphatically, that the reports of Turkish atrocities are, for the most part, unfounded, and that in instances where Greek villages were destroyed the Turks were justified in taking such action in retaliation for the many villages wantonly destroyed by the Greeks. A seemingly specious argument but hardly convincing. . . . Captain Houston [of the *Brooks*, accompanying Captain Haas] told the colonel that the Americans had heard a great deal about the Greek side of the question, but scarcely anything about the Turkish side. Captain Houston expressed a wish to see some of the villages which the colonel claimed had been destroyed by the Greeks, to which the colonel replied that he would give the matter his consideration.

Observed several field gun carriages, large number of rifles and large quantity of small-arms ammunition on dock. Near East Relief received communication from Mutasariff tonight requesting that money and supplies be sent to the relief of Turks in Kamalos whose homes and crops have been destroyed by Greek bandits. Van Toor has requested permission to visit Kamalos tomorrow to ascertain the needs of the people and has invited Captain Houston and myself to accompany him, provided this meets with the approval of the Mutasariff.

July 10, 1921

Went ashore at 10:00 with Commanding Officer of the BROOKS. Met Van Toor and Haidar Bey at Mr. King's office; the former informing us that the Mutasariff would not consent to his visiting Kamalos. The Mutasariff's denial of Van Toor's natural and reasonable request is unmistakably significant and might plausibly suggest an attempt to misrepresent facts in order to obtain funds and supplies which possibly might be turned over to the army, and thus used for other than the intended purposes. It is glaringly apparent that the Turkish authorities are doing everything possible to prevent or delay as long as possible the entry of Americans into the interior which fact would indicate that they are attempting to conceal from the outside world existing evidences of their rapacity, brutality and repulsive methods. Captain Houston and myself motored out into the country for a short distance, but observed nothing of interest.

July 11, 1921

No change in situation. Large number of cattle stolen from the Greeks sold at auction this morning—cows were sold for [....] Turkish pounds apiece. It is the consensus of opinion among the Near East Relief personnel that the Turks are getting ready to deport the Greek women and children under the pretext of sending them into the interior to join the male members of their families who, of course, they will never see. This would appear to be in keeping with the procedure heretofore practiced by the Turks. There is every indication that the Turks are now committing the same atrocities which they committed during the late war and which caused the world to shudder with unspeakable disgust and horror. Abdullah told me to-day that the Greeks who were deported and sent to Amassia for alleged conspiracy about six months ago are now being tried. Eight were hung a few days ago. Observed smoke behind the hills in the direction of Tekekeuy.

July 12, 1921

Captain Houston and myself motored along the coast to the south-eastward of Samsun for a distance of ten or fifteen miles, in the expectation of being able to observe evidences of the recent destruction known to have been effected in that locality by the Turks. The country was quiet and peaceful so far as we could observe. Road practically deserted except for sentries scattered here and there along the road. Passed several small villages which showed outward signs of having been partially burned recently. It would appear that the Turks have carefully refrained from destroying Greek villages bordering on the coast, the destruction of which would be observed by Americans or American ships.

About three p.m. sighted two vessels which subsequently proved to be Greek ships standing in towards Samsun. Both ships, one of which was a large destroyer and the other an armed troop transport or possibly a supply ship, had decks cleared for action and men standing by the guns. In conformity with adopted doctrine, BROOKS got underway and proceeded to meet the incoming Greek ships, whereupon the Greek ships turned around and stood out to seaward. Commanding Officer of the STURTEVANT went ashore and made arrangements to embark Americans in case of bombardment. Received message from BROOKS stating that the emergency was over and I at once returned to the ship. The BROOKS returned to her anchorage at 4:00 p.m. Reported to the Commanding Officer of the BROOKS immediately and learned from him the result of his interview with the Commanding Officer of the Greek destroyer. It appears that the Greek ships, having learned that guns had been landed recently, came here for the specific purpose of investigating the matter and incidentally to prevent the further importation of arms and ammunition. The Commanding Officer of the Greek destroyer, in anticipation of an attack on him by the shore batteries, had made preparations to return the fire and doubtless would have done so had the Turks fired at them. When last seen the Greek ships were hull down on the horizon, but their smoke was plainly visible for some time thereafter, indicating that they are patrolling in the immediate vicinity.

To say that the Greeks were greatly alarmed would be only to express their state of feeling mildly. The entire population assembled on the waterfront and streets were practically deserted and stores closed. Trenches were manned and there appeared to be general activity on the part of the military. The few Turks and Greeks whom I met on the streets appeared to be excited and frightened.

Captain Houston and myself went ashore at 4:15 p.m. to call upon the Mutasariff and upon arriving on the dock we met a Turk (evidently an officer of the Gendarmes) who told us that he had received information this morning that the Greek ships were in the Black Sea, apparently bound for Samsun. The Mutasariff, contrary to his usual attitude, received us very cordially—in fact gave us a very enthusiastic welcome. He made no attempt to conceal his jubilant feelings, and expressed his gratitude and thanks to Captain Houston for having been instrumental in preventing the bombardment of Samsun. He asked many questions regarding the mission of the Greek ships, whether there is any likelihood of their returning, etc., to which Captain Houston gave very tactful replies. Later called on Military Commander who likewise expressed his thanks to Captain Houston for the part he had played in driving the Greeks away.

Captain Houston made it very clear to both the Mutasariff and the Commander the exact reason for his going out to meet the Greeks, and quite wisely, I believe, for otherwise the Turks would undoubtedly have gotten the impression that we were assisting them. The Military Commander told us that he had explicit orders to fire on any Greeks attempting to enter Samsun and that he was fully prepared to do this as soon as the Greek ships came within effective range. Had the Turks fired a single shot at the Greeks, the fire would have been returned and I believe a general bombardment of the town would have ensued.

Considering all phases of the matter I am of the opinion that the non-bombardment of Samsun can be directly attributed to the prompt action on the part of the BROOKS. The promptitude with which the BROOKS got underway—nineteen minutes after the order was given to get underway—enabled the BROOKS to communicate with the Greek ships before they had come within effective gunfire range of the shore batteries, which fact alone prevented what might have developed into a disaster. [The Turkish] Military Commander assured us that in case we should deem it advisable to evacuate Americans in the event of a threatened bombardment, he will place no obstacles in the way of their expeditious embarkation. While talking with the Military Commander he received information that four Greek destroyers had been sighted off Sinope Point.

American colony [was] entertained on board the STURTEVANT.

July 13, 1921

Conditions ashore quiet and peaceful. Reported that Greeks are very excited and alarmed over the threatened deportation of Greek women and children. Large quantities of loot (household furniture, etc.) sold at auction today. Lieutenant Dunn arrived [back from his interview with Mustapha Kemal in Angora].

July 14, 1921

No change in situation. Was informed by Currin that one of his former employees, a Greek who was deported with the third party, and subsequently escaped to the mountains, succeeded in entering Samsun last night. He was found in Mr. Currin's hen-house this morning. He informed Mr. Currin that practically all the men who left with the third party were killed.

USS *BROOKS*, COMMANDER VICTOR STUART HOUSTON, WAR DIARY SET FOR JULY 7-17, 1921

. . . .

July 9, 1921

. . . .

Went ashore to call on the Mutasariff and the commanding officer of the troops, accompanied by Haidar Bey. . . .

The Mutasariff is an ordinary looking Turk with a shifty expression. He started out by saying "How do you do" in French, but when I started speaking French expressed inability to carry on a conversation or to understand me. Haidar Bey also stated that he, the Mutasariff, did not understand French. The Mutasariff was anxious to know what the news was, and in fact that was his only query. He didn't strike me as being beyond doing any of the things that are attributed to the Turks in this Sanjak [county] at the present time.

Called also on the Military Commander, who is very much more cordial, and who impressed me more favorably. He stated the usual thing, that all the outrages were due to the Greek outlaws. Turks always lived in accord until the British, about the time of the armistice, started arming and inciting the Greeks. He was convinced that the British were endeavoring to overthrow any semblance of government by the Turkish race. He stated that there was perfect security in the town and that the Greek women and children were perfectly safe.

Haidar Bey stated that the government had received permission for fifteen of the Greek employees of the tobacco firm to return. It remains to be seen if they will get back.

Mr. Currin stated that Haidar Bey had admitted that the Greek villages in the neighborhood had been systematically burned and plundered. That the refugees who had escaped must be in the mountains where there is nothing to eat and they would probably starve.

Arms, artillery, and ammunition continue to be landed here. We saw two field pieces, two old siege guns, besides quantities of rifles and ammunition on the dock. A Turkish tug, towing a sailing vessel, came in from the direction of Trebizond.

July 10, 1921

. . . .

Went ashore, saw some of the Americans and took a drive out into the country back of the town. I was not stopped by any of the sentries though I went beyond the main barracks.

Continued stories of burning villages being brought in. The Mutasariff requested Near East Relief to give him supplies for some homeless Turkish villagers, he said, who had been burned out by Greek bandits. Van Toor asked for permission to go out and visit the villagers to see what the needs would be, but the Mutasariff would not agree to this. In fact Haidar Bey said he was angry, saying that the Near East Relief did not believe him. Van Toor then said that if they would bring them all in that he would put them in the bread line. That, however, is not what the Mutasariff wants. He wants the money or the supplies delivered to him.

More villages are apparently being burned. Two groups of burning areas and one large column of smoke were visible to the eastward.

Went ashore in the afternoon again. Saw Van Toor, Smith (Socony) [Standard Oil Company of New York manager], Kings, and some of the American women. More refugees are straggling in, both Greeks and Turks. It probably is quite true that the Greek men who had been burned out and hunted are attacking Turkish villages, but they would probably starve unless they went foraging. The Greeks continue to bring in harrowing stories of atrocities. One today told how the Turks had surrounded a village where there were only women and children and were firing into the village. A notice was posted in the Greek church stating that some of the most well-known Greeks who were prisoners in Amassia were to be hung. Mr. King told me that he had heard Osman Agha was expected back, and that there were rumors of deporting the women and children. That, of course, had been talked about for some time, but he never thought it true. Now, however, he was inclined to be afraid of it.

There is very little friendliness shown for any foreigners in town. The place seems to be pretty well filled with irregulars. I noticed a good number of shoe shops engaged in making bandoliers and cartridge belts. . . .

. . . .

July 12, 1921

STURTEVANT and BROOKS at Samsun.

. . . .

At 1410 two smokes were sighted to the northward, one was made out to be a man-of war. As their identity could not be made out, gave orders to get underway. Attempted to signal these ships by searchlight but received no answer. Soon made out these ships to be a Greek destroyer and a transport. Signaled the STURTEVANT to be prepared to act as evacuating ship. At 1449 underway, standing towards the ships which were now identified as one of the five-stack Greek destroyers (PANTHER) and a Greek transport (DAPHNE).

Upon getting underway both ships turned away and stood out. Hoisted international signal "wish to communicate with you," which was answered. After getting well out hailed the destroyer PANTHER and said that I would like to go on board. She answered "Yes, certainly." Boarded her, and was met at the gangway by the Captain, Captain de Frigate C. Liamboy. Had a long conversation with him in the cabin and stated that in the first place I requested sufficient time, in case they intended to bombard, to evacuate the Americans. This he agreed to. He told me that he had heard that guns and ammunition were being landed here, and he was on the lookout for ships carrying on this traffic, and asked me which they were and where they came from.

I told him that of course I could not give me such information. He assured me that they will not bombard, but said that if fired on he would have returned the fire. When they first turned [back] out they were within range of shore but fire was not opened. I explained to the Captain the serious conditions ashore regarding the Greek population, that the men had all been deported, and that the women and children were perfectly defenseless; that an attack would surely precipitate reprisals on these people particularly in view of the weakness of the Mutasariff, who had allowed all sorts of burnings to take place in this Sanjak without putting a stop to it. He stated that he hoped that we, the Americans, might do something for the harassed Greeks.

After leaving his ship, they stood away to the eastward. During the night they were still in the neighborhood as their radio could be heard fairly close. Returned to our anchorage and signaled the STURTEVANT "Emergency over."

. . . .

Another blaze was visible over the mountains to the eastward during the night. . . .

July 13, 1921

STURTEVANT and BROOKS in the harbor, also the Italian steamship ALDO.

Went ashore and saw various Americans. No news. Visited the Catholic priest of the native Doloraosae, and had a long chat with him in French. He is an Italian and has been in the country thirteen or fourteen years; he was at Trebizond during the Armenian Massacres. He stated that the indications here pointed to a similar handling of the situation, and also that he would not be surprised if the women and children were deported after a while. He believed that the Turks would let the effects of the deportation of the men wear off, and then try the next step—women and children. The priest described the present killings as a white massacre; that is, he explained, no orders to kill were given, but only to deport, and that the transportation would probably continue until the individuals would gradually succumb either to fatigue or starvation. Of course the killings by the guards were incidental and due to incidents—attempted escape, etc.

In the afternoon the Turkish steamships "UMID" and the "KRINN" came in. On the UMID was Lieutenant Dunn from Angora via Ineboli.

Went ashore with Dunn to see Mr. King and later Van Toor. At Van Toor's met the Colonel commanding the Troops and various other Turkish gentlemen having tea. The Mutasariff and Haidar Bey had been asked but both excused themselves. Just before leaving, Colonel Osman Senai Bey said that the Colonel of the Troops, Colonel Ismain Haku Bey, asked if I wouldn't stay a little longer, that he wanted to tell me something. He then said that after I had seen him yesterday he had a long conversation on the telephone with Nureddin Pasha at Kavak and told him how we had been instrumental in perhaps preventing the Greeks from bombarding, and that I had suggested that perhaps by the Turks not opening fire first or withholding their fire as they had apparently done that they could put the onus of the fight on the Greeks, or altogether avoid a bombardment by giving the American destroyers a chance to communicate with them. Nureddin had said that he approved highly of the plan and that he was glad to tell me of it. . . .

July 14, 1921

STURTEVANT and BROOKS anchored in Samsun. . . .

Went ashore with [Lieutenant] Dunn about 10 a.m., saw Abdullah, stopped in to see Currin and the Kings. Last night three Greek refugees came in from the hills and landed in Currin's back yard. They were naked when they came in. They tell the usual story of great privations, that they were attacked by Turkish guards and escaped. Currin found them early this morning so allowed them to stay hidden during the day. However, I advised him that it would be very unwise to keep them very long.

Abdullah told us that Osman Agha was reported outside Kavak, and that he was expected here to reestablish order.

Called to see Count Schmecchia, the agent for the Lloyd Triestino, and previously the delegate of the Italian High Commissioner. Asked him about the situation. He is very pessimistic, says that he believes all the stories of atrocities committed to be true. He said that he expected that the deportation of all Greek women and children might be ordered any day. He called my attention to the fact that killings of Greeks occurred in Samsun itself before the deportations, under the leadership of an Albanian named Mshmetscheff, who had apparently come from Angora. When these killings became too much even for the Turks here they complained to the Government and the followers of Mshmetscheff were imprisoned, while he himself returned to Angora. The deportation was the next step, and they happened to follow the bombardment of Ineboli, which was given as an excuse for the massacres.

After the deportations had been completed, Angora [had] issued a statement that the deportations had been carried out in perfect order.

I suggested to him that I would like to quote him in a message to Admiral Bristol describing the existing conditions in regard to the women and children, but he asked instead that I should suggest a conference with the Italian High Commissioner [in Constantinople], to whom he had already described the situation.

Lunched with Currin. After lunch met Count Schmecchia on the street, who said that he had just learned that four ex-Austrian families, now Italians, of orthodox faith, had been given orders by the police to get out of the country. He was going to see the Governor, and asked if we might transmit a message for him perhaps. Told him that we could take a verbal message and he said he might have one tomorrow. He said that upon thinking it over he saw no reason why we should not quote him on the situation.

Following are paraphrases of two messages filed this day, [this first] regarding conditions in Samsun, and [the second regarding Lieutenant] Dunn's trip to Angora [to interview Mustapha Kemal and other Nationalists]:

> MUTASARIFF AGAIN IN CHARGE OSMAN AGHA REPORTED OUTSIDE KAVAK VILLAGE BURNING CONTINUED NO WOMEN AND CHILDREN HAVE ENTERED SAMSUN EXCEPT SIXTY ON THIRTEENTH BEST ESTIMATE AVAILABLE PUTS DEPORTED MEN AT ABOUT THREE THOUSAND IN FIVE PARTIES REPORTS FROM EXCELLENT SOURCES INCLUDING RELIABLE TURKS INDICATE GENERAL CONDITIONS ON COAST NOT EQUALED SINCE 1915 DEPORTATIONS FOUR ITALIAN FAMILIES INCLUDING WOMEN OF GREEK FAITH HAVE BEEN ORDERED TO LEAVE THE COUNTRY WITHIN TEN DAYS SUGGEST CONFERENCE WITH ITALIAN HIGH COMMISSIONER WHO HAS BEEN FURNISHED REPORTS FROM HERE ON SITUATION NEAR EAST RELIEF PERSONNEL STILL DENIED PASSPORTS FOR INTERIOR ON SAMSUN ROUTE REPORTED HERE BY TURKS THAT FIGHTING BEGAN AT CUCHAK JULY TENTH SIGNED DUNN HOUSTON.*

- - -

* These two messages are signed by both Lieutenant (junior grade) Dunn and Captain Houston. Normally, it would be very unusual for Dunn, a very low-ranking officer, to co-author a message as strict seniority normally would prevail. We have already seen how one ship's captain would always bow to the seniority of the other, even when both held the same rank. However, Dunn's status with Admiral Bristol was unique as he was Bristol's highly trusted intelligence officer, one who had influenced many of the admiral's opinions. Dunn's specific situation in this case, having returned successfully from a mission to interview Mustafa Kemal himself, seems also to have resulted in Captain Houston's forbearance.

FOLLOWING OUTLINES SOME POINTS RESULT OF INTERVIEWS WITH MUSTAFA KEMAL AND FIVE CHIEF MINISTERS. SUGGEST CONSIDERATION FOR SECSTATE.*

(1) GOVERNMENT AT PRESENT NOT VERY SOLICITOUS FOR FOREIGN RECOGNITION OR MILITARY AID. REAL DEVELOPMENT POLITICAL ORGANIZATION DURING THE PAST YEAR, ASSURED PERMANENCE OF MOVEMENT BY SUPPRESSION OF KONIA RISING, ETC., HAVE MADE ITSELF RELIANT AND SECRETIVE WITH CONSEQUENT DANGER FUTURE ERRORS TYPICAL OF TURKISH OFFICIALS. COMMERCIAL RELATIONS ADVANTAGIOUS TO FOREIGNERS NOT IMMEDIATELY OPPORTUNE.

(2) MODERATE PARTY APPARENTLY PERMANENT IN POWER WITHOUT SERIOUS POLITICAL DIVISIONS OR OPPOSITION, WHICH MOVEMENT IS YET TOO YOUNG AND UNITED IN WAR PURPOSE TO HAVE DEVELOPED. GOVERNMENT CLINGS CONSISTENTLY AND TENACIOUSLY TO NATIONAL "PACT" RECOG-

* Lieutenant (jg) Dunn has just concluded his interview with Kemal and other Nationalist leaders and will return to Constantinople via the next destroyer from Samsun. He seems to think a quick review of his impressions from his interviews in Angora might be useful to the admiral even before he presents his full report when he gets there in a few days. The full report can be found in the Mark Bristol collection at the Library of Congress.

Dunn's exalted impression of his own importance (he is neither a senior officer nor a diplomat; he is by training, at best, a journalist) is apparent in his suggestion that some of the information he presents here might be forwarded to the Secretary of State.

While this "diplomatic" message is in several respects not pertinent to the incidents recorded in this book, Captain Houston and others aboard the *Brooks* and the *Sturtevant* would have read it, and hence it seems appropriate to present it here.

Dunn's argument in paragraph 6 that the excesses were limited to the Samsun region and his absolution of Nationalist leaders' responsibility for acts of inhumanity have no basis in fact. Dunn was not in a position to know what was happening throughout Turkey, nor could he have known what the Nationalists were aware of. In fact, as noted before, Mustafa Kemal had sent Nureddin Pasha, one of the most brutal of men, to pacify the Pontus region, and the Nationalist leader would have known the likely results. As we have already seen, evidence of Kemal's alignment with Osman Agha during this period is well documented (Mango, 227, 284).

NIZING DEFEAT BY ALLIES AND PERMANENT DETACHMENT MESOPOT (SYRIA, PALESTINE, ETC.), BUT DEMANDS UNEQUIVOCAL CONTROL IN ANATOLIA AND COMPLETE RESTORATION SMYRNA AND EASTERN THRACE.

(3) NO BOLSHEVIK MENACE THROUGH TURKISH MEDIUM APPARENT. BOTH RUSSIANS AND TURKS RECOGNIZE IRRECONCILABILITY THEIR POLITICAL AND SOCIAL AXIOMS AND NEITHER YET SEEKS PRESS SPECIAL INTERESTS. PRINCIPLE IS TO DIVIDE CAUCASUS ON RACIAL AND ECONOMIC LINES MUTUALLY ADVANTAGEOUS. FEAR OF RUSSIANS AND DESIRE NOT TO HAVE ENEMIES ALSO IN NORTH INFLUENCES TURKS, WHO ARE ALSO FLATTERED THAT MOSCOW IS FIRST GOVERNMENT TO RECOGNIZE THEIR PROGRAM, THOUGH MARCH TREATY NOT YET RATIFIED BUT WILL BE.

(4) MARSOVAN AFFAIR* HAS DONE AMERICAN STANDING INCALCULABLE DAMAGE, COMPARABLE

* The "Marsovan affair" spoken of here (to be distinguished from the Marsovan burnings, rapes, and massacre, which are presented in later diaries) involved a Turkish investigator searching out the papers of the American college at Marsovan because of a dismissed laundry worker's complaint and discovering supposedly damning information there. These included, for example, incriminating maps inscribed with the word "Pontus," which the Turks thought related to the scheme for separating a Greek Republic from Turkey, as had been proposed after World War I. But in fact, the maps had been printed in Chicago and simply mapped out the Roman provinces, including Pontus, as they had existed in the time of St. Paul.

Based on this kind of "evidence," the college was shut down by the Turkish government; propaganda about the seditious plots of the Greeks at the college was sent out widely; and only the orphanages on the campus at Marsovan were allowed to continue operating, with a few Americans permitted to stay behind to manage them. (Dunn's comment that the Turks were obsessed by "spy and sedition mania" does make sense here, but the admiral nevertheless continued to consider the American college greatly to blame for its closure and the blow that closure had given to American prestige. However, at one point Admiral Bristol admitted in his own war dairy that, despite Turkish promises to produce the Marsovan "evidence," they never actually had done so; Shenk, *ABSF*, 95.)

TO THAT DONE BRITISH BY SAGHIR EXECUTION,* AND CONSIDERABLE ANTI NEAR EAST RELIEF PROPAGANDA CURRENT.

(5) GOVERNMENT WOULD ACCEPT OFFICAL RELATIONS WITH NO POWER WHICH WOULD REFUSE TO RECOGNIZE ABOLITION OF CAPITULATIONS [THESE WERE BUSINESS AND OTHER PRIVILEGES TRADITIONALLY ALLOWED FOREIGNERS BY THE OTTOMAN GOVERNMENT].

(6) EXCESSES FOLLOWING PRESENT DEPORTATIONS CONFINED TO SAMSUN REGION AND LARGELY RESULT BAD CHARACTER LOCAL OFFICIALS AND USUAL LACK COORDINATION BETWEEN CAPITAL AND PROVINCES. DEPORTATION ORDERS ISSUED BY ANGORA BUT DETAILS CARRIED OUT BY LOCAL OFFICIALS WHO APPARENTLY FAIL REPORT INHUMAN ACTS BY TURKS AND SO ARE NOT HELD RESPONSIBLE. SPY AND SEDITION MANIA WIDESPREAD AND MINOR OFFICIALS SEEK UNCHECKED PROMOTION BY INDISCRIMINATE ACCUSATIONS AGAINST CHRISTIANS. INTENTION NOT TO DEPORT WOMEN AND CHILDREN STATED TO ME.

(7) MILITARY REGROUPING NOW IN PROCESS ON WESTERN FRONT IN ANSWER TO SIMILAR FIRST MOVE BY GREEKS, CONCENTRATIONS TRANSFERRED FROM KUTAIA TO AFION SECTORS. OPPOSED FORCES ABOUT EQUAL IN NUMBERS. APPROACHING QUARTER MILLION EACH GROSS. GREEK EQUIPMENT SUPERIOR, TURKISH MORALE BETTER. CHARGES BRITISH AID IN MONEY, MATERIAL AND MEN MADE FREELY BUT NO PROOFS PRESENTED. GREEK OFFENSIVE AWAITED WITHOUT

---

* The "Saghir" story referred to here has reference to one Mustafa Saghir, a leader of anti-Imperialist Indian Muslims who had met Mustafa Kemal and other Nationalist leaders in Angora. But he was suddenly arrested by Nationalist intelligence agents, interrogated, and executed. He is said to have confessed to being a British spy sent to Angora with the specific aim of murdering Mustafa Kemal and thereby ending the Nationalist movement (Mango, 313).

Whatever actually happened and whoever Saghir actually was, the event provided excellent propaganda against the British.

APPREHENSION AND BELIEF GENERAL THAT ITS FAILURE WOULD PRECLUDE FURTHER EFFORT.

(8) CHARACTER HIGH PROVINCIAL OFFICIALS, VALIS, ETC., SHOWS STEADY IMPROVEMENT, BUT EVILS OF OLD SYSTEM AND TRADITIONS FAR FROM ELIMINATED. USUAL DAB [OF] DIPLOMACY IN PRESSING TEMPORARY ADVANTAGE TO LIMIT AND SO JEOPARDIZING FUTURE STILL APPARENT AS SAGHIR AND MARSOVAN INCIDENTS ILLUSTRATE.

(9) MUSTAPHA KEMAL WAS PERSONALLY VERY RETICENT, SO AFTER EXPLANATION MY STATUS I PRESENTED HIM WITH THIRTEEN WRITTEN QUESTIONS WHICH HE CONSENTED TO ANSWER. ALL BUT TWO OR THREE ANSWERS WERE EVASIVE OR PROPAGANDA.

(10) BOUILLON MISSION WAS TO PRESENT AND RECEIVE NEW PROPOSITIONS FOR FRENCH TREATY. NO DEFINITE RESULT ACHIEVED AT ANGORA.

(11) AT MY REQUEST MINISTER FOREIGN AFFAIRS PROMISED TO ORDER RETURN DEPORTED SAMSUN GREEK TOBACCO WORKMEN. MUTASARIFFF HERE HAD RECEIVED NECESSARY ORDERS AND KING HAS LOCATED MOST WORKERS, BUT FORMER HAS NOT YET TAKEN ACTION.

SIGNED DUNN

July 15, 1921

BROOKS and STURTEVANT at anchor off Samsun; French steamship LAZARETT also here. At about 2:00 a.m. received a priority message to send the STURTEVANT to Constantinople with Lieutenant Dunn. . . .

At 11:02 the STURTEVANT, having paid her bills, gotten the tobacco company and the Near East Relief mails and Lieutenant Dunn, sailed. BROOKS transferred to STURTEVANT for further transfer to the United States via [U.S.S.] SAPELO all short timers, fourteen in all.*

* "Short timers" are American Navy men whose end of enlistment is imminent and who are being transferred home to the States via the fleet oiler *Sapelo.* This vessel had recently called at Constantinople and would soon return to the United States.

Went ashore and visited Lloyd Triestino agent [Count Schmecchia], and had quite a lengthy chat with him. After I saw him yesterday he had gone to the Mutasariff to make protest regarding the four Italian families (19 persons) of Orthodox faith, who had been ordered to leave the country within ten days. The Mutasariff explained to him that explicit orders had been received from Angora directing the expulsion of all foreigners of the Greek Orthodox faith, and that there was no redress. Two of these men are leading workers for the Gary Tobacco Company.* Schmecchia had telegraphed Angora, but was doubtful of any action. He regards the situation as extremely critical. He says that if the Angora government is willing to antagonize foreign countries simply to get rid of people of the Greek faith, what will they do to the Greek women and children, the old men and boys under fifteen of such faith, who are Ottoman subjects? He believes they will be deported before very long.

Schmecchia states that he saw yesterday one of the Mshmetscheff men that was concerned in the killings of Greeks that occurred previous to the deportations: Shukri. He has just been released from prison here, along with others who had been imprisoned at the time. He also says that there are various communistic elements in the town, Georgians, and other people, who have nothing to do, and who, on the slightest pretext, would be ready for anything in the way of plunder [or] excesses.

His estimate of the deportations of men from Samsun agreed with what I had heard already, 3000. He also told me that he understood that all the main parties had been stripped, had all their money taken away from them, and then attacked.

July 16, 1921

BROOKS at Samsun. French steamship L'ANERE also in port. A Turkish side wheeler, painted pea-green, without a name, came in and went alongside the pier to the west of the custom house wharf. She immediately started unloading artillery. She had on board four French field guns and limber [detachable fore parts of gun carriages] together with the horse harness; four Skoda 7.5 centimeter mountain guns; and about two thousand case semi-steel shrapnel ammunition, loaded or fused. This was all sent into the interior in the afternoon.

* These probably included the Cantoni family, whose deposition was presented above. They were listed as of "orthodox faith," and two of them worked for the Gary Tobacco Company.

Landed about 8:30, saw Abdullah who told me that Osman Agha was in Tekekeuy and that some of his men had been seen in town. Saw Haidar Bey and Fitzgerald. Van Toor is still sick. . . .

Osman Agha was expected to come into Samsun between 7 and 8 p.m.

OVERTON arrived about 6:30 p.m. Visited the Commanding Officer, and with him and his passengers for Samsun went ashore about 7:30 p.m. We were met by Haidar Bey and the Kings. On the way to the Gary Tobacco Company's quarters met Mr. King again who had taken the others up to Mr. Johnson's house and he told us that the order to deport the women and children had been given, that they were to go in three days. Haidar Bey said right away, "It wasn't so," that he would see the Mutasariff and let us know. We went on to the Johnson's. A little later Haidar Bey came in to the door and said that it was true.

Today large numbers of refugees from outside have been streaming in; with Osman Agha arriving the situation is really heartbreaking. Everywhere in the Greek quarter one hears women and children crying their lungs out. Never have I seen such a pathetic sight. While we were at the Johnson's women kept coming to the door and asking if America couldn't do something for them. They knew they were going to their death, and worse than that, too.

When I got back to the ship, turned over the diaries to [Captain] Bristol and talked over the situation with him. He prepared a dispatch telling the Admiral of the deportations.

One of my officers, Lieutenant Earle, while out walking by the lighthouse, while going beyond it was fired at by one of the sentries. This officer then turned back after having tried to talk to the sentry, who understood nothing but Turkish. Lieutenant Earle told me that P.M. Smith, of the Socony Company, had heard through some of the postal authorities that the day [the Greek ships] appeared that the military had had a conference, and that they had come to two decisions: One was not to fire on the Greeks unless they opened fire first; second, not to allow the Americans to leave.

There is some possibility as to this last, as the Military Commander when I saw him that day could not give me a definite answer—so that I ended the conversation by saying that "I take it for granted that if we desire to evacuate the Americans, that you will not do anything to make difficulties for us," to which he made no answer. . . .

July 17, 1921

OVERTON and BROOKS at Samsun. During the night the side-wheel Turkish steamer that was moored at the dock went out.

Went ashore accompanied by the Commanding Officer of the OVERTON, Commander Bristol. Visited the Tobacco Companies, and met Count Schmecchia on the street, who accompanied us up to Mr. King's. Met Haidar Bey as well as the Kings, Currin, Smith (Socony) and various others of the colony.

The tobacco work is absolutely at a standstill. Mr. King had his magazines open this morning but not a soul turned up. Mr. Currin said that some dealers approached him with tobacco to sell yesterday afternoon and he told them nothing doing. Mr. English, of the Melechrino Company, notified his Constantinople agents not to ship anything more to Samsun.

Everyone says that the distress in town last night was frightful. Today everyone is carrying their little belongings around to a place of safety. The police have directed that all valuables should be turned into the Greek church before leaving.

The Turkish leaders here are perhaps as much concerned as the Americans and Europeans. I understand from Mr. King that most of them had been to see him and told him that they were having a meeting and were going to the Governor's at two o'clock to protest the deportations.

At 10:30 Bristol and I, with Haidar Bey, went to the Mutasariff. He himself had asked to see us this morning. Strange as it may seem he appeared fairly genial when he came into the room, almost as soon as we had arrived. Bristol opened the conversation by the usual formula of courtesies, glad to see him again, etc. The Mutasariff then said that he was waiting for Bristol to hear what he had to say. Though he had sent for us, apparently he didn't have anything to say, probably anticipating that we would ask to see him.

Bristol then said that he had heard that the women and children, old men and boys were to be deported and asked if that was official. After some fencing which included a statement of surprise as to why we should be interesting ourselves in the matter, he finally admitted that the deportations had been ordered and would take place.

Bristol then stated that in the previous deportations a great deal of suffering and many casualties had occurred and that he hoped that something might be done to reduce this for women and children who of course could not stand the hardships of a journey on foot. The Mutasariff said that they were going to take care of that, that they would all be sent away in arabas, and that there would be sufficient guards; that the casualties in the previous deportations were due to attacks by brigands and were matters for which the government were not responsible.

After more quibbling on the part of the Mutasariff, Captain Bristol stated that as Senior Naval Officer at Samsun and in the name of humanity, he protested the deportations of the defenseless women and children, which were not called for and which would only create a distant revulsion in the feelings of Americans. He asked if steps could not be taken looking to the cancellation of the order.

With Bristol's permission I then made a personal appeal myself in the name of humanity for the cancellation or modification of the deportation order. I requested that he might inquire of Angora whether or not it would be satisfactory to the government to send these people out of the country by steamer rather than deport them into the interior. To my surprise he said that he would ask that by dispatch.

Upon [our] leaving he told Haidar Bey to come back at one o'clock to help him draw up a dispatch to Angora which would cover the points we had mentioned. He also told Haidar Bey in an aside that he had expected a demand that the deportations stop.

Haidar Bey is very much disturbed over the whole matter, says that it will be terrible for the country.

Bristol decided that I had better go right to Constantinople rather than via Trebizond, so as to lay the matter before Admiral Bristol.

Left Samsun at 2:30 p.m.

Sent the following dispatch (paraphrased):

> BRISTOL AND I SAW THE MUTASARIFF THIS MORNING AT HIS REQUEST MADE PROTEST AGAINST THE DEPORTATIONS INQUIRING AS TO POSSIBILITY OF GREEKS BEING ALLOWED TO LEAVE THE COUNTRY MUTASARIFF STATED WOULD REFER QUESTIONS TO ANGORA ENERGETIC AND EARLY REPRESENTATIONS ARE NECESSARY TO SAVE THESE PEOPLE WHO ARE ESTIMATED TO NUMBER ABOUT TEN THOUSAND SCHMECCHIA CONCURS AND ASKS REFERENCE TO ITALIAN HIGH COMMISSIONER.
>
> [MUTASARIFF] APPARENTLY EXPECTED THAT WE WOULD DEMAND THAT DEPORTATIONS STOP.

USS *OVERTON*, COMMANDER A.L. BRISTOL WAR DIARY SET FOR JULY 15-AUGUST 3, 1921

. . . .

July 16, 1921

Captain Houston of the BROOKS called and stated that all preparations for landing of passengers had been made and that Haidar Bey was then waiting for them on the dock. In a brief conversation, he informed me that conditions in Samsun were not improving. In company with Captain Houston, I immediately went on shore with all passengers who were landed and passed through the customs without difficulty. On the way up town I met King who informed me the word had just started around town that the order for deportation of remaining Greeks in the Samsun area had been [issued]. As it was just about dark I sent Haidar Bey to see if he could find the Mutasariff and verify this report. Meanwhile, I went to Johnson's house to wait for an answer. In about an hour Haidar Bey returned, said he had found the Mutasariff, who had [stated] that the order for deportation had been issued. The Mutasariff further sent word to me that he would like to see me at 10.30 a.m. the next morning.

I spent an hour or so talking with the Americans in Samsun and with Captain Houston regarding the alleged killing of men who [had] been sent out in the first deportation. There are innumerable [stories] concerning these killings which may or may not be true, of course. No one with whom I can talk has any first-hand information on the subject, but it seems to be generally accepted that large numbers of men of the first deportation were more or less deliberately slaughtered. A number of Greeks who were in the first movement [had escaped] in the melee and have sneaked back into Samsun where they [are] now in hiding. They arrived in a naked and starving condition and have told tales of the most frightful atrocities. Captain Houston, who has investigated these cases, is convinced that they are in the main true.

At about 9.00 p.m., returned on board, conferred with Captain Houston and read past diaries and otherwise familiarized myself with the general situation. On my return to ship I sent a brief dispatch to Detachment Commander in substance as follows:

> "That I had official information that the order had gone out for the deportation of all remaining Greeks in the Samsun area."

Arthur LeRoy Bristol, photographed here at the rank of captain (he was a commander while at Samsun as captain of the *Overton*). He convinced Admiral Bristol to protest to Mustafa Kemal the deportation of Greek women and children from Samsun, saving many lives. *U.S. Navy photograph.*

July 17, 1921

During the night I thought over the situation and decided to find out from the Mutasariff, if possible, just what the Turks [admit] had happened to the first deportees and secondly, to find out what plans the Turks were making for the deportation of the remaining Greeks, numbering about 12,000 and mostly women and children. It is self evident that if these women and children [are marched] to the interior, as in the case of the first outfit, that a large percentage of them will never arrive; as a matter of fact, many will not survive the trip over the first range of hills back of Samsun.

At 9.00 a.m., went ashore with Captain Houston and near the landing met the Italian Consul, Count Schmecchia. He stated that he considered the situation desperate and that if the deportation was not stopped he considered that the result would be tantamount to a general massacre. He asked me anxiously, if I could not do something to stop the whole procedure. I informed him that I had not yet made any decision regarding any action on my part, but I was then on my way to the Mutasariff and would decide after this interview. He then stated that he had tried to keep his government informed of what was going on but without result and he was convinced that only positive and determined action on the part of some power would prevent a massacre which would be a disgrace to all civilization.

I went to King's office to find Haidar Bey and while waiting for him talked the situation over with most of the Americans here who came drifting in during the wait of about an hour. A dozen or more of the most influential Turks came in to discuss the situation with King and to ask him what could be done. They one and all stated that they were going as a delegation to the Mutasariff at 2.00 p.m. to put in their protest.

At 10 a.m., called on the Mutasariff, usual exchange of greetings. I then waited for the Mutasariff to open the conversation, but after a pause he asked me if I would like to say anything to him. I replied that I had been informed by him the previous evening, through the interpreter, that the deportation of all remaining Greeks had been ordered and I would like to ask if this were true and if so, in what manner the deportation would be carried out. His reply was "Why do you wish to know?" I answered, "Because if a deportation takes place, which will include all the women and children and which will be conducted in the same manner as the previous deportation, it will result in acts similar to those which are known to have taken place in the deportation of the men. As the Senior American Naval Officer on the Anatolian Coast, it is my duty to become informed of acts which take place contrary to the laws of usage and civilization.

"I desire to obtain this information direct from persons who have [matters] in charge rather than rely on irresponsible rumor." The Mutasariff then said he hoped I understood that we were speaking [unofficially] as usual; I assented. Mutasariff then made a statement of which the following is the substance:

> "That the deportation of all remaining Greeks, including women and children, had been ordered by Angora; that the deportation would be begun as soon as arrangements could be made to handle it; that every precaution would be taken to ensure the safe arrival of deportees at destination; that women and children would not be required to go on foot, but would be sent by conveyance—arrabaughs and carts—and that they would be sent in very small parties with strong guard."

I replied that it was known that they were at least 12,000 Greeks in Samsun and that such procedure as he outlined would require an excessively large number of conveyances and would cover a long period of time. I further called his attention to the fact that he had made [many] similar statements in the case of the deportation of the [men]; that none of these conditions had been fulfilled and that it was [well] known [that] large numbers of the men of the first deportation had been killed enroute. The Mutasariff then made a statement protesting [urgently] that the Government could not be held responsible for these [things] as they had furnished a very strong guard for each party. He said that there had been fighting on the road in which many of the [men] being deported had fallen, but that the fact that a strong guard had been furnished was evidenced and proved by the fact that half of [these] deportees had arrived at destination. It will be noted, that [even] the Mutasariff absolutely admitted the killing of many Greek deportees. This is the first admission of such a nature from any official Turk sources; it is further noted, that by inference, half of those sent away were admittedly killed.

I replied to the Mutasariff about as follows—that I did not doubt that they intended to send guards, but past experiences had shown that even with the guards half of the party had been killed, furthermore, that he was aware as well as I was, that in the case of women and children, who in the nature of things could not support such a trip, [many] more than half would perish. Mutassarif replied that he was [powerless] as his orders came from Angora and he could only carry them out to the best of his ability. I replied "In the name of humanity, as the Senior American Naval Officer in Anatolia, I most strongly protest to you as the Governor of the Sanjak of Samsun against this deportation, which will admittedly result in the death of large numbers of non-combatants and innocent women and children."

The Mutasariff replied that he could not do anything himself, but that he [would] inform Angora that I had made such a protest. Captain Houston then asked the Mutasariff whether it was not possible that these Greeks be expelled from the country by water and be allowed, under certain governing regulations, to leave the country by ship. The Mutasariff replied that he did not believe that this would be considered, but that he would also submit this proposal to Angora.

I arrived at the decision to make my official protest as Senior Naval Officer present to the Mutasariff for the following [reasons] – I believe it is the firm intention of the Turks to [carry] out this deportation in the same manner as the last one unless something is done to stop them; I also believe this is part of an official plan which contemplates extermination of the Greeks insofar as they can get away with it. In what I consider to be a [typically] Turkish method, they are going about it in small [tasks], waiting after each attempt to see if any decided action on the part of anyone results in protest. There is no question in my mind that most of the women and children will not survive the trip [from] Samsun to the interior over the mountains under the conditions which the Turks will impose. This, even leaving out of consideration [of any] deliberate massacres, which I am also convinced have happened and will happen again. In view of the above, I felt that was no course open to me other than to protest as strongly as possible against the present movement. I did not feel that I could make my protest any stronger in view of the fact that I was in constant communication with the Detachment Commander and believed him to be fully cognizant of the situation.

After leaving the Mutasariff, I called on the Military Commander and found him out. He was said to be in the hills on a trip of inspection and could not be located.

At about 12.30 p.m., returned to ship and directed BROOKS to get underway and proceed direct to Constantinople, in order to [report] to the Detachment Commander latest developments in the [situation] and to present to him a letter which I hurriedly wrote [containing] an outline of my opinions in the premises (this letter was written in longhand hurriedly and no copy was retained).* As the only object in sending the BROOKS to Trebizond [apparently previously planned] was to land Mr. Brown and to look over the situation, which is believed to be quiet, I decided that she could do better work by getting to Constantinople as quickly as possible.

BROOKS sailed at 2.00 p.m. for Constantinople. At 3.00 p.m., [I] went on shore to endeavor again to find the Military Commander. [Was] unsuccessful as he was still reported to be out in the hills.

* Although Commander Bristol retained no copy of this letter, it was retained in the Admiral Mark Bristol files in the Library of Congress (in the folder marked General Correspondence, July 1921). Having located the handwritten document, we now present it below.

HANDWRITTEN LETTER OF COMMANDER A. LEROY BRISTOL TO ADMIRAL MARK BRISTOL

Below is a transcription of the letter from Commander Arthur LeRoy Bristol to Admiral Mark Bristol concerning the ordered deportations of some ten or twelve thousand Pontic Greek women, children, and old men from Samsun. Captain Houston of the destroyer Brooks *was to hand-deliver it to the admiral, steaming to Constantinople overnight to do so. This memo—after all the previous messages, war diary reports, and conversations during the prior month—seems to have finally convinced the admiral to protest specifically to Mustapha Kemal.*

Commander Bristol was the senior of the two American ship captains present at Samsun, so it would have been his call as to whether to make any recommendation or not.

Whether it was in fact this handwritten letter that convinced the admiral, it is certainly remarkable that the commander puts his assessments as strongly as he does given the admiral's characteristic disinterest in helping the Christian minorities in Turkey in any real way.

18 July [1921]

My Dear Admiral —

I am sending the Brooks direct to Constantinople as I think you should have the most recent news of developments in Samsun. This brief note will give you my opinions in the matter.

As stated by my dispatch of last night the deportation of all remaining Greeks from this area has been ordered. This is naturally regarded as the end by everybody. I gathered what information I could last night, familiarized myself with the situation during the first four weeks, and after thinking it over during the night, decided that I would see the Mutasariff and make [a] protest if the interview warranted. The Mutasariff had sent word asking that I call at 10:00 AM this morning.

Together with Capt Houston I called this AM. After greeting I asked the Mutasariff if this order for deportation was official and when it would be carried out. He replied that the order was in effect, that all Greeks had been notified and that the movement would begin as soon as the necessary arrangements could be made. A long conversation followed of which the following is pertinent.

Following certain comments by me the Mutasariff admitted that many of the Greek men who had already been sent out had been killed. He stated that the Government had sent troops with them and had tried to protect them as evidenced by the fact that one half (1/2) had arrived at [their] destination. The killings had been the results of attacks by Greek and Turk brigands on the columns.

I asked how this deportation was intended to be conducted and called attention to the fact that his assurances to me regarding the past deportation had not been adhered to in any particulars.

He replied that the women and children would be sent in small parties in conveyances well guarded—[they] would not be required to travel on foot.

I replied that he knew as well as I that with the [resources?] at hand this would require a great length of time and was hardly possible.

After further conversation I told him that in view of past experience, he knew as well as I did that large numbers of the present deportees would not survive from one cause or another, and in the name of humanity I as Senior American Naval Officer in Anatolian Waters strongly protested against this intended deportation of old men, women, and children.

He stated at the end that he would send a dispatch to Angora—that his orders were positive and originated there. In this dispatch he would embody my protest.

[Capt] Houston then asked if Greeks under certain regulations might not all be expelled from the country by water and allowed to go to Greece or some other country.

[The] Mutasariff replied that he would also ask Angora about that by dispatch.

This protest was as strong as I felt that I had a right to make under the circumstances—but I am convinced that it was not strong enough to prevent the Government from carrying out the instructions. After the interview Haidar Bey [the Americans' regular interpreter] said to me "Captain, it has not been enough. He was expecting to hear from you a message from America 'You must stop it.' That would have been what he was looking for and on which he would have acted."

I am convinced that the deportations will be carried out practically as the former one was and will result in the death of large numbers of the deportees.

American prestige is now at a low ebb here. We have the only war vessels present in the harbor, and whether true or not are being put in the position of passively standing by and watching what everyone, including Turks, considers a massacre. The officials representing the Government know that we don't believe what they say to us and they also know that we are fully convinced that few deportees will reach [their] destination alive. If this goes through it will at later date when all stories have got assessed be classed with the Armenian affair, and we will occupy in the public mind very much the position of the Germans. Time will impute to us not only doing little to prevent it but actually the attitude of complacency if not concurrence.

There is a feeling among all (Turks included) that concrete action by the Allies or strong action by America can stop it. This must be communicated to Angora. The local Turk will not feel when you are dealing only with him that you are serious in your intentions.

If it is desired that we take any further steps in the matter the action must be quick as I believe that the movement will begin at any time.

The Italian Consul requests you particularly to inform the Italian High Commissioner of the general contents of this letter with the statement that he, Count Schmecchia, has made all protests that he can.

[Capt] Houston will give you full details.

Respectfully
A.L. Bristol

CONTINUATION OF USS *OVERTON* WAR DIARY

....

July 19, 1921

Detachment Commander's message serial number 90 for Mustapha Kemal PASHA [was] received in the early morning and I went ashore, found Haidar Bey and had this message translated into Turkish. At 11.00 a.m., called on the Mutasariff and requested that this message be forwarded by telegraph to Angora. The Mutasariff replied that he would and requested that I call again later in the afternoon. After leaving the Mutasariff's office, Haidar Bey informed me that the Mutasariff intended to put this message in code. I considered that the translation in code would probably [be] too much for the message to survive so went to the telegraph office, saw the head telegrapher and made arrangements with him to send message through immediately on direct wire to Mustapha Kemal in plain English.

MESSAGE FROM ADMIRAL BRISTOL TO MUSTAPHA KEMAL

Although Commander Bristol placed this message at the end of Overton's *August 3, 1921 set of war diaries, we present this message at the chronological point where it originally came to Commander Bristol's attention.*

To: Mustafa Kemal Pasha.
From: Admiral Bristol.

I am informed that the Greek women, children, and old men are to be transported from Samsun to the interior. There is much evidence that when the Greek men were recently transported many perished on the journey. The transporting to the interior of men of military age may be considered as a military measure, but the transporting of old men, women, and children does not seem to be justified by military necessity. This proposed transportation of about 10,000 people under the present conditions must subject these people to great danger of their personal safety in transit. Therefore I trust for the sake of humanity you will prevent the recommencement of transportation from Samsun of these women and children. The world at large is bound to consider that the killing of those who were under guard for military reasons was a neglect of the humane law of war. Any transportation of women and children with loss of life would certainly be viewed with consternation and create a most unfavorable impression against you and your people. I hope for the best interest of Turkey you will reconsider this decision if it has been made. I would be pleased to receive from you an early and favorable answer which I could convey to my government.

/S/Admiral Bristol

The above message, having been received from Constantinople as outlined in the July 19, 1921 Overton *war diary, was translated and forwarded in the clear by telegraph from Samsun to Angora, message's serial number 90—0018. A few minor details from the war diary text of the message have been corrected by reference to a set of messages sent by the* Overton *found in National Archives RG 45 Subj File 1911–27, Box 832, Folder #2, Samsun.*

FURTHER CONTINUATION OF USS *OVERTON* WAR DIARY

July 19, 1921

Then called on the Military Commandant. The Greek men-of-war scare of yesterday had left the command in somewhat doubtful status.* Whenever military operations are in prospect, the Military Commandant immediately assumes control of all governmental functions and this morning I was not able to find out [directly] who was in control. I presented a copy of the message to the Military Commandant and informed him that I was giving him this only for his information, that I had already presented the [admiral's] message to the Mutasariff for transmission to Angora. The Commandant [asked] me to remain awhile and talk over the situation in what he described "a friendly conversation." For a half an hour or more we thrashed out the pros and cons of the present deportation order and I am forced to admit, that aside from the question of humanity [alone] he made a fair case for the Turkish side.

While at the telegraph office several interesting pieces of information were picked up, which may or may not be true. I had a rather long wait there and during this time Haidar Bey and the head [man] carried on a very animated conversation. Afterwards Haidar Bey informed me of the following:

> First, That the Mutasariff had received a telegram on the previous evening from Nureddin Pasha, Commanding General of the Army of the Center, directing him to proceed with all dispatch to carry out the orders which had been given him or that he would shortly cease to be Mutasariff. (This the substance of a very long dispatch).
>
> Secondly, That the Mutasariff had been called to the telegraph office at 3.00 a.m. to communicate with Angora, and had received the following, as I understand, from the Minister of Foreign Affairs: "That the order for the deportation

* Two Greek naval ships had been rumored to be approaching Samsun on July 18, but failed to appear. There was also an unconfirmed rumor that the order for deportations had been rescinded. We have omitted the July 18 war diary.

> of all the Greeks was a mistake and that as a wise man he had better go carefully and make sure of the origin of these orders and verify them before proceeding to carry them out."*
>
> Thirdly, that Osman Agha was expected to arrive in town today and that there were telegraphic orders waiting [for] him to proceed immediately to Angora. Haidar Bey ventured the opinion that Osman Agha would be held in Angora or at the front and not allowed to come to the Samsun area again.

Lunched with Johnson and afterwards had a long talk with [Mrs.] Austin, in charge of all Near East Orphanages. (Van Toor and Compton of the Near East are both in the hospital [with] fever and the remaining Near East man—Wright—can hardly be called a responsible party.) Discussed with Mrs. Austin her arrangements for protection of orphans in case of bombardment. These arrangements are principally a matter of cellar protection. I over-ruled her request that the military be asked to furnish guards for the orphanages. I approved of her decision not to accept in the orphanages Greek children offered by their mothers, under present conditions.

While driving from Johnson's house, passed Osman Agha and [some] of his followers going into the Mutasariff's. Went on to King's office and there found Haidar Bey, who told me that I would [have] to wait a short while before my visit to the Mutasariff as the Mutasariff was then engaged with Osman Agha. At about 4.00 p.m., called on the Mutasariff. I was shown into a small ante-room adjacent to his office and in a few moments the Mutasariff entered.

We had barely begun our conversation when the door was flung open and Osman Agha burst in followed by several frock-coated Turks who seemed to be endeavoring to hold him back. He started on a violent [tirade] apparently directed at the Mutasariff; for

* If taken seriously, this sentence might suggest that perhaps the whole notion of deporting women and children was Nureddin Pasha's idea and did not originate in Angora. The telegram from Nureddin mentioned in the prior paragraph supports this speculation. But there are other possible interpretations as to its meaning or purpose.

about five minutes the room was hardly big enough to hold us all, finally his companions succeeded in leading him away. After leaving the Mutasariff, Haidar Bey informed me that his remarks had been about as follows: "You have broken my heart; you have hurt me to the [quick]. I am the only patriot here who thinks about his country and you are all a bunch of Greek traitors; I am going to leave your [dirty], slimy, blanket-blank-blank country forever." After Osman Agha had departed, I asked the Mutasariff if the telegram to Mustapha Kemal had been sent and he replied that it had. I then [stated] that I was informed that the deportation would begin tomorrow morning (Wednesday, July 20, 1921) and that under the circumstances, I expected that he would delay this move until there had been time for Mustapha Kemal to reply. After a slight hesitation, he said, "I promise you on my word of honor, that no deportation will take place tomorrow." I wished to put further questions to the Mutasariff but at this point he apologized and said that he must move immediately to return to the council meeting which he had left at his office.

While waiting in King's office, several Turks of good repute, in talking to King and Count Schmecchia, had informed them that they had positive information that the deportations had already taken [place] from Bafra and Tcharshamba; that the deportees had gone but a little distance from the town when the killing had begun and that few had escaped. One Turk furnished the following details about Tcharshamba—that many of the women (presumably the good-looking ones) had been roused up at night with no clothes, had been assembled in a church while the rest had been marched off and that these women were being held for the pleasure of the troops under Osman Agha.

This can hardly be classed as reliable information, but it at least serves to show what some of the Turks are thinking. I had intended to question the Mutasariff about Tcharshamba and Bafra, [for] instance, but under the circumstances, I was unable to get my questions in.

It may be mentioned here that large numbers of the influential Turks have done everything in their power to stop the deportations. [Frequent] meetings have been held, protests made to the Mutasariff and several telegrams sent directly to Mustafa Kemal.*

After my interview with the Mutasariff, looked up Van Toor and Plimpton at the hospital and then called for a few minutes on [Mrs.] King. Found her household in an uproar and Mrs. King completely [swamped] by a swarm of Greek women begging for assistance.

At 8.00 p.m., returned to ship and sent one officer ashore to [spend] the night. Gave him a signal lamp with instructions to call [us] for a boat in case of any emergency on shore during the night.

July 20, 1921

Went on shore at 8.00 a.m., and found everything quiet. Was informed by Haidar Bey that the Mutasariff sent me word that there would be

---

* That leading Turks of Samsun had protested this deportation of women and children is confirmed by a report heard at the British committee at Constantinople a month later:

> On his return to Samsun towards the end of July, [Osman Agha] ordered the expulsion of all Christian women and children. Seventy Turkish notables, however, intervened and telegraphed to Mustafa Kemal stating that women and children could not be considered as enemies; that it was against their religion to massacre such persons and recommended their deportation to Greece, otherwise the notables were ready to share the fate of these unfortunate people. Mustafa Kemal had replied that he had just returned from the front where he had seen the crimes committed by the Greeks; that the exile of these people, was a merciful act and he regretted that there existed wicked Turks who sided with the enemy. Nevertheless, the notables obtained a "Fetva" (a religious decision) from the Moufti of Samsun that the massacre of these people could not be permitted and Osman Agha was recalled. (Yaghiayan, *British Reports*, 221)

As we have seen, this same war diary entry above manifests the animosity of Osman Agha toward those Turks he considered "Greek traitors." Possibly the protest by Turkish leaders played a part in moving Mustafa Kemal to recall the brigand to Angora.

The absurdity of Kemal's alleged assertion that the death marches were "merciful" and that the seventy brave leaders of Samsun were "wicked" is a signature of some of the worst Kemalist propaganda. This statement also suggests, however, some of the great risk that the local Turkish civilian leaders in Samsun might have been running by standing up against the deportations.

no deportation. In the course of the forenoon the same [word] was brought in from several sources, including many influential Turks and Count Schmecchia. Haidar Bey further informed me that no telegram had been received from Angora, so I decided not to see the Mutasariff until the afternoon. . . .

I learned that Mr. Fuller of the Near East Relief had just arrived in Samsun, coming through from Harput. I sent for him to [hear] his story as to what he had noticed or heard along the road. [I may] remark here, that never had I encountered such colossal ignorance and lack of observation in any person. It is not to be [believed], unless he spent the entire month on the road in a sound sleep; a perfect imitation of the three Japanese monkeys. After a great deal of effort, I dragged out of him the following facts:

One, that well into the interior in the neighborhood of Malatia, he had [seen] numerous bands of Greek men, numbering about fifty in each band, [marching] along under Turk guard and apparently in excellent order. Two, that just north of Amassia he had passed a column of Greek women, children and old men marching along under Turkish guard in very good order and condition. He estimated the number at three thousand and further estimated that there were some arrabaughs numbering between twenty and a hundred in the column carrying household goods and sometimes women and children (these may be Greeks from the villages surrounding Samsun or perhaps people from Tcharshamba and Bafra). Fuller [however] made no effort to find out or could not. Three, he had heard tales from Marsovan that only two hundred of the first column - [male] deportees from Samsun —a thousand in number—had reached their destination, the others had been killed; also that the third column of equal strength had been destroyed. He knew no [details].

Lunched with Currin and during lunch, Haidar Bey came in and informed me that the Military Commandant had received a wire from Trebizond stating that five Greek destroyers had bombarded Trebizond for an hour this morning and had sailed away at 9.00 a.m.*

After lunch waited until 4.00 p.m., to see if any message would come from Angora and then thought of calling on the Mutasariff but found he was engaged in council meeting. Then decided it would perhaps be

* For details, see *Williamson* Trebizond WD, July 27, 1921, below.

better not to call on the Mutasariff until I was informed that a reply from Angora had been received.

At 1.00 p.m., Osman Agha with his personal bodyguard left Samsun headed for the interior.

There are rumors in town that the Turkish forces are suffering [reverses] at the front. One report was brought to me by Count Schmecchia, who said he had reason to trust his informant, [that] the Turks were preparing a final line [of] Amassia, Marsovan, Sivas, and Cesarea with headquarters at Sivas and that Mustapha Kemal had been in that area himself locating positions. A glance at the [map] leads me to believe that this information can hardly be called trustworthy.

Further scraps of information during the day under the heading of unreliable rumors: First, as soon as the Turks had rid themselves of the Greeks, they would make a final and complete clean-up of the Armenians. Secondly, that Osman Agha had his appointment as colonel and would be given a command at the front. This last may be quite true, but he has probably been appointed a colonel of irregulars.

July 21, 1921

Shortly after midnight heavy squall struck Samsun with severe and [....] wind from northwest. Hoisted all boats and got up steam as quickly as possible. Squall lasted about half an hour followed by [severe] rains for an hour or more. At 2.30 a.m., secured.

At 6.25 a.m., sighted Greek destroyer hull down, apparently standing towards Samsun. Made preparations for getting underway and sent Executive Officer, with motor sailer, on shore to round up Americans who were not held by their various duties. (Already had one officer sleeping ashore in Currin's house.) At 6.55 a.m., got underway and stood out to meet the Greeks. By this time, I was able to note that there were two [fleet] vessels—one auxiliary cruiser and one destroyer. They lay to and [awaited] my approach. It was seen that the auxiliary cruiser was flying the flag of a Commodore. I went within hail and stated that I would like to go on board to speak with the Senior Officer Present. He replied that he would be glad to see me. At about 7.30 a.m., I went aboard the Greek auxiliary cruiser "NAXOS," and was met at the gangway by Captain Charles L. Vriacos with the brevet rank of Commodore, in command of the Cruiser [division]. He conducted me to his cabin and there we had coffee.

I [informed] him I was Captain Bristol of the U.S.S. OVERTON, Senior American Officer Present in Anatolian Waters, and stated that if it was his intention to bombard Samsun, I requested sufficient time to move all of the Americans as I desired; that there were many Americans in Samsun engaged in relief work and other peaceful pursuits and I was there to protect their safety and interests. He replied that he did not [intend] to conduct a bombardment, but only to fire sufficient shell for reconnaissance purposes—sufficient to draw fire from shore in order that he might locate the number, type and range of the guns of the shore [emplacements]. Captain Vriacos then stated that he could assure me, that before [any] bombardment of Samsun took place, the American war vessel in harbor would be notified in order that they might take such steps as necessary for the protection of Americans. He then asked me if I knew how the town was fortified. I replied that I was unable to give him any such information and he then stated that he would give me such time as I desired to [arrange] the affairs of the Americans. He then asked me what the local [situation] was in regard to the Greeks.

I told him that transportation of Greeks to the interior had been ordered but was in abeyance; that I had protested in the name of humanity against the moving of women and children to the interior and that I believed the order would be rescinded [and] that the movement would not take place; that the situation was very [shaky] and that any aggressive move on either side would unquestionably precipitate trouble which would affect principally innocent women and children. After hesitating a moment, he informed me that he had changed his intentions and would not open fire on the town.

We had a further lengthy conversation about general subjects in the midst of which he [asked] for further particulars on the American situation. I informed him of the three orphanages and the hospital which we were operating and the tobacco magazines in which in which business men were engaged. At the conclusion of the interview, as I was about to leave, he made the following statement—That he wished to thank me for my humanitarian act; that he was particularly able to appreciate this, because as all the world [knows] the Greeks had a most delicate appreciation of the consideration due to peoples in the cause of humanity; that the American and Greek ideals were one and the same and that they were in fact brothers. Quite overcome, I stumbled down the gangway and left the ship.

OVERTON returned to harbor and I recalled boat and officers from shore. Later in the forenoon I went on shore and saw Haidar Bey. He informed me that no news had yet been received from Angora and asked if I had any information for the Mutasariff concerning the Greek visit of this morning. I told him to inform the Mutasariff that I had called on the Greek Senior Officer and to the best of my belief there would be no bombardment.

After standing away from Samsun, the Greek men-of-war stopped and boarded a steamer believed to be the Turkish steamer "KRIM" of Constantinople. Although the vessels were hull down [far enough away that the vessels' hulls were obscured because of the curvature of the earth, and only their superstructures were visible], it appeared that they boarded this steamer and later took her along in company with them. Greek men-of–war and this steamer could still be seen from the masthead [a position high on a destroyer's mast where each ship of this destroyer class had a lookout position] until about 3.00 p.m., when they finally departed. Information from several sources on shore, considered reliable, is to the effect that the "KRIM" was coming from Kerasunda and had on board certain arms and ammunition and ninety-two of Osman Agha's men.

Up until 8.00 p.m., no information had been received from Angora and I returned to ship.

July 22, 1921

On shore during the day with no news of any importance. Everyone going about their business and the alarm occasioned by the deportation order and the appearance of the Greek fleet, is passing away.

Count Schmecchia informed me that he had reliable information that the present Mutasariff would be relieved and he stated that this time he felt that it was straight information and that the move would be carried out. If the move goes through and another man of the same general type is appointed, I would be sorry to see it, as I feel that we are beginning to get the bulge on [get the upper hand with] the present incumbent. If the change results in a man of distinctly superior type, who has a mind of his own and acts on his own initiative, it will be a good thing for Samsun and particularly for the Americans here.

Sufficient time has now elapsed for a calm review of present events in their proper perspective and apart from the bias caused by harrowing stories of atrocities. My conception of the situation is as follows:

1. For months past and probably for more than a year, there has been a distinct anti-Greek movement looking to the extermination of the Greeks. This movement [is] local in its conception and sponsored by Osman Agha and other men of his type, principally of the military. While I have no direct knowledge of events other than at Samsun, it is generally accepted that Osman Agha's district of Kerasunda and the adjacent district surrounding Ordu were pretty thoroughly cleaned out of Greeks many months ago, attended by killings and village burnings similar to the present ruction. This excited no particular [argument], was carried out little by little and without protest from [any] source.

2. Recently, that is, within the past three months, the Government, for military reasons, decided to move the Greeks from the sea-coast to the interior. They were considered a menace because of their proven disloyalty to the Turkish cause. This move on the part of the Government had no connections with previous anti-Greek actions. The orders from the Government had in mind more particularly the Samsun area, because of the preponderance of Greeks and because of past Greek agitations in this area.

3. It happened that this order of the Government came at about the time that Osman Agha and others of the same viewpoint (Nureddin Pasha, for example) were planning to extend their Kerasunda and Ordu activities into [the Sanjak] of Samsun. This may have been a coincidence or it may have been that this crowd seized upon the opportunity.

4. There is very little direct evidence in regard to what happened to the villages to the south and west of Samsun about two months ago, but it is now commonly accepted by everyone here Turks and Greeks alike that the Greek villages were thoroughly wiped out and this [was] attended in most cases by atrocities and killings. It was in no sense

a deportation. There is no question but that these attacks on villages were accomplished by the military, but it has never been shown that they were regular troops and on this point the reports are even now conflicting.

5. Following hard upon this general Greek village destruction, came the order from Angora to deport all male Greeks between ages of fifteen and fifty. I believe that this actually was a legitimate order of the Government and that the Government intended that full protection should be given these deportees; unfortunately, the man charged with the deportation, the present Mutasariff, was a weakling and thoroughly terrorized by Osman Agha and certain others who represented a lawless element in this district. I am convinced that he was fully aware that this lawless element intended the massacre of the deportees and had not the strength of character enough to stop it.*

6. These deportees were sent out of Samsun in five columns. It seems fairly well established by reports from many and various sources and by what is generally believed here, that two of these columns were subject to attack when they had progressed only a small distance from Samsun, namely, as far as Kavak. Three columns [passed] through safely and there is evidence to show that this was the result of a pre-emptory order from the Angora Government to afford proper protection and to take steps to insure that no further atrocities be committed. This

* Commander Bristol's belief, above, that the massacres near Kavak were not intended by the central Nationalist government—reasonable as this conclusion may be from one aspect—may be qualified by these considerations: (1) that Nureddin Pasha, who Commander Bristol thought was *at least* "amplifying and hastening" the deportation, had been put in his place by Mustapha Kemal, and Osman Agha, who no doubt was doing all he could to promote it, and was himself on the spot in Samsun, was to continue to provide Kemal's bodyguard for two more years; and (2) that American reliefers, once they left Angora en route elsewhere in the interior, were horrified to see that a general deportation with death marches had been taking place for months during the same time the Nationalists in Angora had been contending that no such thing would occur. Finally, (3) other atrocities—equivalent to massacres in many respects—the labor battalions and simple killings to which Greek men throughout Pontus were subjected to upon deportation—were the equivalent to the Kavak massacres of a couple of thousand ethnic Greek men but on a much larger scale.

belief of mine is based on piecing together rather vague information, but there is evidence to show that Greeks were being moved about in the interior without [molestation] and it is reasonable to suppose that the Central Government itself intended that the coastal Greeks should not be molested.

7. After the situation had quieted down from the deportation of the men, there came the order to deport the women and children. The situation is not yet clear, but the preponderance of evidence seems to indicate that whatever the order of the Central Government might have been (if indeed there were any such orders), that these were amplified and hastened by Nureddin Pasha. It is possible that the Angora Government had issued some orders for a small percentage or for certain persons by name. Again the Mutasariff was brow-beaten and terrorized by Nureddin Pasha and Osman Agha and would in all probability have yielded to their wishes had [we] not interfered. When I first arrived here this time, in every interview which I had with the Mutasariff, he appeared as a man at his wits-ends and ready to jump overboard. The change which has occurred in him since the departure of Osman Agha is extraordinary.

8. As no reply has yet been received from Mustapha Kemal to the note of the Detachment Commander, this summing up of the situation may prove to be a bit premature. I am making it, however, while events and conversations are still fresh in my mind and yet sufficiently past to get away from the weeping and wailing and the general excitement.

9. One point, which I have not touched on and which may have been a deciding factor, is the appearance of the Greek ships at Samsun. The Turks of Samsun are vitally concerned for their own safety and they realize that the presence of Greek women and children carries with it a measure of protection.

10. It appears at this writing, that the affair is finished, at least for the present, but I am quite convinced that it is only temporary and that as long as the present Greek-Turk war goes on, a similar situation may arrive at any moment. Only the extermination of the Greeks or their removal from this district will settle the situation.

July 23, 1921

Went on shore in the afternoon and received from Haidar Bey, communication from the Mutasariff written in French, which proved to be the reply from Angora to the Detachment Commander's message. This was signed by Youssuf Kemal, Minister of Foreign Affairs. The reply was translated into English, coded and sent by radio to Stanav.

NATIONALIST MINISTER OF FOREIGN AFFAIRS'S REPLY TO ADMIRAL BRISTOL

This document is presented here at the date and time it was mentioned in the war diaries. It had originally been added to the war diary set of the Overton *on August 3, 1921.*

Admiral Bristol American High Commissioner at Constantinople,

I have the honor to advise you of the following consideration as answer in reply to your telegram to Mustafa Kemal Pacha: The information which you have received relative to the transfer to the interior of the country of women children and old Greeks of Samsun is completely in error. Absolutely no measure of this kind has been taken.

This information could have had its birth directly from the fact that the Greeks which were able to carry arms, as consequence of activities of secret Greek societies, mostly the society whose name is "PONTOS," were transported to the interior. The same fate has been borne equally by the inhabitants of some villages which had hidden the bands in the pay of the above mentioned societies and those which helped in the accomplishment of their crimes.

I can assure you that only the measures which were urgently called for by a military necessity were taken and that in no case on our side would we go further than the urgency of the justice of the obligation to guarantee the safety of the country.

I take this occasion to ask you to be so kind as to interest yourself equally in the Musselmen of all ages and of both sexes in the struggle with the incredible acts of barbarity of the Greek Army and the Greek population in all parts of our country which is occupied by our enemy.

That which happened at the end of June at Ismid* both known and

---

* Youssuf Kemal's main reference is to Greek atrocities that had taken place recently (in 1921) at cities near the Sea of Marmara near Ismid in which Greek Army commanders had either countenanced or encouraged killings and burnings of Turkish villages by local minority bands. Lieutenant Dunn, Admiral Bristol's intelligence officer, claimed that up to 2,000 Turks had been killed in these episodes.

Inexcusable as they were, these actions may have been retaliations for terrible massacres of Greek villagers in this region that had been committed in the recent and more distant past. The nature of the Turkish atrocities seen by the representatives and the troops of the Occidental Powers was only a pale reflection of the horrors which the Greeks have committed and are committing daily in the interior of Anatolia where very few come forward to witness against them.

The massacre and the "devastation" perpetrated by the Greeks either on the coast or in the interior was verified by numerous American French and other citizens, and the Occidental Press, in spite of their prejudice against us, spoke of this at length and unanimously. Consequently my Government will be grateful to you if you will have the kindness to take effective steps which will permit us to hope that the Greek atrocities will be stopped.

The Turkish nation which defends its life and independence and which fights with all kinds of aggression will be grateful to all those who will endeavor, though without success, to save some of the Turkish children and women which our enemy daily assassinate.

/s/ Youssuf Kemal
Minister of Foreign Affairs

This document, handed to Commander Bristol by the Samsun Mutasariff and then forwarded to Admiral Bristol in Constantinople, is the Nationalist reply to a telegram sent by Admiral Bristol to Mustapha Kemal and is attached to the Overton *war diary set of Aug 3, 1921. The text has been checked by reference to a set of messages sent by the* Overton, *found in National Archives RG 45 Subj. File 1911–27, Box 832, Folder #2, Samsun.*

committed in 1920 are described in Kostas Faltaits's interviews published in Greek in 1921, and only recently published in an English translation in 2016. See also Shenk, *ABSF*, 96–98, the references cited there, and, especially the conclusion recorded in footnote 36 of that chapter (to be found on 305–06), that is, Winston Churchill's judgement in *The Aftermath*, vol. 5 of the *World Crisis*, 430, "that these Greek atrocities were 'on a minor scale' when compared to the 'appalling deportations of the Greeks from the Trebizond and Samsun districts.'"

FURTHER CONTINUATION OF USS *OVERTON* WAR DIARY

July 23, 1921

. . . .

News from the front, according to Turkish information, is decidedly unfavorable to the Turks and the Turkish population seems rather discouraged and down in the mouth. It has occurred to me [that] now is a good time to investigate the answers to the following questions, and I have put this up to the Intelligence Officer of the ship and to certain sources of information on shore. The questions follow:

1. What is the attitude of the local populace and particularly of Turks of influence, towards Mustafa Kemal Pasha and towards the Angora Government as a whole?

2. What is the attitude of the Turks, as represented by local men of influence, towards bolshevism, now that they are confronted with possible defeat? Will they call on the bolsheviks for assistance other than money and material?

3. Are any steps being taken for or is there any talk of local self-government in case of the defeat of the Turks? Will they hold with the Angora Government in defeat or will they break away?

I have neglected to mention in my diary the case of the Greek, Nicholas Tetheophilon, who was received aboard the WILLIAMSON and who is now in the ST. LOUIS (mention will be found of this case in the WILLIAMSON'S diary). I reported the circumstances to the Mutasariff as directed by the Detachment Commander's memorandum.*

* The memo from Admiral Bristol likely required American naval commanders to notify the Turkish authorities of Greek swimmers who had contact with the American ships. He may have required them, further, to give the Greeks over to the Turks as they did in a later instance, which might be considered consistent with American neutrality. See later diaries of the *Sturtevant* (circa August 11–24, 1921) in which it is argued that the three young men who had then swum to and were taken aboard the *Sturtevant* and then were given over to the Turks were likely deported and murdered

The Mutasariff was inclined to make much more of this case than the circumstances warranted. He stated that he considered it very unfortunate that the affair had not been investigated before the WILLIAMSON left Samsun and that it would cause, when known, general attempts on the part of the Greeks to escape to the American destroyer who would receive them. I replied that there was no reason for its being known, unless the Mutasariff desired to give it publicity, but that in any case we did not stand ready to receive Greeks and did not anticipate any such action, but that in any case, each circumstance would be decided on its merits as this had been. The Mutasariff then stated that he would probably want to speak with me further about this matter at a future time. I replied "certainly" and that we were prepared to consider anything which the Mutasariff might propose.

July 24-27, 1921

In the next three days, the Williamson *arrived and was sent by Captain Bristol to investigate conditions in Trebizond after the reported bombardment there (see the* Williamson *Trezibond WD, July 27, 1921). Soon the* Williamson *came back to Samsun. Reports were heard that the Turkish Army at the front was in full retreat, while others claimed a new local government was being prepared in case the present government fell. No particular news was heard in the town except a call for the mobilization of a band of 300 armed Turkish men sent to the front on the morning of the twenty-seventh. Given the possible dramatic change in circumstances, Captain Bristol decided to prepare an estimate of the situation, which begins as follows:*

ESTIMATE OF SITUATION, SAMSUN, 27 JULY 1921

MISSION - To protect American lives and property in Asia-Minor, Turkey, in general and in the Samsun area in particular.

---

despite the Samsun Mutasariff's specific assurance they would receive responsible treatment.

It is uncertain how Tetheophilon ended up on the *St. Louis*, which was not at Samsun until September. See the September 21–23 personal diary of Captain William Leahy of the *St. Louis*, presented among the September war diaries, in which Leahy also mentions the young man.

FORCES OPPOSED – The Mustafa Kemal Government controls Asia-Minor, Turkey, including the Samsun area. This government is at war with the Greeks and according to recent reports, the Turkish Army has suffered serious defeat between Eskisheher and Angora. Further reports that Angora is about to be evacuated and that the Kemalist troops intend to withdraw to a line of Samsun, Amassia, Sivas, and Cesarea, giving up the capital Angora. These reports are not authentic and from sources which cannot be considered reliable, but insofar as they come from Turkish sources, they must be given some credence. Greek men-of-war, including battleship "KILKIS," are in the Black Sea and for the past several days (judging by radio) have been lying off fairly close to Samsun. Within the past month, Trebizond, Ineboli and more recently, Sinop, have been bombarded by the Greek men-of-war with the object of searching out their defenses. Samsun has not been bombarded, probably because of the presence of American destroyers and also because of the large Ottoman-Greek population.

Recently, there has been much anti-Greek movement in and around Samsun. All Greek men have been sent to the interior and Greek villages in this area have been burned. Killings and atrocities have attended this anti-Greek movement.

Numerous bands of brigands are reported in the hills surrounding Samsun. No authentication of this, but probably some truth in it.

There has been much evidence of late, that a large lawless movement exists in Samsun, who have concerned themselves almost with impunity in murder and robbery.

There are numerous Bolshevists in Samsun with no apparent business. A strong connection seems to exist between these Bolshevists and the lawless element previously mentioned.

The Mutasariff representing the Kemalist Government is not considered to be a strong character. He has been brow-beaten by the lawless element in times past and probably will not make a determined stand in any emergency.

Until recently, there have been numerous troops in and around Samsun. There is no proof, but much evidence, to show that most of these have been withdrawn and sent to the front and that now the military in this area number very few.

The rest of this "Estimate of the Situation" suggests possible courses of action should Turkish military reversals continue. As this did not occur, we omit the rest of this "Estimate"; it may be found in the Overton *war diaries of July 15-August 3, 1921.*

July 28, 1921

At 6:30 a.m., Greek men-of-war [were] sighted on the horizon. I signaled WILLIAMSON to take charge on shore and with the OVERTON got underway and stood out towards the Greeks at 6:50. The Greeks apparently [swung?] to, three ships present—"KILKIS," destroyer "PANTHER," [and a] small [converted] cruiser, name not known. I approached within half a mile and lay to. After a wait of about fifteen or twenty minutes, "KILKIS" [hoisted] international signal "Have you any messages for me?" I answered "NO". I then wrote out a wireless signal which I sent in about twenty minutes:

> "To KILKIS:
> Captain Vriacos informed me, that if bombardment of SAMSUN was intended, I would be notified in order that I might take steps to protect American lives. I am here in order that you may communicate with me if you desire".

I took this method of procedure in dealing with the Greeks for the following reasons: This was the third time that we had met the Greek [Navy] ships off Samsun harbor. I did not want to be put in a position [of] trying to stave off a bombardment of Samsun, which from a purely military point of view, is perfectly legitimate. I felt that we were in danger of compromising the dignity of the United States.

[Upon] Receipt of my message, the "KILKIS" sent the "PANTHER" close aboard the OVERTON and the Captain of the "PANTHER" came on board as boarding officer. My conversation with him was in French through interpreter. He presented the compliments of the Captain of the "KILKIS" and informed me that the Greek men-of-war would bombard the hills around Samsun to search out its defenses. I replied that there were about [thirty] Americans on shore and that I requested time to make dispositions for their safety. I informed him exactly as regards the American activities and the location of each. I further informed him that Americans would remain in the hospital and orphanages and in such other [places] as considered necessary; that there were about half the Americans not needed on shore whom I would remove to the ships and I would then move the two destroyers out of his line of fire. Captain of the "PANTHER" stated that he would transmit this information to Captain Lambros of the "KILKIS" and would give me a [reply].

Just as he was leaving, the Captain of the "PANTHER" inquired if I could give him any information about the situation of the Greeks here. I replied that I would be glad to do so and I outlined for him the general Greek situation in the town. He left the ship and boarded "KILKIS". In about half an hour I received a signal from the "KILKIS" as follows: "Thanks for your kindness. I will not act". I answered by signal: "My compliments to Captain Lambros, OVERTON returning to Samsun. Signed Bristol".

The remaining material on this date deals with two British destroyers anchoring at Samsun and contacting Captain Bristol, inquiring about the possibility of British merchant ships doing business at the harbor.

. . . .

July 30, 1921

While Bristol had offered the Mutasariff a boat so he could visit the British ships, it appears he decided not to use it. Bristol concluded that the British were likely on an inspection tour, and in fact the British destroyers soon left the harbor. Captain Bristol moved on to his discussion with the Italian count in the port.

. . . . Count Schmecchia then gave me several bits of information as follows:

That he had very reliable information that Osman Agha, on his way from Samsun to the front, had pillaged and burned every Greek village and town that he came across, killing all the Greek inhabitants that he could get his hands on. Kavak and Marsovan had both been burned. (Note: The report that Marsovan had been burned has been current in town for the past two days and is generally believed here. Just before returning to the ship tonight, I received further confirmation of this in a letter written to a Greek woman here, from Marsovan and dated four days ago. In this letter it was stated that Marsovan was still burning.)

Count Schmecchia informed me confidentially that the "REMO" had brought some Russians, bringing with them gold to the amount of three million paper pounds. He stated that he was absolutely certain of this because of certain trouble about it which the Captain of the "REMO" had had in Batoum. The money did not appear in the ship's manifest, but was handled by the Russians as baggage. He had no further information as to the consignee or destination of the money.

A party of eight Russians sailed from here a few days ago in the "REMO" for Batoum. He showed me the "REMO'S" manifest of passengers, in which it appeared that all the Russians travelled first class and that every name, without exception, was Jewish, three of them being German-Jewish names.*

He said that he had information from Tcharshamba, that all the Greek women and children had been deported from that place and that he had further information that there was constant communication between certain elements in Tcharshamba and Samsun in regard to the most favorable opportunity for an uprising and general pillage of Samsun.

I may here remark, that while I do not class the above information as reliable, with the exception of the story about the Russians and gold, that the information I received from Count Schmecchia has invariably proven good, in most cases has been absolutely accurate and in others has had a great deal of foundation in fact. . . .

July 31, 1921

Went ashore in the afternoon and joined the swimming picnic. [There] were gathered here practically all the foreigners in Samsun. I heard from several sources that a message had been received from Marsovan stating that the town was almost completely destroyed by fire. I could learn nothing regarding Americans in Marsovan. Van Toor sent a dispatch yesterday to Marsovan, asking information about the health and well-being of the Americans, so far no reply has been received. I believe that the news about Marsovan is true.

---

* The information provided here about these Russians being Jewish is perhaps meant to augment the preceding information: that considerable monetary support was being provided to the Turks by the Russians.

Incidentally, there are many references in the diaries about Russian gold arriving in Samsun, paralleling similar mentions of Russian aid to Turkey in memoirs spoken of by Göçek. She says that Russia sent both gold and armaments to the Nationalists because Russia "was intent on funding another revolution it regarded as similar to its own" (280).

Van Toor informed me today that he had received a telegram from Miss Allen in Angora, that permits would be granted [for] two Near East personnel to proceed to Harput. This is the [first] authentic case of a telegram coming through from Angora in the past three days and would indicate that Angora conditions are [getting] back to normal. I told Van Toor that even if these [visas] should come through, that I wished him to consult with me before permitting anyone to proceed to the interior. Conditions in Samsun are unchanged. Everything quiet in and about the town.

August 1, 1921

Went on shore in forenoon and found there was no particular news. Van Toor informed me he had received telegrams from Harput, Caesarea and Sivas, showing that the telegraph is working normally.

Returned to ship about noon. In the afternoon, fires were noticed in the hills, and through the glasses, four or five villages were seen to be on fire. There is a report current in Samsun, that quite [a few] of Osman Agha's men deserted on the [way] to the front and returned to the Tcharshamba plains. The fires may be the work of this band.

. . . .

August 3, 1921

Went on shore in the forenoon to collect mail and say goodbye to everyone. Saw Van Toor and was informed by him that he had received a dispatch from Miss Allen in Angora, stating that all Americans in [Mardin] were well. I told Van Toor to make every effort to get information regarding conditions in Marsovan, [and] if possible to secure permission to send a truck through to Marsovan with supplies which [NER now] has on hand for that place.

To date, I have not secured enough information to give definite answers to the questions propounded on 23 July 1921, but from the information which I have, the following is my opinion regarding each:

1. The attitude of the local populace towards the Mustapha Kemal Government, is in general antagonistic. The Angora Government maintains a strong control, and fear of this control influences all of their ideas. If they had any alternative which would insure their personal safety and the safety of their property, they would instantly break away from allegiance to Mustapha Kemal.

2. There is no distinct tendency for or against coming under the influence of the Bolshevists. This phase of the matter, however, is being constantly considered, and an expression which is frequently heard is "better the Bolsheviks than the Greeks."

3. Distinct steps are being taken for the local protection of Samsun in case of a breakdown of the Angora Government. I believe that this applies not only to Samsun, but to all population centers. . . .

While I have no definite information on the subject, I believe that in case of an attempted landing by Greek forces, that the town of Samsun will be set on fire in accordance with a deliberate plan before it will be given up to the Greeks.

U.S.S. STURTEVANT arrived at 7.00 p.m., 3 August 1921 and at 7:30 p.m., OVERTON sailed for Constantinople.

THE ATROCITIES AT MARSOVAN
–*TESTIMONY OF GERTRUDE ANTHONY AND CARL COMPTON*

Toward the conclusion of the Overton *war diary, after reports that the order for a deportation of the women and children at Samsun have been "completely in error," we hear that much of the city of Marsovan has been burned.*

Although Osman Agha was said to have been ordered to report to Angora by Nationalist officials there, he did not report there immediately. Instead he initiated a reign of terror, his men first killing, burning, and looting various villages en route to Marsovan (Yeghiayan, British Reports, *221 and* Williamson *WD, July 30, 1921) and then descending upon Marsovan itself. It would be neither the first nor the last time that Osman Agha's forces would devastate the Greeks in towns along their route (see Fotiadis, 390). Only after these would Osman report to Angora.*

A couple of Americans wrote about the Marsovan atrocities and the part Osman and his men played in them, and it is fitting to present portions of their accounts here. This is especially pertinent given that the atrocities at Marsovan might well have taken place at Samsun had the Americans' presence and protest not interfered with the Nationalist plans there.

Marsovan is a small city some sixty miles southwest from Samsun, and its American mission was then the site of Anatolia College, one of a few missionary-run colleges in Anatolia. As mentioned earlier, Anatolia College had been closed by the Turks some months back, but the NER orphanages at Marsovan were allowed to continue operating under the management of a few Americans.

NER worker Gertrude Anthony had eventually been allowed to travel from Samsun on to Marsovan to help with the orphanages at the closed American college. She and NER nurse Sara Corning joined the current Marsovan NER director Carl Compton, his wife Ruth, and another NER worker named Donald Hosford, already working at the place. Anthony wrote a detailed report about her experiences in Samsun and Marsovan, and Compton eventually would describe his experiences at Marsovan in a memoir. Excerpts from Anthony's report about the Marsovan events are included here, as well as selected passages from Compton's book.

From Gertrude Anthony's Report on Marsovan

On Monday, June thirteenth, Miss Corning and I went to Marsovan, accompanied by Ismael Haki Bey, one of our employees in Samsun. . . .

Several days later a group of men deported from Samsun was brought through Marsovan. We secured permission to have our Samsun bookkeeper spend the night with us. He reported that they had come through from Samsun to Khavza in one march of about twenty hours; that they had had all of their money and blankets and most of their clothing, rings, watches and some gold teeth stolen by the gendarmes but no life had been taken. Part of their group went on by the Amassia road, the others were being sent to the front. His was the fourth group—the first and third [of] which had some ten or twelve hundred men, he reported, had lost many men near Kavak. He said he had not seen any bodies but the smell was awful at one point on the road. This, I am satisfied, is true, for when I came out I talked with a Greek woman who said she had secretly sent an old Turkish servant to see if she could find any trace of her husband. She reported on his return, that in a valley near Kavak he had counted two hundred bodies and there were many more, but he was so he sickened he couldn't stay to count them.

In Marsovan we found the same terror. Every few days there were reports of Greeks being killed in the vineyards, until almost no Christian went out.

We heard constantly of villages being destroyed and the people "deported". As nearly as I can remember, it must have been early in July that the men from the village of Gelensin were deported and the women and children came to Marsovan for safety. A short time after, they were ordered to go back and care for their crops. They were afraid of the neighboring Turkish village. The foreman of our workers asked us to take the children into the orphanage, at least the smallest ones. We feared a little that it might make trouble for the orphanage work, but consented to take all under ten years if they came to us in such a way as not to attract attention. There were about thirty of them. We have heard that many of the mothers and older children were killed. . . .

Then on the twenty-third of July, Osman Agha's men came. On the afternoon of Sunday the twenty-fourth, Osman Agha came personally. It was reported that they began to rob shops and houses as soon as he came. We gave no gate-passes that afternoon for our workers to leave the Mission compound. We saw the Laz passing up and down our street all afternoon and did not have our usual Sunday night sing for fear of attracting their attention, but not even then did we anticipate any real danger. About half past nine we heard screaming in the Greek quarter which is just north and east of the compound. Someone reported that the Laz were robbing the house of an employee which was just over the wall from one of the boys' dormitories. I went down to keep the children quiet and watched the sacking of the house. Everything was ripped up in search of valuables—clothing, rugs, the cloth covers of yorgans [quilts] and anything of any value that was not too bulky, was piled on the wagon of the house owner, his horse was hitched to it and they drove it off.

While we were watching, terrified screaming of many women came from near our house. Hohannes, our foreman, whose family had come into the compound early in the evening, had allowed Greek women and children to stay in his house. There were about forty of them and the Laz had found them. Many of them found refuge for a few minutes in Saduk Bey's garden, which is just across the street from ours. But Saduk had them gathered together and he himself kicked them out into the street. Many ran up to the main gate of the compound and begged to be admitted. Mr. Compton had run up, on the inside to let them in, but the gendarme whom the Gendarme-Commandant had sent to help guard the compound, would not permit it. Mr. Compton said surely the government would not prevent our giving refuge in case of lawless mob action, but he shrugged his shoulders and said, "The Government knows." During the argument, many slipped in and were hidden behind buildings before he could stop them.

We organized a big-boy guard and patrolled the walls of the compound. Many people came in over the walls at various low places. Turks whose gardens adjoin the compound are said to have assisted them over for a price. Screaming and crying kept up all night, mainly in the Greek quarter, but also in the Armenian district, to some extent. Just at dawn the crying was worse. Women who had hidden in the shrubbery were discovered. During the night there had been much inquiry on the street for both our foreman and pharmacist. The foreman went out to Saduk Bey's to find out what was wanted, and came back safely. He deliberately put himself in danger because he had heard them threaten to search the [college] compound for him.

Monday morning the Police commissar and two gendarmes (not chetehs) came to the gate and took our foreman, our master of the tailor shop, and our former bath master. We never saw them again. The gendarme commandant's brother said the foreman was beaten to death. They asked for our pharmacist but he heard of it and hid. No American was present when they were taken. All of these were Armenians.

During Monday things were somewhat quiet. Some people crept into the compound at one corner or another. They said the chetehs had said to them, "Why do you cry? We are good to you. Tomorrow others will come who will kill. We are only taking your money and the Americans will give you more." This first group of chettahs left on Monday and others came. . . .

Monday night there was less prolonged screaming, but there was shooting, and those who came in over the wall reported much killing with knives. . . .

At about ten o'clock [Saduk Bey] appeared at the compound office with our man, Ismael Haki Bey, who said he had rescued him from prison, and asked us to take Osman Agha and some officers to Chorum. We debated some time, but thought the chance to get Osman Agha out of town quickly, was worth the risk. Mr. Hosford got the truck ready, but before he started, the request was made for us to go to Angora instead of Chorum, so we got ready for the longer trip. I will state here, out of chronological order, that Mr. Hosford got but little beyond Chorum. In spite of promises not to delay they stayed in Chorum until Saturday, then loaded up too heavily, cracked the front spring, and finally permitted Mr. Hosford to return. He arrived Saturday night.

About noon on Tuesday the wife of one of the wealthiest of the Armenian merchants came over the wall. She said that Saduk Bey with one of the Laz' leaders came to her house and said they would give her twelve hours to find her husband and Hyrabed, the manager of the Ibranosian store, and send them out of the compound. A servant told where they had gone. Also, some Turkish women sent word that the chettah leaders threatened to kill them and search the compound if three women who had been entrusted to them were not sent out. One of these was our Armenian Professor's wife, the others I have forgotten. We found them all, and the result of the conference was that they went out. The Professor's wife returned on Saturday, the two other women we never heard of again and the two men were reported killed soon after they went out. . . .

Tuesday night there was much shooting and the house of a prosperous Armenian merchant was burned. There was terrible screaming at intervals all night, in the direction of the French school which stands to the south of the compound, in the Armenian district.

Wednesday, while we were at lunch, word came that there was a fire just outside the compound near the girls' school. We went out and found four separate and distinct fires, one just two houses away from our wall. One was the Armenian Professor's house—he was probably burned in it. . . . It is said that women who tried to save things from their houses were shot or beaten and taken away. One old white hatted woman who had been a teacher in the college for years, went out to see if she could save anything, and came back badly bruised, in the custody of a gendarme who demanded money before he would release her. Her grandnephew, a young boy, was brought to the gate by a gendarme and offered to her for twenty bank notes. She gave it and they took boy and money. People who came into the compound on Saturday said that dead bodies were thrown into the fire, that people escaping were shot and that some live people were seen, being thrown in. The fire burned all Wednesday night. Thursday there was a heavy rain which left only smoldering ruins. It is said four hundred houses were burned.

Wednesday afternoon the chetehs left.

Wednesday night, for the first time, we heard crying and screaming and some shooting at the barracks to the west of the compound. Thursday night there was more crying. We heard men's voices outside the walls, and people walking up the road past the compound, toward the hills. There was shooting some time afterward in the same direction. We were told that a hundred and twenty men were shot just beyond the compound and thirty more just in the hills.

Friday night women cried and screamed frequently at the barracks. On Saturday and Sunday the Armenians were released and some allowed to come in the compound. The Greek women and children were sent to [....] and Hadji Keuy, two villages about fifteen miles west, and the men were sent to Amassia. There were said to be only fourteen men of both nationalities. The people who came to us were in wretched condition. We had not been allowed to send food to them and they had had no food and little water for three days, except a few who had bought bread at ten times the usual price, and water at fifty piastres for a small cup. At the end of three days they received a donation of one loaf each from a kindly Turkish merchant. On the second day they had been driven down to a fountain where they all drank. Their stories were essentially the same. They had been taken to two places—a big house and the French school. If there had been men in the group they were usually taken ahead and either not seen again or found dead in a room of the first house. Later, the women were gathered in the French school. All night the chetehs moved them from room to room and up and down stairs. In this way, they prevented the mothers from concealing their daughters and they picked and chose as they liked. Some of the prettiest were taken away, others were raped and left. . . .

At the barracks some of the gendarmes were as brutal as the chetehs had been. We are told that most of the young women and girls who did not get into the compound Sunday afternoon were raped, and some <u>many</u> times. We know certainly, that most of those who came to us afterwards were in fearful condition.

In the latter part of the week (I cannot remember whether it began Thursday or Friday) they began to carry out the dead to the Christian cemetery across the little mill stream. I do not know how many cartloads there were, for I watched it only at times. They dug five big pits and at least one load was dumped into a shallow hole by the steep roadside, because the horses couldn't pull the load. Through glasses, I saw them strip the bodies, and discovered that they were not all dead. It is impossible to say how many were killed, but I think about a thousand or half of the Christian population is not too big an estimate.

From Thursday, through all the next week, and as I remember it, even longer, the roads were alive with villagers carrying off loot. Stoves, pots, windows, doors, tiles and masses of bundles were carried by donkeys, carts, and men, women and children. Cartload after cartload, for days, went up the hill past our house. Many stopped at Saduk Bey's house before going on. I have been told by several Armenian women that the Turks of Marsovan did more killing and looting than the chetehs. . . .

After seeing these things in Marsovan, I feel certain that a similar plan had been made for Samsun, and that it failed of execution, I am sure was due partly to your protest [this report of Anthony's was originally sent to Admiral Bristol] and partly to the combined action of the influential Turks [of Samsun] who were brought together by Mr. MacDowell's urging and their fear of losing American capital.

From my knowledge of one small corner of the situation, I am convinced that the plan of the Young Turk Committee in 1915 has not been abandoned by these Turks who are now in power, and that unless there is some unforeseen intervention the Christians in Asiatic Turkey are doomed. . . .

Everything points to a settled policy of extermination. . . .

A. Gertrude Anthony

Gertrude Anthony submitted this report (dated Nov 1, 1921) to Admiral Bristol originally. Then on December 12, she submitted a copy in person to the State Department in Washington, D.C. A cover note indicates that Admiral Bristol had not forwarded the report to the State Department. The State Department copy is filed under 867.4016/448.

Events During the Marsovan Massacre as Written by Carl Compton

Carl C. Compton had been a teacher, athletic director, and YMCA advisor at Anatolia College before the college was closed by the Turks. Then, with his wife, Ruth, he oversaw the NER orphanage work, which the Turks had allowed to continue. He would spend the rest of his career at Anatolia College when it was reopened at Thessaloniki in Greece, where it still exists today. Compton was president of the institution from 1950 to 1958.

Our rather isolated peace on the campus one day came to an abrupt end. Rumors began to filter in about a company of Turkish soldiers under the command of Topal (Lame) Osman, who were reported to be coming our way, brutally devastating the Christian communities through which they passed. One Sunday evening, late in July . . . we had just gone to bed when we heard in the street below us the shattering of glass, the crashing of doors being broken open, and piercing screams. We dressed in great haste and I ran to the college gate outside of which was a crowd of crying women and children. We threw open the gate and they came rushing in. A few minutes later we saw soldiers coming up the street and we slammed the gate shut just in time. They pounded on the gate, demanding that it be opened, but I slipped out through a little side door and told them that this was American property. To my astonishment and relief they saluted and said they had been given orders to stay out of American property.

For the next four days and nights, we lived in constant fear. The days were fairly quiet, but the nights were filled with terror. All night long we could hear the sound of running feet, the breaking open of doors, the screams, and occasional gun-fire. We five Americans made no attempt to go to bed at all but took turns snatching such sleep as we could. We organized the older boys into a day and night patrol and stationed them at intervals all around the campus walls. We Americans distributed ourselves at easily accessible spots. The boys had the delicate task of ascertaining whether people they heard outside the wall were fleeing Christians, or Turks bent on murder and loot. If they were Christians, that is Armenians or Greeks, the boys would help them over the wall as quietly as possible and lead them to shelters that had been made ready for such cases. If they were Turks, the boy would rush to a nearby American who would go to the place where the invaders were trying to climb over the wall and tell them: "This is American property." Invariably the Turks would reply that they had orders to stay out of American property and would go on their way.

In the city the killing, raping, and looting continued. The Greek and Armenian men and older boys were dragged from their homes and marched away, never to be seen again. Sometimes groups would be driven up the hill past the college, and whenever I could, I would open the gate in hopes that some of them would be able to slip inside. One night a few men did, but they were seen by their guards and before I could get the gate closed some soldiers with drawn guns rushed in and forced the men back onto the road. . . . On the fourth day of the massacre the Christian area of the city was set on fire. . . . During the fire a group of about thirty haggard looking women appeared at our gate led by a young Turkish officer who had been a student at the college. We found a place for them in our already crowded buildings and afterwards heard their story. They had been driven from their homes and herded into a school building which soon caught fire. Thinking this was the end, they made no effort to escape and tried to find comfort in singing hymns. Just at this time, [this] young Turkish officer came along and when he realized what was happening, he was so furious that the surrounding crowd gave way before his wrath. He threw open the door and shouted for the women to come out. At first they hesitated, thinking it would just prolong the agony. But when he shouted, "I'll take you to the college," their courage was revived, and they came rushing out, just before the floor of the room in which they were imprisoned collapsed.

During these days, we added about twenty-five babies to the refugees on the campus. At night, some families succeeded in escaping from their homes and fled to nearby hills, passing the college on their way. As they felt little babies could not survive the uncertain days ahead, and that they would be safer with us, they wrapped them in blankets and left them outside our walls. In the mornings, we would gather them up and take them to our "Baby House." (We often wondered why the whole family did not take refuge with us.) A few of the babies had names attached but most did not. We never heard from the families and never knew who they were. Later, I joined with a Turkish judge in providing each unknown infant with a certificate, giving a name and a birthdate. . . .

Anatolia College faculty, with x's marking those who were killed by the Turks. Carl Compton is shown in the right center of the front row. *Permission from Anatolia College Archives & Special Collections.*

During these days, we received word that six of our Greek teachers and two students had been taken to the provincial capital in Amassia, condemned as traitors, and hanged in the public square. Mr. Pavlides, pastor of the local Greek Protestant Church, suffered the same fate. A Turkish friend told us that at his execution the rope broke, and he fell to the ground. He jumped to his feet shouting, "You see, Allah himself says I am not guilty." His executioners paid no attention to his pleas and produced another rope. . . .

The presence of the refugees on the campus was known to the authorities and I received an order to give them a list of all the men. I called the men together and explained the situation. They agreed that I had no choice but to give such a list, but they asked me to delay answering for a few days so that those who were afraid to have their names known could slip away to the mountains. Most of them stayed, but a few chose to escape. One Greek with his two sons, who had been students in the college, had fled from their village just before it was completely destroyed. They were afraid to have their names on the list. Late that night we took them to a remote spot on campus, gave them some food, a blanket each, a little money and boosted them over the wall.

We often wondered what became of them but never knew until many years later. One day a middle-aged man appeared at my office in Thessaloniki. He said, "You of course don't recognize me, but I can describe an incident which will identify me." He then described in detail the night I had boosted him over the campus wall in Marsovan. They had somehow survived and finally reached Greece. . . .

Late in July 1922, the Near East Relief succeeded in getting permission to send new workers to Marsovan. As soon as they were familiarized with the work, Ruth and I left for Constantinople. Soon after we arrived I called on Admiral Bristol, who was acting U.S. High Commissioner, to tell him about events in Marsovan. To my surprise, I found that he was very skeptical about the reports of a massacre. He asked me: "Did you, with your own eyes, see anyone being killed?" "No," I replied, "but all night long for three nights we heard gun shots, crashing doors, and screams which suddenly ceased. And desperate people came fleeing to the campus sobbing with words of the terrible things that were happening. In the mornings we saw wagons hauling dead bodies to be buried in mass graves in a cemetery across the valley. On the last day of the massacres, we watched the Christian section of the city being burned."

The High Commissioner and some other Americans who had never been outside Constantinople or Smyrna had great sympathy for the Turks. They said the minorities had always been disloyal and would welcome a chance to revolt. It is undoubtedly true that the minorities had no feeling of loyalty to the Turkish government, but the way they had been treated gave them no reason for feeling otherwise. . . .

This passage is from pp. 36-41 of Carl C. Compton's memoir, The Morning Cometh: 45 Years with Anatolia College, © 2002 Trustees of Anatolia College. *Used with special thanks to the Anatolia College Archives & Special Collections, respectively.*

DEPORTATIONS CONTINUE . . . AS DOES GREAT FEAR OF THEM

After the Nationalist Foreign Minister issued a response to Admiral Bristol saying that the information having to do with deporting the noncombatants was "completely in error," one would have thought that the fears of Greek women would have diminished. But they did not, and for good reason.

Reports in the war diaries note continued efforts by an anti-Greek faction among the Turks in the city to deport all the women and children in Samsun (Williamson *WD, Aug. 8, 1921). Additionally, the diaries report how women and children from burned villages seeking food and shelter within Samsun were deported regularly, along with boys and older men. At one point it was said there were 4,000 women and children in the city who would be deported soon, and apparently all these people too—none of them, one assumes, residents of Samsun proper—were also sent out.*

Beyond that, news came in from Bafra of no fewer than 6,000 women and children being deported from there. Tobacco merchant William King received several reports of plans for a Bafra deportation (Sturtevant *WD, Sept. 1 and 5) and then reports of its actual implementation* (Sturtevant *WD, Sept. 20), along with related occurrences of robbery and rape* (Sturtevant *WD, Sept. 21). One prominent Turk from Bafra told King that "the things which had happened made him ashamed to be a Turk. That not only had the women and children been murdered and subjected to various kinds of torture but that the women had been violated"* (Williamson *WD, Sept. 28). Conditions worsened even more at Bafra after that,* *amounting to a massacre of almost all the refugees there except for some women temporarily kept for pleasure—this according to a survivor of the massacre (*Williamson *WD, Oct. 5).*

Earlier in the diaries, we read of Lieutenant Dunn making light of the fears of some Greek women who were preparing to poison themselves rather than suffer Turkish rape and murder. However, after the burning of Smyrna in September 1922, the American State Department received a letter from an Italian man thanking the American Navy for helping bury his sisters at Smyrna following their suicides by poison to avoid rape and murder (Shenk, ABSF, *221-22). In fact, what the Samsun women feared became the actual fate of many minority women during the terrible debacle at Smyrna. But a reading of these war diaries suggests that such things were already taking place in the Pontus region.*

So it is no wonder that the Greek women in Samsun remained terrified. Compared to such terror, other matters found in the upcoming diaries seem mere footnotes. For example, there were reports that the Turkish government was requisitioning forty percent of the stores from all businesses, including charitable organizations like the Near East Relief, all this to aid the war effort, and that several more young Greek men had swum to the American ships . . . only to have some of them given over by an American ship captain to the Turks!

Captain Haas of the Sturtevant, *hearing of the latter decision by the captain of the* Williamson, *comments in his August 16, 1921 war diary, "I am certain that in so doing we shall send them to certain death."*

In making this prediction, Captain Haas seems much more in touch with the state of Turkish officialdom than the other navy captain currently in the port or than the adamant admiral in Constantinople whose directive had probably provoked the Williamson's *captain to take this action. The verbal promises of the current Mutasariff to treat the Greek lads well and fairly and keep them in Samsun are reported in the diaries, along with that man's outright denials of these very promises a few days later. After that, the three Greeks are brutally deported, and it can be assumed they were soon "tortured and ruthlessly butchered in cold blood" as Captain Haas had predicted.*

The consensus of the ship captains present at Samsun during some part of this period (which included not only three destroyer captains but also Captain William Leahy, the Commanding Officer of the cruiser St. Louis, *which large combatant the admiral sent to Samsun for a few days) is that a further large deportation of noncombatants was likely to take place before long with the aim of final extermination of the local Greeks. However, somehow no one among these four officers was able to summon the conviction or rhetorical power that Commander Arthur LeRoy Bristol's earlier handwritten missive to Admiral Bristol had possessed. But any action at all on the part of one or more of these officers would probably not have been enough, at this point, to convince the admiral to do anything further about the terror now facing both the Greek women and children and elderly of Samsun proper and the Greek women and children from villages near Samsun. Many of the latter groups were being sent inland even as these specific war diaries were written, and myriads of Greeks and Armenians throughout Pontus from Bafra south were facing similar circumstances.*

As we will see, Captain Leahy says in his personal diary that he hopes that his arguments at Samsun about the deploring mistreatment of noncombatants have "induced the Turkish Commander to postpone indefinitely the proposed deportation of Greek women and children. . . ." However, not only will this reported plea of his fall on deaf Turkish ears, but apparently nothing Leahy says in his formal report to the admiral nor anything the ship captains themselves say—either in personal protest to the Mutasariff or by way of reports in their war diaries, which the admiral would soon read—will awaken any real sympathy in America's High Commissioner in Constantinople. Despite hearing of the desperate situation of the remaining Greeks in or near Samsun, the admiral apparently chose not to bother Mustafa Kemal any further. (If the admiral had hoped to awe or daunt the Turks by his action of sending the relatively big guns of the cruiser St. Louis *to Samsun, that maneuver would also have no deterring effect.)*

*Finally, it is true that one of the ship captains in the diaries will say, roughly, that he cannot see how the Turks can do much else than deport the remaining Greeks in or near Samsun given the various attacks by the Greek chettahs in the area and the help given to the Greek chettahs by the Greek women and children in the city (*McFarland *WD of Sept. 3, 1921). However, all these things—the initial creation of the Greek bandit groups, the need of food and other resources for all the displaced villagers in and out of Samsun, the need of Greek male escapees or bandits who sometimes entered the city to attain resources, and the continuing support of such Greek partisan groups by the remaining noncombatant Greek population in Samsun—all these were circumstances mainly of the Turks' own making.*

USS *WILLIAMSON*, LIEUT. COMMANDER J.C. CUNNINGHAM WAR DIARY SET FOR JULY 26-AUGUST 16, 1921

Upon arriving at Samsun, Williamson *was immediately sent on to Trebizond by Captain Bristol and submitted a separate report about that brief visit. When* Williamson *returned to Samsun, rough seas inhibited it from lowering a boat for a day. On July 29, three Greek warships arrived, which seemed to require taking the American civilians to safety—but the Greek ships quickly departed. In his war diary, Captain Cunningham notes that "[t]here was practically no excitement ashore, the people evidently thinking that the Greeks will do nothing so long as the American destroyers are here."*

After describing all this brief though insignificant flutter, which we have quickly summarized, the diaries report a few new rumors.

. . . .

July 30, 1921

Heard well founded rumors from several different sources that Osman Agha, who has received orders to proceed with his forces to the front, had destroyed two villages enroute to Marsovan and had killed all the Greeks in them and that he had also destroyed a number of houses and had killed a number of Greeks in Marsovan.

. . . .

August 1, 1921

At different times through the day observed three villages burning, all to the eastward of and only a few miles from Samsun. Went ashore at 10:00 with Commander Bristol. Saw the tobacco people and Haidar Bey. Nothing new. Late this afternoon, my Commissary Officer observed newsboys selling communiqués in town. Abdullah, the Contractor, reported that in these, Mustapha Kemal and his staff announced that the Greeks were in the town of Tehair Khan, four hours from Angora; that he (Mustafa Kemal) and his staff were withdrawing to the gates of the city; and that the Turks were going to make a very determined stand. This message implored the Turks to be confident as they were sure to deliver a crushing blow in view of the fact that the Greeks had advanced so rapidly that they were not only exhausted, but had also depleted their ammunition.

. . . .

August 3, 1921

. . . STURTEVANT stood in and anchored at 7:00 p.m. The OVERTON left shortly thereafter.

. . . .

August 7, 1921

. . . Went swimming with the American Colony. Haidar Bey told Johnson that the Italian destroyer "POERIO" came in here as an escort for the Italian S.S. AVENTINO, and that the AVERTINO brought in a quantity of ammunition furnished by the Italian Government.

August 8, 1921

Went ashore at 9:30 with Captain Haas. Had a long talk with Count Schmecchia in French, Ensign Robbins of the STURTEVANT acting as interpreter. Count Schmecchia is extremely pessimistic. He considers the situation here very critical. He stated that he had received information from several sources which he considered reliable to the effect that there are two factions in Samsun: one composed of the military, the unemployed, and a few fanatical Moslems who desire to deport all Greek women and children; the other composed of the law-abiding and local influential Turks who are opposed to this deportation. Count Schmecchia further stated that the deportation of Greek women and children was likely to take place at any time and without previous warning; that it is the policy of the Angora Government to exterminate the Greeks; and that although the local influential Turks are opposed to any further deportation, they would not dare attempt to prevent such for fear of being brought before the "Tribune of Justice" [the Nationalist "Independence Tribunal"] which is supposed to meet here very soon.

Schmecchia went on to say that 20,000 troops were concentrated at Ineboli; that Nureddin Bey is expected in Samsun at any moment; that three regiments have been ordered here, one of which has already arrived; and that both the military and the civilian population not only expect, but greatly fear, a landing on this coast by the Greeks. I am convinced that the Turks do believe that the Greeks are going to attempt a landing along this coast and have made what preparations they can to forestall it. I also think that a landing by the Greeks would precipitate a general massacre of the local Greeks. . . .

Villages could be seen burning to the eastward today. Reported to be Tsar-chamba and Tekekeuy. . . .

. . . .

August 11, 1921

The Mutasariff has just issued an order, which originated in Angora, directing all business houses in Samsun to submit a list by tomorrow evening of the amounts of certain articles (there is a long list of these articles enumerated by name covering practically everything serviceable for military purposes) which they have on hand. This order states that the government is going to commandeer 40% of the articles enumerated. Tobacco is not included in the list, but as oils and merchandise are included, both the Standard Oil Co. and the American Foreign Trade may be affected. The order states that anyone failing to submit a list by tomorrow evening will be considered a traitor and will be dealt with accordingly. So this order has caused much anxiety among the local merchants as it will practically ruin many of them. . . .

August 12, 1921

Last night about 2:00 a.m. three Greek refugees (George Konstintinou, John Arristide, and Lazaros Geofirides), were rescued from the water alongside the STURTEVANT. They were in an exhausted condition, having swum from a point outside the limits of the town. Four originally started for the ship, but it is not known what became of the fourth one. They were brought to the WILLIAMSON this morning and are being held on board pending instructions from STANAV. . . .

These Greeks have been hiding in the hills for such a long time and are besides so ignorant that they are unable to give any intelligent or reliable information. They were driven out of Samsun on July 6 with about 800 other Greeks and escaped into the hills. Most of them have been killed. They stated that practically all Greek villages had been burned and that the Turks generally put the women and children in a house and then burned it up. . . .One of these refugees was wounded in the arm about two weeks ago, having been shot by a Turkish soldier. The wound was infected but with proper treatment will heal all right.

The next paragraph deals with the order for property confiscation and also the American officers' desire to meet with Nureddin Pasha, then in Samsun. There follows an interview with an Armenian doctor just arrived from Mardin.

This doctor, who is enrolled in the Turkish Army, was granted leave to come to Samsun in order to sign papers for the sale of some property here, which the Turks are anxious to get. He passed though Marsovan after Osman Agha and his band had finished their operations there. For about five days, Osman Agha and his followers were engaged in murdering Greeks and destroying their property. About 400 houses were burned and several hundred Greeks killed, including women and children. The Valli [Governor] of that Province, having heard of this, immediately proceeded to Marsovan, stopped Osman Agha's operations, released a number of Greeks which were under guard, and reported the affair to Angora, whereupon Osman Agha and his forces were ordered to proceed to Angora.

August 13, 1921

Unable to get the Mutasariff to arrange a meeting with Nureddin Pasha, the ship captains get their contractor Abdullah to intercede, and the contractor is able to schedule an appointment for the officers with him.

Captain Haas and I called at 3:00 o'clock, Ensign Robbins of the STURTEVANT acting as interpreter in French. Nureddin Pasha was extremely frank and courteous throughout the interview—surprisingly different from any other Turk whom I have met. He appears to be both intelligent and clever.

. . . [The] General asked for my private opinion as to the probability of the Greeks landing on this coast. I replied that I considered that it depended entirely upon the conditions at the front and that, since I knew nothing about those conditions, I was not even able to express an opinion. He then stated that he understood the American ships had probably prevented the bombardment of Samsun and did not wish to see the place bombarded; that even though the people feared a bombardment, he would like to see Samsun bombarded in order to accustom the inhabitants to the firing of guns; and that he hoped the American ships would do nothing to prevent a bombardment.

I replied that we were entirely neutral in this matter; that we were here solely for the purpose of protecting American lives and property;

that in going out to meet these Greek ships it was with that end in view; and that, although the question of embarking the Americans in case of a bombardment had been taken up with both the civil and military authorities, no definite answer had been received. He stated that the Americans would not be allowed to be embarked since there were various other foreigners here and no discrimination could be made. . . .

I believe that Nureddin Pasha and all the Turks here feel that the presence of Americans in Samsun is an assurance against a bombardment and are consequently determined that they shall remain, and that his expressed desire for a bombardment was bluff. If he really does desire that this place be bombarded by the Greeks, it is most likely [from] a desire for a pretext to exterminate the Greeks.

Nureddin and Captain Haas then traded speculations as to why the British destroyers had recently come to the port, Nureddin commenting incidentally that the Turks hated the British. The visit ended this way:

Nureddin Pasha inquired particularly into the antecedents of all Americans, and was told that they were all of Anglo-Saxon extraction except Mrs. King, who was Greek.

On several occasions he expressed his admiration for America and spoke of the friendship existing between America and Turkey.

August 14 and 15, 1921

The war diary set of the Williamson *ends with reports that Nureddin had proceeded on to Amassia and that three Italian families of the Greek faith had recently been deported in accord with Nureddin's order to deport all people of Greek faith.*

August 16, 1921

. . . .

Went ashore with Captain Haas at 8:45. . . . I told the Mutasariff that I had been trying to see him for the past four days. . . . I stated that three Greeks had swum to the STURTEVANT and were rescued from the water in an exhausted condition about 2:30 a.m. on Friday, and that, in order to show our good faith, I wished to turn them over to him but requested his written assurance for their safety in as far as political offenses were concerned. At first, Heidar Bey [the interpreter] evidently did not hear the word "written" and the Mutasariff replied that he would gladly give me his word of honor that no harm would come to them, but that, like the other Greek men, they would have to be deported to the interior. He then entered into a discussion about this, stating that the ships would be swamped with refugees and asked if it would not be much better to refuse to receive them at all. Upon [my] replying that these men were so exhausted that it was necessary to pull one of them out of the water and that the only humane thing to do was to receive them, the Mutasariff suggested that they be sent ashore in a boat. He went on to say that the ship would be filled with bandits, both Turk and Greek, as well as other refugees, once this was known, and tried to exact a promise not to receive any more. I replied that I saw no reason why this should be known . . . I could not make a promise not to receive them; and that each individual case would have to be decided upon its own merits.

When the question of turning over these refugees was again taken up, Heidar Bey upon grasping that a written assurance was desired, immediately advised me that the Mutasariff would never give his written assurance and would undoubtedly feel that his word was being questioned if I asked it. Heidar Bey suggested that I request that these men be left in Samsun. I replied that I was in no way questioning the Mutasariff's word and did not wish to leave such an impression under any circumstances but that I desired a written assurance in order that I might include it in my report to Admiral Bristol. When this was communicated to the Mutasariff, he refused to give a written assurance and after some discusssion, agreed that if these three refugees were turned over to him:

(a) That he guaranteed, upon his word of honor, their personal safety in so far as political offenses were concerned.

(b) That they will remain in Samsun.

(c) That the Commanding Officer of the station ship at Samsun is at liberty to see them any time he desires.

(d) That should Admiral Bristol not approve of this agreement that he, the Mutasariff, will return these refugees to one of the ships if it is so desired.

After more discussion, the Mutasariff said that we should settle this as friend to friend and wished them turned over to him merely upon his verbal assurance for their safety. . . . So I felt that, although the message from the Detachment Commander had directed that these refugees be turned over on the Mutasariff's writtten assurance for their safety, to insist upon such written assurance or to postpone this matter any longer would only result in antagonizing the local Turkish authorities and diminishing the few privileges with the Americans now enjoy. . . .

The refugees were sent to the STURTEVANT to be turned over to the local authorities at 3:00 p.m. . . .

Collected the mail, returned to the ship and sailed at 2:30 for Constantinople.

USS *STURTEVANT,* LIEUT. COMMANDER E.G. HAAS WAR DIARY SET FOR AUGUST 2-25, 1921

Sturtevant *had departed Constantinople for Samsun on the second, but little that is substantive was reported on the first three days of his visit. Captain Haas does comment that the Americans ashore are disgusted with the general situation and are ardently hoping the Greek-Turk conflict will end soon, not caring which side wins. At the same time, Haas is convinced that the detention of passports ("vesicas") for Near East Relief personnel, which keeps them for weeks or even sometimes months from traveling on to their inland stations, is deliberate and "is the direct result of [the Turks'] recently adopted policy of not allowing foreigners to enter the interior"* (Sturtevant *WD, Aug. 4).*

August 6, 1921

WILLIAMSON and STURTEVANT at Samsun. Went ashore at 11:00 a.m. with Commanding Officer, WILLIAMSON. Met Abdullah on dock who informed us that five Russians had arrived from Sevastopol with considerable gold with which to purchase flour. . . . [Count Schmecchia] appeared to be rather apprehensive as to the immediate and further safety of the Italian subjects (thirty-five in number), who are residents of Samsun. He told us that he had impressed upon the Commanding Officer of the Italian destroyer R.N. POERIA the imperative necessity of keeping an Italian destroyer here permanently. Was informed by Near East personnel that a commission of three Turks headed by Nureddin Pasha with full plenipotentiary powers had been appointed to Samsun by the Angora Government. It is feared that the leading Turks in Samsun (eighty-five in number), who strongly opposed the threatened deportation of the Greek women and children and who previously opposed the deportation of the Greek men are to be tried and hanged. This organization of Turks is regarded by Angora as of a revolutionary character.

August 7, 1921

No apparent change in conditions ashore. Officers from WILLIAMSON and STURTEVANT joined the American colony in picnic ashore. Was informed by Abdullah that Kemal Pasha has been appointed Commander-in-Chief of the Turkish forces for a period of three months. It is rumored that preparations are being made to move the seat of Nationalist Government to Kaissarye.

August 8, 1921

WILLIAMSON and STURTEVANT in Samsun. Went ashore with Commanding Officer of WILLIAMSON AT 9:30 a.m. Called on Count Schmecchia with whom a lengthy conversation ensued in French, Ensign T.H. Robbins, U.S. Navy, acting as interpreter. Information conveyed to us had for the most part been derived from Shefick Aveni (this name has probably been spelled incorrectly) who was formerly Military Governor of Samsun district and is now the leader of what is regarded as the law-abiding and anti-Kemal party in Samsun. Shefick Aveni is exerting his influence through his newspaper which is printed here, his outstanding slogan being "Anatolia for the Anatolians." He declares that the present ruler, Kemal Pasha, is from Saloniki and is showing favoritism to a very strong party of ex-Saloniki Jews who, disgruntled at the capture of their city by the Greeks, are attempting to rule Anatolia for their own selfish purposes. Shefick Aveni's main argument and complaint is that Kemal Pasha has taken their men and money and has given them nothing in return. The following information was obtained:

Three days ago a move to deport the Greek women and children was made by the local citizens (a party composed of influential Moslem fanatics, soldiers and Turks out of work) in favor of deportation. Though not then approved by the authorities, the matter has not been dropped. Shefick Aveni is of the opinion that the threatened deportation will be carried out ultimately, inasmuch as it is the recognized policy of the Angora Government to exterminate the Greek strain by any means possible; and that owing to possible interference and protest, whether on the part of Americans or local law-abiding citizens, the deportation will take place without any preliminary warning, other than the direct order to leave immediately, which order will be given probably during the night.

Kemal Pasha would do anything to keep in power, even going so far as to import Russian money and Bolsheviki troops, thus making the Bolsheviks his subservient weapon. The abdication or murder of Kemal Pasha is anticipated.

Nureddin Pasha is expected here any moment. He is the rival of Kemal himself and is regarded as a very brutal man, and the instigator of most of the atrocities committed in Anatolia. . . .

Osman Agha, the leader of the Outlaws and Bandits is expected to return to Samsun and according to Shefik Aveni his return will be resisted by the law-abiding citizens. Osman Agha's parting words were if he returned and found a single christian here he would hold the Turks in power responsible.*

The above information which cannot be regarded as well authenticated information is nevertheless of sufficient trustworthiness to merit consideration. Due allowance must of course be made for the Count's emotional nature and personal prejudice which sometimes, but by no means always, colors his remarks. I have, on the whole, found the Count's information to be fairly correct.

. . . .

August 11, 1921

WILLIAMSON and STURTEVANT at Samsun. No change in general condition other than the fact that Nureddin Pasha and assistants have arrived. Learned today that Osman Agha while on his way to Angora stopped at Kavak long enough to kill all Greek women and children and defenseless old Greek men whom he found in the town. About 2:30 a.m., three naked Greeks swam to the ship. They were dragged out of the water physically exhausted and one of the party collapsed upon reaching the deck and passed into a state of semi-unconsciousness. They, being unable to converse in any language other than the Greek language, were unable to give us any information. They were delivered to the Commanding Officer, U.S.S. WILLIAMSON this morning.

. . . .

August 13, 1921

We have omitted Commander Haas's account of the meeting with Nureddin Pasha, which is very similar to the Williamson *account.*

. . . .

August 15, 1921

The rumor about the Greek deportation still exists. Nureddin Pasha told the local Turks officially that because the Americans persisted in protesting against the deportations, he or the central government (he did not specify which) had requested that the Americans themselves

* Commander Bristol said above that he believed the current Mutasariff was terrified of Osman Agha. If this is what Osman had said, no wonder.

deport the Greek women and children to a place of safety; but that the Americans refused to do this. It would appear that Nureddin Pasha is attempting to disclaim, in advance, responsibility for the deportations, should they occur, and especially to conciliate the Turks who opposed it.

Haidar Bey no longer enjoys the confidence of the local authorities and it is thought that he has lost his position as official censor. During the afternoon Commanding Officer of the WILLIAMSON and myself called on the Mutasariff and Military Commander to pay our respects. . . . Was notified by Commanding Officer of WILLIAMSON that he had received orders to proceed to Constantinople and would sail tomorrow morning.

August 16, 1921

WILLIAMSON and STURTEVANT at Samsun.

The question of the disposition of the three Greek refugees now on the WILLIAMSON was taken up with the Mutasariff. Captain Cunningham vainly endeavored to carry out the Detachment Commander's wishes in this matter but did not wholly succeed. The Mutasariff assured Captain Cunningham that he would assume full responsibility for the safety of the Greek refugees and would see no harm is done them. He refused to give his written assurance for their personal safety, inasmuch he had given his word of honor that he will afford them suitable and adequate protection which pledge he deemed sufficient. They will remain in Samsun and the Commanding Officer of the Station Ship will be at liberty to see them any time he so desires. The Mutasariff further stated that the immunity from punishment (for political offences) will not apply, should it later develop that they committed criminal offenses prior to seeking asylum on board the destroyers. Should the Detachment Commander [Admiral Bristol] regard with disfavor the agreement entered into between the Mutasariff and Commanding Officer of the WILLIAMSON, he the Mutasariff will abide by any suggestion or decision the Detachment Commander offers.

The stipulations were repeated just before we left, the Mutasariff emphasizing his promise to afford the refugees humane treatment and protection from bodily harm. Considering the frailties and temperament of the Turks as a race and their erroneous conception of the moral code of civilized nations, it can be said without fear of successful contradiction that their written pledge is no more sacred and binding than their verbal pledge. It is my personal conviction based on intimate knowledge of the Mutasariff's character that he will find a specious pretext for breaking his pledge.

I venture the assertion that within a week the Greek refugees will have been surreptitiously conveyed to the interior, tortured and ruthlessly butchered in cold blood. I feel that in turning these refugees over to the Turks we shall be guilty of an inhumane act, for I am certain that in so doing we shall send them to certain death. The Greeks in question were received on board the STURTEVANT at 2:30 p.m. and in accordance with written instructions received from the Commanding Officer, U.S.S. WILLIAMSON, original appended,* they were delivered to the representative of the local government who took them to the Mutasariff's Office.

About 1:00 p.m. Near East Relief automobile driven by the Georgian chauffeur, (known as Larry) containing Captain Cunningham, Mr. Currin and Van Toor as passengers, struck and injured a small Turkish boy that crossed the street ahead of the automobile. The boy was immediately taken to the hospital where an operation was performed. Received station ship files and diary from Captain Cunningham and relieved WILLIAMSON as Station Ship at 2:30 P.M. WILLIAMSON sailed for Constantinople at 2:35 p.m.

August 17, 1921

STURTEVANT at Samsun. Went ashore at 9:30 a.m. The Turkish boy who was injured by Near East automobile died this morning and the chauffeur has been arrested. Learned definitely that [the] order relative to commandeering 40% of all goods in shops and

---

* Admiral Bristol's specific directive, which the *Williamson's* captain sought to follow, has not been located. However, in view of the Mutasariff's later violation of his promises and the eventual deportation and likely execution of the three Greek men, Lieutenant Commander Haas's expectation proves not only quite prescient but also provides an implicit criticism of Cunningham's turning the Greeks over to the Mutasariff. Beyond that, perhaps they also implicitly criticize—in a war diary that would be read by the admiral—the admiral's apparent attempt to deal with the typical local Turkish authorities as if they always could be trusted to act responsibly.

According to brief letters following this war diary set, the names of the three Greek men who had been turned over to the Turks were George Constantinos, John Aristides, and Largaros Grofurides.

warehouses has not gone into effect nor is it known when this order will become effective. It is thought that all Greek stores which have been closed since the deportation of the Greek men will be opened by order of the Mutasariff and contents commandeered for government use. The three Greek refugees who were delivered to the local authorities are confined in the guard house near the Mutasariff's office and are being kept under surveillance. It is my intention to see them tomorrow.

American colony entertained aboard the STURTEVANT.

August 18, 1921

STURTEVANT at Samsun. Went ashore at 9:30 a.m. Was informed by Van Toor that vesicas [passports] have been received for all ingoing Near East personnel: Miss Sweeny and Mr. Plimpton are leaving today, the former going to Sivas and the latter to Cesarea. Miss Thompson and Miss. Dingledine and Mr. Wright will leave for Harput in a few days. Vesica for Mr. Smith has not been received.

Visited the guard house in which the three Greek refugees are confined and found them in a very weak and hysterical condition. They were complaining of not having received sufficient food and of having been grossly maltreated. Van Toor has offered to feed these refugees which matter I took up with the Mutasariff who readily gave his consent to this arrangement. I called at the council chamber and had a short interview with the Mutasariff concerning the Greek refugees. I told him that rumors were current to the effect that the three Greek refugees are to be removed to the interior and for my own peace of mind or satisfaction, I should like to have him assure me that such rumors were without the slightest foundation.

I pointed out to him that if he allowed their removal from the city, such deportation would be a violation of the stipulation of the agreement entered into between Captain Cunningham and himself and a breach of faith on his part, since he had assured Captain Cunningham that the refugees would be kept in Samsun and the Commanding Officer of the Station Ship would be allowed to see them any time. He replied that he had not made such a promise and Captain Cunningham and myself evidently misunderstood what he said. He requested that I call on him tomorrow morning at which time he will discuss the matter with me. . . .

August 19, 1921

STURTEVANT at Samsun.

Received two bags of mail addressed to Near East Relief from Italian steamer "CARNIOLIA". Went ashore at 9:30 a.m. and interviewed the Mutasariff, Mr. King of the Alston Tobacco Company acting as interpreter. . . . Took up the subject of the three Greek refugees with the Mutasariff, with a view to ascertaining whether the rumor concerning their deportation is true. The Mutasariff assured me that he has no intention of deporting them, but he pointed out the possibility of the Angora Government taking a hand into the matter. He does not anticipate such a thing, but should it occur and their deportation be ordered by Angora, he will be powerless to prevent it. He denied and disavowed that part of his agreement stipulating that the refugees will be kept here and the Commanding Officer of the Station Ship allowed to see them at any time.

Learned this morning that the order to commandeer certain items for military use became effective yesterday. Receipts are given to cover articles seized. Several Greek shops were opened yesterday by the Turkish military authorities and contents removed.

August 20, 1921

STURTEVANT at Samsun. Went ashore at 10:00 a.m. and found Van Toor waiting for me on the dock. He informed me that he had just been notified that his supply of gasoline in storage at Socony [Standard Oil] warehouse would be subject to the 40 percent commandeering order. I hastened to the Socony warehouse and upon my arrival there found that the confiscation of gasoline was already in progress. Several native wagons, each carrying five or six cases of gasoline, were drawn up in front of the warehouse. Interviewed Smith of the Standard Oil Company whom I found there and learned from him that he had not been definitely notified until 6:00 a.m. today that 40 percent of his gasoline would be commandeered. The Government has confiscated and will ship to Angora 266 cases of gasoline belonging to the Socony and 53 cases belonging to the Near East Relief which seizure represents 40 percent of the stock of gasoline of the Socony and Near East Relief respectively. The Socony has approximately (7000) seven thousand cases of petroleum here which have not been requisitioned yet.

. . . .

August 23, 1921

STURTEVANT at Samsun. Owing to heavy sea did not attempt to go ashore this morning. Received message from the Mutasariff at 2:30 that Messrs. Thurber and Garside could land at 4:00 p.m. Took them ashore. Met Mr. Smith of the Standard Oil Company on dock who informed me that the Mutasariff sent for him this morning and made overtures to him, with a view to purchasing the Socony supply of gasoline (400 cases) in storage here, the Mutasariff particularly wishing to know Smith's lowest price for the entire stock. Smith upon being approached previously (before the 40 percent tax order became effective) concerning the sale of his oil, told the Mutasariff that he would be willing to sell his stock for $8.00 per case; but subsequent to the seizure of 266 cases of his oil, he raised the price per case to $14.67 per case, in anticipation of the Government purchasing his oil, hoping to cover the loss previously sustained. The Mutasariff considered the price extortionate and told Smith he would refer the matter to Angora. He practically told Smith that it is the government's intention to commandeer 40 percent of the Socony supply of kerosene (7000 cases). . . .

A former employee of Mr. Currin who was deported last June and who had been in hiding since his return a month ago turned up at Currin's house today, disguised as a Turkish woman. He told Mr. Currin very distressing tales of Turkish brutalities and atrocities; according to his statement practically all of his party was killed.

August 24, 1921

STURTEVANT at Samsun. Went ashore at 10:30 a.m. Was informed by Van Toor and others that the three Greek refugees who were delivered to the Mutasariff by the STURTEVANT were sent into the interior last night. Eyewitnesses to the exit state that they were handcuffed together and under guard of five men. I have learned from many different sources that during their imprisonment here they were grossly maltreated and improperly fed; food that was sent to them by Mr. Van Toor was stolen and eaten by the prison guards. Mr. Van Toor and others have informed me that the Turks, in general, are rejoicing over the outcome of this affair which they consider a conspicuous triumph over the dissidents [probably refers to those Turks in Samsun who oppose the deportations].

Persistent efforts are being made to create the impression that the Mutasariff virtually compelled the Commanding Officer of the Station Ship to surrender the refugees and furthermore that the Commanding Officer was ordered by the local government not to receive any more Greek refugees. It is possible that their reports are being disseminated among the native population with the idea of discouraging others from seeking asylum on board the American destroyers. It is more probable that they were part of the wily Mutasariff's propaganda to create a favorable impression in Angora and thus justify his tenure of office, which according to all accounts, is none too secure.

At 9:30 this morning all Greek men over fifty (50) years of age were rounded up—many being removed from the tobacco magazines and others from their homes—and marched to a former Greek school, where they are to be kept until tonight, when they will start for the interior. While in Van Toor's office I saw fourteen (14) poor old Greek men under guard marched down the street, followed by their wives and children who were crying and wailing. It was indeed a pitiful and pathetic sight and one which could not but excite pity for these poor unfortunate people. A little later, while passing through the Greek part of the city, I observed a considerable number of Greek women in groups in front of their houses engaged in animated conversation. One poor old woman upon seeing me approach, detached herself from the group and approached me talking in Greek and gesticulating madly. Although I was unable to understand one word she said I believe I received the impression she attempted to convey. She and all the other Greek women are undoubtedly apprehensive as to their future and feel that their turn will come soon. I firmly believe that the deportation of all the Greek boys under 15 years of age will be ordered shortly and this will be followed by the deportation of Greek women and children.

French steamer "Korniloff" which came in last night is under Russian charter and brought five hundred (500) soldiers.

August 25, 1921

STURTEVANT at Samsun. MCFARLAND stood in and anchored near STURTEVANT at 8:30 a.m. Went ashore with Commanding Officer of the MCFARLAND at 9:45 and visited Tobacco and Near East offices, hospital and other places. . . . Learned this morning that the old Greek men will be deported to-night or to-morrow morning; approximately one hundred and twenty-five (125) have been arrested.

Both Tobacco Companies have now lost their experienced workers and both King and Currin have decided not to purchase any more tobacco for the time being. If the Greek women and children are deported, both Tobacco Companies will be forced to shut down. King and Currin saw the Mutasariff yesterday afternoon and endeavored to save their old employees, but to no avail. The Mutasariff told them he could not prevent the deportation and referred them to the Military Commander who likewise evaded the issue and disclaimed all responsibility for the order which, he claimed, originated in Angora. Smith had been officially notified that his remaining stock of gasoline will be commandeered. The American Trade Company has not, as yet, been affected by the 40 percent order. . . .

Delivered Station Ship files and diary to Captain Haines. STURTEVANT was relieved by MCFARLAND at 8:00 p.m.

Handwritten, unsigned page dated August 27, 1921 (placed after the August 16 *Williamson* WD entry):

Nureddin Pasha has informed the Greeks through the Americans that he will kill a Greek for each Moslem killed by any bombardment.

USS *MCFARLAND*, LIEUT. COMMANDER P.B. HAINES WAR DIARY SET FOR AUGUST 25-SEPTEMBER 15, 1921

August 25, 1921

. . . .

The Turks are listing all Greeks (male) between 10 and 60, and searching Greek houses and stores for anyone who may be hidden. At 8:00 p.m., took over radio traffic and relieved STURTEVANT as Station Ship.

August 26, 1921

. . . .

The Turks have rounded up about 350 Greek boys and men and have them under guard in jail. This takes practically all of the tobacco men's foremen. . . .

Rumors around town that village women and children are to be deported. I do not believe it is imminent as men over 60 have not yet been taken and it looks as if some tobacco foremen would be left to each company.

August 27, 1921

Called on Military Commander. [This would be the local military commander, not Nureddin Pasha.] Found him very pleasant and a different type of man from Mutasariff. Nothing of importance in conversation. About 300 Greek men and boys were sent out of town late last night. About ten tobacco foremen were not sent. During the day some of these men were released temporarily to assist at warehouses, but as yet have not been fully released. They may be held while awaiting instructions from Angora. Learned from semi-reliable source that the remainder of the Bolshevik mission now in town was establishing a consulate and listing Russian subjects. [...], Bolshevik delegate to Turkey, has not been with the mission.

H.M.S. Montrose (Commander Crabbe) and H.M.S. Trinidad [British naval vessels] stood in and anchored about 4:30 p.m. Sent boarding officer. The Commanding Officer of the H.M.S. Montrose and his executive returned in boat with our boarding officer. The Commanding Officer stated he was in to see if there was an answer to the British note left for the Mutasariff by two British boats a few weeks ago. Also, he wished to go ashore and buy provisions and cigarettes. Told him that orders had been received here from Angora that no foreigners could land without permission from Angora. He stated that he had sent a boat ashore with an Armenian interpreter to inquire. He also made inquiries about Bolsheviks, but [I] did not give him the information on hand. These [British] boats have been all along the coast of Anatolia attempting to establish communication with the Turks, but were permitted to land only at Trebizond, where the Commanding Officer went ashore and called on the Military Commander, who was also acting Valli. He told me that two Greek destroyers and 3 auxiliaries have left Constantinople for the Black Sea, which was confirmed by radio from STANAV.

Went ashore for dinner at 6:00. About 75 wagonloads of ammunition were being moved through the streets and into the country. This may have been brought by several small auxiliaries which came in today.

The British boat with interpreter was lying off dock when we went in. They were not permitted to land and no answer, so far as I have been able to find out, was given to their last note.

The Turks here are very anti-British and consider that Great Britain is practically at war with them.

August 28, 1921

H.M.S. Montrose and H.M.S. Trinidad sailed at 5:00 a.m.

Visited tobacco men and Near East. List of all village women and children now in Samsun being taken today. Count Schmecchia informed me that Military Governor had received orders to deport all women and children from the villages, these orders coming from Nureddin Pasha. He stated that his informer had seen the order and seemed absolutely certain that this was so. If this is so, there is nothing we can do but protest in the name of humanity and I am sure that once the Turks decide upon this deportation a protest will be ineffective. Before making a protest or notifying the Admiral, decided to visit the Military Commander and ascertain if possible if such an order had been received. With Mr. P.E. King as interpreter, called on the Military Commander. We conversed about different subjects, gradually leading up to the question of deportation of the village Greeks, women and children now living in Samsun. The Colonel replied that for some time there had been orders to send the women and children from the country villages into the interior but that he knew nothing of any order to deport the village women and children in Samsun and had received no such order, that possibly in the future it might be necessary to do this, but that at present there was nothing of the kind in view. As this seemed to answer our question, there was nothing more to be said on this subject. We talked about the war and the Colonel stated that the Greeks were being held all along the line. He spoke about the two British ships which came in yesterday, said no one was permitted to land and that he was surprised that the British who were enemies of the Turks could come here, although he well knew that the British had no sense of what was right. The Colonel is a strong Anti-British man.

Price of food, meat, bread, vegetables and fruits have advanced from 20 to 30 per-cent since the 40% Commandeering order.

August 29, 1921

Called on Near East and Tobacco personnel. Town quiet, but rumors persist that women and children of the villages are to be deported. This I believe is due to them being registered, as there are still Greek men over 60 who are free, and today five men were retained to work for Mr. King and three men to work for Mr. Currin. The final papers have not been given to these men, but it looks as if they would be permitted to stay and work, as all others in the age limit [of] 60 have been deported. If the village women and children are to be deported as a military necessity it does not seem logical to keep these men here. Therefore I think that for the present, the women and children will remain in Samsun.

Numerous village fires (12) in the hills around town. These villages have been evacuated for some time. The Turks say the Greeks that are hiding in the hills come down into these villages at night, so that it was necessary to burn them.

The three Greeks who swam out to the STURTEVANT and who were later turned over to the Turks were tried by court martial at Amassia for disobeying government order and escaping from convoy. They were all sentenced to 3-1/2 years confinement in the prison at Bitlis. *I believe these three Greeks have been killed and that report of their court is just a "sop" to the Americans.**

* This sentence about the deaths of the three Greeks is handwritten on the August 29 sheet (3), National Archives copy.

About 500 soldiers came into town along the west road from the eastward this afternoon. The men were regulars. They had no baggage train. Late last night about 100 drafted men were brought in from the westward.

The Djeilan Bahn, Turkish auxiliary schooner, arrived from Constantinople with 2000 cases of oil for the Standard Oil Company. She has been enroute for over a week, travelling only at night. The Captain reports Greek ships off Inebolu and says they are sinking Turkish vessels without even examining their papers. This I do not believe. They may have fired a shot to make a ship stop. The rest is undoubtedly exaggeration. . . .

While returning to the ship at 10:30 last night I passed fifty wagons, each containing about sixty rifles, unboxed.

Saw Count Schmecchia in the afternoon. As usual found him very pessimistic over the situation, though it seems about the same to me. He is sure the women and children will be sent out tomorrow.

August 30, 1921

Visited town. . . . Police still taking names of villagers in Samsun, but otherwise town quiet. The five men who were released to work for the Alston Tobacco Company and the three for the Gary Tobacco Company are continuing to work for their companies, having been released from confinement. Talked over situation with tobacco men. I believe it is only a question of time before the village women and children are taken from Samsun, as when the villagers were deported from near Samsun they were ordered to go into the interior. Instead many came into Samsun and are now living here. The registration will show about 4,000 of them in town, and as the orders from Angora were to send the village women and children to the interior they will undoubtedly have to go. . . .

August 31, 1921

Visited town. Saw Gary Tobacco man (Mr. Fitzgerald). Then visited Alston Tobacco Co. Mr. Johnson told me that the village women and children were being collected and assembled in the Greek school house and that deportation would take place soon, the order having been received last night. Saw Mr. King and Mr. Van Toor who also reported that village women were being assembled. Attempted to see Mutasariff, but found him out. Made appointment for 3:30 to see him. Saw

Count Schmecchia who also stated that order for deportation had been received. . . . At 2:00 with Mr. King as interpreter, called on Military Commander. He stated that order to deport village women and children in Samsun had been received, but that it was a civil order and not a military one and that the Mutasariff was in charge of carrying it out.

At 3:30 called on Mutasariff, Mr. P.E. King acting as an interpreter. Abdullah is persona non grata with the Mutasariff and in addition I find it hard to understand his English.

I told the Mutasariff that I had been informed that the Greek village women and children in Samsun were being assembled and that orders to deport them had been received and I had come to him as the head of the local government to get my information from him direct. The Mutasariff replied that if we were speaking officially he could not answer me, but that if I would consider we were speaking unofficially as usual he would answer. I replied that I was speaking as the Senior American Naval Officer in Samsun, and that as the Mutasariff knew about a month ago when Admiral Bristol was informed of a proposed deportation of women, children and old men from Samsun to the interior, the Admiral had sent a telegram to Mustapha Kemal Pasha. I then quoted from the telegram and from the answer sent by Yousouf Kemal, Minister of Foreign Affairs, with both of which I was familiar.

The Mutasariff replied that orders had been received from Angora to deport into the interior all Greek village women and children in Samsun, but no orders had been received to deport the women and children who were actual residents of Samsun. I stated that this would involve about 5,000 women and children, that many of the women were very old and many of the children very young. In the last deportation of men many had been killed or had died on the journey. That with women and children, who were much weaker, many more would undoubtedly die and that this deportation would be depreciated by the whole world.

The Mutasariff replied that every possible precaution would be taken, that strong guards would accompany each party, that conveyances would be provided for those who needed them, but that he had received orders from Angora and must carry them out.

I then said that, as the Mutasariff well knew, in spite of all care and precautions he might take that many women and children would die from the hardship of the journey, and that I could not see how military necessity justified the deportation of innocent women and children. Therefore in the name of humanity, as the Senior American

Naval Officer in Samsun, I protest most strongly to you against this deportation, which will [result] in the death of large members of innocent women and children.

The Mutasariff replied [that] he was powerless, that he had received these orders from Angora and must carry them out, that he would see that strong guards were furnished and conveyances provided for those who needed them.

He then spoke in what he intended to be a conciliatory manner, saying he was sorry that he had to take the tobacco company employees, and that he had excused from the deportation certain old women who were too old to stand the journey.

I do not believe he intends to do all he said. I think he was simply talking for my benefit. I am sure very few of the women and children will arrive at their destinations. I am also sure that it is only a question of time before an order will come to deport all Greeks in Samsun. The Turks are evidently determined to have no Greek question. Their solution is to exterminate all Greeks.

I then returned to the ship and sent radio [message] to Detachment Commander (copy of radio [message] in radio diary). On my way back Count Schmecchia asked to have a radio [message] sent for him to the Italian Commissioner and also gave me one for the French Commissioner from the French priests in Samsun. Copy of both these [messages] are in the radio diary. . . .

September 1, 1921

About 3 a.m., a Greek boy about 16 swam out to the ship and came on board. Sometime before morning he disappeared and could not be found. He evidently swam over to the Italian steamer CARNIOLIA, which was anchored nearby, and which left for Constantinople this afternoon.*

* The *McFarland* commander has learned from earlier diary reports, as well as his own experience, that the three young Greeks turned over to the Turks by the captain of the *Williamson* were probably dead, a result apparently from strict adherence to directions from Admiral Bristol.

Lieutenant Commander Haines's solution? Perhaps to point out the ladder of the nearby Italian ship, mention its destination of Constantinople, and maybe even pay for the young man's ticket. He certainly chose not to say anything about the Greek swimmer to Turkish officials ashore, nor did he ask Admiral Bristol for instructions on how to treat Greeks who swam out to his ship!

Visited Tobacco men and Near East. Town quiet. Remainder of Greek village women and children being gathered up and kept in buildings on hill near outskirts of town. I believe the deportation will start tomorrow. Sent radio to Detachment Commander outlining present situation of Greeks in town. A Turk from Bafra reported that about 6,000 Greek women and children, who are working for the Turks in the fields around Bafra, are [also] to be deported into the interior.

Intended to go ashore at 6 p.m. but sea was running too high. Hoisted in boats to save them from pounding. At about 8 a.m. Italian steamer CARINTHIA stood in and anchored.

S.S. CARNIOLIA (Italian) sailed for Constantinople at about 6 p.m. Mr. Smith, Standard Oil Company, left on this ship for Constantinople.

September 2, 1921

The Italian CARINTHIA sailed about 11:30 last night. Shortly before midnight two men claiming to be Russians came on board over the boom. They had life belts from CARINTHIA, so they had evidently jumped over from the CARINTHIA as she passed our bow. They gave the names of Leon Gritsay and Leon Prosoroff. They say that they were arrested in Constantinople by the French, accused of Bolshevik plots, and sentenced with 20 others to be deported to Batoum. As they were investigated by the French and deported, I believe they are or were Bolsheviks, or had these tendencies, so they were simply being returned to their friends. They were not under duress and the French had undoubtedly made arrangements for their landing in Batoum. As they cannot be disposed of for the present, they will be retained on board until the CARINTHIA returns and then sent on board.

Visited Near East and tobacco men. Early this morning about 900 women and children from the Greek villages, who have been living in town, were deported. A guard was provided and a few carriages, but most of them will undoubtedly succumb to the hardships of the road. In the crowd there were numerous old women and young children. About half a dozen women apparently too weak to travel were left in the school house and a number were sent to the Turkish hospital here. Also, about 150 women in "Samsun" clothes returned to the Alston Tobacco Company today while the Gary people have about 250. Apparently the Mutasariff is doing this to make the Americans think he is being lenient, and by leaving some old women here and letting some others work for a time, he hopes to get away with this deportation without too much foreign attention. I believe if nothing more is done about this deportation that in a short time the remaining Greeks will be sent. . . .

I sent a telegram to the Detachment Commander, with a copy in the radio diary, reporting the deportation this morning, and stating that I believe it is only a question of time before all Greeks in Samsun are deported.

So far no answer has been received to my radio message of August 31 to the Detachment Commander stating that deportation of village women and children in Samsun has been ordered. The [atmospheric] conditions are very bad at present and what communication we have had has been [conducted] with difficulty. However, [since] this message, as well as the ones sent for the Italian consul and the French priests were acknowledged on the evening of August 31, I am sure the Admiral is cognizant of the situation.

The following code message was received last night from STANAV. Quote For Miss Allen—[at] Angora—"Informed relations between Americans and Turks at Marash strained due to absence of troops. Can you obtain any information regarding the uncertainty of Americans in Marash? Bristol."

September 3, 1921

Visited town, Near East personnel and all orphanages. Tried twice to see Count Schmecchia, but found him out each time. According to reports in town today, a total of about 1,500 Greek village women and children were deported. Haidar Bey returned yesterday from Amassia in Near East truck. He reports passing the refugees and that the deportation was orderly and guarded, with numerous women riding in conveyances. By itself I would not give much weight to this statement. It is confirmed, however, by the report of the driver of the Near East truck.

Many of the village workers in the tobacco companies have returned today, most of them wearing "Samsun" clothes. . . .

Sent telegram to Miss Allen through Near East inquiring about welfare of Americans in Marash. Van Toor told me that he had a telegram from Marash, about a week ago. Sent this information to the Admiral.

Two German officers, one aviation captain and one infantry lieutenant, came into town today. They were imprisoned in 1918 by the

French and were confined in prison camp in Beirut, where the French have about 20 German officers and 400 men. They said [they had been] badly treated by the French, but it developed that they had beaten a French officer and later tried to escape. They both looked very well and showed no signs of mistreatment.

The Turks are now taking a census of all Greeks who have lived in Samsun less than 20 years. I believe the quiet in town today is merely a lull and that eventually all the Greeks here will be deported. In a way I do not see how the Turks can do much else as it is a well-known fact that many Greek chettahs are in the hills and that every day some of them come in town with forged or stolen Turkish passports.

The cook at Mr. Johnson's is a village woman and while in the market the other day saw and talked with her brother, a village Greek now in the hills. Her brother said that there are many Greeks in the hills and that they are in communication with the Greek fleet. He told her not to worry about the deportation as the Greeks would protect them and that the Greek fleet was going to land. As a sign that protection would be given to the deported women a signal fire would burn on a high hill back of town that night. At the time he said this fire was actually lighted.

This chettah undoubtedly exaggerated the facts, but this incident is cited merely to show that Greek chettahs are coming into town in disguise.

The Turks claim that that the villagers in town are giving food and shelter to Greek men who are hiding out in the hills and who come into the outskirts of town at midnight. About 9:50 this evening about 50-100 shots were fired on the edge of town in the Greek quarter. A heavy patrol was placed in this section and everything quieted down. Several stories were told to account for it. The Turks were celebrating, or the Gendarmes were searching for some Greek men from the hills said to be in town. Personally, from the size of the patrol thrown into this section of town, I am inclined toward the latter view.

In the afternoon I met with Haidar Bey. He had no news. Had tea at Osman Sinai Bey's with several of the tobacco people. The tobacco men claim that Osman Bey [this Osman Sinai, though also called Osman Bey, is a different man than Osman Agha] is the head of the Turks' Secret Service in Samsun. He is very friendly, but it might be well to remember that he may be in the Secret Service and looking for information.

The 40% order is still being carried out. The American Foreign Trade store had its turn today and the government intends to take 40% of practically everything in stock. . . .

. . . .

September 5, 1921

Visited town, tobacco men, Near East Relief and Count Schmecchia. The situation in town is apparently quiet, but it is the lull before the storm. The Turks are listing all people who have lived in Samsun less than 20 years. This will cover practically all Greeks in Samsun. Semi-reliable reports from the Bafra district state that deportation of Greek women and children is well underway. Most of the stories come to me from the tobacco men who state that Turks from near Bafra give them the information. I therefore consider that the report is in the main true and that deportations are now taking place in and around Bafra where there are supposed to be around 6,000 women and children.

Haidar Bey visited the Mutasariff and Military Commander today. He told Mr. Johnson confidentially that the Mutasariff told him that he, the Mutasariff, had orders to deport only certain of the villagers, but that the Military Commander said he, the Military Commander, had orders to deport all villagers. This would account for the new lists being taken. Information was also received from various sources that the people being listed have been told to be prepared to leave in three days. . . .

At about 5 p.m. French destroyer BAMBARA, Capitaine de Corvette Le Brun, stood in and anchored. Sent Boarding Officer. The BAMBARA seems to have no definite mission, but inquired about French Merchant ship TADLA, which sailed from here September 4. The Captain states that he had heard a rumor that a Greek destroyer is on the way to Trebizond with orders to bombard the town if the deportation was not stopped. He intends to leave for Trebizond on Wednesday.

No more news of the Bolshevik mission that is supposed to be establishing a consulate here. Have started more inquiries to see if there is any further development. As regards to Bolshevik attitude [toward?] the Turks it is difficult to obtain accurate information. The following which I picked up from time to time is given for information. Count Schmecchia who has been making discreet inquiries states that in Angora are two parties, one headed by Mustafa Kemal who is conservative, the other the extremists, which numbers men like Nureddin Pasha and Osman Agha. The extremists are to a great extent terrorists, and are not far removed from Bolsheviks. The Army Officers are divided, but in a case of national disaster or fall of the government the extremists will undoubtedly come into power.

The two German Officers who escaped from the French in Beirut and made their way here state that numerous officers in the Turk Army have Bolshevik tendencies.

On the other hand a Turkish Naval Officer and an Army Major, in discussing this among other matters at tea, said emphatically that Bolshevism could have no place in Turkey; that the Turks were too attached to the family and the home. These men belonged to the old Turkish regime. . . .

September 6, 1921

The Commanding Officer French destroyer BAMBARA called at 9:30 and at 10:30, I returned his call. Visited town, tobacco men and Near East officers. The town is quiet, but the new registration of Greeks continues. I do not consider the Americans in Samsun are in the slightest danger from the Turks. I would characterize their relations with the Turks as friendly. . . .

. . . .

September 8, 1921

Visited tobacco personnel and Near East. Reliable information that TADLA brought about 20-25 boxes about 1-1/2 ft. x 1-1/2 ft. x 1-1/2 ft. of Russian gold from Batoum.

Yesterday afternoon Greek chettahs attacked small village 8 miles from Samsun. The band numbered between seventy and one hundred. The houses were burned and a number of villagers killed. Five women and three men of the village are now being treated for wounds in the Samsun hospital. Two of the women had nursing babies. There were no powder stains around the wounds, and as the Turks made no statement to the contrary I assumed that these people were wounded in the defense of the village or in retreating. The gendarmes later attacked these chettahs and drove them into the hills. Five gendarmes were killed in this fight.

Yesterday afternoon about seven Greek chettahs came into town and collected about 20 of their women from the villages. When attempting to leave town after dark they were discovered and four killed. The rest escaped. These chettahs say they have a stronghold in the hills and are prepared for the winter. More village women are drifting back to work in the tobacco warehouses, and conditions in town are quiet.

A new procedure was started today in regard to censoring mail. Haidar Bay after censoring outgoing mail must take it to the post office where it is officially sealed. I am of the opinion that the local government is somewhat suspicious of Haidar Bey's censorship and is limiting his power.

For information the names of the following officials are given:
Mutasariff – Sezayee Bey
Military Commander – Ismael Hakki Bey
Chief Police – Tevfik Hady Bey
Civil Censor – Haidar Bey
Military Censor – Schefi Bey
Vali – Trebizond – Hassan Bey
General Commanding Samsun District – Nureddin Pasha

Mrs. Austin, Near East Relief, left this afternoon on the French steamer TALDA for Constantinople.

Count Schmecchia informed me that the Italian steamer CARNIOLIA had a Greek swim to her while here last and had taken him to Constantinople. This was evidently the Greek who stopped on here and later disappeared.

. . . .

September 10, 1921

Sent the two Russians who swam to the MCFARLAND from the [CARINTHIA] when in here before back on board with the two life preservers which they had taken from that vessel. At 3:00 p.m. French steamer Ararat stood in and anchored. Blowing and too rough to land.

. . . .

September 13, 1921

Visited town. Many Turkish flags in evidence and the Turks are celebrating a victory over the Greeks. The Turkish communiqué states that the victory is the most decisive of the war, sixty motor lorries, many machine guns and prisoners being captured. . . .

A rumor was going around in town that the Greeks had bombarded Vona, a port between Samsun and Trebizond. This I was unable to verify.

September 14, 1921

At 8:10 French steamer L'Aucre stood in and anchored. Visited town, Near East and tobacco men. It is reported on good authority that some Greek men and women have, on several occasions, escaped from Samsun at night in small coasting boats. . . .

September 15, 1921

Visited town, tobacco men and Near East in company with Commanding Officer, U.S.S. STURTEVANT. Called on Mutasariff to tell him good-bye. Found him very agreeable, probably glad to see the MCFARLAND go, or to see the STURTEVANT back. He informed us that the Angora Government had called all men from nineteen to forty-five to the colors. . . .

Seventeen Greeks suspected of being connected with the "Pontus Republic" were hanged in Amassia recently. They had been confined in prison at Amassia during their trial. Among them was the Greek Professor at Marsovan. . . .

At 8:00 p.m. U.S.S. STURTEVANT took over radio guard and relieved U.S.S. MCFARLAND as station ship Samsun.

USS *STURTEVANT*, LIEUT. COMMANDER "E. G." HAAS WAR DIARY SET FOR SEPTEMBER 13–28, 1921

. . . .

September 15, 1921

. . . . Observed several field pieces of English origin and large quantity of ammunition on the beach near the Custom House landing which I was informed came from Trebizond. Messrs. Mackenzie, Yowell, Gregory and Zimmerman of the Near East Relief arrived on steamer "REMO" and will leave for Harput upon the receipt of their vesicas [passports]. Received Station Ship files and diary from Commanding Officer of the MCFARLAND and at 8:00 p.m. relieved the MCFARLAND as station ship.

September 16, 1921

Count Schmecchia informs Lieutenant Commander Haas that several members of a Bolshevik commission have just sailed for Batoum. Haas comments: One would naturally incline to the belief that the object of their mission was the dissemination of Bolsheviki propaganda, but there are no outward signs or indications that their mission was productive of the desired results. It is known that the commission spent money freely. I am not disposed to believe that the Turks in Samsun, as a whole, are in sympathy with the Bolsheviks or their pernicious ideas. It is known that there are a few Turks here who have Bolsheviki tendencies but they are in the minority and not very influential. No change in general situation. Everything quiet and peaceful. At 10:30 a.m. the MCFARLAND sailed for Constantinople.

September 17, 1921

STURTEVANT at Samsun. Went ashore at 9:30 a.m. No change in situation. I am informed that the Turks captured ESKISHEHIR yesterday. I talked with former Mutasariff Nafus Bey whom I met in Currin's office and learned from him that the Turks are preparing to make simultaneous drives on Usak and Afimkarahisar, in an attempt to regain control of the railroad lines. He gave as his opinion that should the campaign be successful, it would prove to be the beginning of the end so far as the Greeks are concerned. The Government has commandeered approximately 2,000 [Arabas] to convey ammunition and guns from Samsun to the front which would indicate that a considerable supply of war material is now in Samsun. . . .

. . . .

September 19, 1921

. . . .

Went ashore at 9:30. Situation remains unchanged. I am informed that the house to house census of Greeks has been completed. There are still many Greek village women and children in town, some of whom escaped from the recent deportation party and returned to Samsun.

September 20, 1921

STURTEVANT at Samsun. French steamer L'ANCRE arrived with large quantity of ammunition.

Went ashore at 9:30 a.m., experienced great difficulty in landing owing to the high sea and breakers. Received following report from Mr. Farqua, Samsun agent for the Standard Oil Company, as to the status of his stock: to date the government has requisitioned 266 cases of gasoline and 2721 cases of kerosene. 398 cases of gasoline were sold to the government for which payment has not been received. The company has 5995 cases of Kerosene in its warehouse here.

Called on Mr. King who informed me that he had just learned from reliable source that Greek women and children are being deported from Bafra. 2,500 were sent away yesterday in one party and other parties will follow. There are no outward indications for further deportation from Samsun occurring in the immediate future. Conditions in Samsun are very peaceful and quiet. ST. LOUIS stood in and anchored at 6:10.

September 21, 1921

ST. LOUIS and STURTEVANT at Samsun. Went ashore with Commanding Officer of the ST. LOUIS at 9:30 a.m. and called on Tobacco and Near East Personnel with whom Captain Leahy discussed situation in Samsun, its effect upon American interests and the extent to which American interests here and in the immediate vicinity have suffered as a result of the deportations of Greeks. Accompanied by Haidar Bey we later called on the Mutasariff and Military Commander, both of whom received us warmly. . . . Captain Leahy told the Mutasariff that he was making a short cruise in the Black Sea and had stopped at Samsun to call on the Americans and pay his respects to the representative of the de facto government.

While we were at the Military Commander's Office, the Military Commander received a telegram from Angora giving the latest developments at the front, the contents of which he read to Haidar Bey who translated same for us. The message stated that the Turks have again taken the offensive and are advancing in the direction of ESKISHEHIR, inflicting heavy losses on the Greeks. They have captured SEIDGHAZI and the Greeks are retreating in disorderly fashion, leaving considerable ammunition and food behind. The Military Commander affirmed that he deplored the present war which he stated is a war of self-preservation so far as the Turks are concerned. He expressed disappointment that the ST. LOUIS will not remain here longer and hoped Captain Leahy would return to Samsun soon. . . .

Information received from all available sources confirms the recent reports that the Greek women and children are being deported from Bafra. A Turk from Bafra with whom Mr. King has been doing business for a number of years and in whom he has implicit confidence arrived in town today and told Mr. King that the deportation commenced three days ago and is being conducted in a very cruel manner. It is believed that all Greeks will be deported from Bafra district. He told Mr. King that the Turks in Bafra were unalterably opposed to the deportation and had done everything in their power to prevent it, but their efforts were unavailing. It is reported that the women have been despoiled of all their personal possessions, grossly abused and in many cases their bodies violated.

There is little reason to anticipate that the Greeks here will be spared. All Americans here are agreed that the Greek women and children in Samsun will be deported eventually; they regard the deportation as inevitable. It is the general belief that Nureddin Pasha has issued the order for the deportation of the Greek women and children from Samsun, but for reasons unknown to us the Mutasariff is holding the execution of the order in abeyance. The Turks give as their reason and justification for the deportation of the Greeks, the alleged treachery of the latter whom they believe will assist the Greek Army to overthrow and subvert Turkish control should the opportunity arise. The reasoning is illogical and untenable when applied to the Greek women and children who are totally lacking in the intelligence necessary to carry out such a scheme. The deportation of men is to be expected as an inevitable consequence of the war, but to treat poor women and helpless children, innocent victims of the war, in such a cruel and inhumane manner is an unpardonable sin against civilization.

September 22, 1921

St. LOUIS and STURTEVANT in Samsun. Went ashore with Commanding Officer of the ST. LOUIS at 9:30 a.m. Called on Count Schmecchia and confirmed the report concerning the deportation of Greeks from Bafra. He gave us his personal belief that the Greek women and children in Samsun will be deported very soon and expressed hope that the Allied Powers will act to prevent it. Visited the magazine of the Gary Tobacco Company where approximately 700 Greek and Turk women and children are employed. It was noted that there were but 5 men working in the magazine, all of whom were over 50 years of age; of these men two are Turks and the remainder Greeks.

Later visited the American Trade Corporation. Mr. J. English who is in charge of the American Foreign Trade activities here told us that he anticipates the government's requisitioning more of his stock. His stock is valued at 35,000 Turkish pounds and consists of shoes, cotton and woolen goods and toilet articles. He told us that he recently learned that the Turks are sending requisitioned goods of a non-military character into Russia in exchange for ammunition. However, this report has not been confirmed.

Took luncheon at the Hospital and after luncheon Captain Leahy inspected the Hospital which as usual was spotlessly clean. There are at present 124 patients, Greeks, Turks and Armenians, all of whom are receiving good care and treatment. Messrs. Mackenzie, Yowell, Gregory and Zimmerman left for Harput this afternoon. ST. LOUIS sailed at 7:00 p.m.

PERSONAL DIARY OF CAPTAIN WILLIAM LEAHY, CAPTAIN OF THE CRUISER *ST. LOUIS*

Copies of Captain William Leahy's personal diary for this period can be found in many places, including the Naval History and Heritage Command in Washington, D.C. and Special Collections at the Naval Academy in Annapolis. The following selection covers only his cruiser's visit to Samsun on September 21–23, 1921.

September 21, 1921

Yesterday [on September 20] at 5:55 A.M., sailed from Constantinople, speed eleven knots, for Samsun, to investigate for the American High Commissioner present conditions in Anatolia and a reported prospective deportation of all Greek women and children from the seacoast to the interior. Upon entering the Black Sea, ran into a N.E. wind in squalls and a heavy sea. The sea moderated at midnight and this morning the weather was clear with fresh N.E. wind. At 4:40 P.M., anchored in an open roadstead off the town of Samsun (ancient Amisus), finding the USS STURTEVANT, Commander E.G. Haas, in port.

At 9:00 A.M., accompanied by Commander Haas, visited the town and interviewed the following persons: Haidar Bay, interpreter and censor, Sezayae Bey, Mutasariff, Colonel Ismail Hakki Bey, Military Commander, Mr. King of the Alston Tobacco Co., Mr. Currin of the Gary Tobacco Co., and Mr. Van Toor of the Near East Relief.

All adult Greek males have been deported and their wives and daughters employed in the tobacco warehouses are in constant terror of being also deported, which would result in the death of many by starvation, exhaustion, and cold. It is the opinion of all foreigners that the Turks intend to exterminate all Greeks, and the appalling prospects of these women and children can be definitely and permanently corrected only by concerted action of the allied powers.

I could take and hold the city indefinitely with the force and guns available on the ST. LOUIS.*

* In considering the opinions of virtually all the foreigners in Samsun that only "concerted allied power" could save the Greeks who remained in the city and then suggesting his own cruiser could hold the city indefinitely, Leahy provides a possible answer to the present situation, which he may have included in his formal response to the admiral. Leahy knows he could take

The Turks give as a reason for wishing to deport the women that they give refuge and information to relatives and spies who get into the town. This is true and to my knowledge, one Greek male who had come in from the country was during my visit concealed in the cellar of a house, though it is difficult to think of any information of value to the Greeks he could impart should he be fortunate enough to succeed in getting out of the town safely.

Small arms, artillery, and ammunition come in freely to Samsun by steamer from the Russian seaports. I saw one consignment that has not yet departed for the interior. I could not learn how the Turks get money with which to pay for the armament or how they pay for it. It is certain that allied powers with their full control of the Black Sea make no effort to stop the importation, and it is said here in Samsun that Italians are providing the Turks with munitions in the area south and east of Smyrna.

September 22, 1921

This morning I talked with Mr. English of the American Foreign Trade Corporation and with Count Schmecchia, the Italian consul. Mr. English said that the Turks have prepared a requisition for forty percent of his remaining stock and that they have previously taken stock valued at $3500.

Count Schmecchia, who is very much excited and concerned about the conditions and prospects here, asked me to carry a communication from him to the Italian High Commissioner in Constantinople. In view of the probability that such service would be considered un-

---

effective steps, should America consider action, to protect the women and children at least in Samsun itself.

Such forthright thought as his was particularly lacking among those naval officers stationed aboard over twenty allied warships in the great harbor of Smyrna in September 1922. Despite possessing enormous gunnery power and staffed with a potential landing force of a few thousand sailors, Allied forces did little in the way of protecting the masses ashore who were completely at the mercy of vengeful Turkish mobs, although an American relief team did endeavor to feed as many as they could. Hundreds of thousands of ethnic Christian refugees waited vainly for succor while rape, robbery, looting, and much killing were the order of things *each day* for almost three weeks, to say nothing of the terrible conflagration set by Turkish soldiers that consumed much of the city and maddened the multitude. See the Epilogue for a very brief description of the events at Smyrna, including the final rescue of a portion of the vast horde of pitiful refugees.

neutral, I declined with a suggestion that he address the communication to me, which he has done. The information contained therein may eventually reach the Italian Commissioner.

I took lunch at the Near East Relief Hospital with Miss Blackwell, its very competent and attractive manager. This modern and up-to-date hospital, a credit to Miss Blackwell and to American philanthropy, has now 130 patients, Turks, Greeks and Armenians. Some of the patients, women as well as men, were being treated for gunshot wounds. The one doctor that I met was a Turk who spoke French.

At 3:30 P.M. I returned to the ship in the STURTEVANT'S motor boat which had some difficulty in taking us aboard because of an increasing sea from the north. At 7:00 P.M. we sailed for Constantinople, having obtained the information desired by Admiral Bristol and having also, I hope, induced the Turkish Commander to postpone indefinitely the proposed deportation of Greek women and children.

Before my arrival, a Greek youth about fifteen years of age appeared on board the STURTEVANT with the story that he and a companion had come along the coast several miles by water with the purpose of obtaining assistance for some Greeks who need help and food. His companion had disappeared during one of the nights and he was nearly exhausted when he reached the destroyer.*

It is plainly unneutral service to harbor such an emissary, but delivering him to the Turks would result in his prompt execution as a spy, so I have taken him on board dressed in American sailor's clothes and have told nobody.

Upon clearing the harbor we saw some burning houses to the eastward.

---

* This Greek had swum to the *Sturtevant* on July 5, had been delivered to the *Williamson* (the senior ship), and then was given by the *Williamson's* commanding officer to the captain of the cruiser *St. Louis* for further disposition—though when that happened is unclear. (It has been two months since he boarded the *Sturtevant*. Leahy eventually had him put ashore in Constantinople.)

It may have been this much earlier event, which appears in three of the ships' war diaries, that provoked the admiral to write the directive for dealing with Greeks swimming to the American destroyers, mentioned by the captain of the *Overton* in his July 23, 1921 entry. This directive probably caused the captain of the *Williamson* to give the three swimmers, who arrived after this first Greek swimmer, over to the Mutasariff for disposition, resulting in their deportation and likely deaths. (See the *Sturtevant* WD, Aug. 11–24, 1921 for an account describing these events.)

September 23, 1921

After a pleasant passage we reached Constantinople at 10:00 A.M., finding the harbor so full of British ships that it was necessary to anchor a mile above Dolma Batche [the American fleet landing at Constantinople].

Captain William Leahy. Leahy was captain of the USS *St. Louis* when Admiral Bristol sent his cruiser to Samsun. During World War Two, he would become President Roosevelt's most trusted advisor, and the first American admiral to be promoted to Fleet Admiral.

CONTINUATION OF *STURTEVANT* DIARY

September 23, 1921

STURTEVANT at Samsun. Went ashore at 9:30 a.m. Situation apparently unchanged. It is interesting to note that there is much speculation on the part of the population as to the purpose of the ST. LOUIS' visit here. Rumors are rife and one rumor has it that the ST. LOUIS brought ammunition for the Turks. Haidar Bay undeniably believes that the Commanding Officer of the ST. LOUIS had an ulterior motive in visiting Samsun; he asked Mr. King and Mr. Johnson this morning if they thought she was likely to return soon.

It is rumored that the Greek men who were sent to Amassia last February for alleged activities in connection with the Pontus Republic scheme were hanged yesterday. Received no war news to-day.

September 24, 1921

STURTEVANT at Samsun. Went ashore at 9:30 a.m. Informed by Haidar Bay that an official dispatch received from Angora last night confirms the report that the Greek men who were sent to Amassia last February for alleged activities in connection with the Pontus Republic scheme have been hanged, as a result of a court-martial. Haidar Bay was unable to tell me the exact number who have been hanged, but I have learned from other sources that at least 69 men suffered this fate. It is reported the names will be published soon. . . .

September 25, 1921

STURTEVANT at Samsun. Situation unchanged. . . .

The Greek population, I am told, is greatly excited as a result of the publication of the names of the Greeks from Samsun recently hanged at Amassia. These names were posted on a bulletin board in front of the Mutasariff's office this morning and were also published in the daily paper, a translation of which is appended [We present it after this ship's war diary]. It will be noted that the names of many prominent Samsun men appear in this list. Mr. King and Mr. [Currin] told me that many of these men were in no way connected with the "Pontus Republic" scheme.

There are growing indications that the deportations of Greek women and children from Samsun will occur soon. Several Greek women who have received the power of attorney from their husbands who were deported have been told by the Government that they cannot dispose of any property owned by their husbands. This applies particularly to tobacco of which Mr. King estimates there are approximately 30,000 bales in private magazines. This tobacco, for the most part, is owned by Greeks who were sent to Amassia last February or deported last June. One woman who recently agreed to sell her husband's tobacco to Mr. Currin was told by the local government that she could not dispose of it. . . .

September 26, 1921

STURTEVANT at Samsun. Went ashore at 9:30 a.m. General situation unchanged. There is an unmistakable feeling of incertitude and apprehension on the part of the Americans concerning the future safety of the Greek population. They are of the opinion that all Greeks now in Samsun, about 10,000 in number, will be deported within three or four days. A house to house census of all Greeks was started this morning—this being the third census within the past month—and it is generally believed this is being done preparatory to the deportation. Captain Kamal Bay of the Turkish army who was in charge of the deportations from Bafra arrived here yesterday, but the purpose of his visit is unknown. However, his visit to Samsun at this particular juncture is not without significance. When I spoke to Haidar Bay about the reported deportation he denied it most emphatically and stated that such a thing is not even contemplated. I was unable to see the Mutasariff this morning.

September 27, 1921

STURTEVANT at Samsun. Went ashore at 9:30 a.m. Situation apparently unchanged—outwardly at least. Indications of the early deportation of Greek women and children are not wanting and in fact, continue to multiply. Haidar Bay saw the Mutasariff last evening and asked him if there was any foundation for the persistent rumors concerning the impending deportations and the Mutasariff replied that such rumors are absolutely false and without the slightest foundation in fact. I construe this to mean that the deportations are not only contemplated, but certain to occur. Mr. King and Mr. Currin told me that many of their employees have beseeched them to request the American Government to take them away from Samsun. They told King and Currin that they are willing to give the government everything they possess: their property, money, and personal effects, if only they and their children are allowed to leave.

The anguish, misery and depressed state of mind of these people is pitiful to a degree and beyond the power of words to describe. They cannot understand why the Americans who have done so much for humanity in all parts of the world do not come to their aid and succor. If the Turks are unwilling to allow the Greek women and children to remain here, I believe they should at least give them permission to leave the country. I am informed that among those who will be deported, there are many who possess the means of financing the transportation of all the Greek women and children and in Samsun to Greece. The majority are employees of the Tobacco Companies and if they were sent to the Tobacco districts in Greece (Cavalla, Drama, Dollo, and Seros) they could find employment for which they are fitted by training and experience and thus become self-supporting. . . .

According to reports received from the Near East Personnel at Sivas, conditions there are anything but satisfactory. It would appear that the Turks, instead of assisting the Near East Relief in its benevolent work, are placing every obstacle possible in their way. A copy of a letter received by Mr. Van Toor today from Mr. Thurber who is in charge of Near East work at Sivas is appended. This letter was given to Mr. Van Toor by a Turkish doctor who arrived from Sivas today and was not censored.

About 7:00 p.m. was attracted to the deck by the report of a loud explosion followed from the report of shots fired from rifles. Observed smoke and flames rising from one or more buildings in the Greek section in the city. . . .

It appears that five Greek men who were deported some time ago and who subsequently returned to the city had been in hiding in one of the buildings destroyed. They were discovered yesterday and were ordered out of the buildings after the buildings were surrounded by Turkish gendarmes. They refused to come out and promptly opened fire on the Turks who then set fire to the building. It is not known how many lives were lost. I endeavored to see the Mutasariff this afternoon to protest against the threatened deportation, but he was attending a council meeting and could not see me.

PLEA OF THE RELIEF DIRECTOR AT SIVAS

The following September 15, 1921 letter is mentioned in the diary just above and is located at the end of the Sept 27 report of the Sturtevant *war diary in the National Archive file. It comes from C.C. Thurber, the Director of the Near East Relief at Sivas. This letter reminds us of the state of so many thousands who were not just fearful of being deported, like those in Samsun, but were now walking the deportation trails, their fears realized. Moreover, it also shows how Americans at most of the mission stations were doing all they could to help the most helpless ones—despite frequent Turkish efforts to prevent their aid.*

My most urgent problem here has been one of relief. We are having one endless stream of exiles, refugees, prisoners and deportees daily, and conditions are not only undesirable, but beyond anything you can have possibly imagined. The 10,000 Ltg. [Turkish pounds] appropriation [is] absolutely essential for:

Relief – 5,000 Ltgs. This will surely enable us to survive the next few months, although it will be far from sufficient to prevent the inevitable in 1000's of cases. The Government is demanding 2,000 Ltgs. (for Turkish refugees) almost daily. I have thus held them off with 300 Ltg., but they are not at all satisfied.

2,000 Ltgs. will be necessary if we are to continue the Day Schools of former years for 500–800 children. Practically no one can pay tuition as has been the case previously.

2,000 Ltgs. will cover taxes just levied which must be paid on all homes, buildings (even the hospitals). One eighth of our grain and potatoes, two horses and all our gasoline have been requisitioned and the latest request is for our shoe shops, tailor shops, etc. Of course the country is at war and we must help??

The Government also desires alterations and additions to the Turkish Orphanage at an expense of 1,000 ltgs. to provide for 150 more orphans. They claim to have some 1500–1800 orphans that [they] are unable to provide for.

I beg of you to advise Jaquith [Director of the NER in Constantinople] of the serious conditions here and please wire me as soon as possible in regard to the appropriation requested. If we cannot meet this crisis it is a waste of time (if not our lives) to remain here.

As I wired you soon after my arrival, Miss Ryan, nurse, and Miss MacFarland of the Shelter Home and Women's Industries are to leave immediately, and Miss Kime and Van Velsor are to leave November 1st, but the two latter are now anxious to go with the others (as soon as possible) owing to the lack of transportation which seems to grow worse each day. Just now it is impossible to hire an Araba or a Yailli [carriages]. Miss Monroe is expected from Caesarea and is contented to relieve Miss Ryan (and stay on without Miss Kime); we would be able to get along even if Miss MacFarland could not be replaced at once. I hope you can send us Mr. Mackenzie to replace Van Velsor. I know him and know he would gladly do other things to help out as well as his work as accountant which would not take all of his time. On the whole, the regular work, orphanage, and hospitals are in splendid shape and the work here is in tribute to Miss Graffam's* unusual ability.

Van Velsor is not at all well and if he can go with the first party to go out I would secure M. Karfounche the bank accountant to fill in until an accountant comes. Please advise Van Velsor as to your wishes. Above all else, try to realize the serious conditions here with every prospect of the same throughout the winter unless peace comes at once. Prices are extortionate for everything and it will be a struggle to keep within our appropriation.

Jaquith cannot intelligently solve "in Angora" any problem here [Jaquith was planning to travel there] unless he sees conditions here and knows all I could tell him.

Sincerely,
C.C. Thurber

---

* Mary Louise Graffam was the long-term educator at the American mission at Sivas who, during World War I, heroically accompanied student deportees until she was prohibited from going with them further. She hid hundreds of Armenian girls with families in nearby towns, and did all she could to resist the ethnic cleansing being carried out then by the Young Turks. She stayed through all of World War I in Sivas.

After the war, Graffam unsuccessfully fought for a separate American Mandate for Armenia against Admiral Bristol and others and remained in Sivas until she died of a heart condition in August 1921. Susan Billington Harper's short biography of Graffam, "Mary Louise Graffam: Witness to Genocide," can be found in Jay Winter, ed., *America and the Armenian Genocide of 1915: Studies in the Social and Cultural History of Modern Warfare* (Cambridge: Cambridge University Press, 2004), 214–239.

P.S. It is really vital that we be allowed to aid Greek refugees which we are not now permitted to do. Perhaps Mr. Jaquith can arrange for this in Angora!

We have reliable information that over 50,000 deportees and exiles are enroute to Sivas and now on the road between Amassia and here. Convoys are coming in daily—1000-2000, often 3000. Clothing and food here are to be had at prohibitive prices and we dare not contemplate what the cold weather will mean to scores of thousands. We all feel the situation is far worse than anything in the past. We beg you to make Constantinople realize our plight. None of our wires or letters seem to get through and of course we cannot really go into details in the messages we send.

Orphans at a soup kitchen by Americans in Samsun. From *The Care and Sheltering of Refugees in Turkey, European War, Constantinople*, 1921, p. 37.

CONTINUATION OF *STURTEVANT* DIARY

September 28, 1921

STURTEVANT at Samsun. WILLIAMSON stood in and anchored at 9:15 a.m. Called on Commanding Officer, U.S.S. WILLIAMSON with whom I later went ashore. Called on the Tobacco and Near East Personnel. We had hoped to see the Mutasariff, but were unable to see him as he was attending a meeting of the Council. Learned that eleven houses located in the Greek section of the city were destroyed by fire last night. Eight Greek men, one Greek woman and two Turkish gendarmes were killed and three Turkish gendarmes seriously wounded.

This morning a cordon of Turkish troops were placed around a large area adjacent to the destroyed buildings, and it is believed that the Greek houses lying within this area were searched for Greeks, believed to be in hiding. Several Greek women and children who live in this area were taken from the Tobacco magazines this morning and conducted to the police station. It is not unreasonable to suppose that the Turks will employ the incident of last night for propaganda purposes. Everything points to the early deportation of Greek women and children. A company of Turkish cavalry arrived this morning presumably for the purpose of conducting the deportation.

Delivered Station Ship files to the Commanding Officer, U.S.S. WILLIAMSON. U.S.S. WILLIAMSON relieved U.S.S. STURTEVANT as Station Ship at 8:00 p.m.

THE HANGINGS AT AMASSIA
–*THE TURKISH REPORT POSTED AT SAMSUN*

Toward the beginning of World War I, on April 24, 1915, a great many Armenian leaders in Turkey had been arrested. Some were put on trial; most were executed. These were mostly businessmen but also included Armenian political leaders, intellectuals, and religious leaders (Shirinian, Genocide, *49–50). With this example as precedent, the Turkish Nationalists were now using "Independence Tribunals" as the instrument whereby leading ethnic Greeks of Pontus were removed (Hofmann, "Cumulative," 75–76; Psomiades, "Bombardment," 142).*

On January 18, 1921, many Greek religious figures in Amassia were arrested, and the following day, seventy-two civilian Greek leaders from Samsun, Alaçam and Bafra were also detained and charged with connection to Pontus Republic plots. They were initially imprisoned in Samsun but then sent to Amassia (Fotiadis, 381–82). Virtually all of these men were tried and executed by hanging in September 1921. A few weeks later, a list of their names was posted at Samsun and published in Turkish in the local newspaper. The document found below is the Samsun newspaper version found in the Sturtevant *war diaries of September 13–28, 1921, as translated into English.*

Virtually all of the trials advertised here were kangaroo courts. As Akçam notes, "Many executions were carried out, even without trial" (332).

It is possible that it was Nureddin Pasha who devised this scheme in order to rid the Pontic Greek community of its leaders, as the arrests had begun after he arrived in the Pontus area. If the concept originated in Angora, certainly Nureddin promoted this method locally.

Nureddin might well have exceeded the Angora government's orders. For example, referring to the order to deport all the Greek women and children of Samsun, Captain Bristol had pointed out, "the preponderance of evidence seems to indicate that whatever the orders of the Central Government might have been (if indeed there were any such orders) that these were amplified and hastened by Nureddin Pasha" (Overton *WD, July 22, 1921). In a later diary, Captain Haines of the* McFarland *reports what "the better class of the Turks" said of Nureddin's operation:*

"they say that Nureddin interpreted orders from Angora as he wished, that he disregarded many of them. . . . As an example of how he misapplied orders from Angora they give the one which started yesterday from Angora to 'permit Greek women in Samsun to visit their families in the interior' and which when sent in by Nureddin read that 'all Greek women in Samsun must be sent to their families in the interior. . .'" (McFarland *WD, October 30, 1921).*

Nureddin had also been behind the trumped-up investigation of Anatolia College at Marsovan. The investigation not only resulted in the college's closure but also in the imprisonment of four Greek teachers and two Greek students who were later interrogated by the Independence Tribunal. All six of these men faced Turkish military trial due to membership in a debating organization called the "Pontus Literary Society" at the Marsovan college. As one researcher noted, "the court judged [the debating club] to be a subversive group that aimed to join the Pontus region to Greece. [These defendants] had no benefit of counsel, right of appeal, or any foreign intervention on their behalf." Five of the six were hanged in the public square at Amassia among the other Pontic leaders.

A British committee in Constantinople reported that the executions had been carried out with studied cruelty: The men were hanged in batches, and afterwards their clothes and valuables were stripped from them, and their gold teeth extracted. The aged Abbe Platon—Metropolitan Vicar, or head priest, of Samsun—was the first man led to his death (Yeghiayan, 230).

*Note that this list may not be complete. Hofmann reports that 168 Greeks and 3 Armenians were killed at Amassia ("Cumulative," 75). Gavriilidis lists the names of 177 Greeks executed in Amassia (*Pages from the Black National Tragedy of Pontus, *80-83). Note below that one reason for this action is said to be the "Pontus Republic" proposal mentioned in our General Introduction.*

Sentence of the Amassia Court Martial

September 1921

THE SENTENCE OF THE AMASSIA INDEPENDENCE COURT-MARTIAL TO MUTASARIFF OF SAMSUN

PLEASE PUBLISH AND NOTIFY TO THE PUBLIC THE FOLLOWING:

After the armistice of the World War, the Greeks of Samsun and Bafra, in order to increase the Greek element in Turkey, spent great sums of money to bring and locate there old Greek refugees from Russia. They brought arms and ammunition, armed the Greek people and formed special [bandit groups] bearing the name of "JESUS CHRIST" and "PATRIE." They also formed a court-martial to try anyone who would be an obstacle to Greek ideas and forced the young Greeks older than twenty years to be armed and prepared and arranged everything for realizing these ideas. They are silent and quiet when the Turkish Government is powerful and while it is powerless they become active to proclamate an independent state in a part of the Ottoman Kingdom, that is, from Zunguldak on the Black Sea to Batoum on the Black Sea and including Sivas, Tokad, Amassia, Chorum, and Yozgad and to designate it by the name of "Pontus Republic." At the end of the investigation at Amassia, from reports of the military and civic authorities and searches made in the Metropolit building, their homes and offices, all kinds of documents and papers that had been exchanged between several committees of many towns and villages having been found, it was proved that the following persons were acting as active members of the "PONTUS COMMITTEE" of Samsun and Bafra and were condemned to die.

1. Constantin Constantinidis, Assistant director of Regie.
2. Kiryako Oglou Lavrandios, Lawyer.
3. Yordan Oglou Yanko, Lawyer.
4. Karalambos Oglou Alego, Regie employee.
5. Dimitraki Oglou Theolos, Druggist.
6. Enfieji Oglou Theoyani, Tobacco merchant.
7. Yango Oglou Christaki, Druggist.

8. Yorki Oglou Sava, Druggist.
9. Panayot Oglou Tlia, Doctor.
10. Yango Oglou Theodor, Grocerer.
11. Boraki Oglou Panayot, Church employee.
12. Papadoplos Oglou Kocho, Insurance agent.
13. Perikli Leonida Oglou, Shipping agent.
14. Hadjiyani Ogulou Platon, Tobacco merchant of Bafra.
15. Vassil Oglou Sokrat, Clothing merchant.
16. Dimostokli Oglou Yorki, Tobacco merchant.
17. Simonaki Oglou Demistokli, Tobacco merchant.
18. Yorki Perlides, Clothing merchant.
19. Dolli Oglou Nikola, Timber merchant.
20. Tinek Ogulou Hadji Yorki, Tobacco merchant.
21. Hadji Karalambos Oglou Kosti, Farmer.
22. Tinek Oglou Kocho, Farmer.
23. Panayat Oglou Vassil, Chief editor of newspaper "DIOGENE".
24. Momol Oglou Lafter, Tailor.
25. Totor Oglou Kosti, Tobacco worker.
26. Karalambos Oglou Yorika, Tobacco merchant.
27. Yorki Oglou Gregore, Clothing Merchant.
28. Tktiar Oglou Alexandros, Clothing Merchant.
29. Hadji Yor Oglou Chirsto, Coffee House Proprietor.
30. Nikola Oglou Estavri, Clerk.
31. Demiji Oglou Espir, Tobacco Trader.
32. Alesciades Oglou, Tobacco Merchant.
33. Sophoclos Andovalli, Tobacco Merchant.
34. Bandeli Oglou Karalambos, Tobacco Merchant.
35. Bariss Oglou, Doctor.
36. Lazar Oglou Perikli, Tobacco Merchant of Alla Chamba.
37. Ystovri Oglou Yoriki, Farmer.
38. Sava Oglou Yorki, Farmer.
39. Papadoplos Oglou Papadoplos, Director of Ottoman Bank.
40. Yelkendji Oglou Yorki, Tobacco Merchant of Bafra.
41. Gregorides Karalambos, Doctor.
42. Plosidas Grifolides, Doctor.
43. Yordan Oglou Nikola Grifolides, Expert of Regie.
44. Bodour Oglou Youven, Moving Picture Producer.
45. Nikola Oglou Platon, Chief Priest of Church of Samsun.
46. Arzo Oglou Lazari, Merchant of Bafra.

47. Andon Oglou Mikalaki, Of Bafra.
48. Arab Oglou Youvan, Of Bafra.
49. Allego, Druggist of Bafra.
50. Demistokli, Chief Secretary of Bafra Metropolit.
51. Lazan Oglou Panavot, Treasurer of Samsun.
52. Kara Kash Oglou Karalambos, Clerk Metropolit House.
53. Avraam Khristaki, Doctor.
54. Pavlos Oglou Oyamandos, Doctor.
55. Anesti Malides, Timber Merchant.
56. Andavalli Youvan, Banker.
57. Hodjiandon Oglou Andraki, Of Bafra.
58. Saraph Oglou Bandelli, Of Bafra.
59. Yordan, Acting Chief of Metropolit House.
60. Bodour Oglou Kiryako, Motion Picture Producer of Kovak.
61. Cheumlekji Oglou Mourad, Of Keupei.
62. Anastas, Doctor of Sivas.
63. Dimitraki, Doctor.
64. Apostalaki Oglou Andon, Clerk of Samsun Metropolit House.
65. Cheumlekji Oglou Allego, Merchant.
66. Anastas Oglou Miltiades, Merchant.
67. Bodos Oglou Andon, Merchant.
68. Brother of Momol Oglou Lafter, Tailor.

The following men who are not at present in Turkey are condemned to die as soon as apprehended and their properties were confiscated:

1. Arzo Oglou Theodoraki, Deputee of Samsun.
2. Tktia Oglou Simonaki, Merchant.
3. Yelkenji Oglou Barashkeva, Merchant.
4. Demosti Lagarides, Merchant.
5. Atanas Lagarides, Merchant.
6. Proplos, Tobacco Merchant.
7. Yorki Tkliad Effendis and Son, Tobacco Merchant.
8. Pavlos Pavlides, Tobacco Merchant.
9. Alexandre Pachalides, Tobacco Merchant.
10. Yermanos Mikallides, Chief of Metropolit House of Samsun.
11. Dekermenji Zakaraplos, Of Samsun.
12. Djamji Oglou, Doctor.

The following were sentenced to fifteen years in prison at hard labor:

1. Gregors, Accountant of Regie.
2. Anastas Oglou Simounaki, Lawyer.
3. Anastas Oglou Vassil, Lawyer.
4. Thevator Oglou Tilia, Tailor.
5. Hadji Yovan Oglou Yorki, Of Bafra.
6. Sava Oglou Lazori, Of Bafra.

The above persons are to be send to the prison of Erzerum.

Momoul Oglou Stavri 18 years old has been sentenced to 10 years imprisonment and has been sent to the same prison.

The following suspected will be kept in the Sivas jail until the end of the war:

1. Yid Oglou Antovan, Lawyer.
2. Sava Oglou Banjou, Hotel Keeper.
3. Kristo Oglou Pachol, Tobacco Trader.
4. Vassil Oglou Ayasilios
5. Andonios Oglou Lambo, Barber.
6. Zemzeki Oglou Yorki
7. Zemiki Oglou Vassil
8. Sava Oglou Perikli, Trader.
9. Hadji Sava Oglou Atanas, Trader.
10. Bunyed Oglou Bunyed, Tobacco Merchant.
11. Irakli Oglou Kostaki

The following are part of the above suspected persons who have already been sentenced by a former military court-martial:

1. Polivedes Kocho
2. Yovan Oglou Kozma
3. Anastas Oglou Ovakoff
4. Dimitri Oglou Kocho, Clergyman of Metropolit of Samsun.
5. S[a]phokli Oglou Stavri
6. Kristodeilli Oglou Pandelli, Teacher.

The above have been sent to prison at Erzerum.

The following were condemned to death but died in prison before execution of the sentence.

1. Zelos Eftimios, Acting Preacher of Samsun.
2. Pandelli Oglou Vassil
3. Collaro, Agent of French Paquet Shipping Company.

THINGS GETTING WORSE AND WORSE

With the posting of the Independence Tribunal's notice of the execution of prominent Pontic Greeks, things seem to be getting worse and worse. Captain Cunningham of the Williamson *reports it likely that the families of those hung would also be deported—and we learn later that even more Greeks have been condemned by the Amassia court, which before long (as we hear in other war diaries) transfers its activities to Samsun, with Nureddin Pasha apparently presiding.*

Cunningham's war diary repeats what all recent war diaries seem to confirm: the Americans' continuing expectation that Samsun's women and children will be deported despite the Nationalist Foreign Minister's letter of assurance. There were also reports of the existence of a written order calling for all Greek men of military age to be put to death.

Cunningham later notes that a number of Greeks were eventually deported, including some men who apparently had been in hiding. A later McFarland *diary reports that Greek families related to escapees were imprisoned in retaliation and later deported and that a mere similarity in names was sufficient grounds for selecting those families.*

Although greatly sympathetic toward the Greeks, Captain Cunningham had been impressed by the Turkish argument that Greek women who gave aid to Greek bandits when they came down from the hills must necessarily be treated harshly. The Turkish argument seemed to be supported by a later report that Turkish villages to the east of Samsun had been raided by Greek bandits, resulting in 89 Turkish deaths, 50 wounded, and 150 captured. Turkish bodies would be displayed in the city to whip up anger. Adding to the growing complexity of the situation is a diary statement that some Americans were said to be helping

Greeks escape, although this had not as yet been discovered by Turkish officials—and apparently never was.

None of this seemed to bode well for local Greeks.

In the third diary in this set, Nureddin Pasha is reported to have ordered that all Greeks who had relatives in Angora were to be sent to the interior, which would amount to virtually all the Greeks in Samsun. He also has been getting on the case of local Turks who had written him, objecting to the deportation of women and children. Suddenly, though, a telegram arrives—relieving Nureddin Pasha of his command! This striking announcement, soon confirmed, signals a dramatic change in affairs at Samsun.

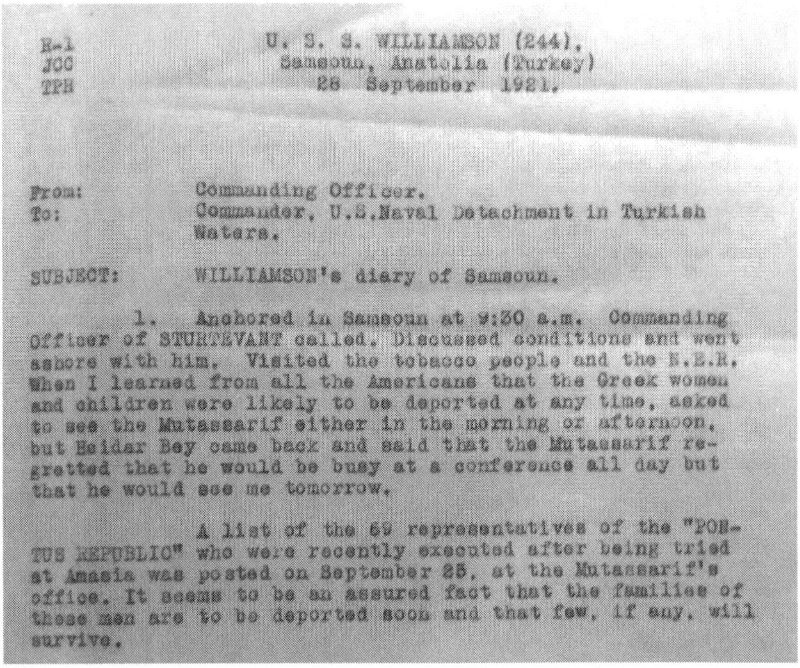

H-1
JCC
TPH

U. S. S. WILLIAMSON (244),
Samsoun, Anatolia (Turkey)
28 September 1921.

From: Commanding Officer.
To: Commander, U.S.Naval Detachment in Turkish Waters.

SUBJECT: WILLIAMSON's diary of Samsoun.

1. Anchored in Samsoun at 9:30 a.m. Commanding Officer of STURTEVANT called. Discussed conditions and went ashore with him. Visited the tobacco people and the N.E.R. When I learned from all the Americans that the Greek women and children were likely to be deported at any time, asked to see the Mutassarif either in the morning or afternoon, but Heidar Bey came back and said that the Mutassarif regretted that he would be busy at a conference all day but that he would see me tomorrow.

A list of the 69 representatives of the "PONTUS REPUBLIC" who were recently executed after being tried at Amasia was posted on September 25, at the Mutassarif's office. It seems to be an assured fact that the families of these men are to be deported soon and that few, if any, will survive.

Another original diary page, this one mentioning the predicament of Greek families of men who had been executed. Even if someone were to be executed, his family might find themselves punished by being deported south.

USS *WILLIAMSON*, LIEUT. COMMANDER J.C. CUNNINGHAM WAR DIARY SET FOR SEPTEMBER 28-OCTOBER 10, 1921

September 28, 1921

Anchored in Samsun at 9:30 a.m. Commanding Officer of STURTEVANT called. Discussed conditions and went ashore with him. Visited the Tobacco people and the N.E.R. When I learned from all the Americans that the Greek women and children were likely to be deported at any time, asked to see the Mutasariff either in the morning or in the afternoon, but Haidar Bey came back and said that the Mutasariff regretted that he would be busy at a conference all day but he would see me tomorrow.

A list of the 69 representatives of the "PONTUS REPUBLIC" who were recently executed after being tried at Amassia was posted on September 25, at the Mutasariff's office. It seems to be an assured fact that the families of these men are to be deported soon and that few, if any, will survive.

Yesterday afternoon several Greek men, who presumably had come in from the hills to see their families and in search of food, were discovered in hiding in a house in the Greek section of town. This house was surrounded by soldier and gendarmes, the Greeks were ordered to come out but instead of complying with the order, they opened fire on the Turks. This house and from six to ten others were burned. Two soldiers, one gendarme, seven Greek men and one Greek woman were killed in the fight which resulted.

Today everything indicated that the Turks were making all possible anti-Greek propaganda out of this in an endeavor to arouse public sentiment against the Greeks. A big funeral was given the soldiers and the gendarme and the dead Greeks were exhibited for public inspection. A large area near the burned district was surrounded by a cordon of soldiers, no one was allowed to leave and later in the afternoon all occupants of this area were being arrested and imprisoned. Eight women employees of the Alston Tobacco Co. were removed from the magazine and probably imprisoned. 140 employees of the Alston Tobacco Co., were not working and Mr. Currin stated that they all either lived in, or near the burned district.

The consensus of opinion among Americans is that all Greek women and children will be deported very soon and that the incident of last night will be used as a pretext for expediting the deportations. It seems to be practically an assured fact that all Greek women and children in this vicinity, except in the town of Samsun itself, have already been deported. This afternoon a prominent Turk from Bafra was in Mr. King's office and in relating to me what this Turk had said about the deportations, Mr. King said, "He told me this without making any bones about it at all." This Turk said that the things which had happened made him ashamed to be a Turk. That not only had the women and children been murdered and subjected to various kinds of torture but that the women had been violated. Mr. King had received similar reports from other sources.

Mr. King, Mr. Currin, and Mr. Johnson, all of whom speak Turkish and in whom many Turks confide, feel certain that all Greek women and children will be deported soon and that the Turks' policy is to exterminate the Greeks. I concur in this belief but I will do everything I can to prevent it.*

In case the Greek women and children are deported, both Mr. King and Mr. Currin will close down their magazines unless they receive instructions from headquarters to continue operations.

September 29, 1921

Went ashore at 10:30. Was unable to see the Mutasariff as he was engaged in a council meeting. Everything was very quiet ashore. Saw all the tobacco people. There was no further information about deportations, but names of Greeks are still been listed and some arrests are being made. While at Johnson's for lunch, the police came to arrest his Greek cook. Johnson promised to take this girl to the police station after lunch. This girl's brother-in-law was one of the men involved in the affray of the night before last, and several days ago her mother and sister visited Johnson's house to see her. So when Johnson went to the police station he stated that his cook has been with them three years,

* This outright statement of concern and resolution is remarkable for having been expressed in a document that the pro-Nationalist American admiral (Cunningham's boss) will read. No similar statement is found in the diaries. However, Cunningham's concern and resolve seem representative of the feelings of several of the naval captains, at least as revealed in the first six months of war diaries.

that she had lived in his house all this time and had done nothing to warrant her arrest, but she was nevertheless retained.

This afternoon about 5:30, two men and four women of the N.E.R. arrived from Harput and Sivas. My commissary officer, who was ashore at the time, talked to them for a few minutes but did not get their names. They reported conditions in the interior as being very bad, particularly at Sivas where all N.E.R. cars, gasoline and horses have been requisitioned. The military authorities are demanding money—Ltg. 2000 [Turkish pounds]—to support Turks who escaped from territory held by the Greeks but [they] refuse to allow any assistance for Greeks or Armenians. Even the salaries of the N.E.R. personnel are being taxed.

September 30, 1921

. . . .

There is no change in the situation ashore. About twenty Greek men, who had evidently been found hiding in Greek houses, were seen near the police station today. There are from 200 to 300 women and children in jail. They were all presumably rounded up in and around the burned district. It is thought that they will be deported tomorrow.

The following Americans of the NER arrived yesterday afternoon: Mr. Hawkes, Miss Ryan, and Miss McFarland from Sivas; Mr. Hopkins, Miss Bailey and Miss McClelland from Harput; and Mr. Hosford from Marsovan. Mr. Hawkes [was] returning to the interior, the others to Constantinople. All of them impress me as alarmists and picture the conditions in the interior as much worse than they actually are. They passed several thousand Greek refugees while enroute to Samsun and saw a few dead bodies. They reported that these people were being badly treated and thought that anyone who was unable to keep up was shot.

At Harput there are five or six thousand Greek deportees, mostly women and children, who are sleeping in the open. Most of them have no blankets, few clothes and no shoes, but due to lack of funds, the N.E.R. cannot help them very much.

At Sivas, the conditions are about the same as reported in Mr. Thurber's letter (the director's letter to Van Toor), a copy of which Captain Haas carried to Constantinople [this letter is included at the end of the prior set of war diaries]. The N.E.R. are not allowed to assist any deportees in any way. All N.E.R. cars, spare parts, gasoline, and horses have been requisitioned and the salaries of the N.E.R. personnel have been taxed. Mr. Hawkes attributes all this to Nureddin Pasha.

Mr. Hosford, a very young but apparently intelligent chap, described the activities of Osman Agha and his band in Marsovan last July. It was even worse than as reported in the diary at that time. A reign of terror prevailed for four or five days during which time several thousands were killed, houses were burned and many young girls 16 and 20 were violated. The picture which he painted is almost inconceivable. He told of brutal robberies, such as cutting off fingers to get a ring, knocking out gold teeth with a bayonet, etc., etc. It seems that conditions are quiet in Marsovan at present.

October 1, 1921

Went ashore at 10:00. Delivered N.E.R. mail which had been received from the Italian steamer PALACKY. Saw Johnson who had been to the jail to see about his cook. Johnson said there were from 350 to 400 women and children in jail, that some of the women were 60 years old, and that some had babies in their arms. Johnson further stated that these women had been told to get ready to be marched out of town. He got this information from an ex-gendarme who works for him. Later I saw a number of Greek women outside the jail and was told that they were delivering clothes, money, and food to their friends who were going away. Everything indicated that these women and children were to be deported probably tomorrow morning. . . .

Called on the Mutessariff. . . . [I] stated that I had heard rumors to the effect that the Greek women and children were to be deported. . . . The Mutasariff stated that no decision had been made to deport women and children. He tried to leave the impression that no women and children would be deported but did not say so. He stated that families who shielded Greek men in their houses were a menace to the Turkish cause and would be deported, that such men were always armed and were a source of constant danger, particularly since they would communicate with the Greeks hiding in the hills. His reasoning was logical and I admitted as much.

He said that all kinds of rumors about deportations were being circulated. Then I stated that I had even heard a rumor to the effect that three or four hundred women and children were to be deported very soon but that as such seemed to be an excessive number to be implicated in hiding Greek men in their houses, I had not placed much credence in this report. . . . The Mutasariff tried to evade the issue and at the same time attempted to leave the impression that the women and children would not be disturbed. I believe that the policy is to deport them all, and this will be accomplished by sending away a few at a time.

A few days ago an order was issued saying that all Greek men who surrendered themselves by today would be sent into the interior without anything else happening to them, but that after today anyone found who had failed to comply with this would not only be dealt with very severely, but also the family guilty of hiding such person. The Mutasariff stated that 100 had surrendered as a result of this order. Mr. King placed the number at 210, but I think this excessive. . . .

. . . .

October 3, 1921

Went ashore at 10:00, and saw all the Americans. Mr. King reports that about 300 Greek men who have been in hiding in houses in town have given themselves up. There is a rumor that all these men and the 350 or 400 women and children who were arrested in and around the burned district are to be deported tomorrow, but I have heard this same rumor every day that I have been here. . . .

October 4, 1921

Went ashore at 10:00. . . . Called on Count Schmecchia. He reports that some men, women and children were deported this morning. Ten arabas left with these deportees and the Count estimates the number of people at 60. . . .

October 5, 1921

Went ashore at 10:00 and called on the Americans. Yesterday morning there were 150 Greeks deported instead of 60 as was reported in my diary of yesterday. Practically all of this party were men. Mr. King states that he has information from a very reliable source that an order has been issued to kill all Greek men of military age. He is trying to get a copy of this order for me. At first he said this order originated in Angora, but when I asked if it might not have come from Nureddin Pasha, he said that it might and that he was not sure of its source. He stated that he thought the order specified men between the ages 18 and 55 but that all will be killed regardless of age. The above information came from a gendarme. Mr. King further stated that the Greek men in Bafra had been deported in three parties. The first party, after being assembled in a valley, was surrounded by soldiers and shot; the second party was burned; and the members of the third party were killed with knives. A man who escaped from one of these parties and is now in Samsun is authority for the above.* This man also said that the women were murdered and that the good looking girls were either carried [off?] by soldiers or else violated and then killed.

There is a rumor in town that the English, French, and Italians have submitted terms of peace to Turkey and Greece and have demanded that they accept them. The civilian population hope that this is true. They are extremely anxious for peace. . . .

. . . .

October 8, 1921

. . . .

Last night, about eight Turks, men and women, reported to the hospital suffering from gunshot wounds. None were seriously wounded. These Turks, who were from a nearby village, had been in Samsun buying provisions. In returning to the village a band of Greek chettahs from the mountains approached them and demanded their provisions. They resisted and the chettahs opened fire, took all their provisions and escaped.

It is reported that the flour is 25 pounds per sack in Bafra owing to the fact that chettahs attack and confiscate the food in all conveyances going to the town.

October 9, 1921

Went ashore at 10:30. Saw King and Johnson and was advised that some women and children were deported this morning—the number was estimated at 60, but might have been greater. They were allowed to leave in arabas. While these women and children were being marched out of the jail, a Turkish soldier pointed to some mutilated bodies of dead Turks on exhibition just outside the jail and said, "That is what your people did to us and is what you may expect to happen to you." This was reported to Johnson by one of his servants who was at the jail at the time.

* This report seems to be related to an original deportation of the Greek men from Bafra, perhaps weeks or months earlier. Possibly it is reported only now because the escapee has just turned up.

Some dead Turks, the number estimated from 6 to 24, were exhibited at one or two places in town apparently to arouse anti-Greek feeling here. I saw several bodies on carts in the lot between the Government building and the jail, as I passed enroute to Currin's house for lunch. There was a big crowd around theses corpses. Abdullah reports that the two Turkish villages to the eastward—Tekekeuy and Tcharshamba—were raided by Greek chettahs and that 89 Turks were killed, fifty wounded and 150 captured and carried into the hills. Abdullah also reports that 24 bodies were brought into Samsun in a badly mutilated condition such as having their eyes gouged out or their ears cut off.*

There is a rumor that another house to house canvas will begin tomorrow to round up any Greeks in hiding. . . .

The OVERTON arrived at 7:05 p.m. Called on the Commanding Officer, discussed condition with [him], and delivered the Samsun diary to him. . . .

* This report by the contractor Abdullah obviously seems to conflict with earlier reports of the destruction, deportation, and/or killings that took place at Tekekeuy and Tcharshamba, said earlier in the diaries to be *Greek* rather than *Turkish* villages (see, for instance, the *Williamson* and *Sturtevant* war diaries of early July, 1921, and the July 19 war diary of *Overton*). The exaggerated numbers and general vagueness suggest Abdullah's report is Turkish propaganda having to do with some local battle in which a number of Turks had been killed.

USS *OVERTON*, LIEUT. COMMANDER BRUCE R. WARE WAR DIARY SET FOR OCTOBER 9-27, 1921

The original Overton *report from this date included three items: (1) a dated set about commercial vessel comings and goings, about reports of Greek warships operating offshore (detected by radio), and about fires detected and at what direction—this set we have omitted; (2) a summary estimate of the situation—which we include just below. Although it includes little new information, it provides for us a convenient summary; and (3) the ordinary war diary for October 9–27, pertinent information from which follows the formal estimate of the situation, below.*

ESTIMATE OF THE SITUATION, SAMSUN, OCTOBER 10, 1921

MISSION. – To protect American lives and property in the Samsun area of Turkey.

SITUATION IN GENERAL. – The Turkish Nationalist Government under Mustafa Kemal Pasha is at war with the Greeks. Neither government is recognized by the United States other than as de facto governments. During the summer the Turkish Army was consistently on the defensive and the fall of Angora was expected by many. However, the Greek offensive before reaching that objective [failed], and since about 1 September 1921, the Turks have been victorious, pushing the Greeks back from their advanced positions. It is not known how far the Greeks have been driven back but it is practically an established fact that Angora is safe, and that the Greeks will launch no more offensives for the present at least. It is the general opinion that both factions will "dig in" for the winter, but no authentic information regarding this has been received.

Greek men-of-war are known to be in the Black Sea operating off the Anatolian Coast. Their intentions are not known, but it is believed that their mission is to stop the transportation of arms into Turkey.* Several months ago they bombarded Ineboli, Trebizond and Sinop, but so far have not bombarded Samsun, undoubtedly due to the presence of American destroyers here who notified them that there are

* One actual Greek naval mission was to inhibit the shipment of ammunition and weapons to Turkish soldiers at the front.

many Americans in Samsun, engaged in peaceful pursuits. The Greek Commodore commanding the Greek Naval Forces informed us that his object in bombarding these towns was to "feel out" the shore defenses, in order to find out their range, location and number. If this is true, his motive in collecting this data must have been to determine the feasibility of sending landing forces ashore. This based on the fact that very little damage has been done in the places bombarded, and no other advantage was gained by this bombardment.

There has been much anti-Greek movement around Samsun since last May. The entire male population between the ages of fifteen and fifty has been deported to the interior, a great number of whom were massacred. Some of them succeeded in escaping, and returned to Samsun and hid themselves. Recently a proclamation was issued requiring all Greeks hiding in Samsun to surrender themselves, promising them safety provided they do so before a set date—now past. It is known that there are some Greek men who failed to surrender and are still in hiding. These men if caught will be put to death and their families deported. Those concealing them will probably either be deported or put in prison.

Numerous bands of brigands are supposed to be in the hills around Samsun. There is very probably some truth to this due to the numerous houses that have been burned recently outside the city of Samsun. These fires are plainly visible from the ship. The presence of these brigands creates terror in the minds of the Greek civilian population. It is quite certain that most of the atrocities [are] by bands of brigands who swoop down, rob and massacre the deported Greeks after they are a few miles outside of Samsun. The present government existing at Samsun will in all probabilities survive for some time to come, and the presence here of regular troops will undoubtedly prevent the brigands [from doing] wholesale violence in the town. There is a lawless element in town and also a number of Russian Bolsheviks, but so long as the present government survives it is not believed that any dangerous disorders will take place.

There are about twelve Americans in Samsun engaged in business and other peaceful pursuits who are looking to us for protection in case of certain events which may develop here.

POSSIBLE COURSE OF EVENTS THAT MAY DEVELOP. –

1. Landing from Greek ships and occupation of the town by the Greeks.

2. Collapse of local government in Samsun.

3. Uprising and seizure of local government by one of the various factions in town.

4. Attack and pillage of town by brigands from the hills.

5. Act of some Americans in town, such as harboring fugitive Greeks, which might antagonize the Turkish authorities to such an extent that the lives of one or more Americans ashore might be jeopardized.

<u>OUR OWN FORCES</u>

(a) U.S.S. OVERTON. This destroyer can land a force of about forty-five men, fully armed.

(b) NEAR EAST RELIEF. – The personnel of the Near East Relief are operating a base headquarters, one hospital and three orphanages. The operations of the base can be suspended, but the hospital and orphanages must carry on.

(c) TOBACCO INDUSTRY. – The tobacco personnel have offices and magazines stowed with tobacco. The offices can be temporarily closed, but the magazines must be guarded, if possible, after the question of personnel safety has been considered.

(d) AMERICAN FOREIGN TRADE. – Warehouse and store will not be guarded. (Not considered feasible).

BEGINNING OF *OVERTON* WAR DIARY ENTRIES

October 9, 1921

Arrived Samsun at 7:10 p.m. Commanding Officer of the U.S.S. WILLIAMSON reported on board with station ship diary, and latest news. Studied all matters pertaining to our mission, and made estimate of the situation.

October 10, 1921

OVERTON and WILLIAMSON at Samsun. WILLIAMSON sailed for Constantinople at 6:00 p.m. Fires burning to left of town during night.

I called on all Americans here, the Mutasariff, and the Military Commander.

Six 3" ex-Russian field pieces with limbers left for Angora overland. Three 20 burro trains heavily laden with wheat arrived in town. Turkish sailors searching all Greek homes for men in hiding and ejecting all families with furniture. Families are not being allowed to return.

Fires noticed of no consequence.

Unfounded Rumors

1. At daybreak 25–40 Greek persons were deported—6 men killed while leaving town—not substantiated.

2. A feeling of unrest and impending disaster overhanging town—no cause event—expecting to happen within three days, namely before Friday, 14 October.

October 11, 1921

I called on the Mutassarif this morning. . . .

During the day further search of Greek houses continued, with robbing of the inhabitants by Turkish soldiers conducting the search.

October 12, 1921

I interrogated peasants and soldiers and endeavored to confirm a rumor that Osman Agha, with his band were coming to Samsun. The story now is that four of his officers have been wounded and killed at the front and Osman [himself] is enroute Samsun for recruiting purposes. . . .

I dined and spent the evening at the Hospital.

October 13, 1921

Samsun quiet. Many villages around the outskirts of Samsun, and among the hills burning.

During the day, 8:00 a.m. to 4:00 p.m., covered the area to the east of the city. One party of five men, two on horseback, were seen along the beach. Upon approach four of them took to the bushes, the fifth galloped hard down the beach towards the south of Yoshil Irmak river.

Heard intermittent firing up in the hills, Very probably 3 inch guns.

I spent the evening with Mr. Sinai Bey [perhaps the head of the Turkish secret service in Samsun; see *McFarland* WD, Sept. 3, 1921] and confirmed my opinion that he not only understands but can speak English. He has studied it for five months. He is very pleasant and talked freely, in French, of Mustafa (Kemal) Pasha, Angora and the front, being careful however not to give any information of value. His daughter, who speaks English fluently, is expecting to visit Constantinople towards the end of this month. I am convinced that he uses her as a means not only to obtain information, but [also to obtain] our opinions on various subjects pertinent to the present situation.

. . . .

October 17, 1921

A number of fires broke out before daybreak this morning bearing 130 degrees true from the ship, distant about 10 miles. These fires were in the general direction of Tcharshamba.

Mr. Johnson of the Alston Tobacco Company reported having seen a number of Greek women, about 55 in all, outside of the Samsun prison. It is believed they have been or will be deported.

October 18, 1921

Expecting deportation of 20 Greek women. I went ashore at 4:30 a.m. and remained until 6:30 a.m. Nothing out of the ordinary occurred. Samsun and vicinity quiet. No rumors.

It is reported that the output of tobacco this year is 20,000 bales—20% of normal. Each day the fields surrounding the city are full of large bands of sheep and cattle. They are being shipped to Constantinople.

A predicted food storage is being investigated by me and will be covered later.

A caravan of small arms ammunition left the city today via the Marsovan road. About sixty regular size boxes.

Two motor trucks containing two 3" field pieces and limbers arrived from Bafra. I obtained three maps for my intelligence report. *We have omitted some entries on shipping and war reports from Eski-Shehir, and shipping reports have been omitted in several of the succeeding entries.*

The following war communication was received in Samsun:

"In accordance with sentence of Amassia court-martial, Commaglou Aleko, Greek of Bafra, was shot to death before the troops, having been found guilty of desertion.

"The following Greeks of Tcharshamba, who were members of the Pontus Committee, and who later joined the Greek bandit party in the 'Vampire' mountains, were captured and tried by court-martial and condemned to death:

Baba Yirom Oglou from Kerim,
Papas Oglou from Cosma,
Lazare Oglou from Yordan,
Yani Oglou from Anastas,
Sapor Oglou from Djenjek,
Yarika Oglou from Djenjek,
Sari Yani Oglou from Kosti.

"The above named men, after having joined the Greek bandits in the Vampire Mountains, attacked the village of Tunkel, plundered the whole village and killed Ahmed and Mustapha. They were found guilty not only by the testimony of bona fide witnesses, but by their own confession."

October 19, 1921

Samsun and vicinity quiet.

Captain and Officers engaged in collecting intelligence report data. A large number of merchants from Bafra came into town today bringing general merchandise and tobacco.

October 20, 1921

Expecting deportations, I visited the city before breakfast, but all was quiet.

During the afternoon I called on the Mutasariff and questioned him relative to the deportation of four hundred men, women and children, who, it is supposed, are soon to be deported. A prison guard informed me that these people were to be deported as soon as an escort of gendarmes arrives from Amassia, probably on Saturday, October 22, 1921. However, I think it will be postponed.

The Mutasariff said that all prisoners would be deported; that if there were any women and children they would be put on wagons with springs. Our conversation lasted one hour and a quarter during which time he was consistently on the defensive and quite evasive in answering my questions. He finally stated that there were neither women nor children in the prison—only a few robbers, liars and murderers.

The Mutasariff refused to allow me to go through the prison but said that he could prove that there were no old men, women and babies there. Then he went to the telephone, called up some one, said a few words, and turned around, informed me with his usual characteristic smile that he was correct. Not being in a receptive mood for any further comedy, I left him to amuse others outside.

About 5:00 p.m. another village was burned down about three miles to the eastward of Samsun. This was done by government troops who could be plainly seen from the ship. There were about 150 troops in all. These troops marched back to Samsun after firing the village.

October 21, 1921

At 7:30 a.m., a large number, about 200 men, women and children of all ages, were deported from Samsun. These noncombatants were gathered in the prison yard and, escorted by mounted gendarmes, left the city via the Tcharshamba road, for Tokat.

Samsun city and vicinity quiet, and orderly. Many new soldiers are arriving in town. These men are easily recognized as they salute when passing.

It is estimated that there is a force of 5000 Greek "Chettahs" gathering in the mountains. In order to attack and repress them, all men from 37 to 40 are actually being drafted. The order reads that at the end of one month of service they will be released from duty, and men from 40 to 43 drafted in their place.

It is reported that the "Tribunal of Three" which tried the "Pontus Republic" conspirators at Amassia, are coming to Samsun. They will try for treason the families of Greek bands at Dua-Bogaz, two hours distance from Samsun. The chief of this band of brigands was called Cosmo Oglou Istill of Kadi-Keuy, Samsun. About twenty families are implicated and it is of a certainty that they will be jailed, then hanged. I enclose two photos with attached explanatory notes. These photos are authentic and from the Mutasariff's personal collection.

In passing, I wish it emphasized that the Mutasariff is disliked and called a "wooden blockhead" by many of the Turkish population. He is an ideal "Governor" for Nureddin Pasha, however, as he is a deliberate liar and scoundrel.

I sent a request to the Mutasariff today, asking permission to have all Americans in Samsun visit the ship Sunday afternoon.

MR. HAIDAR BEY IS FALSE TO US AT ALL TIMES. I recommend that as soon as diplomacy permits, he be discharged, and another interpreter employed, of whom there are several available. I believe that if a very important question was to be discussed with the Governor, an American understanding some Turkish should be present. It is further recommended that all Commanding Officers be required to learn a smattering of Turkish. I have found that a small booklet "Turkish Self-Taught" by Prof. J. Hagopian is very good for this purpose.

Continued gathering intelligence data.

. . . .

October 24, 1921

Samsun and vicinity quiet.

The following is a synopsis of the Kerasund daily paper, "Kerasund" appearing after date of 16 October 1921:

"The following Greeks belonging to the 'Pontus Republic' society, were tried and sentenced to be hung for having organized [special] bandits and for having incriminating documents in the their possession:- . . . ."

The list that follows, of some eighteen ethnic Greeks, is not entirely legible in the photograph made from the war diary, so we have omitted it here. We have also omitted partially illegible names of six others who were sentenced to lose their possessions as punishment for desertion.

USS *MCFARLAND*, LIEUT. COMMANDER P.B. HAINES WAR DIARY SET FOR OCTOBER 26-NOVEMBER 11, 1921

. . . .

October 27, 1921

. . . .

At 4:15 Commanding Officer of the OVERTON called and turned over Station Ship files and latest information. Read over late files and at 5:00 p.m. relieved U.S.S. OVERTON as Station Ship Samsun. At 5:20 U.S.S. OVERTON got underway for Trebizond. . . .

At 5:10 went ashore. Visited Mr. King of Alston Tobacco Company and Mr. Currin and Mr. Fitzgerald of Gary Tobacco Company. Found everything quiet in town. There are a few Greeks, those who have been shielding relatives in their houses, in jail. Dined at the Kings and returned aboard at 10:00. The Americans are still sheltering some Greek refugees in their houses, in spite of Turkish orders and searches, and have aided others to escape. While I can understand their doing this from a humanitarian standpoint, it will change the Turkish attitude towards Americans if discovered. This attitude now is friendly and since our mission here is to protect American lives and property, any act which may tend to jeopardize either should be stopped.

A modified campaign order covering procedure in case it becomes necessary to land [apparently the admiral's policy on delivering a landing party of armed sailors in case of need] was published today and is in effect.

. . . .

October 30, 1921

Visited all tobacco personnel. Lunched with Mr. Johnson and dined with Mr. King. Town quiet.

During the morning an order came in via Nureddin Pasha from Angora to send to the interior all Greeks who had male relatives there. This would comprise practically all Greeks in Samsun. Before any excitement was aroused, however, a telegram from Angora was received by certain influential Turks saying that Nureddin Pasha had been relieved from his command. A little later the first order was modified to permit any Greeks with male relatives in the interior to go to them.

There are many Turks in Samsun who believe Nureddin Pasha is too radical and who disagree with many things he does. When the question of deporting all the Greek women and children from Samsun first developed, about sixty-five of these influential Turks got up a letter to Nureddin Pasha and asked him to stop the deportation, giving among other reasons, their fear of bombardment by the Greek Fleet, if the deportation took place. Nureddin Pasha was very angry with these Turks and called them traitors to their country. Since that time there has been bad feeling between these men and Nureddin Pasha. A short time ago, some of these men wished to leave Samsun for Constantinople, Trebizond, etc. In answer to their request Nureddin Pasha sent each one a written questionnaire in regard to their protest against the deportation of Greek women and children. He asked questions about as follows: (a) Who started the meeting which led to the writing of the letter? (b) Who was present at the meeting? (c) Who made speeches? (d) What was said? Etc.

No reply was made to these questions but each Turk answered that there are several law courts (naming them) in the country who alone are entitled to ask these questions and asked Nureddin Pasha which one he represented. In the meantime the matter was taken up with Angora direct and the Turks here believe that Nureddin Pasha's removal is partly because of his treatment of them. In addition they say that Nureddin interpreted orders from Angora as he wished, that he disregarded many of them, and that he is not popular among the better class of the Turks. They say that no matter who is appointed to command the District he cannot but be a better man than Nureddin. As an example of how he misapplied orders from Angora they give the one which started yesterday from Angora to "permit Greek women in Samsun to visit their families in the interior" and which when sent in by Nureddin read that "all Greek women in Samsun must be sent to their families in the interior. . . . "

. . . .

November 2, 1921

Visited town, all Tobacco Personnel and Near East. Conditions normal, town quiet and no rumors. Called on Count Schmecchia and on Osman Sensi Bey. Had a long talk with each about nothing in particular. Both agreed that with the removal of Nureddin Pasha conditions should be better in Samsun for the Greek refugees.

Another reason for the removal of Nureddin Pasha was being circulated in town today. The Greek chettahs have been very active in the hills and the Samsun people have made many complaints to Angora about them. It is now being claimed that Nureddin Pasha was removed because he failed to take proper measures to capture or kill them.*

At 8:22 French steamer L'Anere stood in and anchored.†

. . . .

November 5, 1921

Visited town, Tobacco Personnel and Near East. Town quiet and conditions normal. From time to time Greek families who are supposed to be relatives of different men who had escaped from those deported and were later were recaptured are put in prison and later deported. This is done on the slightest [pretext], a similarity in names alone being sufficient.

At 4:30 p.m. Greek sloop "N" flying Commodores flag and destroyer PANTHER stood in, circled the harbor very slowly and stopped. At 5:00 MCFARLAND got underway and stood out toward Greeks. The Greek gun crews were at their stations and both ships were [ready] for action.

After lying to off [from] the Greeks for half an hour, I sent the following message by radio to the Greek Commander:

Have been informed that you will advise us before bombardment so we can remove Americans. Have you any message?

This was reported to the sloop "N" by the PANTHER.

The sloop then stood close aboard the MCFARLAND, hailed, presented the Commodore's compliments and asked if we had any message. I repeated the message given above. The Commodore replied, "It is useless for the present, good bye," and both ships stood out to sea.

I interpreted this message to mean there would be no bombardment, stood in and anchored at 5:53.

The Greek ships remained about ten miles outside all night, signaling each other and using searchlights.

---

* This motive for Nureddin's relief has some credibility, for (as we will see in the book's next section), early in the next year, the Nationalist Minister of the Interior comes to Samsun, along with a strong force that campaigns in the mountains against the Greek partisans.

† Note that besides what has been omitted here for lack of pertinence, a page from the *McFarland* war diaries that included some text from the November 4, 1921 entry was missing in the original war diaries at the National Archives and hence could not be read or reviewed.

There are three possible reasons for the Greeks coming in:

(a) They may have wished to draw the fire of the Turks as an excuse to bombard the town themselves or with the [Greek battleship] KILKIS.

(b) They may have been making a demonstration to alarm the Turks and to write up for their weekly military and naval report.

(c) They may have expected to pick up some refugees who would come out to them when they were lying off during the night. . . .

November 6, 1921

Visited town, Tobacco Personnel and Near East Relief. Town quiet and conditions normal. Had all the Americans in town out for luncheon on board. Permission readily obtained from the Mutasariff.

Sent liberty party of ten men ashore yesterday and today. No difficulties were experienced.

The Near East Relief have a new interpreter, N. Arif Bey, a former Lieutenant Commander in the Turkish Navy, who acted as a [liaison?] officer with the Allies in Constantinople immediately after the Armistice. Arif Bey is a better man to deal with than Haidar Bey, speaks better English and has a better personality. In view of the general dissatisfaction with Haidar Bey as interpreter, I recommend that if possible the services of Arif Bey be secured instead.

At 9:50 a.m. Italian steamer ALDO stood in and anchored. At 12:40 Italian steamer ALDO got underway and stood out. At 8:15 sighted glow from a fire over the hills in back of town.

November 7, 1921

Visited town, Tobacco Personnel and Near East Relief, called on Count Schmecchia. Conditions in town quiet and normal. . . .

At 6:25 p.m. fire broke out on hills in back of town. During the night these fires continued, but were not always in the same place.

The activities against the chettahs in the hills have been increased and these fires may have been caused by the troops burning houses which might shelter the chettahs. There is a story in town that about fifty Greek chettahs have been surrounded by soldiers and are now being attacked. The chettahs are reported to have their women and children with them.

. . . .

November 9, 1921

Visited town, Tobacco Personnel and Near East Relief. Conditions quiet and normal. There seems to be a general quiet condition throughout town now. From time to time a few Greek families, relatives of some Greek who was hanged at Amassia, who had been captured after escaping while being deported, or who are themselves sheltering some male Greek in their houses, are put in jail and later deported. There is, however, no general deportation and no talk of it. In fact there is talk of certain of the refugees being permitted to return in order to take up their work with the Tobacco Companies. While this is not general at present, it indicates the tendency.

This change I believe is due to the constant pressure which has been applied by many of the leading Turks in Samsun, headed by the director of the Regis Tobacco Company [a Turkish company]. These men realize the necessity of retaining their old employees, most of whom are Greeks, and for some time have been working for that end. In addition they have been dissatisfied with the Mutasariff, who was controlled by Nureddin Pasha, and have opposed most of the things done by these men. Whether it was because of their efforts or not I am unable to say, but Nureddin Pasha and the Mutasariff have been removed and I believe that for the present at least conditions will remain the same in Samsun.

Djevid Pasha, who takes Nureddin's place and Fiek Bey, who replaces the present Mutasariff, are expected in Samsun by boat in the near future. Both of these men were, I understand, formerly held at Malta by the English. . . .

. . . .

WHAT THE RELIEFERS REPORTED
–*TESTIMONY OF STANLEY HOPKINS AND WILLIAM HAWKES*

In his informative war diary of September 28 to October 10, shown above, Captain Cunningham of the Williamson *reported two somewhat contradictory views. On September 28, he commented that "Mr. King, Mr. Currin, and Mr. Johnson, all of whom speak Turkish and in whom many Turks confide, feel that all Greek women and children will be deported soon and that the Turks' policy is to exterminate the Greeks. I concur in this belief but I will do everything I can to prevent it." This is a very unusual resolution in the diaries. No other ship's captain makes this kind of a commitment, which might have caused the admiral to frown a bit when he read it.*

In his diary of two days later, though, Cunningham mentions dire reports from several Americans he met with who had just come from the interior. For example, "they passed several thousand Greek refugees while enroute to Samsun and also a few dead bodies. They reported that these people were being badly treated and thought that anyone who was unable to keep up was shot," and more. But then he dismisses these concerns, saying of the Americans, most of whom were associated with the Near East Relief, "All of them impress me as alarmists and picture the conditions in the interior as much worse than they actually are." So was the Nationalist policy all that bad, really?

Since Captain Cunningham expresses a bit of doubt here, it seems reasonable to present the reports of two of the specific Americans who Cunningham thought alarmist but who eventually wrote about what they had seen. Presenting these testimonies just after reports of Nureddin Pasha's relief of command will help us understand the nature of the situation Nureddin had helped create.

Report of Stanley Hopkins:
The Thousands of Greeks on the Deportation Trails

One of the Americans apparently thought by Cunningham to be an alarmist was Stanley Hopkins, who returned from Turkey to New York on November 12, 1921. Hopkins had been tasked by the Near East Relief to travel between stations, which gave him considerable opportunity to witness the circumstances of the deportees.

I have been in the interior of Anatolia in the employ of the Near East Relief for about a year. My work has been automobile transportation which has carried me many times over the road from Samsun to Marsovan, Sivas, Caesarea, Oulou Kichla and Harput. During the winter of 1920-21, I was a member of the Harput Unit of the Near East Relief and did industrial and transportation work there in connection with the large orphanages maintained by the Near East Relief.

About September 1st 1921, I started on a trip by automobile from Harput to Samsun. On the roads between Harput and Malatia I passed a large number of Greeks being deported from the south coast region of the Black Sea, to the east. I estimated them to be about twelve thousand persons. They consisted of entire families and villages that have been uprooted and started on the road with whatever property they could carry on their backs and ox-carts. They were guarded by Turkish gendarmes, and they were moved slowly so that they would be unable to reach any point where they could settle before the winter snow would come. As regards health, clothing and food, the gendarmes and Turks along the way took every possible advantage of them. One man sold a cow for one hundred silver piasters, the equivalent of about $3.00, in order to obtain food. After leaving Samsun on my return to Harput I passed the old men of Samsun, Greeks, who were being deported. Many of these men were feeble with age, but in spite of that fact they were being pressed forward at the rate of thirty miles a day and there was no transport available for those who were weak or ill. There was no food allowance for them, and any food that they could obtain had to be procured by money or sale of small articles that they could carry with them. On the trip I passed many corpses of Greeks lying by the road side where they had died from exposure. Many of these were the corpses of women and girls with their faces toward the sky, covered with flies. About October 1st I started from Harput toward Samsun being accompanied by Miss Bailey and McClellan, all of us planning to return to America. On this trip we passed what I estimated to be about ten thousand Greeks. I remember one group of about two thousand, being women alone, most of them with no shoes, many of them carrying babies on their backs and in their arms. A driving cold rain was falling at the time I passed them and they had no protection whatsoever and their only place to sleep was the wet ground. These women were on the road within a day's automobile journey of Harput.

On this, our last trip out from Harput, we passed similar groups all along the way.

Harput seems to be a gathering and forwarding center for these Greek refugees. There are between fifteen and twenty thousand Greeks in Harput from all regions to the west and north. They are absolutely without help, and in the nature of the case large numbers of them are dying. They are allowed to stay in Harput a short time and are then sent forward to the east where their fate is not known. The Near East Relief is not allowed by the Turkish Government in any of its centers in Anatolia, so far as I know, either to hire Greeks or to help them by giving food, clothing or money. In Sivas the Americans of the Near East Relief were not even allowed to go and see the conditions in which the Greek refugees were. I was given an account by someone in Samsun of the way in which a large number of Samsun men, said to be fifteen hundred, were treated near Kavak. Kavak is about half way between Samsun and Marsovan on the main road. The road out of the town toward the south descends a valley, crosses a bridge, and ascends the hill on the other side. The valley is that of a stream which flows down from the west. These fifteen hundred men were marched out of Samsun on August 15th, and as they left Kavak were diverted up the valley and shot down by fire of Turkish troops. It was stated that of the fifteen hundred, thirteen hundred were killed in two and a half hours. These are conditions and incidents all of which except the last I witnessed. They seem to indicate that the Greeks of Anatolia are suffering the same or a worse fate than did the Armenians in the massacres of the Great War. The deportation of the Greeks is not limited to the Black Sea Coast but is being carried out throughout the whole country governed by the Nationalists. Greek villages are deported entire, the few Turkish or Armenian inhabitants are forced to leave, and the villages are burned. The purpose is unquestionably to destroy all Greeks in that territory and to leave Turkey for the Turks. These deportations are, of course, accompanied by cruelties of every form, just as was true in the case of the Armenian deportations five and six years ago.

Signed— Stanley E. Hopkins
November 16, 1921

Hopkins's November 16, 1921 report is an attachment to the November 17, 1921 letter of Charles W. Fowle to the Secretary of State, NA 867.4016/432.

Report of William Hawkes: Conditions in Sivas and the Deportation Trails

Another American NER veteran who Cunningham spoke to was William Hawkes. Hawkes had been working in Turkey for three years, mostly at Sivas. In July 1922, Charles W. Fowle, foreign secretary of the Near East Relief, wrote Allen Dulles at the State Department to notify him that William E. Hawkes could corroborate the reports of Dr. Mark Ward, Theda Phelps, and others who Dulles had already seen.

Hawkes had not traveled as widely as Hopkins, nor had he seen as much, but all of the details he reports are telling.

One year ago the Government called all the big boys of our Orphanage and set ages for those who had no birth certificates. It was practically impossible for those boys to get their certificates from their original homes, and ages were set according to the caprice of the official. Most of the boys were made from one to four years older than their real age. Most of those boys were called and taken during the year. This spring our Commissaire with a military officer picked out about eight of our boys, none of whom could possibly be over nineteen years old, and their ages were all made twenty-one or twenty-two, which is above soldier age. When these boys or any Armenians are taken as soldiers, they could be exempted by paying Ltq. 300 (paper) for one year. If this could not be done, they were sent to Erzerum, supposedly to work on the railroad, but in reality to starve or freeze to death. The stories we heard from Erzerum during last winter were all sad ones, as the majority of those we sent that way did not survive.*

Some exiled men went to Harpout and Erzerum were granted permission from Angora to return to their homes in Samsun or Konia, as in certain cases I know about. These men were allowed to travel as far

* In his memoirs, the Armenian survivor Varteres Mikael Garougian reported dire conditions in the Erzurum region similar to those Hawkes mentions. As Garougian reports, "All the soldier-laborers had been specifically sent to this area [Korucuk, near Erzerum] so that hunger, thirst, and cold would precipitate our deaths. Why use bullets to kill? . . . Instead, let the soldier-workers die off. . . ." (Hofmann, "Cumulative Genocides," 74, quotes this from Mikael Garougian, *Destiny of the Dzidzernag*, Princeton: Gomidas Institute, 2005, 169).

Many others, like teachers, were also sent to Erzerum in terrible condition, as Bruce Clark's researches and interviews note (121, 114).

as Sivas and in two cases were stopped there and in three other cases were sent back to Malatia. . . .

Our Commissaire, Jevdet Bey, the Sivas Sanitary Inspector, always hectored us and hindered our help for needy people continually. He is one of the most immoral and really bad-minded men I have ever known, but was always so suave and apparently the best friend one had that he often deceived us. There is a peculiar custom among the Turks of painting a man's door red when he is outrageously immoral and disliked by his fellow-Turks, and that happened to this man.

The Greek deportations began about a year ago and until November we, in Sivas, were helpless to assist the deportees passing through Sivas except through other people. Many Armenian people from Konia and Eski-Shehir were allowed to remain in Sivas in care of the Bishop, and through him we were able to help them and to take many children into the Orphanages. In November we were given permission to help Greek exiles who were allowed to stay in the city and those who were sick. . . .

We were allowed to rent three large houses for the use of Greek people, and there we attempted to care for those sick of typhus, pneumonia, dysentery, small-pox and starvation. These people were piled (literally) into an old Armenian church and Miss Phelps was able to remove them to our houses after begging and beseeching the Commissaire, who did not want such help given. This old church was a real "hell-hole," where sick and living and dying and dead were all mixed up together. . . . It was in this place that both Miss Phelps and Mr. Thurber got typhus germs. . . .

The deportations have continued for one year and were still in progress when I left the interior, May 1922. Within twelve miles of Sivas we passed a group of about two hundred women and children trudging along in a cold rain. The next morning as Mr. Beach came out to where our car was stranded he passed fourteen dead bodies. We passed bodies in several places and saw two women and one little boy left by the roadside to die.

All these we passed were ragged and barefooted and looked almost starved to death. We probably saw fourteen or fifteen hundred people.

We were told by members of the Tokat Armenian Orphange Committee that the exiles as they stopped in Tokat were not allowed to be given or to buy bread or water.

In Amassia we passed a group of thirty persons, one old man, three women and the rest children from five to fifteen years of age. In Samsun there was shooting in the streets and outskirts of the city every night as the Greeks in the hills attempted to enter the city to get food.

As far as I have been able to find out it would seem that all the Greeks from the coast to the interior as far as Sivas, from every little village as well, have been rounded up and sent on the road towards Malatia, Harput, and beyond.

Hawkes's report was filed under State Department number 867.4016/583; Fowle's introductory letter is dated July 18, 1922; Hawkes's report itself is dated "Constantinople, June 5, 1922."

SUMMARY OF SAMSUN WAR DIARIES FROM NOVEMBER 1921 TO JUNE 1922

ATTACKS UPON GREEK PARTISANS, A BOMBARDMENT, AND CONTINUED DEPORTATIONS

To this point, we've presented the relevant material from some six months' worth of Samsun naval war diaries in considerable detail. The next eight months or so of the war diaries include less material of importance to the focus of this book, and accordingly we summarize the diaries rather than present them verbatim. (Note that we do not have the war diaries of the Childs *or* Hatfield, *two additional American Navy destroyers that came to Samsun for a couple of weeks apiece during 1922.)*

Relatively Minor Issues

Topics of relatively minor importance that the war diaries present may be mentioned briefly here.

The ship captains on a few occasions mention how the Greco-Turkish War is going but not necessarily with accuracy. They also continue to monitor the arrival of weapons or ammunition on the docks and caravans moving inland, offloading that happened frequently, although as Captain Leahy notes, "It is certain that the allied powers with their full control of the Black Sea make no effort to stop the importation" (personal diary, St. Louis *captain, Sept. 21, 1921). The Americans also continue to notice shipments of Russian gold coming through the docks. Occasionally delegations from other countries pass through Samsun while en route to or from Angora, such as a group of*

Italians returning from Angora or a Russian mission en route there (Sturtevant *WD, Jan. 2, 1922;* Sturtevant *WD, Jan. 12, 1922).*

A more important issue arises concerning possibly fake telegrams sent home by men deported earlier from Samsun for the purpose of extorting money from worried families. This question appears in the November 30, 1921 war diary of the Sands, *for example, quoted earlier in our first Testimony section. An answer appears in the recently published letters of Lieutenant Arthur D. Murray of the* Overton. *He reports an interesting discovery—that before one massacre at Kavak, "the men were asked if they wished any telegrams sent to relatives or friends. They were then asked to turn over all their money to the guards for safe-keeping. Telegrams were then sent to the names and addresses given by the men, worded about as follows: 'I am at —- and am all right. In two days I will send a man back to see you. Please give him —- (naming a sum of money) —- which I will need to complete my journey.' This note came to the home of one of the men who had returned home safely after escaping from the massacre" (Murray, 365).*

The diaries of this period also report on Osman Agha's continuing activities. After burning, looting, raping, and killing, Osman Agha with his chettahs had traveled from Marsovan to Angora, where he had been made a colonel in the army. There he apparently took part in the war against the Hellenic Army, for he is mentioned as having been wounded at the front. In January 1922, he arrives at Samsun accompanied by a bodyguard of fifty mounted men to embark on a steamer for his home base at the port city of Kerasund, east of Samsun. In the war diary that reports this, Captain Cunningham notes that Osman was "hated and feared by all factions in Samsun" and that several local Turks were overheard wishing that he had been killed rather than merely wounded (Williamson *WD, Jan. 31, 1922).*

A couple of months later, Osman comes back to Samsun on a French steamer, along with a newly recruited force of 600 men, returning to the front. The Overton's *captain, Bruce Ware, (WD April 2, 1922) expresses hope that it is only a coincidence that a group of refugees is to be deported that same day—Osman's cutthroats usually being death to unprotected Greeks. The groups apparently leave on different days, however, and there is no more mention of Osman Agha in the Samsun diaries.*

The Visit of the Nationalist Interior Minister

Captain Cunningham mentions in his diary of February 1922 that the Nationalist Interior Minister, Ali Fethi (Okyar), visited Samsun for several days and that Cunningham decided to visit him. It is worth presenting the Williamson *war diary entry of this visit.*

February 12, 1922

Called on the Minister of the Interior. I explained that I had not called before on account of the bad weather. He was very courteous and an extremely intelligent looking man. He looks more like a European than a Turk. He speaks French fluently and English fairly well, having been a prisoner in Malta for some time.

The following is a translation by Arif Bey of a communique issued by the Minister of the Interior and published in the local papers on the 12th. Instant:-

> Copy of translation. Samsun, Feb. 12, 1922
> Circular-letter.
>
> To the Greek insurgents in the mountains.
>
> "You enjoyed [a] very prosperous and luxurious life since centuries under the safeguard of the Turkish Government. You now moved to establish a Government in the name of the Pontus and revolted against the Turkish nation and the Turkish Government by the mischievous intrigues and selfish ambition—ambitions of the outside world which is neither your friend nor ours.
>
> "As you were a beneficial element in Agricultural and commercial life in this country, you began to burn the Mohammedan villages and kill their inhabitants; particularly you burnt some of them alive with their children. You devastated all the Mohammedan villages and spread an awful misery in all parts of this country.
>
> "As the Turkish nation is struggling at the front (against the enemy) you are using your arms against Home on account of our enemy. The government will urgently take necessary and stringent measures (Military) against your rebellious actions.
>
> "I bring to your notice that, in considering from the point of view of humanity with a view to avoiding further bloodshed, you will at once surrender to Bafra, Tcharshamba, Ladik and

> Vizier-Keupru Governments without any conditions and restrictions within a week from this declaration, I therefore invite you as a God-fearing and law-abiding people of this country. This is my last remark."
>
> (Sd) Ali Fethi,
> The Minister of the Interior.

Copies of this message have been sent to the Greeks who are hiding in the mountains.

In reference to this entry, it is notable that, as "Minister of the Interior," Ali Fethi, who had been appointed to this position under the Nationalists in mid-1921, held the same position under the Turkish Nationalists that had been held by the infamous Talaat Pasha, the prime architect of the Armenian genocide, in the Young Turk government. So perhaps it is not surprising that this Interior Minister speaks as if one of his principal missions is to root out all enemies of the Nationalists, calling for Greek guerillas to surrender as he does here and threatening their utter destruction if they do not.

The minister's warning to the Greek fighters, of course, is both Nationalist propaganda, omitting any mention of the absolutely egregious Turkish atrocities, and a threat. Captain Cunningham makes no notice in his war diary (it is possible that he does not know) that the Minister of the Interior has brought with him a significant military force—perhaps it preceded him—to attack Greek guerillas in the Samsun-Bafra region. This force is said to have been composed of 2,500 troops and 1,000 Laz chettahs.

The minister would eventually report back to Angora that he had wiped out the remaining Greek fighters and seized much in the way of arms and ammunition. A later Greek military account from Constantinople would report that 4,000 of 10,000 Greek bandits had been killed (Psomiades, "Bombardment," 146, note 27). To be sure, both the complete annihilation of the Greeks in the mountains reported by Fethi and the figures reported by the Greek military may be doubted.

But significant military conflict certainly had occurred, which indicates a couple of things: (1) the American Navy captains had few sources of information about regional Turkish military actions or about Greek guerilla activities, for that matter; and (2) although Kemal's biographer gives the impression that all was quiet in the Pontus region by the end of 1921 (Mango, 330), actually the Greek guerilla presence had remained a concern even after the dismissal of Nureddin Pasha in November. One is also struck by Captain Cunningham's very positive impression of the Turkish Interior Minister, Ali Fethi, despite the minister's dire mission, huge propaganda effort, and threat. Was Cunningham utterly naive?

Threatened and Actual Bombardments and the Possibility of a Greek Landing

One of the primary concerns voiced throughout the Samsun war diaries, of course, was a possible bombardment of Samsun. As we have seen, each time Greek ships were seen approaching, the senior American officer at the port got his ship underway and sped out to meet them, requesting time so the Americans could withdraw from the line of fire if a bombardment was planned. Sometimes the American warship's captain also would mention the perilous condition of thousands of Greek women and children remaining in the city and the danger a bombardment would present to them. By doing so, he was implicitly or overtly asking the Greek Navy's forbearance, for Turkish anger might visit itself on the local ethnic Greeks.

Earlier Greek Navy visits to Samsun had occurred on July 12, July 21, July 28 and November 5 in 1921. However, on June 7, 1922, the Greek commodore was not dissuaded as others seem to have been, and he went ahead to shell the city (see the long Sands *WD, June 7, 1921). This bombardment, which Psomiades says was intended to draw some Turkish troops away from the battlefield far to the west, failed at that and accomplished little else. Strategically, it was altogether a "blip," according to this scholar ("Bombardment," 153). After the Greek ships fired some 400 rounds, which were returned by some 25 Turkish shells, they withdrew, having done little more than damage several buildings and destroy some oil and gas supplies, although four Turks were reported killed and three wounded (*Sands *WD, June 7, 1922, p. 11). The next day, a Russian ship entered the harbor and unloaded ammunition (Psomiades, 153), and two days after this, on the ninth of June, a horse race took place at the Samsun track. According to the* Sturtevant *diary of June 9, the race was attended by virtually the whole population of the city. Obviously, Samsun had quickly returned to normal.*

Ironically, the Sturtevant *war diary mentions that had the bombardment gone on a bit longer or aimed more widely, it might have explod-*

ed some 400 mines stored in a building near the NER hospital. This would have caused "a catastrophe of appalling magnitude," including the potential destruction of both the hospital and that entire area of the city (Sturtevant *WD, June 8). Knowing this, the American ship captain therefore was not persuaded by the Mutasariff's contemporaneous argument that the hospital would be a good refuge for Americans to assemble at should future bombardments occur.*

Incidentally, a dispute between the American naval officer on site and the Turkish officials prior to the bombardment was whether the Turks would allow the American civilians in the city to board the American destroyer present in the harbor, which could then ferry the civilians away to safety. The Turks forbade it. There were at most twenty American civilians working in the city during this period, although if one allows for a few wives and children among the families of the five or six American merchants at Samsun and a couple of NER workers awaiting permission to go inland, there might have been a total of thirty non-naval Americans in Samsun at any one time. It was, anyway, a small enough group that all these civilians had clustered in Currin's house ashore during the Samsun bombardment. (Commander Ghormley, incidentally, had taken care to point this house out to the Greek captain so that the Greek gunners might avoid hitting it; Sands *WD, June 7, 1922, p. 8).*

It seems that martial ineffectiveness of this naval action was typical of the Hellenic Navy's shelling of the several Pontic ports over the year. Actually, the greatest impact of the shellings may have been the secondary effect they had upon Ottoman Greeks in those ports. In the minutes of the British committee meeting of August 17, 1921 in Constantinople, Dr. Theotokas's argues this case, saying that:

> *[M]uch of the fanaticism displayed by the Turkish population on the Black Sea Littoral was due to the ineffectual and senseless bombardment of towns and ports there by the Greek Naval forces. The report above [a letter dated August 1, 1921 from Samsun] expressed the fervent hope that Greek Naval forces would follow up the bombardment immediately by landing troops to protect the Christian inhabitants. (Yeghiayan, 218)*

Of course, the Greek navy never landed troops, and so this allowed the Turks to retaliate for the bombardment upon the local Greeks, as they sometimes did.

The Hellenic Navy's strategic ability was hampered by the Allied powers denying them certain warmaking powers, to be sure. Otherwise the Hellenic Navy might have attempted blockades or other tactics rather than be limited to the occasional bombardments we report here. However, Psomiades points out that "the Allied powers denied Greece these rights, including the occupation of the Black Sea ports" ("Bombardment," 153).

*Yes, according to the war diaries, the Turks greatly feared the possible landing of a strong Hellenic military force (*Williamson *WD, Aug. 8, 1921). As we have mentioned before, theoretically such a force might have have provided a second front for the Hellenic Army, adding strategic complication to the Turkish Army's deployment inland.*

It would have been very difficult to implement such a second front. For one thing, current Turkish-Greek forces were faced off hundreds of miles, and many weeks' march, away from any Pontic landing site. Even more important, the Pontic mountains lay between any Pontic port and the dug-in Greek and Turkish Armies. Just by remembering the historic lessons of Thermopylae, Hellenic naval officers should have known that the Pontic mountains would give Turkish soldiers many strong defensive positions from which to ambush invading forces. Also though Greek bandits might have supported a landing force, their effectiveness was unlikely to be substantial given the limitations posed by their lack of military arms and training, as well as the presence of their families. But much of the above is theoretical, and to our knowledge, actual information about the Greek guerillas is hard to come by. As Fotiadis notes, "The activities of the partisan forces and their battles with the Kemalist army and irregular Chetes have yet to be documented" (Fotiadis, 484; an assessment written in 2015).

On the other hand, while a second front seems unlikely to have succeeded militarily, *the mere landing of a Hellenic force in Pontus might have provided* political *difficulties. The diaries make it clear that there was little support for Mustafa Kemal's leadership in Samsun, at least, and on his stumbling, another Turkish leader (like Nureddin) might have arisen to challenge him.*

In any case, the Greek warships that had bombarded Samsun withdrew after receiving return fire.

A common speculation in the diaries was whether Samsun was a "fortified city" (see also, for example, Overton *WD, July 1, 1921), but most American officers took a position that it was indeed fortified given the Turkish gun emplacements they had often observed. They argued to the Mutasariff that the city could be legally bombarded under international law. For some reason, before the bombardment of Samsun, Captain Ghormley of the* Sands *repeated the Turkish claim that the city was unfortified to the Greek captain he contacted, even though a glance at the entries in the war diaries covering earlier Hellenic naval visits would have told him differently. A couple of days after the bombardment, Captain Haas would express to the Mutasariff his amazement at the continued Turkish claim of nonfortification despite the return fire that had bellowed from a few Turkish guns during the actual Hellenic bombardment (*Sturtevant *WD, June 10, 1922).*

*One minor contention among the Americans was whether Captain Ghormley might have evacuated American civilians in defiance of Turkish orders during the shelling. A tobacco manager thought the navy should have forced the issue, believing that the Turks would have allowed it. However, Captain Haas, whose vessel arrived shortly afterwards, thought Ghormley had been right not to attempt it (*Sturtevant *WD, June 11, 1922).*

The Continuing Deportations

Most important of all the issues during the eight months covered by the war diaries of November 1921 to June 1922 continued to be the regular deportations occurring at many Pontic and Anatolian locations, including Samsun. Greek women and children from the Samsun vicinity were regularly sent inland.

We have read of the June 1921 deportations and massacres of Samsun's Greek men and, shortly after that, of the Nationalist order to deport the remaining women, children, and elderly from the city. Then, suddenly, apparently in response to Admiral Bristol's protest, the Nationalists backed off, disavowing the order that had originally been promulgated, probably at the insistence of Nureddin Pasha and others of like mind.

Overall, the war diaries document that Greek women and children who were originally residents of Samsun proper never were actually deported, although they continually feared being sent away. The 10,000 to 12,000 who were allowed to stay at Samsun, even until the burning of Smyrna and after, seem to have owed their safety and their lives both to the regular presence of the American destroyers at Samsun, as well as to continued Nationalist restraint following the protest made to Mustapha Kemal by Admiral Bristol.

However, the admiral issued no additional objection to the deportations from most of the rest of the Pontus region or, for that matter, to deportations of Ottoman Greeks and other Christians from much of the rest of Anatolia, which also continued apace. Moreover, even refugees who had sought food and shelter in Samsun after their nearby villages had been destroyed continued to be deported south, and the admiral made no objection to these deportations either, though they were reported regularly in the war diaries over the next year. When families of partisans came down from the mountains near Samsun after being sheltered for a time there—they were probably near starvation—they were also deported without American protest.

*The war diaries record local Samsun deportations of 700 women and children in November 1921 and further deportation of 1,500 in January 1922. Then groups of 1,400 and 1,300 of these poor people were deported in April 1922 (*Fox *WD, Nov. 17, 1921;* Sturtevant *WD, Jan. 7,* Fox *WD, April 10, and* Sturtevant *WD, April 25, 1922). Another 500 were deported the day before the Samsun bombardment, that is, on June 6, 1922 (as reported in the* Sturtevant *WD, June 8, 1922). This total of some 5,400 deportees no doubt fails to include all of the women and children deported over this period, both because the Americans may not have witnessed it all (deportations from or through Samsun sometimes took place at night) and because war diaries for some short periods over this eight month-stretch are missing. For example, we do not have any diaries for March 1922.*

In this respect, it is important to note that not all authors of the diaries understood what deportation actually meant. As we have seen, Captain Bristol of the Overton *had no illusions; he doubted whether some deportees would survive even over the next mountain! Captain Leahy was also quite certain about the Greeks' poor prospects. As he noted in his personal diary: "All adult Greek males have been deported and their wives and daughters employed in the tobacco warehouses are in constant terror of being also deported, which would result in the death of many by starvation, exhaustion, and cold" (Sept. 21, 1921).*

Many Americans like these two men might have had access to Ambassador Morgenthau's book and the Bryce Report, which described in great detail the manner and extent of the Armenian genocide or perhaps in some other way had heard in detail how terribly Christians in

Turkey had suffered during the Great War. They may have expected that the resumption of deportations in Pontus would resemble what had happened in 1915–1916.

But we continue to read of such American officials as the two NER hospital directors being naïvely impressed by the good order and condition of the deportees leaving Samsun (Mr. Van Toor in the Fox *WD, June 18, 1921, and ten months later, Mr. Green in the* Sturtevant *WD, April 25, 1922). More noteworthy yet, we read of Captain Harry Pence reporting in the* McFarland *war diary of June 2, 1922 that Faik Bey, the new Samsun Mutasariff who had taken his position after the dismissal of Nureddin Pasha as regional military commander, was "apparently a fine type of Turk. For one thing, he* has not permitted any atrocities here" *(emphasis added).*

True, once Nureddin left Pontus, the tone of the war diaries is no longer as dark as it had been before. Until that time, every single ship captain had commented ominously about the likely fate of Samsun's women and children. Faik Bey does seems to have been a bit less brutal. Indeed on May 29, he expresses to Captain Harry Pence his desire "to have the Greek women who work in the tobacco houses remain, in order that they could earn a livelihood" (McFarland *WD). Such a humane hope is seldom heard from Turkish officials, and these Greek women and children were actually to stay until evacuated to Greece sometime after the burning of Smyrna. It is likely that Faik Bey's promise to spare these Samsun resident Greeks eased tensions in the city somewhat.*

But tensions would have been very different in the "wretchedly bad" conditions of the "detention barracks" on the hillside beyond Samsun (Sturtevant *WD, April 25 and 23, 1922), where starving women and children coming down out of the mountains were temporarily camped. Their subsequent deportation, ordered by Faik Bey, likely sent them into the standard dangers of starvation, exposure, robbery, rape, and death and certainly constituted an atrocity despite Captain Pence's impression.*

Faik Bey had assured the Sturtevant's *Captain Haas that "no civilized country desiring peace and security could countenance or tolerate the depredations of bandits," to which that captain had commented favorably in the diaries: "The logic of this is impregnable" (WD, Dec. 31, 1921). To such an argument, the more knowledgeable Pontic Greeks would probably have responded that no civilized country could countenance massacres, death marches, and the "death-sentence" conditions of the labor battalions in the first place, which fatal circumstances, from the point of view of those not yet exterminated, had given rise to the Greek guerilla groups.*

Early in the war diaries, even Captain Bristol of the Overton, *upon hearing the local Turkish military commander offer the pros and cons of the then-current deportation order, noted that he was "forced to admit, that aside from the question of humanity [alone] he made a fair case for the Turkish side" (WD, July 19, 1921). Of course, that's like saying, "except for the ovens, the Germans in 1940-1945 had military reasons for treating the Jews as they did." Such a statement would not be true even accepting the qualification, but most important, the use of the ovens would contradict any such tentative approval. Finally, the fact that the Turks sometimes in these deportations might, in their minds, just be letting innocents die of starvation and exposure rather than killing them outright obviously makes no difference in the overall equation. They put the deported Greeks in the position to die. Hence they were guilty of bringing about their deaths.*

The children of deported Greeks that had dropped out exhausted and were picked up by the NER and taken to Beirut some 750 miles away. *The New Near East*, Nov. 1922, 15.

WHAT CONSTITUTES AN ATROCITY? *–TESTIMONY OF EDITH WOOD AND ETHEL THOMPSON*

Lack of understanding as to what was actually happening in Anatolia no doubt sometimes resulted partly from a lack of imagination on a captain's part. However, certainly these captains were also influenced by Admiral Bristol's mantra as to what the realities in Turkey had to be. *Whatever the reason for such ignorance, the* actual *nature of the deportee experience can be shown by a couple of additional testimonies.*

Neither of the testimonies that follow are new, and not all of the deportees mentioned here come from the Samsun region. However, the tens of thousands of Greeks who were marched inland from the Pontic coast all endured similar conditions of hopelessness, particularly when they had just entered a city only to be marched off into a snowstorm the next day—or suddenly discovered that the children carried on their backs had frozen to death on their most recent journey (something, incidentally, which various memoirs indicate happened many hundreds of times on the death marches).

It is hard to imagine how the "Turkish case for the deportations" that is spoken of in the diaries might possibly justify the conditions described in the following accounts of two American reliefers who witnessed the ordeal of deportees hundreds of miles into their journey inland.

Edith Wood's Testimony — from Malatia

Having entered Turkey as a nurse with the Near East Relief, Edith Wood first worked at Harput and then moved on to Malatia, where conditions were "even more horrible." Unlike at Harput, where she was forbidden to provide relief, she was able to attend to Greek orphans in Malatia. But as she found for many of them, that made no difference, as a reporter who talked to her noted.

Housing the children only prolonged their agony. . . as only half of those under 12 were temporarily saved.

From four to seven of those who passed the initial test of being able to stand food and washing passed away each day after Miss Wood thought they might be pulled through. Their constitution was too greatly undermined by the journey from the coast. "It was like an endless chain," said Miss Wood. "The children would often be gone before I had taken their names. Forty to fifty of the older women passed on each day also. You see, starvation, exposure, exhaustion did their work before these deportees arrived at Malatia. They came to me in the last stages.

"Food and medicine were no good, although I tried my best. The Turks were doing nothing at all for them. In Malatia bodies lay around in the streets and fields. No attempt was made to bury them. Deportation is worse than a sentence of execution. Unless one sees these things, it is difficult to believe that such monstrous cruelty and barbarity exist in this world. Making women and children suffer that way until they drop and expire seems incredible. But that is Malatia. And they receive us coldly in Constantinople when we want to tell what we know for the benefit of our Government, and let it appear very clearly that my story is unwelcome and that I am a hysterical woman, exaggerating or falsifying—that is the way it is.*

"It took me fourteen days' constant travel to get from Malatia to Samsun on the Black Sea coast, where I took a vessel for Constantinople last Thursday. All the way it was a heartrending journey, passing women and little children on their long road to Calvary. And I knew what was at the end of it! I hardly pitied those who had given up *en route*. Bodies lay along the roadside and in the fields everywhere. There was no hope for the Greeks from Malatia to Samsun, and the most fortunate were those who perished at the start."

Reporter Herbert Gibbons told Wood's story and quoted her (as shown above) in the Christian Science Monitor, *July 13, 1922, in an article entitled, "Near East Relief Prevented from Helping Greeks."*

Ethel Thompson's Testimony — Her Experience at Harput

Ethel Thompson of Boston worked in the city of Harput, deep in Asia Minor, for almost a year. She had entered the interior of Turkey in August 1921 in the midst of the death marches.

I entered Anatolia to do orphanage work for the Near East Relief unprejudiced regarding race or religion. I have come out with a feeling

* Edith Wood was not the only female American relief worker to be denigrated and ignored by Admiral Bristol in such a way (see, for instance, Shenk, "Ethnic Cleansing," 94).

of horror and misgiving that in 1922 such conditions are allowed to exist under any Government or people. . . . We were supporting the Turkish orphanage and helping the Turkish poor as well as supporting the Armenian orphanages and aiding with clothes and food, when we were allowed to do so, the ghastly lines of gaunt starving Greek women and children who staggered across Anatolia through the city of Harput, their glassy eyes fairly protruding from their heads, their bones merely covered with skin, skeleton babies tied to their backs, driven on without food supplies or clothing until they dropped dead, Turkish gendarmes hurrying them with their guns. My eyes still ache with the sights I have seen and I hope my brain will sometime forget that open graveyard around Harput as it was last winter. People ask if these reports are true! After a year of these experiences, the very question amazes me. My orphanage work took me out to the villages where outlying buildings were situated, and I can merely swear that I am telling the truth concerning what I saw daily.

On June 30th, 1921, I left Constantinople for the interior of Anatolia. At Samsun I was held for two months awaiting permission from the Kemalist Government in Angora to continue the journey to Harput, about 500 miles across the interior of Anatolia. During my stay in Samsun, in the early part of July, the Greek villages round about were burned and the inhabitants deported, including the women and children. In June, before our arrival, the young Greek men were deported from Samsun, and soon after our arrival the old men were notified and tramped away in the night. We were kept awake at night by the crying of the Greek women—their wives and daughters. Night after night, from the Armenian orphanage where I spent most of my time, I watched the burning of villages and thought what a hell on earth human beings could make of this really beautiful section of the country. In August, word came that the women were to follow the old men. Our house was surrounded by these poor women, hammering at our doors, holding out their children, begging us to take the children if we could not save the women. They threw their arms about our necks and we never felt as helpless in our lives. About this time the Greek fleet threatened to bombard the town and this saved for a time the women.*

* As we have seen, it was the American protest—and the presence of destroyers at Samsun—that probably saved the Greek women and children who were residents of Samsun proper. Any Greek bombardment of the city was more likely to have brought about deportation than to have stopped it.

Our permission arrived the last of August, and we were allowed to proceed. We crossed Anatolia under a blazing sun, passing groups and groups of the old men of Samsun and the inhabitants of other Black Sea ports walking on, God knows where, driven by Turkish gendarmes. The dead bodies of these who had dropped during the hard tramp were lying by the roadside. Vultures had eaten parts of the flesh so that in most cases merely skeletons remained. When I arrived in Sivas, I was ill with the intense heat and our party was supposed to rest three days. After resting one day, however, word came that the Turks were to [appropriate] our American trucks in which we were travelling, so we quickly left the city before dawn the next morning.

Upon arriving in Malatia, we found the remainder of a group of young men who had been deported from Samsun in June. These men told us that the balance of their party had been killed. Upon arriving in Harput, September 3rd, we entered a city full of starving, sick, wretched human wrecks—Greek women, children, men. These people were trying to make soup of grass and considered themselves fortunate when they could secure a sheep's ear to add to it. When the poor things heard of the killing of a sheep, they tried to secure the ear—the only part of the animal thrown away in Anatolia. I shall never forget the look of a black hairy sheep's ear floating in boiling water and these poor wretches trying to obtain nourishment by eating it. The Turks had given them no food on the 500-mile trip from Samsun. Those with money could bribe the guards for food or buy a little on the way—until they were robbed. Those without money died by the wayside. In many places, thirsty in the blistering sun and heat, they were not allowed water unless they could pay for it. The Near East Relief stations tried to give them bread as they passed through Cesarea and Sivas but the amount they could carry was small. It would have been more humane to give them a bullet than bread, however, because death would mean a release from intense suffering which would in time end in death.

When a woman with a baby died, the baby was taken from her dead arms and handed to another woman and the horrible march proceeded. Old blind men, led by little children, trudged along the road. The whole thing was like a march of corpses—a march of death across Anatolia which continued during my entire stay. First the young men, then the old men, then the women and children who had committed no crime against any one. Numbers who had travelled in winter and thousands who had typhus were afflicted with gangerine feet. These were lying about Harput camps in helpless groups.

The heaviest winter weather, when a howling blizzard was raging, during a blinding snowfall, was the favorite time chosen by the Turks to drive the Greeks on. Thousands perished in the snow. The road from Harput to Bitlis was lined with bodies. I saw women with transparent lips who did not look human. They were gaunt shadows. The roads over which women and children travelled were impassable for any kind of travel excepting pack mule. . . .

On February 5th, 1922, I and another American were riding horseback to visit an outlying orphanage when we came to an old watershed five minutes outside the city of Mazereh. We heard a different kind of cry than the usual moan of the refugees, and riding nearer we saw about 300 small children who had been driven together in a circle. 20 gendarmes who had dismounted from their horses were cruelly beating the children with their heavy swords. When a mother rushed in to save her child she was also beaten and driven out. The children were cowering down or holding up their little arms to try to ward off the blows. As an Armenian interpreter was with us, we did not linger.

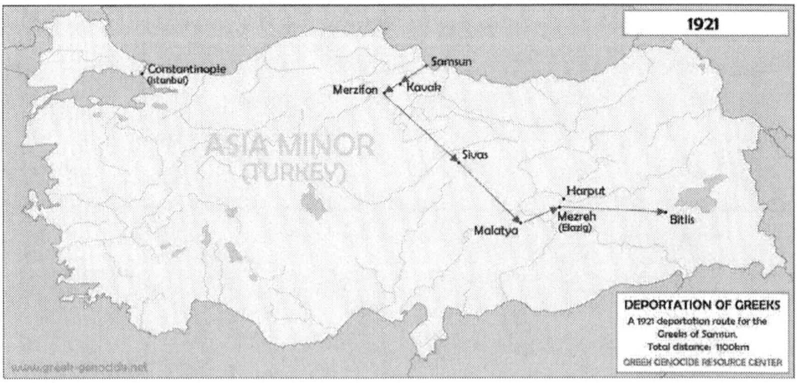

A standard deportation route (upon which Greek women, children, and elderly were herded on foot) ran from Samsun inland for over 500 miles. Thousands who survived such journeys would die at Malatia and Harput from exposure, starvation, and disease.

Our Director had begged for permission to take into the orphanages the Greek children whose mothers had died on the way. It was always refused. Finally, after many weeks of continual appeals, they promised that we could take an old building formerly belonging to German missionaries and keep the Greek children there. We did this and issued a week's rations of food and gave them some clothes, but in a very few days the building was empty. The Turks had driven the children over the mountain. Finally we were permitted to open a camp for those unable to move. The camp was two miles from the city. We could not admit one of these people into our hospital, no matter how serious the case, without payment of L40.00 [forty Turkish pounds] by the patient to the sanitary inspector. The patient, no matter how sick, was forced to go in person to make the payment. Some of the patients, too sick to be out of bed, went time and again to the sanitary inspector and were sent back because they did not have sufficient money. Many died before permission was granted. The roads round about were covered with dead bodies who died from disease and exposure. Flocks of vultures continually hovered about the city. Anatolia has been for the past year an open graveyard.

The attitude of the Turks toward the Greeks who were deported from the Black Sea coast has been one of extermination. From statistics obtained from reliable American sources, we have accounted for the whereabouts of at least 30,000, who passed through Sivas. 8,000 died on the way to Harput and 2,000 remained in Malatia up to last March. More than 2000 refugees died in Harput during the past winter. If they died in Harput, they were wrapped in cotton cloth and carried out by cartloads and buried. In our refugee camp the same method was followed. If they died in the streets or by the road, they were thrown to one side and the vultures ate them. 15,000 were sent to Diarbekir during the freezing winter blizzards. Three-fourths of this number were women and children and they marched out of the city of Harput without food or covering over mountains where no shelter could be found. The best looking girls were taken into Moslem harems by Turks who boasted openly of the number of women who they had taken for this purpose. They then sent them to us for bread, stating they were refugees. Some of the girls whom I knew in Samsun disfigured their faces with dye to hide their good looks in the hope that they would not be taken. 3000 of these, sent to Diarkebir, died on the road, and 1000 after arriving there. Some were put to work on roads and were given a little thin soup or bread each day. If they were too ill to work, their food was stopped and they died without medical aid. 9000 Greeks went toward Bitlis but their whereabouts is unknown. They are probably dead as Bitlis is partially destroyed and is incapable of supporting more than 10,000 people. We were told when passing through Diarbekir that not one child under eight years of age arrived in Diarbekir alive.

In the Villayet of Harput we were not allowed to employ any Greek. Some Greeks with money bought the permission to work for a Turk. Money was the only means of temporarily securing safety.

When we were preparing to leave, the Turkish Governor sent for us and asked us to deny the reports given by Mr. Yowell and Dr. Ward when we arrived at Beirut or Constantinople. At that time we did not even know what reports Mr. Yowell had given. The Vali threatened that unless we promised, he would not give us permit to leave. Finally we obtained the permit without giving any promise other than to tell the truth as we saw it and I am herewith living up to my promise to that Turkish Vali back in Harput.

In submitting this statement, I wish that the women of America who have a voice in the Government could do something for the women and children of Anatolia who are dying and suffering untold agonies. Trade interests, petty jealousies, greed for territory, etc., should be set aside for the cause of humanity. I think it is a disgrace that in 1922 such things have happened. . . .

When she left Anatolia and the Near East Relief, Ethel Thompson sent the above statement (dated Aug. 4, 1922) to Charles W. Fowle, Foreign Secretary of the Near East Relief. He forwarded it to the Allen Dulles at the Department of State, Washington, D.C., index 867.4016/626.

TREBIZOND WAR DIARIES FROM JUNE 1921 TO JUNE 1922

INTRODUCTION TO TREZIBOND WAR DIARIES

Of Turkish ports other than Samsun, Admiral Bristol only sent his destroyers to Trebizond with any regularity. Typically, Admiral Bristol had his destroyers stop over briefly there, about once a month or so. This port was smaller than Samsun but was famous as a Western terminus of the great camel caravan route (known as the Silk Road) from the East. Marco Polo, for instance, had returned to Venice from his great journey to China via Trebizond.

In one of the first of these Trebizond diaries, we find a brief report of the Greek naval bombardment of the city. This shelling, which occurred in July, seemed to have been as ineffectual as other Hellenic Navy shellings of Pontic ports, but it triggered Turkish deportation of some Greek males.

Beyond the shelling, in this group of Trebizond diaries we hear of a Valli of Trebizond (a Valli was the civilian governor of a large province) being relieved from his job for refusing to deport the Greeks. In the McFarland *diary for August 1921, Captain Haines reports that the Turks had yet to deport Greeks and Armenians. However, by December, all Greek men of military age had been deported from the city. Even later, deportations of men are reported taking place gradually, fifty at a time every few days, supposedly to allow these smaller groups of deportees to find food. (Perhaps the initial deportation at Trebizond took men of a relatively narrow range of ages, while the later ones took older and younger men, or maybe these later deportations involved men seized from nearby villages.) Strikingly, both in December 1921 and then again in late May and early June 1922, the ship captains report that there had been no reports of Greek women and children being deported from the Trebizond district.*

A report worth noting is one that mentions Turkish destroyers capturing a vessel containing many Greek refugees who were trying to flee the country. The captured men were deported inland. (Such Turkish warships had not been reported in the war diaries prior to this. Apparently, whenever the Greek Navy was active in the Black Sea, they usually stayed in Batoum.) In this connection, although only a single report in the Samsun diaries speaks of Greeks fleeing Turkey by coastal boats, still, as Americans during this period came across great camps of Greeks in several Russian ports, it is likely that waterborne escapes from Pontus were often attempted and that some of them were successful.

In late May 1922, Captain Pence of the McFarland *recounts the "Gibbons" incident and also refers to a man named Yowell. These mentions require some explanation.*

Forrest Yowell had been the Director of NER activities in Harput, a city deep in the interior of Turkey. As reported in the Sands *war diary of November 30, 1921, Yowell had been so horrified at the condition of the minorities he encountered there that he had sent a message to Samsun, which he hoped would be sent on to President Harding, begging the president to intervene in the war between Greece and Turkey so as to stop the "untold suffering and death to the noncombatant population both Moslem and Christian in Anatolia." Nothing came of that, but Yowell and Dr. Mark Ward and the other Americans in Harput did their best to aid the deportees passing through Harput.*

Perhaps because of such activities, Yowell and his team were suddenly ordered to leave Anatolia entirely. The expulsion of the four Americans occurred in March 1922, and it would take them two months to reach Constantinople (traveling via Aleppo).

On arriving at the old Ottoman capitol city, they met with Admiral Bristol, who asked them what they planned to report. He advised them to say nothing at all, arguing that their reports would just be used for propaganda. Bristol also convinced American newspaper representatives in Constantinople to keep Yowell's and Ward's reports about conditions in the interior from being published in America.

During this period, American relief officials at various sites had resisted giving out information about the death marches and other atrocities, lest the local Turkish officials stop their local relief operations. But as recounted elsewhere (Shenk, ABSF, *113–14), leading Near East Relief officials from Constantinople and the Near East region as a whole now met in Constantinople and decided to abandon that policy and instead to encourage Yowell and Ward to get the news out about the terrible circumstances of the deportees that they had witnessed. Specifically they told them to ignore the American admiral's counsel and send their stories through British channels (Shenk,* ABSF, *113–14). These men also decided to scrub their committee's minutes, so there would be no local record of this decision.*

Thus, Ward's and Yowell's reports about the terrible circumstances of the Greek deportees were soon published in British papers. Admiral Bristol was irate at this development, calling Yowell's statements "Yowell's yowl" and publicly calling the mens' veracity into question—pronouncements that, as shown in the Sands *war diary at Trebizond of June 3, 1922, were used by Turkish officials to support their denial of these reliefers' reports. To this day, Admiral Bristol's regular slightings of reports about the death marches, his arguments that all the ethnic groups in Turkey were equally bad, and his scoffing at the many troubles of the Christian minorities in Turkey continue to be used by Turkish propagandists to deny the details and nature of the Greek genocide.*

Still, American papers had published nothing about the atrocities the Greeks were suffering. Then, as recorded in the McFarland *war diary of May 24–26, 1922 (below), the American scholar-turned-journalist Herbert A. Gibbons got ashore. (He was on his way east to see Yowell, who was now working at the Near East Relief station in Tiflis, Georgia.) Gibbons's access to uncensored knowledge in the Trebizond region horrified Director Crutcher of the Near East Relief at Trebizond, who had been doing all he could to keep quiet all knowledge of Turkish atrocities in the Trebizond region.*

Crutcher failed to dissuade Gibbons from speaking out. When he returned to Constantinople, Gibbons sent his stories to the Christian Science Monitor *via British wires, and so in late May and July 1922, one prestigious American paper published two of Gibbons's articles about the atrocities, which were again occurring in the interior of Turkey. Specifically, Gibbons published the horrible news of "the Moloch jaws of Jevislik" at Trebizond (see the succeeding testimony in our book for that article), although the story he told there was even less horrific than Crutcher's own June 18, 1922 report about what was happening in the same place. Crutcher had this latter report sent to the admiral via the war diaries, as will be seen below, asking that it be kept confidential. Of course, the admiral buried it.*

To summarize, it appears that despite the efforts of a Turkish official at Trebizond to shield Ottoman Christians from deportation, which ran counter to Nationalist policies elsewhere in Pontus, once that Turkish official was turned out of office, there were few roadblocks to regular deportations of minority men. Consequently, most of the Trebizond Greek men were also swallowed into the black hole reserved for hundreds of thousands of minority men in Turkey, never to be heard from again.

USS *HUMPHREYS*, COMMANDER W.O. SPEARS TREBIZOND DIARY FOR JUNE 21-22, 1921

June 21, 1921

Arrived Trebizond about 6:30 P.M., 21 June. Saw Miss Gillespie and Mr. Stapleton on dock, sent boat over to bring them off to dinner.

June 22, 1921

Went ashore 10:00 A.M. 22 June. Was met by Mr. Stapleton and escorted to N.E.R. offices. Delivered mail to N.E.R. Had private conversation with Miss Gillespie. She stated that Mr. Stapleton was very unpopular with all hands in Trebizond. At the present time he is engaged in a silly controversy with the Armenian prelate connected with the Armenian Orphanage. She was of the opinion that he was stirring up a lot of fuss about nothing. . . .

Met Nihad Bey, Red Crescent Doctor, who arranged and interpreted for me in an interview with the Valli. The Valli, very congenial, seemed pleased that I had called. After I had told him that I was surprised that the Turks didn't make more propaganda to present their side of affairs to the world, he informed me that his government was contemplating sending a mission to American for that purpose. . . .

There was no information about Russian submarines at Trebizond. About a week ago a dead body was found on the beach, which was washed in from sea, and as some native had said he had seen a periscope that day, the two events were somehow connected in the native mind and it is thought that this started the rumors. . . .

The Russian refugees on the Mariannina did not land at Trebizond. These were the refugees including the five who swam aboard the HUMPHREYS at Samsun and were returned. The ship arrived but the Russians were not permitted to land.

All military stores and ammunition are being removed from Trebizond to a place about three miles in rear of the city. There is at least one regiment for the defense of Trebizond. Placards are posted all over the town telling the inhabitants what to do in case of bombardment by the Greeks.

The Americans in Trebizond have no restrictions, they can visit destroyers by first getting permission, which seems to be only a matter of form. . . .

USS *WILLIAMSON*, LIEUT. COMMANDER J.C. CUNNINGHAM TREBIZOND DIARY FOR JULY 8, 1921

July 8, 1921

1. This ship anchored in Trebizond at 9:28. The Commanding Officer went ashore soon thereafter, and was met on the dock by Mr. Stapleton, Director of the Near East Relief. We drove to the N.E.R. office and there met Miss Gillespie. Discussed the situation in Trebizond with both Mr. Stapleton and Miss Gillespie, then drove to the N.E.R. personnel house and saw three other members of that organization. Mr. Stapleton and Miss Gillespie then came off to the ship to lunch. After lunch had another talk about local conditions with Miss Gillespie. She said that Mr. Stapleton by his method of handling things had become persona non grata with not only the Americans but also with the natives, and she emphasized the fact that she was entirely impersonal in expressing this view and that she was leaving soon anyway. From what I saw of Mr. Stapleton, I am inclined to think that Miss Gillespie is right.

2. The conditions in Trebizond are practically the same as they have been for the past month. The Americans have practically no restrictions placed upon them, and the Greeks have not been interfered with in any way. Although the Americans have to get permission to visit the ships, it is a mere formality. There are some troops here and some recruits are being taken in, but everything is quiet.

3. The N.E.R. feel that they should be allowed more money. The demands upon them are growing but there has been no additional allowance for this place.

4. Miss Gillespie stated that the local people here were not satisfied with the way the Angora authorities were handling things, that the people felt that they were being too heavily taxed, that shops manufacturing or dealing in luxuries were being closed, and that the people felt the need of a strong hand and thought the Government was accomplishing nothing. . . .

6. It was also reported that Yiaha, the Kaif or Chief Boatman, was opposed to deporting Greeks from Trebizond as he says that nothing was gained by deporting the Armenians.

7. At 4:00 p.m. sailed for Ineboli. . . .

USS *WILLIAMSON*, LIEUT. COMMANDER J. C. CUNNINGHAM TREBIZOND DIARY FOR JULY 27, 1921

July 27, 1921

Anchored at Trebizond at 10:30 and went ashore at 11:00, was met on the dock by Miss Gillespie and walked to the Consulate Building—the NER headquarters. Mr. Stapleton and Mr. Barnum Brown had gone into the interior in the car. They made a trip of about twenty miles on the road to Erzeroum. Miss Gillespie made arrangements for us to see the Vali, Nedji Bey, and the Military Commander, a Colonel named Seyfi Bey. Discussed conditions with Miss Gillespie.

Trebizond [had been] bombarded about 8:00 a.m. on July 20 by a Greek destroyer and a cruiser, and although the inhabitants were very much terrified, practically no damage was done and only one person was wounded—cut on the face by shattered glass. About 10 or 12 shots were fired by the Greek ships. The fire was returned by a shore battery consisting of probably only two guns of small calibre, and as soon as shells began to fall close to the ships, the Greeks withdrew.

On the day following the bombardment, a house to house canvas was made and all the male Greeks were rounded up; on July 24, a similar canvas of the surrounding villages was made. Very early this morning, about three hundred Greeks were marched out of Trebizond towards Erzeroum. This was observed by both Mr. Brown and Mr. Stapleton. Although a number of Greeks such as interpreters, employees of the hospitals and orphanages, and old men have been released, a considerable number are still held on the presumption is that they will be impressed into the military service. About two thirds of the shops in Trebizond are closed.

USS *MCFARLAND*, COMMANDER P.B. HAINES TREBIZOND DIARY FOR AUGUST 23-24, 1921

August 23, 1921
1. The U.S.S. MCFARLAND anchored off Trebizond breakwater at 8:00 p.m. August 23, 1921. Due to the state of the weather, raining and blowing, no attempt was made to land that night.

August 24, 1921
2. At 9:00 a.m. the Commanding Officer went ashore with mail and five packages of books for the Near East. Delivered mail to censor, books were passed through. Called on Mr. Stapleton and all Near East personnel. Arranged to call on the Military Governor, Colonel Tesik Bey at 2:30 in the afternoon. Colonel Tesik Bey is also acting as Valli, as the former Valli has been removed. According to Near East reports, his removal is due to his being unwilling to deport Greeks and Armenians.

3. In company with Mr. Stapleton, Near East Relief, visited market, town, Turkish orphanage and American Mission House. The following American personnel are in Trebizond: Mr. Stapleton, Miss Gillespie, Mrs. Crawford, Mrs. Cole, Miss Daniels. . . .

5. There is still the same dissension among the Near East Personnel which is most unfortunate as the Turks must surely be aware of it.

6. Business conditions in town are bad. There was practically no business and not much market. The 40% commandeering order has increased prices. There is very little money in town. Many filberts are now coming in and the shelled nuts are being exported. Visited a "factory" where the shelling and sorting is done. The Turkish owner filled my pockets with the kernels. The relations between the Americans and the Turks are cordial. This is due mostly to Miss Gillespie. More freedom is allowed Greeks and Armenians here than in Samsun or Ismit. A number of Greek stores are open and one sees numerous Greeks and Armenians on the streets. (I saw two Armenian patriarchs in costume.) The Commandant has even exempted from the draft the employees of the N.E.R. who are of the draft age. The military Commander was very pleasant and friendly. He stated the Greeks had been held in their advance on Angora as I was also informed by the Commandant at Ineboli. The Greek battleship KILKIS and a destroyer were off the port yesterday and caused considerable excitement.

7. The commandant stated that, believing President Wilson at Paris, the Turks had given up their arms and now the Greeks were attacking them. He wanted to know why America would not send arms now to the Turks, in view of this fact. I replied that the Greeks held control of the sea and the arms would not get to Turkish ports. He asked how the Greeks could take arms from ships. I told him that if consigned to the Kemalist Government they were contraband of war and liable to seizure. The Commandant stated that he would like always to have an American destroyer here and that the reason the Greek ships left yesterday was because they heard an Ameircan ship was coming in....

10. A Lieut-Commander, ex-Turkish Navy, told me that guns have been mounted to defend Trebizond from attack by Greek boats. No landing has been made along the coast by the Greeks. A large mass meeting was held this afternoon in the public square, roughly 1500 men being present. This meeting was to protest Greek atrocities and devastation of villages and country through which they pass.

11. There are according to my information about 5000 Greeks, 400 Armenians (five Trebizond families) and 300 Russian refugees in town.

USS *OVERTON*, COMMANDER BRUCE WARE TREBIZOND DIARY FOR OCTOBER 29, 1921

October 29, 1921

The OVERTON arrived Trebizond at 7:30 a.m. I went [ashore] and called on the Mutasariff and Military Commander; they were in the country for Sunday and I did not see them.

The people of the Near East Relief, Dr. Stapleton, [Mrs.] Crawford, Miss Cole and Miss Daniels, were very glad to get the mail. Their joy in seeing the ship was evident. I made an automobile tour of Trebizond and environs. Was very quiet and orderly.

The following news items were obtained:

(a) A British dreadnought is due to arrive here 1 Nov. 1921, with the Turkish Ex-War Minister from Yalta. It is understood he will be exchanged for Colonel Rawlinson, British High Commissioner of Erzeroum.

(b) On 23 October 1921, Miss Ostend, Miss Sinburn, and Miss Jordan were allowed passage to the Caucasses.

(c) The Head (King) of the Kayikas, becoming rich during the war, has fled into the hills and become a refugee for (1) Aiding Greeks to escape, (2) Avoiding customs.

(d) The orphanages now total as follows: Armenians 140, Turks 200, Greeks 120.

(e) Three divisions of Turkish infantry attacked the Greek refugees in the hills and completely routed them last week. Twenty-two women entering the city were given employment husking corn by the Near East Relief.

(f) Very little, if any, deportation is being done here, What there is consists of drafting Greek men for the Army, getting them into the Hills, then turning them loose to drift for themselves.*

* Our photographic copy of this single page, which is labelled "(1)" of the *Overton*'s October 29, 1921 visit to Trebizond, did not have the customary signature of the captain at the end. If there was a second page to this war diary, we did not find it.

USS *SANDS*, COMMANDER R.L. GHORMLEY TREBIZOND DIARY FOR DECEMBER 17, 1921

December 17, 1921

1. .... SANDS arrived at Trebizond 0745. Went ashore at 0845. Called on Americans and government officials; called on Americans attached to the Near East Relief, Mr. Crutcher, Miss Daniels, and on the American Mission House, Mr. Stapleton, Mrs. Crawford, and Miss Cole. Inquired into the general conditions here and all stated that everything was quiet; that most of the Greek men of the town between the ages of 20 and 46 have been deported. About ten days ago another call was issued for Greek men 15 to 50 years of age; however, the latter have not been deported and no definite orders have been issued that they will be deported; as yet, no women have been deported. A total of about 2,000 Greek men have been deported. Of Greek men from 25 to 30 years of age there are ten remaining in the city; four are connected with the Near East Relief; three are connected with the Ottoman Bank; and three are connected with the Greek church. There are a few Armenians in the city, who have apparently not been molested.

2. The Russian Bolshevists maintain a Mission or Commission here and are going and coming constantly. My impression, however, is that there is little or any chance of this section of Anatolia becoming Bolshevist. Recently 1-1½ tons of Russian new gold coins, dated 1920, were received from Ukraine en route to Angora. It is reported that these were coined at the old Russian mints in Moscow which are now [back] in operation. This money was accompanied by a Bolshevist mission from here to Angora. . . .

6. Mr. Crutcher stated that the officials and people of Trebizond have been very kind to him and assisted him in every way possible. He is allowed to go hunting for birds and rabbits and states that guns and dogs are available for such purpose. His mail is not censored, and he has been invited to call and to have tea at the homes of various officials. . . .

12. My general impressions were that everything here is quiet and orderly and that there is little tension in the minds of the people. The shops were open and seemed to be bounteously supplied with food of all kinds. . . .

USS *STURTEVANT*, LIEUT. COMMANDER E.G. HAAS TREBIZOND DIARY FOR APRIL 18, 1922

April 18, 1922

Anchored off Trebizond at 6:55 A.M. Went ashore at 8:00 A.M. and called on Mr. Crutcher, Director of the Near East Relief activities at that port, to whom I delivered mail for Trebizond and Batoum. Mr. Crutcher in reply to my query as to conditions in Trebizond reported that the city was very quiet and peaceful. He told me that all Greek men of military age are being deported in small drafts; on an average, fifty are being deported every three or five days. He believes this will continue until the entire Greek male population has been deported. Got underway for Samsun at 6:50 P.M. and arrived there at 7:00 P.M.

USS *MCFARLAND*, COMMANDER HARRY PENCE TREBIZOND DIARY FOR MAY 24-26, 1922

. . . .

May 25, 1922

Talked over situation with Crutcher, and he seemed very much perturbed over the Gibbons incident with which I believe, the Detachment Commander is already somewhat familiar. It seems that last Sunday, May 21, a Mr. Herbert [Adams] Gibbons* was on board the "ADRIA" on his way to Tiflis with three young ladies of the Near East Relief. He was going to Tiflis at the invitation of [Forrest] Yowell to see conditions there. Crutcher had them come out and spent the day with him. Mrs Crawford and Dr. Stapleton were at Crutcher's house for lunch. It happened that at the time Crutcher was absent, giving an examination in English at the Sultana high school. When he returned they were at lunch.

Mrs. Crawford had been much perturbed because of a Greek boy of about 15 years of age who had been in her household since he was a baby. The government had picked this boy up and he was to be deported. Mrs. Crawford went to see the authorities. The Valli Bey informed her that it was not in his hands to release the boy. Mrs. Crawford returned very much put out over the boy's leaving and she expressed her opinion to Mr. Gibbons. Mr. Gibbons has spent several years in the Near East and he is a well known writer and has written several books on the Turkish atrocities, and he began inquiring around trying to get other information. He spent the whole afternoon with Mrs. Crawford and Mr. Stapleton. Mrs. Crawford said it seemed as though the Lord had answered her prayers and sent a man here who was willing to write up the Turkish atrocities going on here in Trebizond. Mrs. Crawford hopes, through the information she gave Mr. Gibbons, to obtain $1,000 a month for relief work here in

* Gibbons would report his observations from Trebizond in articles published in the May–July 1922 issues of *Christian Science Monitor*, for which he was a correspondent. He was especially concerned about the atrocities committed at Jevislik or Jivislik (see the Gibbons testimony following these Trebizond diaries).

The Near East Director at Trebizond had also heard terrible reports from Jevislik (see the *Fox* diary of June 18, 1922, below).

Trebizond. This was all that took place until Mr. Gibbons was ready to return to the "ADRIA".

Crutcher took Mr. Gibbons off and explained the situation it would cause in Trebizond if any story was published in the European papers. Gibbons said that he realized it but that he was going ahead with the story. He said that he was not going to send it through the American High Commissioner [Admiral Bristol], but would send it through the English High Commissioner. He stated that he would send the story by radio as soon as he got back on the ship. Crutcher pleaded with Mr. Gibbons, told him that it was through him that he came ashore, and that if it had not been for him, he could not have gone ashore. He told Gibbons that as long as he had been in Trebizond he had been on good terms with the officials and that if his story was pubished it would put everyone in an awkward position with the officials. . . .

There are two Turkish destroyers that run between here and Batoum and Samsun regularly, carrying ammunition. They run quite often, probably about twice a week. When there is a rumor that the Greek fleet is in the Black Sea, these destroyers go into Batoum and remain there. Two small Greek boats were captured by one of these Turkish destroyers and brought into Trebizond, first stopping at Resur. These two Greek ships had quite a number of Greek refugees on board, men, women and children. The women and children were left at Resur and the men were brought to Trebizond to be deported. The two small boats are now being used by the Turkish government and have been taken to Samsun.

There is not a full division of Turkish soldiers here. Ammunition is sent from here through to Samsun. There are about [. . .] Russian refugees and practically all have work. They are mostly men, very few women and children. . . .

There is no typhus or cholera in Trebizond. About 30% of the population are affected with malaria.

The Turkish government is deporting Greek refugees in lots of fifty, sending them into the interior. Deportation parties leave Trebizond on each Monday and Thursday. This is done, that is, sending them in groups of fifty, in order that they might find food and shelter on the way. There are about 500 Greeks remaining in the city and when they are deported there will be none left. Among this 500 there are some of the age of thirteen and upwards. There are no women or small children [deported] so far. . . .

May 26, 1922

. . . . As a matter of interest, the Greek boy of Mrs. Crawford mentioned earlier in this diary has been returned. . . .

USS *SANDS*, COMMANDER R.L. GHORMLEY TREBIZOND DIARY FOR JUNE 2-3, 1922

June 2, 1922

The vessel arrived Trebizond at 1630, 2 June. Went ashore and delivered NER mail and called at the NER office. Saw Mr. Crutcher and Dr. Stapleton, and talked over the situation with them. Crutcher is greatly worried over his standing as a result of the Gibbons affair, reported previously by the Commanding Officer, MCFARLAND. He is afraid that the military commander may be relieved for permitting Gibbons ashore.

I asked about Russian girls being sold into harems here. They both said there is nothing in it. Some Turkish prisoners of war have recently returned from Russia bringing Russian brides with them, and a few other Turks have Russian wives.

A few German prisoners still work their way back through here.

The Russians are not sending any soldiers into Turkey through Trebizond. They are, however, sending in ammunition.

Some Greeks have recently been deported, but it is reported that yesterday some deportees were returned in view of the possibility of an Allied investigation.

June 3, 1922

Ashore at 1000. Went to NER headquarters and saw Mr. Crutcher and Miss Murless. Crutcher is greatly disturbed over the Gibbons incident and feels that whatever good he may have done in regard to establishing friendly relations with the officials and prominent Turks may be offset by Gibbons' articles. He thought that he should go to Samsun and thence to Marsovan and see Mr. Jaquith [Manager of the NER in Constantinople], who is expected there soon and will go from there to Angora. He thought that if he could personally explain the whole thing to Mr. Jaquith, that Mr. Jaquith could then see the Angora officials about the matter. He asked my advice. I told him that in view of the fact that he had discussed the entire question with the Valli it would be best to see what the Valli thought before making a decision as the Valli might think he had some ulterior motive.

At 1100 in company with Crutcher and Munir Bey, the local censor [acting] as interpreter, called on Sami Bey, who is an army colonel.

He is the Military Commander, but the regular Valli is away on an inspection trip and so Sami Bey is acting. After the usual exchange of greetings, the Gibbons question came up. The Valli said he had been asked by Angora how Gibbons got ashore and the Valli had sent a reply. Pending further word from Angora, Mr. Crutcher's privileges would go on as before and he would be permitted to bring any of his personal friends ashore from steamers passing through.

The Valli expressed a hope that the incident was closed. He then said that the local paper yesterday contained an article to the effect that Admiral Bristol had made a statement in regard to the Yowell case, which had entirely settled it. He expressed a desire that Admiral Bristol would take such action so that Gibbons' story will be squashed or discredited. The Valli believes that Gibbons is in the pay of the English and was sent to get a story. He apparently got ashore by giving the impression that he belonged to the NER; for this Crutcher wants to take the responsibility, but the Valli says he should not. Crutcher took up the question of his going to Marsovan to see Jaquith. The Valli said he would have to get permission from Angora for him to go inland, and that he would suggest that it would be better for him not to go unless he heard more from Angora.

The Valli then proceeded to make a statement which he said he hoped that Admiral Bristol knows. It was in substance as follows:

> The Greeks this side of the line of battle have lived here many years, but they are now taking up arms in many cases and assisting the Greek army by such actions that may be considered attacks on the Turkish army from the rear. At the same time they are getting their daily bread from the Turks. That he had found 500 rifles in the hands of Greeks in this vicinity, and that right now there were 800 armed Greeks in the hills near here. The Turks are at war with Greece and therefore they have a right to take action against the Greeks of military age. This they have done by deporting men (no women from this district) between the age of 16 and 50 years. That they had all been fed, well treated, and no one had molested them. That they had done nothing here but what would have been done in any civilized country, under similar conditions. That all have been treated as any civilized governor would treat them.

Crutcher said that things here in regard to deportations had been very quiet; that no women had been deported. When I asked him whether the Turks were feeding deportees, he did not seem so sure.

USS *STURTEVANT*, LIEUT. COMMANDER E.G. HAAS TREBIZOND DIARY FOR JUNE 6, 1922

June 6, 1922

Arrived at Trebizond at 9:10 a.m. Went ashore at 10:00 a.m. and visited the Headquarters of the Near East Relief where I met all the Americans residing in Trebizond. Mr. Crutcher reported that conditions were very satisfactory and that the city and environs were very quiet and peaceful. He stated that the deportations of the Greeks had ceased. About three [weeks] ago, fifty three boys were deported and sent into the interior but were brought back about a week ago. He is of the opinion of a British commission having being sent to Turkey to investigate the alleged Turkish atrocities was the direct cause of the virtual cessation of deportations and the return of the these boys.

I asked him if he knew whether or not Russian girls had been brought to Trebizond and sold into harems. He said he was absolutely certain that not a single instance of this nature had occurred in Trebizond. . . .

In company with Mr. Crutcher and his interpreter, Muni Bey, I called on [the Acting Valli] Leghabib, the new military Commander, on Houssein Effendy, Mayor of the city, and on Hamdoula Soudhai, Minister of Education [from] Angora. I was very favorably impressed with these officials who appear to be very intelligent and efficient men. The new Military Commander is of very striking appearance and every inch a soldier. The relations existing between the Americans and the Turkish officials appear to be very orderly and harmonious; the officials are not only willing but very anxious to cooperate with Mr. Crutcher in every possible way.

It was noted that the Americans here enjoy more freedom of movement and are not subjected to [any] petty restrictions to which the Americans in Samsun are subjected. Mr. Crutcher gives one the impression of being very tactful and discreet, as well as extremely courteous, in his official intercourse with the local authorities, and I believe that the friendly feeling existing between the Turks and Americans can be attributed, in no small measure, to his excellent judgment and tact. . . .

. . . .

USS *FOX*, LIEUT. COMMANDER WEBB TRAMMELL TREBIZOND DIARY FOR JUNE 18, 1922

June 18, 1922

Arrived Trebizond at 3:00 p.m. and went ashore to call on the Americans. Commander Atkins accompanied me and we had tea with Dr. Stapleton and Mrs. Crawford at the Mission. They are the only Americans there at present, Mr. Crutcher and Miss Murless having been called to Samsun.

The population expect the Greek Fleet to bombard Trebizond, and they believe that several hundred people were killed in the bombardment of Samsun.*

The following report was left by Mr. Crutcher, local director of the Near East Relief.

"On June 14 two Greek women called at the N.E.R. Personnel House begging for food. These two women were from a village near Trebizond by the name of "Livadia." This village four months ago was entirely Greek and consisted of about one hundred and eighty families with an average of about six persons to a family. About four months ago some Turkish officers and soldiers came into the village. The people of the village took them in, gave them food, housed them and showed them every hospitality that they were able to render. The officers and soldiers treated them with due courtesy. But after a few days they left the village. Shortly after they left another bunch of officers and soldiers came in and surrounded the village. They moved all the families of the village together in forty of the houses, in all there were one hundred and eighty houses in the village, but they concentrated the whole village only into forty of the houses. They were kept there a few days, not allowed to come out of the houses, to make a fire in any of the houses to cook food. Finally the soldiers came down and told them that they could come out. Coming out of the houses they found to their amazement all of their belongings, furniture and food packed up. The people of the village asked just "what does this mean?" The soldiers replied, that they were going to be moved and told them to load their personal belongings on their backs. Some of the people

* Apparently Turkish propagandists had been hard at work. The Samsun war diaries quote reports from Turks in Samsun that four Turks had been killed and three wounded.

refused, the soldiers [then] threatened to massacre them and began beating some of them.

"This frightened them so that they began loading all their belongings, and with the soldiers they marched to the central village, 'Jivislik.' There most of the men were deported including boys from eleven years up. These have not been heard from since.

"These two women state that they have seen and witnessed seventeen [Greek] men taken out and killed by cutting their heads off. After the heads were cut off, the soldiers ran a bayonet through from one ear to the other, a long stick was placed through each head, and then the soldiers paraded before the officers with these heads, showing who was killed and how many. The officers looked them over and then told them to take them away and bury them. These two women also saw four girls from fifteen to eighteen years of age taken by officers for immoral purpose who afterwards were put to death. They claim to have witnessed their execution. There were also three children, nine, ten and twelve years of age killed before the eyes of these two women. In this village there are only three old men left, all boys and men from eleven years of age up have been deported and massacred.

"The women that are left in this village have absolutely nothing to eat. What food they had and the seeds for planting have been taken away by the soldiers. These women tell that some of the families are actually starving and that they are eating grass.

"This story has been told to me by these two women, and also Mrs. Crawford has heard this story from five other Greek women, who arrived in Trebizond from this village. The women that came to Trebizond said that if they had remained in this village, they would starve. They came to Trebizond to beg. I myself have heard several such stories from the surrounding villages, just a few hours from Trebizond.

"Kindly treat this story confidentially."

/s/ J.H. Crutcher,

Director Trebizond Unit

Note: Several words were obscured in the Trebizond part of the original file of this message in the National Archives (the Fox *war diary report dated June 18, 1922 for June 18–24, which includes both Samsun and Trebizond visits). That copy has been corrected by reference to a copy that Trammell kept personally among a small set of* Fox *war diaries, which was kindly sent to Dr. Shenk by Trammell's son.*

ACTUAL CONDITIONS IN HARPUT AND TREBIZOND
–*TESTIMONY OF MARK WARD, FORREST YOWELL AND HERBERT GIBBONS*

As noted above, when Turkish officials expelled American relief workers Forrest Yowell and Mark Ward from Anatolia, Admiral Bristol did his best to see that anything they said or wrote was kept out of the American press. Eventually their stories were wired to British newspapers. Before long, Herbert Gibbons, the scholar and writer who was traveling through the Near East for The Christian Science Monitor, *got a couple of articles about the Turkish atrocities published in that American paper.*

It is important to hear some of what Ward, Yowell, and Gibbons had to say.

Dr. Mark Ward's Memorandum on Greek Deportations May 1921 to January 1922

Both Dr. Ward and NER director Yowell had been working at Harput before being expelled by the Turks there. Below is the report of Dr. Mark Ward (Director of the NER Hospital in Harput) about the situation where he had worked, written upon his arrival in Constantinople in May 1922.

BEGINNING with May 26th, 1921, and up to January, 1922, there were a total of 20,378 deportees that reached Harput. About 18,000 were Greek Ottomans and the remaining 2,000 were Armenians. They were from the following places, named in the order in which the deportees reached Harput:—

Konia, Cesarea, Amassia, Bilijek, Eskishehir and villages near Brussa, Eregli, Afium Karahissar, Alishar, Kutahia, Sivri-Hissar, Akshehir Keroman, Haymans, Ordu, Kerasun, Samsun, Khanza, Topejuk, Marsovan, Koppy, Vozir-Kupru, Sparta, Burdur, Endemish.*

According to the reports we received, there must have been 30,000 sent down the Harput road from Sivas during this time. Some 5,000 of them were able to escape from the convoys while passing through

* It is important to note that not all of those deported to Harput came from Pontus, though most did. The others came from a broad range of locations in Anatolian Turkey.

the various villages and towns along the road. In Malatia alone, there were 4,000 refugees during the fall and winter months. From these the Near East Relief was taking care of over 600 children in an orphanage and feeding 400 refugees at a soup kitchen. There were another 1,000 whom the Americans could not reach or care for.

The remaining 2,000 who remained at Malatia all died either from starvation or typhus during the winter.

As the deportees were driven down the road, many dropped by the roadside from exhaustion, and during the winter nights these froze to death as they had no covering. One American saw 1,500 dead bodies along the side of the road as he journeyed from Sivas to Harput during the month of December last. Another, going from Malatia to Harput earlier in the same month, saw 150 bodies of women and children. Some of these bodies were on the roadway itself, just where they had stumbled and fallen. Others appeared to have had just enough strength to crawl to the side of the road so they would not be crushed by passing wagons.

In all, fully 5,000 of the 30,000 who started from Sivas died on the road, so that, together with the 5,000 who escaped from the convoys, only 20,000 reached Harput.

The Near East Relief was able after a hard struggle to give bread to most of the thirty-eight convoys of retugees as they passed on the road. Some 5,000 of them remained in Harput and nearby villages, and 3,000 of these received the Near East Relief ration of bread regularly. During the cold winter months, however, many died from starvation and exposure. Typhus broke out and spread like wildfire in spite of quarantine. In Harput during seven months over 1,300 refugees were received in our American hospital, and out of these, even with the best of care, 341 died, a death-rate of 25 per cent. In the largest isolation camp 600 died. In the entire Vilayet fully 2,000 died. Nothing was done for them except by the Americans.

Some 15,000 refugees were sent over the high mountains south to Diarbekir, but the Americans there reported that only 12,000 arrived. The remaining 3,000 perished in the snow on the mountains. Food and bread was given to them as they passed through Diarbekir. Two thousand remained there during the winter and half of them died from starvation, disease or exposure.

Thus, out of the 30,000 who left Sivas, only 10,000 passed over the bridge of the Tigris river at Diarbekir into the Vilayet of Bitlis.

Beyond this point we know nothing—no word has ever come back. From the nature of the country and the barrenness of the mountains we know that very few can possibly have survived the winter.

Of the 30,000 refugees, there remain, so far as we know, about 6,000: 2,000 in Malatia, 3,000 in Harput and 1,000 in Diarbekir.

The earlier convoys of refugees consisted of men, many of them in the prime of life. These were mostly put to work on the roads between Harput and Diarbekir. They received no pay and their entire food allowance consist of 200 grams of bread and a little thin soup daily. They were allowed no shelter and were compelled to sleep out of doors in bitter cold weather without bedding or covering. When they were too ill to work, their food allowance was cut off and they were left to die without medical care. In some cases, by paying gold, a refugee was able to remain in one of the larger towns and work locally. Some were thus able to get in touch with friends and receive money through the agricultural bank.

But after the earlier deportations, the convoys consisted almost entirely of women and children, with a scattering of old men and boys. In some cases they were permitted to travel with their ox-carts or donkeys, but mostly they were forced to walk, and their baggage consisted of what they could carry on their backs. This was especially hard on women with children. The little children had to walk, for their mothers were obliged to carry the food and bedding for the journey on their backs. Therefore, it was the children who gave up first and fell behind, and later crawled to the side of the road to die. Many babies were born along the road, but as the mothers had to keep up, they did not survive. Even in the American hospital, out of 33 babies born from among the refugees, only 13 lived and half of those have no chance of growing up. Ten of the babies were born prematurely and, of course, died.

Some of the sick among the refugees we were permitted to take into the American Hospital, but only after they had personally been examined by the local health officer and given a permit to be admitted. Sometimes they would have to wait four days for a permit and sometimes they would have to pay a bribe to the official. We were not allowed to give the refugees any work and it was only after difficult negotiations that we obtained permission to give out clothes to those who came to us with hardly rags enough to cover their nakedness,

This sping, as soon as the roads were passable over the mountains, new convoys began to pass through Harput. These convoys were mostly made up of the survivors who had managed to live through the winter in some of the towns along the road. They were being pushed on, we learned, in order to make room for new convoys who were to be started down from the North and condemned to exile in the mountains of Bitlis. The deportees all knew that they were being sent there to die. The Turkish officials all knew it. There was no possibility that many could find shelter or food among those high mountains.

(Signed) MARK H. WARD

From Ward's short book, The Deportations in Asia Minor, 1921–1922, *London: Anglo-Hellenic League and British Armenia Committee, 1922.*

Forrest Yowell's Statement upon Arriving in Constantinople from Harput

Forrest Yowell had been Director of the Near East Relief at Harput before he was expelled by the Turkish officials. Here is the statement he made upon arrival in Constantinople, about May 3, 1922.

I have been Director of American relief work in Harput since October. I was arrested March 5 for reasons which the Turkish officials refused to divulge and forcibly deported from the country, preceded by my three chief assistants, who were informally notified that unless they left the country they would be forcibly deported. We were nearly two months reaching Constantinople.

All the twenty American relief workers in the Harput district have been consistently treated by the Turkish officials with the utmost discourtesy and injustice despite the fact that they were doing a large relief work for Moslem orphans and refugees as well as for Christians. Our 200-bed hospital was operated virtually under the orders of the Turks.

The Armenians in this district are now in a state of virtual slavery. They are not permitted to travel even within the country, and they are absolutely forbidden to leave the country. Since I have been in Harput I have been compelled to return $75,000 to people in America who had forwarded it to pay the traveling expenses of relatives desiring to leave the country.

All the property of Armenians who died in the deportations has been confiscated by the Turks. Armenians have no rights in the courts. A recent Turkish law prevents Armenians from inheriting property except from a father or brother; all other properties go to the Government. If the rightful heirs are deported to any other district they are prevented from taking possession by the law which forbids them to travel.

Armenian men and boys are thrown into jail without any reason except to extort money. Armenian women today are being forced into Moslem homes without the right of appeal to any tribunal. The Turkish officials, who are six months behind in their salaries, state frankly that the only way they can get money is by blackmailing Armenians.

The condition of the Greek minorities is even worse than that of the Armenians. The sufferings of the Greeks deported from the districts behind the battle front are terrible and still continue. These deportees began to reach Harput before my arrival in October. Of 30,000 who left Sivas 5,000 died before reaching Harput. One of the American relief workers saw 5,000 bodies on the road to Harput. Two thousand died on the roads east of Harput.

The Near East Relief has been giving aid to these refugees at stations located along the road from Sivas to Diarbekir. No American is permitted east of Diarbekir. All along the route the Turks are permitted to visit the refugee groups and select women and girls whom they desire for any purpose.

The deportations are still in progress. If American aid is withdrawn, all will perish. Their whole route today is strewn with the bodies of dead, being consumed by dogs, wolves and vultures. The Turks make no effort to bury these dead, and the deportees are not permitted to do so. The chief causes of death are starvation, dysentery and typhus.

The Turkish authorities frankly state their deliberate intention to exterminate the Greeks, and all their actions support these statements.

At the present time fresh deportations and outrages are starting in all parts of Asia Minor, from the northern seaports to the southern districts.

From British Foreign Office Archives, FO 371/7878.

Herbert A. Gibbons's Article on the Situation in the Trebizond Region

After getting ashore at Trebizond in late spring of 1922 (as discussed in the Trebizond diaries, above) and perhaps visiting NER workers elsewhere, Gibbons would write at least two articles on the situation in Turkey's interior for The Christian Science Monitor, *for which he was a correspondent.*

Gibbons had written the thesis for his Princeton PhD (awarded in 1913) while lecturing at America's Robert College in Constantinople. Earlier, while serving as a missionary in Adana, Turkey, he and his wife, Helen Davenport Gibbons, had witnessed the 1909 Turkish massacres of Armenians. Gibbons wrote a book about those atrocities and later penned another book about the 1915 atrocities committed against the Armenians.

In 1922, Gibbons traveled by steamer from Constantinople to Batoum, hoping to arrange transportation to Tiflis, Georgia, where he meant to visit and probably interview Forrest Yowell. His steamer stopped at Trebizond for several hours. Nationalist authorities in the Turkish ports of the region were keeping most foreign travellers on transiting vessels from debarking in the region, lest they discover what was happening there, but Gibbons somehow got ashore anyway. After learning of the situation in the Trebizond area, Gibbons would defy Trebizond NER Director Crutcher's plea that he say nothing of what he had learned there. He would also evade Admiral Bristol's efforts at keeping news of Turkish atrocities out of American newspapers by using British wires to send his stories to America upon returning to Constantinople.

GREEK MASSACRES BY TURKS CONTINUE
Ruthless Policy of Extermination continues—
Evidence of Americans living in Anatolia.
By Herbert Adams Gibbons, Ph.D. (By Special Cable.)

Trebizond, May 24th. (Delayed in Transmission.)
Despite repeated blank denials, the Angora Turks are following a deliberate and ruthless policy of extermination of the Greeks. I find that Trebizond is being cleared of the remaining Christian population.

Two years ago there were 25,000 Greeks here. Today, between the ages of 80 and 14, the male population numbers 6 priests and 10 civilians. Not one doctor, not one teacher is left. The Greek hospitals and Greek schools are closed and even private lessons in the homes are forbidden. There are no Greeks in business. The Greeks were the most prosperous element here, with fine homes, a splendid hospital, owning large summer villas on the hills; but now that the fathers and the husbands and the sons have gone, the women are plunged into deep poverty.

I see the women digging ditches, passing stones to masons, carrying heavy burdens in bare feet and rags. They are the longshoremen of the port. Now, after having deported all the older boys, the Angora Government has ordered the seizure of children of 14 down to 11 years of age. It is a heartrending sight to see the poor little children herded like cattle, driven through the streets to the Government House, where they are being thrown into a filthy underground dungeon. Some 300 were thus collected on May 20th at Trebizond.

Free from Foreign Eyes

This week these will follow their elders to the barbed-wire enclosure near Jevislik, on the road to Erzerum, far from the unpleasantly inquisitive eyes of foreigners, and where they will disappear for ever. For the deportees, once entering the Jevislik camp, never leave it. The Turks give them no food, which of course can only have one result. Not only Trebizond, but all the Greek villages of this region, feed their mankind into the Moloch jaws of Jevislik.

The Armenian villages were long ago destroyed; now has come the turn of the Greek peasants. With no men and boys, having no seed, cattle or farming tools, the women cannot eke out a living, so they come with their children to Trebizond in quest of food, the young girls hiding their youth behind dirt and rags. Whatever outrages may be perpetrated, the authorities make no investigation.

Prominent Turks Protest

Prominent Turks of Jevislik came here to protest. "Jevislik cries out to Heaven against us, we shall be doomed among the nations," one of these declared, while another pleaded with the Vali that the Turkish national honour should be no longer stained with such crimes against humanity, but though Ebou Bekir Hakim, the Vali, and Hushein, the Mayor, feel the shame of making war on little boys, they are powerless to arrest the execution of a decree which has been determined by a secret committee which rules this country.

This Angora committee, after the fashion of the former Committee on Union and Progress, has representatives everywhere who dictate to and watch the Government officials. Whoever does not obey the orders of this committee is arrested and tried for treason, or in some instances assassinated. The valis and the military governors have been changed several times at Trebizond when these functionaries tried to soften the persecutions.

The most fanatical Nationalist agents who have direct charges of exterminating the Greeks are the health commissioners, doctors, and the directors of public education, so it is the educated Young Turks who are directly responsible.

No Future for Christianity

The Turkish hodja, of Cretan origin, when he saw the schools closed and the youngsters going without education, acted on a generous impulse and went to the director of schools of the vilayet and said: "I know Greek and want to open schools for these children."

The director flew in a rage and shouted, "What, when we are working to destroy these people, would you keep them alive?"

There is no hope for the Christians under Nationalist rule; no future for Christianity in the regions of Anatolia outside Greek occupation, unless Europe and America declare their patience at an end and outlaw the Angora Government.

Despite the formal denials of the Nationalist Government and the false or misleading statements purporting to come from the American Relief Workers in the interior which are telegraphed from Angora,* there is overwhelming evidence which indicates that the massacres and deportations of the Greeks is more horrible even than those of the Armenians during the World War, and that these crimes continue unabated.

The above article was published in The Christian Science Monitor *on May 31, 1922.*

---

* This may refer to statements from Angora attributed to Constantinople relief head Harold Jaquith, who had traveled there around this time but who, upon returning to Constantinople, would disown Nationalist press reports of his statements.

The Trekking Train of 5,000 Christians Making Their Tragic Way from Harput to the Sea. *National Geographic*, Nov. 1925.

EPILOGUE:
THE NATIONALIST VICTORY, SMYRNA, AND AFTER

"In spite of our experience in Erivan in 1920, and at Ismid in 1921, we reckoned without the Turk. We should have known better. The deportations and massacres of the Christian population of Turkey had been going on for years. The Turks had manifestly adopted a radical plan for setting the vexed question of the Christian minorities, by getting rid of these minorities during the confusion of the World War, with its aftermath of lesser wars, and oiling the troubled waters later if necessary."

—Dr. Esther Lovejoy

The Situation in Pontus as of Late Spring 1922

By the late spring of 1922, most of the Greek population of the Pontus region had disappeared. Through massacre, forced labor, and widespread deportations, at least some 150,000 Pontic Greeks of an estimated pre-1914 population of somewhere between 450,000 and 485,000 had died, and many more had been deported into the interior of Anatolia or even further south to Syria. This was in addition to some 100,000 who had died because of the deportations and associated events of 1914-1918 (Psomiades, "Pontic Hellenism," 18, 22). Beyond that, almost all the Greek villages in the region had been pillaged and burned, Greek-owned livestock had been appropriated, and even the Greek-owned land, houses, and businesses in the cities had been or would soon be confiscated.

Some Greeks remained in a few Pontic areas. In addition to Greek fighters holding out in the Pontic mountains, the war diaries record that most of the Greek women and children in the city of Samsun proper—maybe 10,000 or 12,000—still remained undeported. As for Trebizond, although the Greek men in that city had all been deported by the end of 1921, as of June 1922, the Greek women and children of Trebizond had not been deported, though the women had now become longshoremen for the port due to the lack of male Greek muscle. Actually, that the Greek women of Trebizond were still living in that city well past the September 1922 burning of Smyrna is known from an interview that Bruce Clark recorded with George Siamanides, a Greek survivor from a very small mountain town some fifty miles from Trebizond, a community so isolated it was completely ignored until the Nansen population exchange in late 1923 or early 1924. Per the interview, much of Siamanides's family managed to get out of Turkey, but his sister had been living in Trebizond. As Siamanides told Clark, "One day in January 1923, all the Greeks who still lived in Trebizond were rounded up and transported by sea to Constantinople" after only a few minutes' notice. These details were remembered well in the family as his sister's infant child had died in her arms during that voyage (Clark, 126).

The threat that the Hellenic Navy would land troops to create a "second front" had turned out to be a mirage, and perhaps it was mostly a pretext to begin with, but some Turkish Nationalist authorities were persuaded by this apparent threat to initiate the deportion of Greek noncombatants from Pontic areas. Others seized on this opportunity to reinstitute the labor battalions and death marches of World War I with accompanying killings and also to reimplement the so-called independence tribunals that resulted in the hangings of Pontic leaders at Amassia. As mentioned earlier, the latter assault upon Pontic leadership paralleled and perhaps took its inspiration from the Young Turks' arrest and disposal of Turkey's Armenian leaders in Constantinople in the spring of 1915.

Despite these efforts, tens of thousands of Pontic Greek women and children remained alive, though most were now far from their homes. In late August or early September 1922, an event of great magnitude occurred, one that enabled Turkish authorities to reverse the direction of the population movement and thereby achieve the removal of Christian minorities from the entire country except for Constantinople itself. This event was the crushing defeat of the Hellenic Army by the Turkish Nationalist Army in western Anatolia, which put an end to the Greco-Turkish War that had lasted over three years.

The Nationalist Occupation and Burning of Smyrna

The Nationalist victory was followed by the Greek Army's disorganized trek toward the sea, the Turkish capture of thousands of Greek soldiers, and the Nationalist Army's march on the great city of Smyrna. Some 150,000 Greek and Armenian refugees accompanied the retreating Greek troops on the roads to Smyrna, seeking safety in that metropolis (Psomiades, "American NER," 265). Refugees were frantic to escape the Turks, especially since the retreating remnants of the Greek Army burned many of the Turkish villages they encountered, stoking Turkish anger. The stunning defeat of the Greek forces—who, since the fall of 1919, had occupied Smyrna and much of far western Anatolia—not only enabled Turkish forces to occupy and loot Smyrna but also enabled them to burn two-thirds of that city, beginning with the Armenian quarter but also engulfing the Greek quarter and the homes of Levantines, Jews, and many others.

The American destroyer *Litchfield*, anchored near the famous Smyrna Quay at the height of the terrible Smyrna fire in September 1922.

In recent years, the burning of the ancient Anatolian commercial and cosmopolitan center of Smyrna has been the subject of several full-length histories. In 1971, Marjorie Housepian Dobkin penned her magnificent history, *The Smyrna Affair.* More recently, Giles Milton wrote *Paradise Lost*, a work that documents the end of the Levantine community of Smyrna that had conducted much of the business of Turkey, and in 2015, Lou Ureneck published his fine book, *The Great Fire*, another look at the causes and effects of the Smyrna conflagration. A substantial chapter of Shenk's *America's Black Sea Fleet* deals directly with the American Navy's involvement at Smyrna, and a follow-on chapter portrays the U.S. Navy's activities in the aftermath of that great fire, for American destroyers not only remained in Smyrna's harbor throughout the crisis and eventually coordinated and helped effect the evacuation of the 200,000 remaining refugees, but they also aided in the evacuation of tens of thousands of Greek women and children from many small Turkish ports afterwards. War diaries of these destroyers (not usually the same ships whose war diaries are reproduced in this book but also post-World I War four-stacker destroyers, all manned by American naval officers and men) have provided the above-named authors with key firsthand resources about what happened in Smyrna and the region in September–October 1922.

Given the quality documentaries on the subject, we need only briefly summarize the basic events of the great Smyrna debacle here. Although there were some twenty-one European and American warships in the harbor of Smyrna, those powerful naval forces made no attempt to occupy the city, protect the inhabitants, or set up an orderly evacuation. In contrast, the lack of atrocities in Constantinople itself, soon to be threatened by the Nationalist Army, can be attributed to the fact that three Allied nations had occupied that city in 1920 and remained there until the fall of 1923.

In Smyrna, however, the presence of all the Allied warships in the harbor throughout the crisis—a small fleet of which included great battleships and cruisers, as well as destroyers, and which might have employed many great guns and deployed large landing parties to effect their will—should have enabled the Europeans and Americans to control Smyrna and ensure a peaceful evacuation. Instead, all those supposed naval leaders allowed the Turkish Army to occupy and ransack Smyrna, to ravage the ethnic Greek and Armenian populations of that utterly glutted city in the process, and eventually to burn the European quarter to the ground.

When Turkish troops, many of them little more than uniformed chettahs, entered Smyrna on September 9, 1922, they began looting the city while bands of bloody-minded Turkish civilians routed the Armenian Quarter in particular, murdering all the Armenians they could find even as horrified American civilians looked on. (One of them later recorded his awful firsthand witness.) Some commercial vessels had taken refugees away before the arrival of the Turks, and other British and American steamships (and an American destroyer) transported a few thousand refugees to safety even after the Turks occupied the city, though very few male refugees were allowed to leave. Even so, hundreds of thousands of refugees remained in a few protected conclaves or houses or hid in attics or graveyards or whatever odd, overlooked shelters they might find.

Several Americans witnessed Turkish troops set the city on fire. The blaze soon enveloped the Armenian and Greek Quarters, and before long virtually the entire non-Turkish population of Smyrna, including maddened horses and flocks of sheep, rushed to the famous, large quay. There, however, they were trapped between Turkish troops, the sea, and the great fire. Some refugees leapt into the sea and swam out to the naval vessels only to find fire hoses turned upon them. During the night of the enormous conflagration, a reluctant British admiral, moved by the impassioned argument of his chief of staff, ordered large power boats and oared boats to rescue as many civilians as possible, saving perhaps 20,000 (Housepian Dobkin's estimate, 172). But those rescued represented only a fraction of the multitude of victims who, after the fire burned out, remained in untold squalor on the quay. Meanwhile, the allied navies in the harbor often played victrolas to drown out the screams from ashore.

Minority Men Simply Slaughtered or Forced into Labor Battalions

Thousands of Greek and Armenian men, residents and refugees alike, had been unable to escape before the Turks entered the city. Among them were some 6,000 Greek soldiers in Turkish custody (remnants of the defeated Greek Army) who were forced to march through Smyrna shouting "Long Live Mustafa Kemal"—this in retaliation for an episode during the Greek occupation of Smyrna in 1919. (Back then, the Hellenic Army had forced captured Turkish soldiers to shout "Long Live Venizelos," the name of the Greek Prime Minister at the time; Shenk, *ABSF*, 216.) It can be assumed that these captured Hellenic soldiers were massacred outright not long afterwards, unseen by foreign eyes. Though measures were taken to keep prisoners out of sight, American officers reported that it was obvious that many Greek, Armenian, and other Christian men had been sorted out and "'marched into the interior'" from Smyrna. At one point, an American official reported ominously that perhaps 40,000 had already begun "'their grim march inland'" (Shenk, *ABSF*, 231, 227).

Shortly after the occupation of Smyrna, the labor battalion into which the Greek writer Elias Venezis had been pressed was ordered to "clear the corpses of 40,000 Christian men, women and children from Manisa and Smyrna, which had been tied to one another with wire, before they were killed and dumped in a huge ravine," in order to hide them from an investigating Spanish official. Hofmann paraphrases Vryonis's account of this event and cites René Puaux's estimate that as many as 150,000 minorities were deported into the interior during the Smyrna suffering, many of them (especially the men) soon to be slaughtered (Vryonis, 284, and Hofmann, "Cumulative Genocide," 92, 91). During the following weeks, American NER workers would come across more than one group of deported Greek or Armenian women and children in terrible condition *four hundred miles east* of Smyrna. One group of wretched deportees they came across had dwindled from 4,000 to a few hundred during their forced journey (Shenk, *ABSF*, 258).

The many Greek males assigned to labor battalions after Smyrna mostly suffered the same fate. As mentioned earlier, members of Ayvalı's labor battalions suffered a death rate of more than ninety-nine percent (from roughly 3,000 to 23). Elias Venezis reported in detail the many ordeals that had so ravaged his group—the disease, the exhaustion, the robbery of their clothes, lack of pure water, murders, and utter dehumanization (Vryonis, 284). Housepian Dobkin similarly details the experiences of three other men, all originally members of a group of male Greek and Armenian deportees from Smyrna. Over many months, they endured long marches, hard labor, little food, little or no shelter, theft of their clothes, beatings by angry Turkish civilians, and a typhus outbreak afflicting prisoners and guards alike. Hence it would seem unsurprising if more than ninety percent of these deportees, too, died before the remainder were released (Housepian Dobkin, 219-222).

A Lowly American Finds 20 Ships for 200,000 Women and Children

After the fire, a great multitude of older people, women, and children, including many orphans, remained on the quay in Smyrna despite the various depredations.

For those who remained, rescue was nowhere in sight, the great warships in the harbor notwithstanding. Some warships ordered bands to play so as to mask the sounds of atrocities occurring only half a mile away. One of the great ironies of the Smyrna tragedy was the fact that the person who finally located ships and brought them to the rescue was a lowly American YMCA worker named Asa Jennings rather than any of the so-called naval leaders present (Jennings' story has been recounted in Housepian Dobkin, Papoutsy, Shenk, Ureneck especially, and elsewhere). Moved by the terrible things he had seen, Jennings went from steamship to steamship in the Smyrna harbor and then traveled further on, eventually discovering twenty Greek transports in the nearby harbor of Mitylene, vessels which had transported the retreating Greek Army out of Turkey a couple of weeks earlier. By arguing, pleading, and bluffing, he eventually got several of the ship captains to bring their ships and the Greek government to release those vessels to his charge, while the American destroyer captain Halsey Powell risked his career by working to convince the Turks to let these ships into the harbor (Admiral Bristol wanted the Americans to let the Allies take the lead).

Jennings then led ten transports into the Smyrna harbor under American destroyer escort, even though all Jennings really knew about ships was to be sick upon them. These vessels were followed by other transports, which went back and forth, onloading refugees from Smyrna and offloading them onto Greek islands for days, with the American officers and sailors organizing the evacuation upon the Smyrna quay itself. (Far removed from the Turks and cooperating with the Americans, British sailors helped load the refugees on the transports.) By September 30, a succession of Greek ships had evacuated almost 200,000 thousand refugees.

Many refugees lost their lives even while the transports were visible from the quay, to be sure. Although most of the Greek and Armenian men at Smyrna had already died or would soon perish, eventually almost all the remaining old people, women, and children among the refugees would be carried on to Greece.

Then another episode unfolded: the trek of hundreds of thousands of Christian refugees from throughout Anatolia toward the sea, in what Lou Ureneck calls. . . .

"One of History's Most Remarkable Forced Migrations"

After the Smyrna cataclysm, orders were issued by the Nationalists requiring all Christians remaining in Anatolia to leave within thirty days, "or they would be deported"—and everyone knew what that meant. From throughout mainland Turkey, all remaining Christians began a trek to the sea. These masses included women and children who had already been deported far inland from the coast; reversing direction, they endured a second prolonged journey (Clark, 72). The whole exodus included NER teams caring for orphans at American mission stations inland, who now began transporting their charges to the coast. By the end of December, the NER had transported 15,644 orphans to Greece, though many more remained. The total number of children (not all of them orphans) under NER care in Turkey exceeded 115,000. Most would eventually get out of Turkey (Psomiades, "Near East Relief," 271).

The massive exodus took many months. Few, if any, of the exiled Christians were allowed to sell the property they left behind. Most were forced to carry what belongings they could on this long trek, and their burdens had to include food to sustain them. Sometimes they traveled on carts drawn by livestock, but often they walked. Thousands died on their journeys to the sea, which many of them living inland had never seen, for they were utterly unprepared for the ordeal, and were subject to further Turkish depredation as they traveled.

Once at a port, the refugees might wait for weeks for room on a ship. Even in victory, the Turkish Army prohibited most men from leaving the country, continuing to press draft-age men into labor battalions, as Efthimios Couzinos writes in his memoir. A young man of draft age, in late 1921 at Anatolia College in Marsovan, had hidden in a small hole under the kitchen where his sister worked, very like Jews in Europe hiding from the Nazis a couple of decades later. For a year Couzinos stayed in that hole while his sister sneaked him food—he would emerge at night to stretch his legs. Not long after Smyrna, he was transported in a carriage with younger boys by American NER workers from Marsovan to Samsun. A Turkish soldier grabbed him at the port, but when the soldier went after another young man, he jumped into the bottom of a boat at the dock, hid, and eventually boarded a waiting ship. For Couzinos, it had been thirty seconds between life and death (Couzinos, 136-37).

This final exodus of the Pontians, Cappadocians, and all other Asia Minor Christians from their ancestral home had begun in November 1922, and the great tide only began to slow in May 1923. Once those traveling north arrived at Samsun and Trebizond, the refugees were fed by Near East Relief workers, but many were forced to work at the port in order to pay the cost of further transport by ship. Asa Jennings and others now brought transports to Pontic ports, though not Hellenic ships this time, for the Turks had barred the Greeks from the Black Sea. American destroyers mainly observed and reported upon the evacuations. A British report noted that in late November 1922, 30,000 refugees had already arrived at Samsun while 500 more were arriving each day (Clark, 68); several ships were en route to Samsun to pick them up. In December 1922, it was reported that nearly all of the evacuees were women, though this likely meant women along with their children (Ureneck, 389).

Even aboard ship, the suffering was not over. As Harold Jaquith of the NER at Constantinople commented, "Weakened by days of travel, by wagon and foot from [the] interior [to the] Anatolian or Black Sea ports, Trebizond and Samsun, these wretched people fall easy victims to disease. Many of those who survived their march of terror to the sea died on shipboard and 60 per cent of those who lived through the voyage on filthy, crowded ships were diseased on arrival [at Constantinople]" (Lovejoy, 267). Then in January 1923, Greece refused the ships entry, for Greece could no longer accomodate the enormous flood of people seeking asylum!

Many refugees remained on these ships for weeks. "To take one example, a ship arriving at Piraeus from Samsun . . . in January 1923 had carried 2000 passengers. Of these 1600 were stricken with typhus, smallpox or cholera, and two of the three doctors on board were seriously ill" (Clark, 142).

Barge carrying refugees being towed out to a ship from which they would be taken on to Constantinople. The city of Samsun is seen in the background.

Prior to that, some 10,000 refugees had been shunted off to Selimiye Barracks in Constantinople, the same enormous building in which, during the Crimean War, Florence Nightingale had worked her miracles. According to Dr. Esther Lovejoy, who on the Smyrna quay had overseen the delivery of dozens of babies, conditions in this building on the Asiatic side of the Bosphorus were worse than anything Nightingale herself had ever seen. For weeks the refugees had had no beds nor care. "The place was a colossal incubator of pestilence. The sick and well were sleeping on the reeking floors with disease breeding among them and Death gathering the harvest." Lovejoy wondered how Nightingale would have viewed such a scene, "What would she have written if she had lived in these days of free speech, witnessed the horrors of Smyrna, and worked among the Christian refugees uprooted and driven from their homes in Anatolia? . . . What would she have written if she had actually seen the outcasts from the Pontus quarantined for typhus fever and smallpox in her old barracks at Scutari?" (Lovejoy, 268-71) Lovejoy's organization (the remarkable American Women's Hospital Association, run by a small number of dedicated female American doctors) turned to, got the place cleaned up, and began saving lives.

It wasn't until the end of March 1923 that the Greek government opened its ports and began admitting Greek and Armenian refugees again.

The Controversial Population Exchange

A final irony about the forced Greek exodus from Turkey, in retrospect, is that people often hear of and praise the 1923-24 population exchange between Greece and Turkey that was negotiated by the Norwegian statesman Fridtjof Nansen, the "High Commisioner for Refugees" for the League of Nations.

Certainly this good man was enormously moved by all the sufferings in Anatolia, and he went to great lengths against much Turkish resistance to propose, organize, and find approval for what he thought was a greatly needed humanitarian exchange of Moslem and Christian ethnic groups between Greece and Turkey. He hoped this would help end further hatred and bloodshed. The subsequent compulsory denaturalization and deportation of Christian Ottoman citizens and Muslim Greek citizens was criticized even at the time as a violation of international law though and was an evolution that involved enormous suffering.

Moreover, the actual exchange Nansen negotiated, moving some 390,000 Moslems from Greece to Turkey and 250,000 Ottoman Greek and Armenian Christians from Turkey to Greece, did not take place until late 1923 or early 1924. By that time, perhaps a million refugees had already been expelled from Turkey, being carried mostly to Greece (Lovejoy, 183, 200-01; Ladas, 724; Shirinian, *Genocide*, 56), something apparently not mentioned by Göçek (263). Not all these refugees survived, of course. Tens of thousands died from malnutrition or disease. Deaths occurred on the trek to the sea or on so-called "death ships" or in Constantinople at Selimiye Barracks (Lovejoy, 200-01; 272; Housepian Dobkin, 214-15). Nor were their problems ended when they actually reached Greece, for by that time, most refugees' physical constitutions had been under great stress for months. Besides hardships during transit, moral and psychological issues from loss of family, friends, and familiar surroundings exacerbated physiological threats to health among all parts of the refugee population, whenever they set foot in Greece.

Nansen's exchange, though, did finally allow some draft-aged Greek men to leave Turkey. In late 1923 or early 1924, labor battalion survivors, some released Greek prisoners of war, and the Greek partisans who remained in the Pontic mountains were allowed to leave Turkey under comparatively benign conditions. Some Greek partisans had made it to Greece in stolen boats before then (Clark, 66), to be sure, and others had already escaped Turkey by other means. However, the vast majority of the tens or even hundreds of thousands of Christian male detainees had already died by this time (Housepian Dobkin, 219). Altogether, over the period 1914 to 1923, maybe a million Asia Minor Greeks had died from the outrages inflicted upon them (Hofmann, "Cumulative," 109).

As for the living, Greece would admit approximately 1,250,000 Greek refugees from Turkey and 100,000 Armenians, accepting the latter without question. This added somewhere between another third to another fifth of the prewar population of that country (Ureneck, 387; Housepian Dobkin, 219). As for Turkey, in September 1923, the Turkish Nationalists forced the occupying European forces to leave Constantinople. By that time, all European naval vessels and the American warships, too, had finally left Pontus and the Black Sea entirely.

THE HORROR ON THE SMYRNA QUAY
–TESTIMONY OF DR. ESTHER LOVEJOY

Dr. Esther Lovejoy was the head of the Medical Women's International Association, which, in the first week of September 1922, was conferencing in Geneva with kindred groups. Her colleagues there were all American and Canadian women M.D.s who, when they discovered that women nurses but no women doctors would be allowed into the United States Army at the outbreak of World War I, decided to build their own organizations. Within a little more than a year, several fine American and Canadian women doctor volunteers found themselves providing hospital care and other services for Armenian and Ottoman Greek refugees throughout Anatolia. Others toiled elsewhere in devastated Europe. Dr. Mabel Elliott became the head of the American Women's Hospitals in Turkey, but she and Lovejoy met and often worked together as the chiefs of their two organizations, and both eventually wrote stunning books about their experiences.

On hearing of the terrible fire at Smyrna in mid-September 1922, Lovejoy immediately traveled to Constantinople, soon to board a tramp freighter that quickly took her to Smyrna even while the inferno was still simmering. For several days, Lovejoy immersed herself as a doctor in the unspeakable squalor, anxiety, despair, and tragedy of the Smyrna quay. The only American woman to be found there, Lovejoy helped pregnant women as best she could, gazed at the "infernal gates" the Turks had set up on the quay, listened to the terrible nightly shrieks that Ernest Hemingway would write about later (but without comprehension; he had not been there), and daily labored alongside American sailors and officers of the American destroyer Litchfield *and a few relief workers. Most of these Americans were doing all they could to help more than 200,000 Greeks and Armenians huddled there, many of whose lives were in great danger. However, as we will see, yet another American naval destroyer captain is portrayed toward the end of this passage who—in striking contrast to the merciful instinct of a sailor who possibly came from his own crew!—finds himself utterly perplexed or stymied by the admiral's orders to "stay neutral," and sends a young Greek lad back to a probable death on the pier.*

A very intelligent and observant witness, Lovejoy by turns effectively expresses outrage, compassion, cynicism, and deep irony in describing the terrible events that had taken place before her very eyes.

. . . the Turks finally notified all concerned that males of military age (17-45) were to be detained and deported to the interior, and that all refugees regardless of age or sex, remaining in Smyrna after September 30, 1922, were to share this terrible fate. This notice was posted in conspicuous places, and scattered from an airplane among the wretched people huddled on the quay.

"Deportation to the interior" was regarded as a short life sentence to slavery under brutal masters, ended by mysterious death. . . .

The people on the quay were panic-stricken. The Allies had forsaken them. The Turks were going to deport them to the interior on the thirtieth of September. What country would help them? Greece had signified her willingness to receive them, but how could they get there without ships? . . .

The night of September 25th had come. Eight ships sailed on the 24th, one on the 25th, and only four days remained until the 30th of September. That evening at dusk, I stood on the balcony of the Relief Headquarters with a native Christian woman, and looked out over the shoal of tragic faces on the quay. There was a strange murmur of many voices rising and falling along the waterfront. The sound was mournful, like the moaning of the sea, increasing in volume as the darkness deepened. The language was unfamiliar, the tone minor and the effect weird and indescribably uncanny.

"What are they doing?" I asked this girl.

"Praying," she answered simply. "Praying for ships."

This girl and her sister, capable, well-educated young women, had been working among the refugees and keeping house for the [American] Disaster Relief Committee, since the opening of the headquarters. I had urged them to take the first ship which they could reach lest they lose the opportunity. But their young brother was in hiding, and they refused to leave, because in saving themselves they would sentence him to certain deportation and probable death. By staying they could give him food, day after day, and they might be able to find someone, some American perhaps, who would help him get away.

That night when I went to my room, which I shared with this young woman, I found her kneeling by her bedside praying to God for mercy—praying for her people, for ships, and for her brother's life. She had been educated in a mission school, and she spoke my language. She asked me to pray with her, but my soul was dumb. As I listened to that strange woman pleading her case with God, so simply, so intimately, even as she might speak to her father, I sensed, in a vague, indefinite way, the meaning of "Our Father which art in heaven" and I realized that I was standing in the presence of the Faith which had sustained her people, age after age, unto this day.

The remnant of the race to which that woman belonged, after eight years of massacre and deportation under the Turks, had joined Soviet Russia in order to survive. She and her family had lost all their worldly possessions. They were facing deportation and perhaps death, but as soon as her prayer was finished she slept peacefully, while I, in personal security, lay awake listening to the terrible sounds from the quay.

Night after night blood-curdling shrieks, such as Dante never imagined in Hell, swept along that ghastly waterfront. From my room-mate I knew what these cries meant. When the Turkish regulars or irregulars, under cover of darkness, came through the ruins to the quay for the purpose of robbing the refugees or abducting their girls, the women and children, a hundred thousand or more in concert, shrieked for light, until the warships in the harbor would throw their searchlights to and fro along the quay, and the robbers would slink back into the ruins.

Darkness and silence followed these outbursts, broken at times by the phonographs on the warships in the harbor, which, of course, suggested Nero playing the violin while Rome was burning. . . . [Since] Smyrna, we should let Nero and his violin rest. He has been outclassed. We have a better story. Time after time, the sweet strains of familar records, including "Humoresque," and the swelling tones of Caruso in "Pagliacci," floating over the waters, were suddenly drowned in that frightful chorus of shrieks from the Smyrna quay.

Well after midnight I heard a sound on the stairs. It was Mr. Jacobs of the Y.M.C.A., bringing good news. Nineteen ships were coming into the harbor. Greece was not only receiving the refugees, but she was sending ships to save them. . . .

Early Tuesday morning, September 26, a terrible struggle to reach the ships docking at the end of the railroad pier began. The quay was separated from the pier by two iron picket fences about seventy yards apart. These fences had narrow gates. The pier extended a long distance out to deep water, and three more fences with narrow gates had been improvised by placing heavy timbers across the pier about two or three hundred yards apart. The purpose of these fences was to force the refugees to pass through the narrow gates, where they could be carefully scrutinized, and all men who appeared to be of military age detained for "deportation to the interior." The gates were guarded, and beween the first and second gates at the north end of the quay leading to the pier there was a double line of Turkish soldiers, in addition to officers and other soldiers moving to and fro among the refugees. . . .

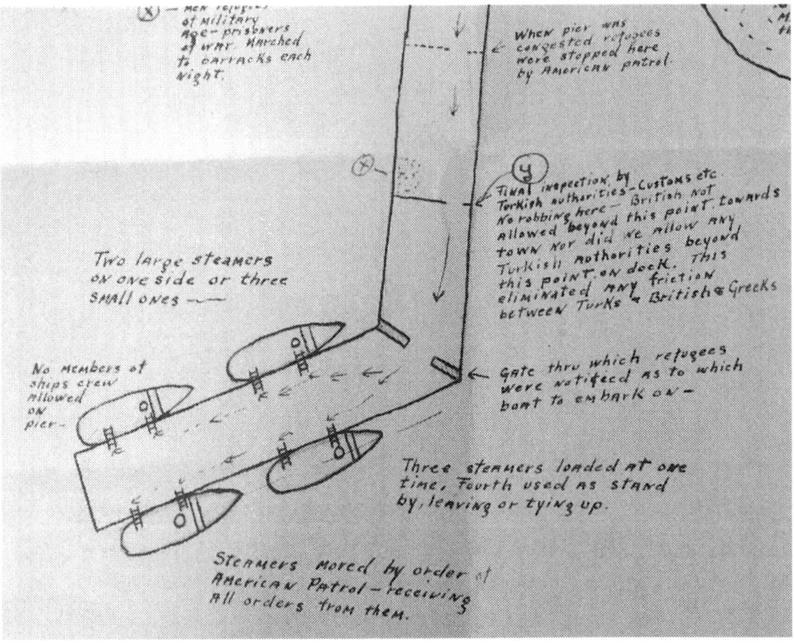

Portion of a large diagram from National Archive files indicating where American sailors were stationed on the Smyrna Quay. These sailors helped load nearly 200,000 refugees aboard transports that finally took them away from Smyrna. Incidentally, a comment next to "Y" indicates "No robbing here." Markings near other gates on the diagram indicate where robbery was "systematically" taking place, something also noted by Lovejoy.

The description of that frantic rush to reach the ships is beyond the possibility of language. Pain, anguish, fear, fright, despair and that dumb endurance beyond despair, cannot be expressed in words. . . .

For six hours on Tuesday, September 26, I stood near the land end of the pier, between the first and second gates, watching this inhuman spectacle. Thousands upon thousands of refugees, with heavy bundles upon their backs, pressed forward along the quay, struggling to reach and pass through the first gate. The Turkish soldiers beat them back with the butts of their guns to make them come more slowly, but they seemed insensible to pain, and their greatest fear in the daylight was the fear of not reaching the ships. . . .

The crush at the first gate was terrible. Many of the women lost one or both shoes, their clothing was torn and their hair hanging by the time they got through. One poor old grandmother, who had become separated from her group, was naked from her waist to her feet and apparently unconscious of this fact, as she ran about in the open space near where I was standing, calling pitifully for her family. Another woman, whose child passed the gate just as a halt was called, was beaten back by the soldiers, but the mother instinct is hard to control. With a wild expression of countenance she turned, dropped her bundle and went over that iron picket fence, which was at least seven feet high, like an orang-outang. . . .

All along this fence there were women attempting to climb over and get their children over. Here and there they were caught on the sharp pickets. A Turkish soldier, who had noticed that the gate receipts were worth while for those who had the luck to be stationed along the line of traffic, improvised a ladder by hooking a bed spring on the pickets, and did a profitable business helping women and children over the fence at this point. . . .

In the space between the first two fences many of the deportees were robbed. Individual soldiers would seize the more prosperous-appearing women, drag them out of the line and rob them in broad daylight. As the men of military age passed through with their families, they were sometimes arrested at once and placed with the group of prisoners for deportation, but frequently a man or his wife would whisper to the solder making the arrest, after which they would pay tribute and the man would be released. Before he had gone far, he would be held up by another soldier and then another, the experience being repeated over and over again. At first I wondered why they temporized in this manner, but as the hours passed the motive became clear. It was evidently a plan of the common soldiers to secure their share of the loot, and to trick the women, who had money or other valuables secreted upon their persons, into buying their husband's or their son's freedom. These men would afterward be arrested at one of the gates farther down the pier, many of them reaching the last gate before they were finally placed with the prisoners for "deportation to the interior. . . ."

The greatest crime against humanity with which I am personally familiar was committed on the Smyrna Railroad Pier during the last week of September, 1922, and consisted in the separation, by military force, of the members of all the Christian families. At every gate during the daylight hours, this atrocity was conducted systematically. As family after family passed those gates, the father of perhaps 42 years of age, carrying a sick child or other burden, or a young son, and sometimes both father and son, would be seized. This was the climax of the whole terrible experience for every family. In a frenzy of grief, the mother and children would cling to this father and son, weeping, begging and praying for mercy, but there was no mercy. With the butts of their guns, the Turkish soldiers beat these men backward into the prison groups and drove the women toward the ships, pushing them with their guns, striking them with straps or canes, and urging them forward like a herd of animals, with the expression, "Haide! Haide!" which means "begone! begone!"

I shall never forget those women with their little children clinging to their skirts as they moved backward, step by step, gazing for the last time, perhaps, upon the faces of their husbands and sons. "Their wives shall be widows and their children orphans" is a prophecy which was fulfilled on the Smyrna Railroad Pier, the Via Dolorosa of those unfortunate people.

Deportation is a common practice during war, but this was not a common deportation. The men were going to the "interior," and the women, children and elderly were going to a strange country to begin life anew without the support of their natural protectors. Day after day the pitiful procession of mothers and their little children, the aged, sick and helpless, moved toward the ships. This was the most cruel, cowardly and unsportsmanlike spectacle that ever passed under the eyes of heaven. . . .

In a city with so large a population there were, of course, a great many expectant mothers, and these terrible experiences precipitated their labors in many instances. Children were born upon the quay and upon the pier, and one woman, who had been in the crush at the first gate for hours, finally staggered through holding her just-born child in her hands.

The [American] sailors soon came to know me and call me in maternity cases. . . . On one occasion . . . I was called to a woman in labor on the quay. There was a midwife in the crowd who promised to stay with the sick woman, if we would see that they were both put aboard a ship later. An American marine [probably a sailor] was with me, and we knocked insistently on the door of one of the few houses standing. Finally it was opened, the woman taken in and made as comfortable as possible. The place was full of frightened people. Just as I was leaving, a woman who spoke English detained me. She was in deep trouble like all the rest. Her sons and several other young men whose parents were in that house were hidden in the attic. Up a narrow stair she led the way to a low space at the top of the house, where these young men were lying flat on their chests looking out through peepholes under the eaves.

After the manner of mothers, this woman begged me to help these boys escape. The older members of the family would gladly die, she said, if only their young could live and be free. These boys were watching the ships in the harbor, measuring the distance and planning to make a swim for life and liberty. But their mothers were afraid. Night after night, young men from the quay, who knew that they could not pass the gates on the pier, were silently slipping into the dark waters, and no one ever knew whether they succeeded or failed in their desperate attempts to escape. It was a long way to swim and hard to beat against the steel plates of a ship in the darkness, when the waves were high. The waters were smooth in the morning, and told no tales of the night, but sometimes on the flooding tide a body was seen floating in the distance, and hundreds of women on the quay whose men had made that swim, said prayers for the souls of the drowned. . . .

Day after day there was a succession of harrowing incidents. Children fell off the pier and were drowned, young men committed suicide, elderly died of exhaustion, and at the end of the pier, when two or three ships were loading at the same time, children were lost and their mothers ran to and fro frantically calling for their little ones, and great was the joy if the lost were found. But in many instances such children were already stowed away in the holds of outgoing ships, crying for their mothers, who were put aboard vessels bound for other ports.

Women whose husbands had been seized and whose sons had swum away into the unknown at night, moved down that pier silently, and sometimes audibly praying for strength and mercy. With seemingly impossible loads on their backs and their little children by their sides, they passed those infernal gates. . . .

On the night of September 29 I left Smyrna on the United States destroyer *Litchfield*. There were, perhaps, fifty thousand refugees still in Smyrna, and approximately a quarter of a million had gotten away. Pestilential diseases were inevitable among these people wherever they went, and our organization would be called on to conduct hospitals for their care. Fortunately, we had a small fund, but it was necessary for me to reach the United States as quickly as possible in order to get more money for this service. Several Americans were leaving, including the United States Commercial Attache and the representative of the Baldwin Locomotive Company. I was detained on account of an accident to Mr. Jacobs of the Y.M.C.A., who had been working day and night since the beginning of the holocaust for the relief of the victims. It was dusk when I reached the small pier used by the launches of the warships, but I saw one of the sailors pass my suitcase to a young boy and I heard him whisper: "Take this suitcase aboard for the lady and don't come back. Listen! Don't come back. . . ."

Dinner was over and the men had lighted their cigarettes when the captain turned to me and asked about the boy who came aboard with my suitcase. I told him that he was a stranger to me, but the captain seemed unsatisfied, so he sent for the boy and questioned him in the presence of everybody, including the vice-consul, who was a guest at dinner. This boy was small in stature, looked very young, not more than twenty, and spoke English well. He was pale and trembling, for it was a case of life and deportation and death, perhaps, to him, although but a light, unimportant matter to those used to this sort of thing from the other end of the game. Mr. Jacobs identified the boy as one of those who had been helping relief workers on the quay. Therefore, we knew that in saving others he had probably lost any chance to save himself. He was a brave boy. Not a word did the captain get out of him about his friend the sailor who sent him aboard. I had not noticed him particularly, but standing before his judge in the bright light of the cabin, his thin, blanched face contrasted strikingly with the the older, harder faces of that company, and strangely suggested the "Judgment" upon which his religion was founded.

There was no fault in this boy except that he was an Orthodox Christian. My plea for him was of necessity denied. In the beginning the captain might have closed his eyes, but having called attention to the case he was bound by the rules and as helpless as Pilate.

The captain of the *Litchfield* was an efficient officer. Wherever he appeared during the evacuation order was maintained. Day after day I met him on the quay and pier. He seemed like a man with a kind heart and a strong defense reaction against this weakness within himself. In the performance of their duties such men are apt to lean backward from their humane impulses.

The boy was sent ashore—two of them, for another had meanwhile reached the ship. This seemed very cruel, but orders are orders, and neutrality is neutrality.

Less than half an hour later, while I was leaning over the rail peering through the darkness at the last refugee ship of the day pulling out from the end of the wharf, a sailor told me that those boys had been put on the pier. The vessel was already well in the stream, and with the pier guarded by Turkish soldiers, it seemed unlikely that they could have gotten aboard—but perhaps they did. Seven months later I was told by a diplomat (formerly the American vice-consul at Smyrna) that those two boys had actually been put aboard that outgoing refugee ship. Strange, how that boy's pale face still lingers in my memory. If I ever meet Saint Peter I shall ask about him.

I was still leaning over the rail when the representative of the Baldwin Locomotive Company, who had been in Smyrna on business for several days, came along and stood with me for a few minutes. He said that he had been on the pier, but did not stay long, because he could not bear to witness the suffering of the children. "Besides," he added, as he turned away, "my business is to sell locomotives." That was the answer. That was the core of the whole wicked game. It was a case of every man for himself, and every company and country for that matter. The ships in the harbor were under instructions to protect the property of their own nationals and otherwise maintain neutrality. Their shadowy forms on the dark water suggested a herd of sea monsters with big bodies and no heads.

They had not saved the property of their nations, unless "futures" may be regarded as property. They had failed. The property had gone up in smoke. But, if in all the ages that men have lived upon the earth, they had found some simple plan of standing together for humanity's sake in times of great disaster, Smyrna would have been saved, and incidentally the precious property. . . .

From the deck of the *Litchfield* after dark, the ruins of Smyrna seemed as spectral and fantastic as a nightmare. I could not see the people huddled at the north end of the quay in the angle they dreaded so terribly, but I knew they were there, and that later in the night they would shriek for searchlights. . . .

From Certain Samaritans, *rev. edition, by Esther Pohl Lovejoy, M.D., New York: Macmillan, 1933.*

SELECTED BIBLIOGRAPHY

The various war diaries published in this edition were located and photographed at the U.S. National Archives and Records Administration in Washington, D.C. The pertinent record or file is entitled RG (Record Group) 45, Inventory 18, Appendix F (War Diaries, April 1917–April 1927 [Entry 254]). They are filed under ship name and date. Note that there are many other naval war diaries from the Turkish period in the National Archives than those reproduced or summarized here. Some describe ship visits to Turkish ports of Smyrna, Mersina, and Inebolu, for instance, while a good many others cover the evacuation of refugees to Greek ports from Turkish ones after the burning of Smyrna. Still others record ship visits to Russia. Naval destroyers were continuously stationed at Odessa and Novorossisk (and wrote war diaries there too) while American grain was being shipped to help end the great famine in Southern Russia—this from January 1922 into mid-1923. The various American destroyer missions are outlined in detail in Shenk's *America's Black Sea Fleet.*

Akçam, Taner. *A Shameful Act: The Armenian Genocide and the Question of Turkish Responsibility.* New York: Metropolitan Books, 2006.

Ascherson, Neal. *Black Sea.* New York: Hill and Wang, 1996.

Balakian, Peter. *The Burning Tigris: The Armenian Genocide and America's Response.* New York: HarperCollins, 2003.

Barton, James L. *Story of Near East Relief (1915–1930): An Interpretation.* New York: Macmillan, 1930.

Beers, Henry P. "U.S. Naval Detachment in Turkish Waters, 1919–1924." In Administrative Reference Service Report No. 2. Office of Records Administration, Navy Department. June 1943. Reprinted in *Military Affairs* 7, no. 4 (Winter 1943): 209–20.

Bierstadt, Edward Hale. *The Great Betrayal: A Survey of the Near East Problem.* New York: Robert M. McBride, 1924.

Braisted, William R. "Mark Lambert Bristol: Naval Diplomat Extraordinary of the Battleship Age." In *A Navy Second to None: The Development of Modern American Naval Policy*, edited by George Theron Davis, 331–73. Westport, CT: Greenwood Press, (1971).

Bristol, Mark L. Papers. The Library of Congress. Cited as MBC; "GC" means "General Correspondence" section.

Bryce, James, Viscount. *The Treatment of the Armenians in the Ottoman Empire, 1915-16*, compiled by A. Toynbee. London: British Government Document Miscellaneous, 1916.

Bryson, Thomas A. "Admiral Mark L. Bristol, an Open-Door Diplomat in Turkey." *International Journal of Middle Eastern Studies* 5 (1974): 450-67.

Buzanski, Peter M. "Admiral Mark L. Bristol and Turkish-American Relations, 1919-1922." Diss. University of California, 1960.

Chater, Melville. "History's Greatest Trek." *National Geographic* 48, no. 5 (November 1925): 533–90.

Clark, Bruce. *Twice a Stranger: The Mass Expulsions that Forged Modern Greece and Turkey.* Cambridge: Harvard Univ. Press, 2006.

Compton, Carl C. Ed. by John O. Iatrides and William R. Compton. *The Morning Cometh: 45 Years with Anatolia College*. New Rochelle, NY: Aristide D. Caratzas, 1986.

Couzinos, Efthimios N. *Twenty-Three Years in Asia Minor (1899–1922).* New York: Vantage Press, 1969.

Dos Passos, John. *Orient Express.* New York: Harper & Brothers, 1927.

Dunn, Robert. *World Alive: A Personal Story.* New York: Crown Publishers, 1956.

Edib, Halide. *The Turkish Ordeal: Being the Further Memoirs of Halide Edib.* New York: The Century Co., 1928.

Elliott, Mabel Evelyn. *Beginning Again at Ararat.* New York: Fleming H. Revell, 1924.

Faltaits, Kostas. *The Genocide of the Greeks in Turkey: Survivor Testimonies from the Nicomedia (Izmit) Massacres of 1920-1921*, translated and edited by Eilene Phufas-Jousma and Aris Tsilfidis. Prologue by Tessa Hofmann. Riverdale, NJ: Cosmos Publishing, 2016.

Field, Richard Stockton. "A Destroyer in the Near East." *Naval Institute Proceedings* 51 (February 1925 and March 1925): 246–67 and 400–23, respectively.

Fotiadis, Konstantinos. *The Genocide of the Pontian Greeks.* Thessaloniki: K. & M. Ant. Stamoulis, 2015.

Gallery, Daniel V., Rear Adm., USN. Diary. Papers of Admiral Daniel V. Gallery. Special Collections. U.S. Naval Academy.

Gavriilidis, Antonios I. *Pages from the Black National Tragedy of Pontus.* Thessaloniki, Greece: Kyriakides Brothers, 2002. (In Greek; the first edition was published in 1924.)

Gibbons, Herbert Adams. "Greek Massacres by Turks Continue," May 31, 1922; and "Near East Relief Prevented from Helping Greeks," July 13, 1922. *The Christian Science Monitor.* These articles were reprinted in Bierstadt, *The Great Betrayal: A Survey of the Near East Problem,* 201-12.

Göçek, Fatma Müge. *Denial of Violence: Ottoman Past, Turkish Present, and Collective Violence against the Armenians, 1789-2009.* Oxford University Press, 2014.

Halo, Thea. *Not Even My Name: A True Story.* New York: Picador, 2001.

Harbord, Maj. Gen. James G. "Mustapha Kemal Pasha and His Party." *The World's Work* 40 (May 1920): 176–92.

Hatzidimitriou, Constantine G., ed. *American Accounts Documenting the Destruction of Smyrna by the Kemalist Turkish Forces.* New York: Aristide D. Caratzas, 2005.

Henderson, George W., and Paul B. Ryan. "Naval Watch in the Mideast." *Naval Institute Proceedings* 103, no. 7 (July 1977): 66–75.

Hofmann, Tessa. "The Genocide against the Christians in the Late Ottoman Period, 1912-1922," 43-67 in Shirinian, George N., *The Asia Minor Catastrophe and the Ottoman Greek Genocide.*

Hofmann, Tessa. "Γενοκτονια εν Ροη—Cumulative Genocide: The Massacres and Deportations of the Greek Population of the Ottoman Empire (1912–1923)," 39–111 of *The Genocide of the Ottoman Greeks. [See just below.]*

Hofmann, Tessa, Matthias Bjørnlund and Vasileios Meichanetsidis, eds. *The Genocide of the Ottoman Greeks: Studies on the State-Sponsored Campaign of Extermination of the Christians of Asia Minor, 1912–1922 and its Aftermath: History, Law, Memory.* New York and Athens: Aristide D. Caratzas, 2011.

Horton, George. *The Blight of Asia.* Indianapolis, IN: Bobbs-Merrill, 1926.

Housepian Dobkin, Marjorie. *The Smyrna Affair.* New York: Harcourt, Brace, Jovanovich, 1971.

Ioannidou, Theodora. *The Holocaust of the Pontian Greeks: Still an Open Wound.* Translation editor, Katerina Garagouni. Athens: Theodora Ioaniidou, 2016.

Kincaid, Earle H. *The History and Cruises of the United States Ship Whipple, Destroyer Number 217,* vol. 1. Privately printed, 1920.

Kirli, Biray Kolluoglu. "Forgetting the Smyrna Fire." *History Workshop Journal* 60 (2005): 25–44.

Ladas, Stephen P. *The Exchange of Minorities, Bulgaria, Greece and Turkey.* New York. Macmillan, 1932.

Leahy, William. Diary. In Papers. The Library of Congress. Also to be found at Special Collections, U.S. Naval Academy.

Lewis, Bernard. *The Emergence of Modern Turkey.* 2nd ed. London: Oxford University Press, 1961.

Lovejoy, Esther Pohl. *Certain Samaritans.* New Edition, New York: MacMillan, 1933.

Lowry, Heath W. "American Observers in Anatolia ca. 1920: The Bristol Papers." *Armenians in the Ottoman Empire and Modern Turkey* (1912–1926), No editor. Istanbul: Boğaziçi University Publications. 1984.

Mango, Andrew. *Atatürk: The Founder of Modern Turkey.* New York: Overlook Press, 2002.

Marcosson, Isaac F. "Kemal Pasha." *Saturday Evening Post* 196 (October 20, 1923), 8–9, 141–42, 144–46, 149.

McCarthy, Justin. *Death and Exile: The Ethnic Cleansing of Ottoman Muslims, 1821–1922.* Princeton, NJ: Darwin, 1995.

Meyers, Jeffrey. "Hemingway's Second War: The Greco-Turkish Conflict, 1920–1922." *Modern Fiction Studies* 30, no. 1 (1984): 25–36.

Milton, Giles. *Paradise Lost: Smyrna, 1922; The Destruction of a Christian City in the Islamic World.* New York: Basic Books, 2008.

Morgenthau, Henry. *Ambassador Morgenthau's Story.* Garden City, NY: Doubleday, 1918.

Murray, Lieut. Arthur. *Black Sea: A Naval Officer's Near East Experience.* Ed. Renee Heideman Murray. February, 2014; Kindle edition.

Nicolopoulos, John. "The Testimony of Mikhail Vasilievich Frunze (1885–1925). Concerning the Tragedy of Pontic Hellenism." *Journal of Modern Hellenism*, N. 4, New York (1987), 37–53.

Oeconomos, Lysimachos. *The Martyrdom of Smyrna and Eastern Christendom.* London: George Allen & Unwin, 1922.

Papoutsy, Christos. *Ships of Mercy: The True Story of the Rescue of the Greeks, Smyrna, September 1922.* Portsmouth, NH: Peter E. Randall, 2008.

Pence, Harry. War Diary of USS *McFarland,* 1922–23. Papers. Mandeville Special Collections, University of California, San Diego.

Psomiades, Harry J. *Fridtjof Nansen and the Greek Refugee Crisis 1922–1924.* Bloomingdale, IL: The Asia Minor and Pontus Hellenic Research Center, 2011.

Psomiades, Harry J. "Greece in Asia Minor: The Greek Naval Bombardment of Samsun [Amisos], June 7, 1922," 135–154 in Shirinian, ed. *The Asia Minor Catastrophe and the Ottoman Greek Genocide.*

Psomiades, Harry J. "Pontic Hellenism and the Asia Minor Disaster, 1908–1922." Paper Presented to the Pontian Society of Chicago "Xeniteas" in Des Plaines, Illinois, May 19, 2006.

Psomiades, Harry J. "The American Near East Relief (NER) and the *Megale Katastrophe* in 1922." In Hofmann, Bjornlund and Meichanetsidis, eds. *The Genocide of the Ottoman Greeks,* 265–75.

Raber, Oran. "New Light on the Destruction of Smyrna." *Current History* 18 (May 1923): 312–18.

Shenk, Robert. *America's Black Sea Fleet: The U.S. Navy Amidst War and Revolution.* Annapolis: Naval Institute Press, 2012.

Shenk, Robert. "Ethnic Cleansing, American Women and the Admiral: Deep in Anatolia during the Turkish Natonalist Revolution." In Shirinian, ed. *Genocide in the Ottoman Empire,* 187–213.

Shirinian, George N., ed. *Genocide in the Ottoman Empire: Armenians, Assyrians, and Greeks, 1913–1923.* New York and Oxford: Berghan, 2017.

Shirinian, George N., ed. *The Asia Minor Catastrophe and the Ottoman Greek Genocide: Essays on Asia Minor, Pontos, and Eastern Thrace, 1912–1923.* Bloomington: The Asia Minor and Pontos Hellenic Research Center, Inc., 2012.

Shirinian, George N. "The Background to the Late Ottoman Genocides." In Shirinian, ed., *Genocide in the Ottoman Empire,* 19-81.

Smith, Michael Llewellyn. *Ionian Vision: Greece in Asia Minor, 1919—1922.* London: Allen Lane, 1973.

Toynbee, Arnold J. *The Western Question in Greece and Turkey.* London: Constable and Company, 1922.

Trammell, Webb. War diary, USS *Fox*, DD 234. Sept. 1921 to June 1922. In possession of the family. Used by permission.

Travis, Hannibal. "The Refugee Crisis." Speech at the National Hellenic Museum in Chicago, IL on May 21, 2017.

Ureneck, Lou. *The Great Fire.* New York: HarperCollins, 2015.

Vryonis, Speros Jr. "Greek Labor Battalions in Asia Minor." In T*he Armenian Genocide: Cultural and Ethical Legacies,* edited by Richard G. Hovannissian. New Brunswick: Transaction Publishers, 2007, 275-90.

Winter, Jay. *America and the Armenian Genocide of 1915.* New York: Cambridge University Press, 2003.

Yeghiayan, Vartkes, ed. *British Reports on Ethnic Cleansing in Anatolia, 1919–1922: The Armenian-Greek Section.* Glendale, CA: Center for Armenian Rememberance, 2007.

INDEX

Savvas "Sam" Koktzoglou is a retired mechanical engineer. He received his degrees in engineering from Villanova University and the University of Pennsylvania. During his career he worked in senior level engineering positions in both the private and public sectors in the United States and Greece. Prior to his engineering career he served as a second lieutenant in the Greek Army Reserve special forces. Sam has been on the Board of Directors of a number of nonprofit organizations in the Chicago area. He is an avid reader of Greek history with special interest in the history of Asia Minor. Sam's parents were both Ottoman Greek refugees from Asia Minor who settled in Greece in 1922.

Dr. Robert Shenk retired in Spring, 2019 as a professor of English at the University of New Orleans. As author or co-author he has published nine books, including *The Naval Institute Guide to Naval Writing*; *Authors at Sea* (a History Book Club selection); and a naval history published in 2012, *America's Black Sea Fleet*. Dr. Shenk is also a retired captain in the U.S. Naval Reserve, having seen duty on a destroyer and on river patrol boats in Vietnam, and as a professor of English on voluntary recall to active duty at both the Air Force Academy and the Naval Academy.